MODERN LEGAL STUDIES

The Informal Acquisition
of Rights in Land

AUSTRALIA
LBC Information Services
Sydney

CANADA and USA
Carswell
Toronto—Ontario

NEW ZEALAND
Brookers
Auckland

SINGAPORE and MALAYSIA
Sweet & Maxwell (Asia)
Singapore and Kuala Lumpur

MODERN LEGAL STUDIES

The Informal Acquisition of Rights in Land

Nicholas Hopkins
LL.B.

London
Sweet & Maxwell
2000

Published by
Sweet & Maxwell Limited of
100 Avenue Road London NW3 3PE.
http://www.sweetandmaxwell.co.uk
Typeset by LBJ Typesetting Ltd, Kingsclere
Printed and bound in Great Britain by
MPG Books Ltd, Bodmin, Cornwall

A CIP catalogue record for this book
is available from the British Library.

ISBN 0421 681004

No natural forests were destroyed to make this product, only farmed timber was used and re-planted.

Dedication

To my Parents, Patricia and Derek Hopkins

Preface

In writing this book I have sought to bring together the diverse range of situations in which rights in land may informally be acquired. This is an area of law which has not previously been treated comprehensively as a discrete topic and which appears, at times, to be subsumed in discussions of the uncertainties and inconsistencies of some of the doctrines applied.

In writing this book a great debt of gratitude is owed to colleagues and friends at the University of Durham and the University of Southampton. In highlighting the contributions of some, I hope not to offend others. The idea for the book and of the approach that it adopts developed through discussions with Carl Emery, Senior Research Fellow at the University of Durham. His support and encouragement in the early years of my academic career are fondly remembered, and I hope that my research reveals at least a degree of the incisiveness and critical perception that Carl always demonstrated. In addition, Rosa Greaves continues to be a valuable source of professional support and advice.

In Southampton my greatest debt is owed to Kit Barker: I could not have hoped for a more generous colleague. Where our subjects collided Kit patiently guided a (sometimes reluctant) property lawyer through the law of restitution. My thinking on a number of topics has benefited from discussions with Kit, who also commented on the entire text. Additionally, thanks are due to Sarah Nield who reviewed several chapters and to Debbie Malson for her excellent secretarial support.

Finally, I would like to express my thanks to the Board of Modern Legal Studies and, in particular, to Alison Clarke for her comments on the text.

As ever, I remain responsible for any remaining errors or omissions. The law is stated on the basis of materials available to me on June 30, 2000.

Nicholas Hopkins
University of Southampton
June 2000

Contents

Dedication	v
Preface	vii
Contents	ix
Table of U.K. Cases	xv
Table of Foreign Cases	xxiii
Table of Statutes	xxv
Table of Abbreviations	xxvii

CHAPTER 1—INTRODUCTION | **1**
I. The Formality Requirements | 3
II. Justifying Informal Acquisition | 5
III. Structure Of The Book | 6

CHAPTER 2—TO GIVE EFFECT TO AN IMPERFECT GIFT | **9**
I. Introduction | 9
II. The First Rule: Where The Door Has Done All In His Power To Complete The Transfer | 10
   1. Development of the Rule | 11
   2. Elements of a Claim | 15
   3. Scope of the Rule | 16
III. The Second Rule: Where The Donee Is Appointed As The Donor's Executor Or Administrator | 18
   1. Development of the Rule | 18
   2. Elements of a Claim | 19
   3. Nature of the Right Acquired | 20
IV. The Third Rule: Gifts Made In Contemplation Of, And Conditional Upon, Death | 20
   1. Is Land Capable of Passing as a *Donatio Mortis Causa?* | 21
   2. Elements of a Claim | 24
   3. Nature of the Right Acquired | 26

V.	Transfers On Trust	27
VI.	Conclusion	28

CHAPTER 3—TO PREVENT STATUTE BEING USED AS AN INSTRUMENT OF FRAUD — **29**
I.	Introduction	29
II.	Elements Of A Claim	30
	1. Use of Statute as an Instrument of Fraud	30
	2. Transfer of Land on Trust	33
III.	Two Party Situation	34
IV.	Three Party Situation	36
V.	Nature Of The Interest Acquired	39
VI.	Application Of The Principle To Other Factual Situations	41
	1. Transfer of a Subsisting Beneficial Interest	42
	2. Agreement Relating to a Non-beneficial Interests	42
	3. Agreements Relating to Non-proprietary Rights	44
VII.	Application Of This Rule In Conjunction With The Rules Discussed In Chapter 2	45
VIII.	Conclusion	45

CHAPTER 4—WHERE A PURCHASER TAKES LAND "SUBJECT TO" A PERSON'S RIGHTS — **47**
I.	Introduction	47
II.	Elements Of A Claim	48
	1. Transfer "Subject To"	49
	2. Intention to Create New Rights	49
	3. Fraud	51
	4. The Implied Requirement	52
III.	Scope Of The Rule	55
IV	Nature And Enforceability Of The Right Acquired	57
V.	Time At Which The Right Is Acquired	58
VI.	Conclusion	59

CHAPTER 5—WHERE THERE IS AN UNCOMPLETED SALE — **61**
I.	Introduction	61
II.	The First Situation: Where There Is A Specifically Enforceable Contract	62
	1. Contracts for Sale of Legal Rights in Land	62

    2. Contracts for Sale of Equitable Interests in Land   65
    3. The Requirements of Specific Performance   68
    4. The Nature of the Proprietary Right   69
      (a) An independent proprietary right?   70
      (b) Dependence upon specific performance   73
III. The Second Situation: Where The Purchaser Has
    Paid the Consideration In Full   74
    1. Authority for the Principle   76
    2. The Scope of the Principle   79
IV. Relationship With Other Means Of Acquiring Pro-
    prietary Rights   83
V. Conclusion   85

**CHAPTER 6—WHERE THERE IS AN AGREEMENT
TO SHARE THE BENEFICIAL INTEREST OR
CONFERRING A BENEFICIAL INTEREST IS
NECESSARY TO PREVENT UNJUST ENRICHMENT 87**
I. Introduction   87
II. Where The Beneficial Interest Is Conferred To Pre-
    vent Unjust Enrichment   92
    1. The Restitutionary Resulting Trust   92
    2. The "Inferred Agreement" Constructive Trust
      and its Relationship with the Resulting Trust   95
    3. Cases Where no Presumption of Resulting Trust
      can be Made   98
III. Where There Is An Agreement To Share The Bene-
    ficial Interest   103
    1. Establishing a Beneficial Interest Where There is
      an Express Agreement   104
      (a) Establishing the agreement   104
      (b) Detrimental reliance   109
    2. Establishing a Beneficial Interest Where the
      Agreement is Inferred   115
    3. Quantifying Beneficial Interests   118
IV. Conclusion   124

**CHAPTER 7—WHERE THERE HAS BEEN A
UNILATERAL ASSURANCE OF RIGHTS**   **127**
I. Introduction   127
II. Elements Of A Claim   128

	1. Assurance of Rights	133
	(a) The nature of the assurance	133
	(b) Establishing the assurance	139
	2. Reliance	141
	3. Detriment	144
	4. The Role of Unconscionability	147
III.	Nature Of The Inchoate Equity	150
IV.	Granting A Remedy To Satisfy The Estoppel	155
	1. The Purpose of the Remedy	156
	2. The Status of the Remedy: Personal or Proprietary?	158
V.	Distinguishing Estoppel From Other Principles	160
	1. Estoppel, Contractual Licences and Constructive Trusts	160
	2. Estoppel and Restitution	163
	3. Different Species of Estoppel	165
VI.	Conclusion	166

CHAPTER 8—WHERE A PERSON HAS ACCEPTED THE BENEFIT OF AN AGREEMENT WHICH HAS A CORRESPONDING BURDEN — 167

I.	Introduction	167
II.	Development Of The Principle	168
III.	Requirements Of The Principle	172
	1. Conditional Benefit and Burden	172
	2. Enjoyment of the Benefit	174
IV.	Effect Of The Principle	177
V.	Conclusion	182

CHAPTER 9—TO PREVENT A PERSON DEROGATING FROM HIS GRANT — 185

I.	Introduction	185
II.	The General Rule	186
	1. The Requirements	186
	(a) Grant of rights in land for a particular purpose	186
	(b) Grantor owns neighbouring land	191
	2. Scope of the Duty	194
	3. Giving Effect to the Duty: The Acquisition of Proprietary Rights	199
	4. Duration of the Right Acquired	202

III. Specific Rules Derived From Non-derogation From
Grant 205
1. Where an Easement is Necessary to Provide
Access to Land 206
2. Where the Easement is Necessary for the Land to
be Used Consistent with the Common Intentions of the Parties 209
3. Where the Easement (or Quasi-easement) was
Enjoyed by the Grantor Prior to the Grant 210
4. Easements Acquired by Statutory Words Implied
into a Conveyance 213
IV. Conclusion 215

CHAPTER 10—TO RECOGNISE USE OF A RIGHT **217**
I. Introduction 217
II. Sources Of The Rules 220
1. Adverse Possession 220
2. Prescription 221
III. Elements Of A Claim 225
1. The Elements of a Claim to Adverse Possession 225
(a) Dispossession or Discontinuance in possession 225
(b) Adverse possession 226
(i) Implied licence 229
(ii) Specific future use 231
2. Elements of a Claim to Prescription 232
(a) Without force 234
(b) Openly 235
(c) Without permission 236
3. Failure of *PO* or *SO* to Assert Their Rights 236
IV. Effect Of Use Of The Right 239
1. Adverse Possession 239
2. Prescription 242
V. Applying Claims Based On Use Of A Right To
Leaseholds 242
1. Adverse Possession 243
(a) Application to registered land 243

(b) Bringing *L's* reversionary estate into possession 245
2. Prescription 247
VI. Claims Based On Use Of A Right And Estoppel 249
VII. Conclusion 250

CHAPTER 11—CONCLUSION **251**
I. Introduction 251
II. The Nature Of The Informality And The Relation-
ship Between The Rules Discussed 251
III. The Nature And Type Of The Right Acquired 254
IV. The Common Background To The Informal
Acquisition Of Rights 255
V. Concluding Comments 256

INDEX **259**

Table of Cases

Abbey National Building Society v. Cann [1991] 1 A.C. 56; [1990] 2 W.L.R.
    833, HL 52, 155
Aldin v. Latimer Clark, Muirhead & Co. [1894] 2 Ch. 437 191
Amalgamated Investment & Property Co. Ltd v. Texas Commerce Inter-
    national Bank Ltd [1982] 1 Q.B. 84; [1981] 3 W.L.R. 565, CA 142, 165
Ashburn Anstalt v. W. J. Arnold [1989] Ch.1; [1988] 2 All E.R. 147, CA .. 2, 49–51,
                                        57, 152, 154, 159, 160
Aspden v. Sedden (No. 2) (1876) 1 Ex.D. 496 .... 169, 172, 175
Att.-Gen. of Hong Kong v. Humphreys Estate (Queen's Gardens) Ltd [1987]
    1 A.C. 114; [1987] 2 W.L.R. 343, PC 138

Basham (Deceased), Re [1986] 1 W.L.R. 1498; [1987] 1 All E.R. 405,
    Ch D 134–136, 142, 144–146, 150
B.P. Properties Ltd v. Buckler (1988) 55 P. & C.R. 337; (1987) 284 E.G. 375,
    CA 237, 239
Bannister v. Bannister [1948] 2 All E.R. 133; [1948] W.N. 261, CA 32–35, 39
Barclays Bank Plc v. O'Brien [1994] 1 A.C. 180; [1993] 3 W.L.R. 786, HL 123
Barry v. Hasseldine [1952] Ch. 835; [1952] 2 All E.R. 317, Ch D 207
Beddington v. Atlee (1887) L.R. 35 Ch. D. 317, Ch D 203
Beswick v. Beswick [1968] A.C. 58; [1967] 3 W.L.R. 932, HL 53
Binions v. Evans [1972] 1 Ch. 359; [1972] 2 W.L.R. 729, CA 39, 49–51, 53–59
Birch v. Treasury Solicitor [1951] Ch. 298; [1950] 2 All E.R. 1198, CA 25, 26
Birmingham Midshires Mortgage Services Ltd v. Sabherwal, judgment,
    December 17, 1999 .... 153, 162
Birmingham, Dudley and District Banking Company v. Ross (1887) 38
    Ch.D. 295 185
Booth v. Alcock (1873) 8 Ch. App. 663 .... 203, 204
Borman v. Griffith [1930] 1 Ch. 493, Ch D 189, 211, 212
Bridges v. Mees [1957] 1 Ch. 475; [1957] 3 W.L.R. 215, Ch D 78–80
Bridle v. Ruby [1989] Q.B. 169; [1988] 3 W.L.R. 191, CA 233
British Leyland Motor Corporation Ltd v. Armstrong Patents Co. Ltd [1986]
    A.C. 577; [1986] 2 W.L.R. 400, HL 198
Brown & Root Technology Ltd v. Sun Alliance and London Assurance Co
    Ltd [2000] 2 W.L.R. 566; (1998) 75 P. & C.R. 223, CA; reversing
    [1996] Ch. 51, Ch D 11, 17, 18
Browne v. Flower [1911] 1 Ch. 219; [1908–10] All E.R. Rep. 547, Ch D   189, 190,
                                          194, 199, 200
Buckingham C.C. v. Moran [1990] 1 Ch. 623; [1989] 3 W.L.R. 152, CA 218,
                                      225–228, 231, 232
Burns v. Burns [1984] 1 Ch. 317; [1984] 2 W.L.R. 582, CA 117, 118
Button v. Button [1965] 1 W.L.R. 457; [1968] 1 All E.R. 1064, CA 112

Central London Commercial Estates Ltd v. Kato Kagaku Co. Ltd [1998] 4 All
    E.R. 948; [1998] 3 E.G.L.R. 55, Ch D 229, 244, 246, 247
Chamber Colliery Co. v. Hopwood (1886) L.R. 32 Ch.D. 549, CA 233
Chamber Colliery v. Twyerould (1893), noted [1915] 1. Ch 268 173
Chartered Trust Plc v. Davies (1998) 76 P. & C.R. 396; [1997] 2 E.G.L.R. 83,
    CA 186, 190, 197
Chinn v. Collins see Chinn v. Hochstrasser (Inspector of Taxes)
Chinn v. Hochstrasser (Inspector of Taxes); sub nom. Chinn v. Collins
    (Inspector of Taxes) [1981] A.C. 533; [1981] 2 W.L.R. 14, HL 77
Chung Ping Kwan v. Lam Island Development Co. Ltd [1997] A.C. 38;
    [1996] 3 W.L.R. 448, PC 245
City Permanent Building Society v. Miller [1952] 1 Ch. 840; [1952] 2 All
    E.R. 621, CA 187–189
Clough v. Killey (unreported, March 7, 1996) 124
Colchester B.C. v. Smith [1992] Ch. 421; [1992] 2 W.L.R. 728, CA 239
Collier v. Calvert, (unreported, July 22 1996) 19
Coombes v. Smith [1986] 1 W.L.R. 808; [1987] 1 F.L.R. 352, Ch D   133, 134, 141,
                                                                142, 144, 146
Costagliola v. English (1969) 210 E.G. 1425 212
Crabb v. Arun D.C (No. 1). [1976] 1 Ch .179; [1975] 3 W.L.R. 847, CA   138, 139,
                                                                147–150, 155, 158, 163

Diplock, Re [1948] 1 Ch. 465 94
D.H.N. Food Distributors Ltd v. Tower Hamlets L.B.C. [1976] 1 W.L.R.
    852; [1976] 3 All E.R. 462, CA 57, 77
Dalton v. Angus, sub nom. Angus Dalton, Commissioners of Her Majesty's
    Works & Public Buildings v. Henry Angus & Co. (1881) L.R. 6
    App. Cas. 740, HL 222, 223, 232
Dalton v. Henry Angus & Co. see Dalton v. Angus
De Mattos v. Gibson (1859) 4 De G. & J. 276 . . . . 54, 58
Dodsworth v. Dodsworth (1973) 228 E.G. 1115, CA 155
Drake v. Whipp [1996] 1 F.L.R. 826; [1996] 2 F.C.R. 296, CA 97, 124
Du Boulay v. Raggett (1989) 58 P. & C.R. 138; [1989] 1 E.G.L.R. 229, DC 36
Duffield v. Elwes (1827) 1Bli.N.S. 497; 4 E.R. 959 . . . . 22, 26
Dyer v. Dyer (1788) 2 Cox Eq. Cas. 92; 30 E.R. 42 92

Ellenborough Park, Re; sub nom. Powell v. Maddison; Davies (deceased), Re
    [1956] Ch. 131; [1955] 3 W.L.R. 892, CA 69, 232
E.R. Ives Investment Ltd v. High [1967] 2 Q.B. 379; [1967] 2 W.L.R. 789,
    CA . . . 72, 84, 144, 147, 152, 153, 155, 159, 166, 168, 172, 176, 177, 179–183
Evans v. Hayward [1995] 2 F.L.R. 511; [1995] 2 F.C.R. 313, CA 116
Eves v. Eves [1975] 1 W.L.R. 1338; [1975] 3 All E.R. 768, CA . . . 107–112, 118, 120

Fry, Re [1946] Ch. 312, Ch D 11
Fairweather v. St Marylebone Property Co. Ltd, sub nom. St Marylebone
    Property Co. Ltd v. Fairweather [1963] A.C. 510; [1962] 2 W.L.R.
    1020, HL 239, 245, 246, 247

Gonin; Re; sub nom. Gonin v. Garmeson [1979] 1 Ch. 16; [1977] 3 W.L.R.
    379, Ch D 19
Gayford v. Moffatt (1868) L.R. 4 Ch. App. 133, CA 248

Gillett v. Holt [2000] 2 All E.R. 289; [2000] 1 F.C.R. 705, CA, reversing
      [1998] 3 All E.R. 917, Ch D 136, 137, 139, 141, 144–146, 149, 150, 155,
                                                                                    158
Gissing v. Gissing [1971] A.C. 886; [1970] 3 W.L.R. 255, HL; reversing
      [1969] 2 Ch. 85, CA 96, 98, 102, 104, 115–120, 123–125
Goldberg v. Edwards [1950] 1 Ch. 247; 94 S.J. 128, CA 212
Goodman v. Saltash; *sub nom.* Goodman v. Mayor of Saltash (1882) L.R. 7
      App. Cas. 633, HL 69
Grant v. Edwards [1986] 1 Ch. 638; [1986] 3 W.L.R. 114, CA 107–109, 111,
                                                                      112, 120, 121, 161
Greasley v. Cooke [1980] 1 W.L.R. 1306; [1980] 3 All E.R. 710, CA   139, 142, 143,
                                                                           146, 155
Greenhalgh v. Brindley [1901] 2 Ch. 324, Ch D 221
Griffith v. Williams [1978] 2 E.G.L.R. 121 155

Habib Bank Ltd v. Habib Bank AG Zurich [1981] 1 W.L.R. 1265; [1981] 2
      All E.R. 650, CA 133
Hall v. Hall (1983) 3 F.L.R. 379 117
Halsall v. Brizell [1957] Ch. 169; [1957] 2 W.L.R. 123; [1957] 2 Q.B. 379,
      Ch D 168, 169, 171–175, 182, 183
Hammond v. Mitchell [1991] 1 W.L.R. 1127; [1992] 2 All E.R. 109, Fam Div . . 105,
                                                106, 108, 109, 111–113, 118, 119
Harmer v. Jumbil (Nigeria) Tin Areas Ltd [1921] 1 Ch. 200 .... 186, 190, 194–196,
                                                                            199–201
Hodgson v. Marks [1971] 1 Ch. 892; [1971] 2 W.L.R. 1263, CA 33, 35, 41, 100
Hopgood v. Brown [1955] 1 W.L.R. 213; [1955] 1 All E.R. 550, CA 165
Hounslow LBC v. Minchinton (1997) 74 P. & C.R. 221; [1997] N.P.C. 44,
      CA 226–228
Hussey v. Palmer [1972] 1 W.L.R. 1286; [1972] 3 All E.R. 744, CA 164, 256

International Tea Stores Co. v. Hobbs [1903] 2 Ch. 165, Ch D 214
Inwards v. Baker [1965] 2 Q.B. 29; [1965] 2 W.L.R. 212, CA 139, 145, 147,
                                                     151–153, 155, 159, 163, 164
Ivin v. Blake [1995] 1 F.L.R. 70; [1994] 2 F.C.R. 504; (1994) 67 P. & C.R.
      263, CA 117

James, Re; *sub nom.* James v. James [1935] 1 Ch. 449, Ch D 18
J.A. Pye (Oxford) Ltd v. Graham [2000] E.G.C.S. 21; (2000) 97(8) L.S.G. 36,
      Ch D 228, 231, 237
J.T. Developments v. Quinn (1991) P. & C.R. 33; [1991] 2 E.G.L.R. 257, CA . . 137,
                                                                                    138
James v. James, *see* James, Re
Johnston & Sons Ltd v. Holland [1988] 1 E.G.L.R. 264, CA 185, 188, 190,
                                                192–196, 198, 200, 202, 205, 207
Jones (AE) v. Jones (FW) [1977] 1 W.L.R. 438; (1977) 33 P. & C.R. 147, CA . . 146,
                                                                                    151
Jones v. Challenger [1961] 1 Q.B. 176; [1960] 2 W.L.R. 695, CA 190

Korvine's Trust,Re; [1921] 1 Ch. 343 22

Lady Hood of Avalon v. Mackinnon [1909] 1 Ch. 476, Ch D 93

Law Debenture Trust Corp. Plc v. Ural Caspian Oil Corp. Ltd [1995] Ch.
    152; [1994] 3 W.L.R. 1221, CA; reversing [1993] 2 All E.R. 355,
    Ch D 172
Layton v. Martin [1986] 2 F.L.R. 227; [1986] Fam. Law 212 135
Lazarus Estates Ltd v. Beasley [1956] 1 Q.B. 702; [1956] 2 W.L.R. 502, CA 43
Leigh v. Jack (1879) L.R. 5 Ex. D. 264 .... 231, 232
Lim Teng Huan v. Ang Swee Chuan [1992] 1 W.L.R.113; (1992) 64
    P. & C.R. 233, PC 133, 150
Lloyds Bank Plc v. Carrick [1996] 4 All E.R. 630; [1996] 2 F.L.R. 600, CA 48,
                  68, 71, 78, 83–85, 133, 153, 157, 161, 166, 253
Lloyds Bank Plc v. Rosset [1991] 1 A.C. 107; [1990] 2 W.L.R. 867, HL 95, 96,
                  104, 107–110, 115–118, 122, 125, 155
Loke Yew v. Port Swettenham Rubber Co. Ltd [1913] A.C. 491 49
Long v. Gowlett [1923] 2 Ch.177, Ch D 214
Lord Strathcona Steamship Co. v. Dominion Coal Co. Ltd [1926] A.C. 108,
    PC 54, 58
Lovett v. Fairclough (1991) 61 P. & C.R. 385; [1990] E.G.C.S. 27, Ch D .. 218, 221
Lowson v. Coombes [1999] Ch. 373; [1999] 2 W.L.R. 720, CA 97
Lyttleton Times Co. Ltd v. Warners Ltd [1907] A.C. 476, PC 185
Lyus v. Prowsa Developments [1982] 1 W.L.R. 1044; [1982] 2 All E.R. 953,
    Ch D 42, 48–55, 57–59

McHardy and Sons Ltd v. Warren [1994] 2 F.L.R. 338; [1994] 2 F.C.R. 1247,
    CA 123
Manchester Brewery Co. v. Coombs [1901] 2 Ch. 608 73
Manjang v. Drammeh (1991) 61 P. & C.R. 194, PC 207
Marsh v. Von Sternberg [1986] 1 F.L.R. 526; [1986] Fam. Law 160 116
Mascall v. Mascall (1985) 50 P. & C.R. 119; (1984) 81 L.S.G. 2218, CA 9–15
Matharu v. Matharu [1994] 2 F.L.R. 597; [1994] 3 F.C.R. 216; (1994) 68
    P. & C.R. 93, CA 133, 144, 145, 155
May v. Belleville [1905] 2 Ch. 605, Ch D 63
Midland Bank Plc v. Cooke [1995] 4 All E.R. 562; [1997] 6 Bank. L.R. 147,
    CA 38, 96, 106, 121–124
Midland Bank Plc v. Dobson [1986] 1 F.L.R 171; [1986] Fam. Law 55, CA 91,
                  104, 112
Midland Bank Trust Co. Ltd v. Green [1981] A.C. 513; [1981] 2 W.L.R. 28,
    HL; [1980] Ch. 590, CA 31, 43, 48
Miles v. Bull (No. 2) [1969] 3 All E.R. 1585; 21 P. & C.R. 23, QBD 50, 51
Millman v. Ellis (1996) 71 P. & C.R. 158, CA 211
Mills v. Silver [1991] 1 Ch. 271; [1991] 2 W.L.R. 324, CA 223, 232, 236
Milroy v. Lord (1862) 4 De G.F. & J. 264; 45 E.R. 1185 .... 9, 11–14, 26
Mollo v. Mollo; sub nom. Mollo v. Diez [1999] E.G.C.S. 117, Ch D 161
Molton Builders v. Westminster City Council (1975) 30 P. & C.R. 182;
    (1975) 238 E.G. 411, CA 198
Montague v. Long (1972) 24 P. & C.R. 240; 116 S.J. 712, Ch D 176
Moody v. Steggles (1879) L.R. 12 Ch. D. 261, Ch D 219
Mortgage Corporation Ltd v. Shaire, judgment February 25, 2000 124
Mount Carmel Investments Ltd v. Thurlow Ltd [1988] 1 W.L.R. 1078;
    [1988] 3 All E.R. 129, CA 236, 238

National Provincial and Union Bank of England v. Charnley [1924] 1 K.B.
    31, CA 63
National Provincial Bank Ltd v. Hastings Car Mart Ltd, see National
    Provincial Bank v. Ainsworth

National Provincial Bank v. Ainsworth; *sub nom.* National Provincial Bank
  Ltd v. Hastings Car Mart Ltd (No.1) [1965] A.C. 1175; [1965] 3
  W.L.R. 1, HL 1, 2, 74, 151, 154, 181
Neale v. Willis (1968) 19 P. & C.R. 836; (1968) 112 S.J. 521, CA 37, 39, 40
Neville v. Wilson [1997] Ch. 144; [1996] 3 W.L.R. 460, CA 67, 68, 76
Newnham v. Willison (1988) 56 P. & C.R. 8, DC 224, 234, 235
Nickerson v. Barraclough [1981] 1 Ch. 426; [1981] 2 W.L.R. 773, CA;
  reversing [1980] Ch. 325, Ch D 206–210
Nocton v. Lord Ashburton [1914] A.C. 932; [1914–15] All E.R. Rep. 45, HL 31
North Eastern Railway v. Elliot (1861) 10 H.L.C. 333; 11 E.R. 1055 ...... 188, 189

O'Cedar Ltd v. Slough Trading Company Ltd [1927] 2 K.B. 123, KBD ... 191, 198,
                                                                       199
Oakley v. Boston [1976] Q.B. 270; [1975] 3 W.L.R. 478, CA 222
Oughtred v. I.R.C. [1960] A.C. 206; [1959] 3 W.L.R. 898, HL ... 65–68, 72, 75, 77,
                                                                    79, 80

Palmer v. Bowman [2000] 1 W.L.R. 842; [2000] 1 All E.R. 22, CA 222
Pascoe v. Turner [1979] 1 W.L.R. 43; [1979] 2 All E.R. 945, CA 134, 139, 145,
                                                                    155, 156, 158
Peckham v. Ellison (1999) 31 H.L.R. 1030; (2000) P. & C.R. 276, CA 206, 210
Pennell v. Payne; [1995] Q.B. 192; [1995] 2 W.L.R. 261, CA 204
Pettitt v. Pettitt [1970] A.C. 777; [1969] 2 W.L.R. 966, HL .. 96, 101, 102, 105, 110,
                                                                112, 118, 123, 124
Phillipson v. Gibbon (1871) L.R. 6 Ch. 428 250
Plimmer v. Mayor of Wellington (1884) L.R. 9 App. Cas. 699, PC 133
Port v. Griffith [1938] 1 All E.R. 295, Ch D 195, 196, 198, 199
Poster v. Slough Estates Ltd [1969] 1 Ch. 495; [1968] 1 W.L.R. 1515, Ch D ... 180,
                                                                             181
Powell v. McFarlane (1979) 38 P. & C.R. 452, Ch D 226–231
Pugh v. Savage [1970] 2 Q.B. 373; [1970] 2 W.L.R. 634, CA 224, 248, 249
Purchase v. Lichfield Brewery Co. [1915] 1 K.B. 184 73
Pwllbach Colliery Co. Ltd v. Woodman [1915] A.C. 634, HL 209, 210

Quicke v. Chapman [1903] 1 Ch. 659 192

Ralli's Will Trusts, Re; *sub nom.* Ralli's Marriage Settlement, Re; Calvocoressi
  v. Rodocanachi [1964] Ch. 288; [1964] 2 W.L.R. 144, Ch D 27
Rose, Re; *sub nom.* Midland Bank Executor and Trustee Co. Ltd v. Rose
  [1949] 1 Ch.78; [1948] 2 All E.R. 971, Ch D 12, 15
Rose, Re; *sub nom.* Rose v. I.R.C. [1952] 1 Ch. 499; [1952] 1 All E.R. 1217,
  CA 12–17, 20, 27, 45, 187, 251, 256
Radstock Co-operative and Industrial Society Ltd v. Norton-Radstock Urban
  District Council; *sub nom.* Radstock Cooperative & Industrial Society
  v. Radstock Urban D.C. [1968] 1 Ch. 605; [1968] 2 W.L.R. 1214, CA;
  [1967] 1 Ch. 1094, Ch D 172, 173
Rafique v. Trustees of the Walton Estate, *sub nom* Rafique v. Trustees of the
  Walton Charities (1993) 65 P. & C.R. 356; [1992] N.P.C. 75, Ch D 238
Rains v. Buxton (1880) L.R. 14 Ch. D. 537, Ch D 226
Ramsden v. Dyson (1866) L.R. 1 H.L. 129, HL 129, 131, 140, 164
Reddaway v. Banham [1896] A.C.199; 13 R.P.C. 218, HL 31
Rhone v. Stephens [1994] 2 A.C. 310; [1994] 2 W.L.R. 429, HL .. 2, 170, 172–175,
                                                                   183

Robinson v. Kilvert (1889) L.R. 41 Ch.D. 88, CA 191
Rochefoucauld v. Boustead [1897] 1 Ch. 196, CA 31–35, 39–41, 43, 51
Romulus Trading Co. Ltd v. Comet Properties Ltd [1996] 2 E.G.L.R. 70;
    [1996] 48 E.G. 157, QBD 191, 196, 198, 199

Sharpe Re; sub nom. Ex p. Trustee of the Bankrupt v. Sharpe [1980] 1 W.L.R.
    219; [1980] 1 All E.R. 198, Ch D 38, 57, 152, 155
Stewart, Re; [1908] 2 Ch. 251, Ch D 19
Salvation Army Trustee Co. Ltd v. West Yorkshire C.C. (1981) 41 P. & C.R.
    179, QBD 138, 141
Sen v. Headley [1991] Ch. 425; [1991] 2 W.L.R. 1308, CA 22–25
Simmons v. Dobson [1991] 1 W.L.R. 720; [1991] 4 All E.R. 25, CA 222, 223,
                                                                                        248
Simpson v. Simpson [1992] 1 F.L.R. 601; [1989] Fam. Law 20, Ch D 19
Singh v. Beggs (1996) 71 P. & C.R. 120, CA 69
Sledmore v. Dalby (1996) 72 P. & C.R. 196; [1996] N.P.C. 16, CA . . 144, 145, 148,
                                                                                    151, 158
Sovmots Investments Ltd v. Secretary of State for the Environment [1979]
    A.C. 144; [1977] 2 W.L.R. 951 . . . . 189, 214
Spectrum Investment Co. v. Holmes [1981] 1 W.L.R. 221; [1981] 1 All E.R.
    6, Ch D 244–247
Springette v. Defoe [1992] 2 F.L.R. 388; [1992] 2 F.C.R. 561, CA . . . 91, 92, 96, 97,
                                                                                    106, 116
St Marylebone Property Co. Ltd v. Fairweather see Fairweather v. St
    Marylebone Property Co. Ltd
Stokes v. Anderson [1991] 1 F.L.R. 391; [1991] F.C.R. 539, CA 105, 120, 121
Strong v. Bird (1874) L.R. 18 Eq. 315 . . . . 19, 20, 24, 27, 45, 254
Sturges v. Bridgman (1879) L.R. 11 Ch. D. 852; (1879) 43 J.P. 716, CA 233
Sze To Chun Keung v. Kung Kwok Wai David [1997] 1 W.L.R. 1232; (1997)
    141 S.J.L.B. 171, PC 221

Tailby v. Official Receiver (1888) L.R. 13 App.Cas. 523; (1887) 18 Q.B.D. 25,
    HL 76, 77
Taylors Fashions Ltd v. Liverpool Victoria Trustees Co. Ltd [1982] 1 Q.B.
    133; [1981] 2 W.L.R. 576, Ch D 128, 129, 131, 140, 147, 150, 164
Taylor v. Dickens [1998] 1 F.L.R. 806; [1998] 3 F.C.R. 455, Ch D . . . 136, 147, 148
Tehidy Minerals Ltd v. Norman [1971] 2 Q.B. 528; [1971] 2 W.L.R. 711,
    CA 222–224, 242
Thamesmead Town Ltd v. Allotey (1998) 30 H.L.R. 1052; (2000) 79
    P. & C.R. 557; [1998] 37 E.G. 161, CA 174, 175, 183
Tichborne v. Weir (1892) 67 L.T. 735 239
Tinsley v. Milligan [1994] 1 A.C. 340; [1993] 3 W.L.R. 126, HL 97, 102, 103
Tito v. Waddell (No.2) [1977] Ch. 106; [1977] 3 W.L.R. 972, Ch D   167–170, 173,
                                                                                174, 176, 182, 183
Tulk v. Moxhay (1848) 2 Ph.774; (1848) 18 L.J. Ch. 83; 41 E.R. 1143 . . . 2, 54, 173,
                                                                                        202

Union Lighterage Company v. London Graving Dock Company [1902] 2
    Ch. 557 . . . . 207, 235
United Bank of Kuwait v. Sahib [1997] Ch. 107; [1996] 3 W.L.R. 372, CA . . 44, 78,
                                                                                        80, 81, 153

Voyce v. Voyce (1991) 62 P. & C.R. 290, CA 151

Wallis's Cayton Bay Holiday Camp Ltd v. Shell-Mex and B.P. Ltd [1975] 1
    Q.B. 94; [1974] 3 W.L.R. 387, CA 229–231
Walsh v. Lonsdale (1882) L.R. 21 Ch.D. 9, CA 63, 73, 253, 256
Walters v. Webb (1870) L.R. 5 Ch. App. 531, Ch D 237
Wayling v. Jones [1995] 2 F.L.R. 1029; [1996] 2 F.C.R. 41; (1995) 69
    P. & C.R. 170, CA 113, 114, 135, 136, 142, 143, 147
Westdeutsche Landesbank Girozentrale v. Islington L.B.C. [1996] A.C. 669;
    [1996] 2 W.L.R. 802; [1996] 2 All E.R. 961, HL .. 14, 23, 64, 71, 74, 75, 90,
                                       94, 240, 254, 257
Westhoughton Urban D.C. v. Wigan Coal & Iron Co. Ltd. [1919] 1 Ch. 159,
    CA 169, 172, 173, 175
Wheeldon v. Burrows (1879) L.R. 12 Ch. D. 31, CA 189, 206, 211–215
Wheeler v. JJ Saunders Ltd; [1996] Ch. 19; [1995] 3 W.L.R. 466; [1995] 2 All
    E.R. 697, CA 212–215
Williams v. Coleman (unreported, CA, June 27, 1984) 141
Willmott v. Barber (1880) L.R. 15 Ch. D. 96, Ch D 130, 132
Wong v. Beaumont Property Trust Ltd [1965] 1 Q.B.173; [1964] 2 W.L.R.
    1325, CA 210

Yaxley v. Gotts [2000] Ch. 162; [1999] 3 W.L.R. 1217, CA 81, 82, 162

Table of Foreign Cases

Bahr v. Nicolay (No. 2) (1987–88) 164 C.L.R. 604 (High Court of Australia)   49, 57
Bayliss v. Public Trustee (1988) 12 N.S.W.L.R. 540   22
Bone v. The Commissioner of Stamp Duties of New South Wales [1977]
    A.C. 511; reversing (1974) 132 C.L.R. 38   18

Chan v. Cresdon Proprietary Ltd (1989) 168 C.L.R. 350 (High Court of
    Australia) 63, 73
Corin v. Patton (1990) 169 C.L.R. 540 (High Court of Australia)   16

Government Insurance Office (N.S.W.) v. K.A. Reed Service Pty. Ltd [1988]
    V.R. 829 (Supreme Court of Victoria) 168, 183

Hofman v. Hofman [1965] N.Z.L.R. 795   95

Vandeleur v. Slone [1919] I.R. 116 (Irish Court of Appeal)   237

Table of Statutes

1677 Statute of Frauds (29 Car.
2, c.3) 30
1832 Prescription Act (2 & 3
Will. 4, c.71) 222–224,
232, 235, 237, 242, 248
s.1 .... 223, 224
s.2 .... 223, 224
s.3 232
s.4 .... 224, 234, 235
1837 Wills Act (7 Will. 4 & 1
Vict, c.26)—
s.9 9
s.11 28
1918 Wills (Soldiers and
Sailors) Act—
s.3 28
1925 Settled Land Act (15 & 16
Geo. 5, c.18) 39, 55
1925 Law of Property Act (15 &
16 Geo. 5, c.20)—
s.1 1
(4) 3
(6) 107
s.40 .... 3, 40, 68, 69
(1) 44
(2) 41, 69
s.52 .... 3, 4
(1) 3, 4, 62, 187
(2) 3, 43
(d) 187
s.53 .... 3, 4, 66
(1) 24
(a) 4, 43
(b) .. 21, 22, 27, 30, 31,
38, 40, 41, 43, 45, 57, 87,
88, 100, 104
(c) .. 42, 43, 65–67, 101
(2) ... 4, 5, 22, 41, 43, 66,
67, 88, 89, 104, 124
s.54(2) 3, 5, 187
s.60(3) 99, 100

1925 Law of Property Act—cont.
s.62 .... 213, 214, 215
(1) 213
s.205(1)(ii) 213
1925 Land Registration Act (15
& 16 Geo. 5, c.21) 244,
246
s.19(3) 213
s.20(1) 10
ss.21–22 246
s.22(1) 10
(3) 213
s.69(1) 246
s.70(1)(f) 241
(g) 100, 155, 159
(k) 187
s.75 .. 240, 241, 243, 244, 246,
247
(1) 240
(2) 240
(3) 240
s.123A 17, 62
(3) 16
(4) 16
(5)(a) 16
1931 Statute of Westminster (22
& 23 Geo. 5, c.4) 222
1972 Land Charges Act (c.61) 72,
178
s.2(4)(iii)(a) 72
s.6 159
1980 Limitation Act (c.58) .. 225, 230,
238, 240, 246
s.15 225
(1) 220
ss.29–30 237
Sched. 1,
para. 1 225
para. 4 243
para. 8 225
(4) 230, 231

1982 Administration of Justice
        Act (c.53)—
        s.17 9
1985 Administration of Justice
        Act (c.61)—
        s.50 19
1986 Insolvency Act (c.45)—
        ss.238–239 20
        s.339 20
        ss.423–425 20
1989 Law of Property
        (Miscellaneous
        Provisions) Act (c.34) .. 41,
                44, 69, 79, 80, 81
        s.2 .... 60, 81, 82
          (1)   3, 4, 69, 75, 79, 81, 82
          (5) 3, 5, 81, 82
            (a) 3, 5

1995 Landlord and Tenant
        (Covenants) Act
        (c.30) 73
        s.28(1) 73
1996 Trusts of Land and
        Appointment of
        Trustees Act (c.47)   39, 43,
                                    190
        s.1(1)(a) 43
          (2)(b) 43
1997 Land Registration Act
        (c.2) 16, 62
1999 Contracts (Rights of
        "Third Parties") Act
        (c.31) 53, 59, 60, 62
        s.1 59

Table of Abbreviations

Gray	Kevin Gray, *Elements of Land Law* (2nd ed., 1993)
Hanbury and Martin	Jill E. Martin, *Hanbury and Martin Modern Equity* (15th ed., 1997)
Meagher, Gummow and Lehane	R. P. Meagher, W. M. C. Gummow and J. R. F. Lehane, *Equity Doctrines and Remedies* (3rd ed., 1992)
Megarry and Wade	Charles Harpum, *Megarry and Wade The Law of Real Property* (6th ed., 2000)
Oakley	A. J. Oakley, *Constructive Trusts* (3rd ed., 1997)
Smith	Roger J. Smith, *Property Law* (3rd ed., 2000)
Underhill and Hayton	David J. Hayton, *Underhill and Hayton: Law Relating to Trustees* (15th ed., 1995)

Chapter 1.

Introduction

The purpose of this book is to consider circumstances in which proprietary rights may be acquired despite a failure to comply with formal requirements. The formal requirements referred to are imposed by statute, and must generally be complied with for the express grant of proprietary rights. The requirements are discussed below, but they are essentially documentary requirements, which provide that proprietary rights must be created, or at least be evidenced, in signed writing. The form of writing may, further, be required to be a deed. The effect of a failure to comply with formality requirements is either to deprive the transaction of any effect, or to limit its effect. It is by virtue of the absence of compliance with these requirements that the subject matter of this book is described as the informal acquisition of proprietary rights.

Compliance with formalities will create a proprietary right only where, in addition, the right is in substance proprietary. The general characteristics necessary for a right to be proprietary were explained in a classic formulation by Lord Wilberforce. He explained, a proprietary right must be "definable, identifiable by third parties, capable in its nature of assumption by third parties, and have some degree of permanence or stability".[1] However, merely to fulfil these general characteristics is not sufficient alone. The right must be a recognised proprietary right. These are relatively few in number, encompassing the rights recognised in section 1 of the Law of Property Act 1925 and, additionally, beneficial interests under a trust,

---

[1] *National Provincial Bank v. Ainsworth* [1965] A.C. 1175 at 1248.

estate contracts[2] and restrictive covenants. The list of proprietary rights is not closed, but it is extended only rarely. The most recent addition remains the restrictive covenant in the nineteenth century case, *Tulk v. Moxhay*.[3] Subsequently, the courts have refused to confer proprietary status on positive covenants,[4] contractual licences,[5] and the deserted wife's equity.[6] In exceptional circumstances, a right informally acquired is not a recognised proprietary right, although it meets the general characteristics explained by Lord Wilberforce. In these circumstances, the right acquired is classified as a proprietary right *sui generis*.

It is important at the outset briefly to explain some of the terminology used in this book. Although these are all terms familiar to property lawyers, their use is not always uniform. In this book, "estate" is used to refer to a right to possession of land (*i.e.*, a freehold or leasehold estate). An "interest" refers to a right exercised over land which is possessed by someone else. For example, a legal or equitable easement. However, "equitable interests" (unless the context determines otherwise) is used generally to refer to all proprietary rights which are classified as equitable. This includes, for example, equitable easements and beneficial interests under a trust. The expression "proprietary right" denotes all rights recognised as proprietary. In most of the situations discussed in this book it is not necessary expressly to distinguish between the transfer of an existing right (for example, the assignment of a lease) and the grant of a new right (for example, the grant of an easement). Unless it is apparent from the factual context that only one of these acts is of relevance, or the distinction is expressly drawn, a reference to the "creation" of a right denotes both acts. The creation of a right, even in this broad manner, is however to be distinguished both from the imposition of a right by the court (for example, as a remedy to an estoppel within Chapter 7) and the original acquisition of a right (for example, by adverse possession or prescription as discussed in Chapter 10).

---

[2] The proposition an estate contract is proprietary is not controversial, but is "so well known that it is difficult to find authority": Simon Gardner, "Equity, Estate Contracts and the Judicature Acts: *Walsh v. Lonsdale* Revisited" (1987) 7 O.J.L.S. 60 at n.26.

[3] (1848) 2 Ph. 774; 41 E.R. 1143.

[4] See, most recently, *Rhone v. Stephens* [1994] 2 A.C. 310.

[5] *Ashburn Anstalt v. Arnold* [1989] Ch. 1.

[6] *National Provincial Bank v. Ainsworth* above n.1.

I. The formality requirements

The need to comply with formal requirements may arise in any one, or all, of three distinct stages of the creation of a proprietary right (in the broad definition outlined above). First, the creation of a proprietary right may be preceded by a contract to create the right. For example, the creation of a lease may be preceded by a contract to create a lease. Where this is the case, formality requirements apply in relation to the contract. Second, the actual creation of a proprietary right is subject to formality requirements. Thirdly, in registered land, there may be an additional requirement of registration for legal title to vest.

In relation to contracts, section 2(1) of the Law of Property (Miscellaneous Provisions) Act 1989 provides that: "A contract for the sale or other disposition of an interest in land can only be made in writing. . .". Exceptions are provided in section 2(5), including in relation to the creation of resulting and constructive trusts. For the purposes of this section, "interest in land" includes estates and interests, in the manner in which these terms have been defined above. Hence, for example, section 2(1) applies equally to a contract to create a lease (except for a contract to create a short lease within section 54(2) of the Law of Property Act 1925)[7] or a contract to create an easement. A contract that does not comply with section 2(1) is void. Section 2(1) applies to contracts entered into on or after September 27, 1989. Contracts made before that date are governed by less stringent requirements provided by section 40 of the Law of Property Act 1925. Under that section a contract for sale of land is not enforceable unless evidenced in writing or coupled with an act of part performance.[8]

The formal requirements for the creation of a proprietary right are provided principally by sections 52 and 53 of the Law of Property Act 1925. Section 52(1) provides that "all conveyances of land or of any interest therein are void for the purpose of conveying or creating a legal estate unless made by deed". "Legal estate" is defined in section 1(4) as including legal interests. The effect of section 52(1) is that legal estates and interests must be created by deed, save for exceptional cases provided for in section 52(2). The requirements of a deed

---

[7] Law of Property (Miscellaneous Provisions) Act 1989, s.2(5)(a).
[8] For a full discussion of these requirements, see Chapter 5 Part II.3.

are explained in section 2(1) of the Law of Property (Miscellaneous Provisions) Act 1989. A failure to comply with section 52(1) has the effect that the conveyance is ineffective insofar as it purports to confer legal title. By section 53 of the Law of Property Act 1925 the creation of (equitable) interests in land, excluding a beneficial interest under a trust, is required to be in writing, signed by the person creating the same.[9] A declaration of trust of land must be evidenced in writing, signed by a person able to declare the trust. Section 53(2) provides, "this section does not affect the creation or operation of resulting, implied or constructive trusts".

It is apparent that formality requirements represent purely a paper exercise. Their effect is that unless a particular form of documentation is used, a proprietary right is not created, notwithstanding the fact that the right is in substance proprietary. In this respect, Patricia Critchley aptly describes formality requirements as "a requirement that matters of substance must be put into a particular form".[10] The Law Commission identified several broad justifications for imposing formality requirements in relation to a contract for sale of land, which may in fact be of more general relevance.[11] One principal justification is that formalities ensure certainty as to the nature, duration and terms of the right created. The requirements also serve related roles in providing evidence of the nature and duration of the right and in ensuring that parties understand the terms of their transaction. The latter may be achieved practically, as the effect of formality requirements is likely to be to ensure that parties seek professional advice prior to a transaction.[12] It is particularly important that the terms of transactions relating to land are understood, as the transaction may involve a significant financial investment and create on-going rights and responsibilities. Formalities also ensure that rights are not created inadvertently, for example in the course of negotiations. Finally, as Peter Birks explains, formalities provide a means of making proprietary rights visible.[13] As proprietary rights are

---

[9] s.53(1)(a). The creation of a legal interest will have to comply with the stricter requirement of a deed in section 52.

[10] "Taking Formalities Seriously" in *Land Law Themes and Perspectives* (Susan Bright and John Dewar eds., 1998) 507, p. 508.

[11] Law Com, No. 164, *Transfer of Land Formalities for Contracts for Sale etc. of Land*, paras 2.7–1.13. See also the discussion by Critchley above n.10.

[12] Critchley above n.10, p. 514.

[13] "Before We Begin: Five Keys to Land Law" in *'Land Law Themes and Perspectives'* (Susan Bright and John Dewar eds., 1998) 457, p. 483.

a form of intangible property, documents serve to make their existence apparent.

II. Justifying informal acquisition

The formality requirements explained above constitute what may be described as a "policy of formality" in the creation of proprietary rights. Given these requirements, the concept of informal acquisition needs to be justified. Specific justifications are dependent upon the different contexts in which informal acquisition takes place, and are considered in each chapter. However a number of general comments can be made as to the legal and policy-based grounds for allowing the informal acquisition of proprietary rights. As a matter of law, the statutory provisions which lay down the requirements themselves provide for exceptions. These exceptions are relied upon in a number of situations discussed in this book. Some exceptions are narrow, providing only for the creation of a particular type of right. For example, the formality requirements do not apply in relation to the grant of certain short leases.[14] Other exceptions are of a more general application. Of particular importance is the saving provided for the operation of resulting and constructive trusts.[15] The broad scope of these trust doctrines has provided a particularly fertile basis for informal acquisition. There is however a limit to the extent to which these legal exceptions can be used to justify informal acquisition. If the need to impose formality was considered of paramount import-ance, then the exceptions could be strictly construed. Further, these statutory exceptions are not relied upon in all situations in which informal acquisition occurs. Hence, policy-based justifications must also be considered.

As has been seen, a number of reasons for requiring formalities have been forwarded. The concept of informal acquisition represents, in essence, a policy judgement that in some situations the desire to enable a proprietary right to be acquired outweighs the reason for generally imposing formalities.[16] This judgement may be based on a

---

[14] Law of Property Act 1925, s.54(2); Law of Property (Miscellaneous Provisions) Act 1989, s.2(5)(a).

[15] Law of Property Act 1925, s.53(2); Law of Property (Miscellaneous Provisions) Act 1989, s.2(5).

[16] See, *e.g.* the list of "benefits" and "detriments" of formalities identified by Critchley above n.10.

number of factors. The guarantees provided by formality requirements may be provided through other means. For example, the
existence and scope of a proprietary right may be apparent because it
has been exercised over a period of time. Or, it may be that to insist
on formalities will defeat, rather than achieve, the purpose for which
the requirements are imposed. This is particularly the case where
proprietary rights are acquired to prevent fraudulent reliance on non-
compliance with formalities. The desire to prevent certain types of
conduct which may be classified as fraudulent or unconscionable may
also represent policy goals superior to the desire for formality, with
the effect that the latter gives way to achieve the former. In this
respect, informal acquisition enables a balance to be achieved
between competing policy interests. As Birks explains, in imposing
formality requirements "pain should not be inflicted except in the
case of pressing necessity".[17] Finally, informal acquisition provides a
means to protect those who are justifiably unaware of the need to
comply.[18] In this respect, Peter Sparkes notes: "Formality favours the
monied, the strong and the well advised, so flexibility is required to
correct the imbalance which exists against the poor and weak".[19]

III. Structure of the book

Each chapter of this book considers a particular situation (or related
situations) in which proprietary rights may be acquired informally,
and the rule through which the right is acquired. The chapters are
separated according to the factual situation in which rights are
acquired, rather than by reference to the nature or the doctrinal basis
(for example, resulting or constructive trust) of the right. Chapter 2
considers three rules which enable proprietary rights to be acquired
pursuant to an uncompleted gift of land. Chapters 3 and 4 are both
concerned with situations in which proprietary rights are acquired to
prevent a particular type of fraud. In Chapter 3, and exceptionally in
Chapter 4, the claimant of the right (in common with Chapter 2)
need not have provided consideration or acted to his detriment.
Chapter 5 then considers the circumstances in which proprietary

---

[17] See above n.13, at 484.
[18] Critchley above n. 10, pp. 522–526.
[19] Peter Sparkes, *A New Land Law* (1999), p. 217.

rights are acquired pursuant to a sale of land which is not formally completed. The focus of Chapters 6 and 7 is the means by which proprietary rights may be acquired by persons in a familial or emotional relationship, although the rules discussed (in particular in Chapter 7) are of much wider application. Chapter 6 considers how a beneficial interest may arise pursuant to an agreement between the parties found to be trustee and beneficiary, or to prevent the unjust enrichment of the trustee by the beneficiary. Chapter 7 looks at the effect of unilateral assurances of rights. Chapters 8 and 9 deal with the consequences of the fact a particular right is enjoyed. The chapters show how proprietary rights may be acquired to ensure that the grantee and grantor of a right acts according to a broad standard of fairness. Chapter 10 considers when a proprietary right is acquired simply on the basis that it has been exercised over a period of time.

Chapter 2

To Give Effect to an Imperfect Gift

I. Introduction

This chapter is concerned with transfers of land which are intended to operate as a gift. The general requirement for a gift to be effective is that it must be made either by a valid *inter vivos* transfer of the land or in a valid will.[1] The gift remains incomplete and imperfect until formal requirements have been observed. Further, equity will not intervene to complete the gift, consistent with the maxim that 'equity will not assist a volunteer'.[2] This chapter discusses three rules according to which, despite this maxim, proprietary rights may be acquired from a gift in respect of which formal requirements have not been observed. The common element in the situations discussed is that the person in whose favour rights are created has not provided consideration.

Equity's general refusal to complete a gift recognises the donor's right to change his mind and the absence of any reciprocity by the donee to justify intervention on his behalf. The rules discussed in this chapter, although disparate in terms of their origin and require-ments, are connected as they identify circumstances in which giving effect to the donor's intent is considered paramount. This is justified in part by the existence of a clear and unequivocal intention of the donor to make the gift. However, the mere existence of such intent is

---

[1] The formality requirements for a valid will are provided by the Wills Act 1837, s.9 (as amended by the Administration of Justice Act 1982, s.17). The will must be in writing, signed by (or on behalf of) the testator, and signed by two or more persons as witnesses.

[2] See, *e.g. Milroy v. Lord* (1862) 4 De. G. F. & J. 264, 45 E.R. 1185; *Mascall v. Mascall* (1985) 50 P. & C. R. 119 at 126, *per* Browne-Wilkinson L.J.

not itself sufficient. In the first two rules discussed, equity is not in fact required to intervene to assist the volunteer. Hence, in these situations there seems no remaining objection to the acquisition of rights by the donee. The third rule, in which equity's assistance is required, is justified by the special circumstances of an impending death in which the rule applies.

The rules to be discussed apply whether the transfer is direct to the donee, or to trustees to hold on trust for the donee. A transfer to trustees raises a particular question which is considered in Part V of this chapter. Therefore, the discussion of the rules in Parts II-IV is made by reference to transfers direct to the donee.

II.   The first rule: where the donor has done all in his power to complete the transfer

The formal requirements to complete a gift, whether of land or personal property, may lie wholly within the donor's control. This is the position, for example, in relation to a gift of unregistered land. A gift of unregistered land is complete following a valid conveyance of the land by the donor. However, there are some situations in which formal completion of a gift is dependent upon action by a third party. In relation to land, this is the case where the gift is of a registered title. Legal title will pass only when the donee is registered as proprietor.[3] This, of course, requires action by a third party; namely the Land Registrar. Where the act of a third party is required to complete a gift at law, equity considers the gift to be complete once the donor has done all that is within his power to transfer the title. From that time equity treats the donee as entitled to the land.

The operation of this rule is not construed in terms of equity assisting the volunteer by completing the gift. Instead, the rule defines the point in time at which equity considers that the parties themselves have completed the gift. In *Mascall v. Mascall*, Browne-Wilkinson L.J. explained that the maxim 'equity will not assist a volunteer' means that equity will not issue an order to complete the donee's title. However, it is not inconsistent with that maxim to treat the gift as complete once the donee's title can be perfected without further action by the donor and, therefore, without the need for intervention by equity.[4]

---

[3] Land Registration Act 1925, ss.20(1) (freehold) and s.22(1) (leasehold).
[4] See above n.2 at 126.

1. DEVELOPMENT OF THE RULE

This rule developed in the context of gifts of shares in private companies. Such a transaction is analogous to the gift of a registered title to land. Legal title to shares vests only upon registration (in the Register of Shareholders) which is, in turn, subject to approval by the directors. Indeed, the application of the rule to land may be considered *a fortiori* as the directors, unlike the Land Registrar, may have a discretion to refuse the transfer.[5] The application of the rule to land was first considered in *Mascall v. Mascall*.[6] There, in the Court of Appeal, it was not disputed that if the rule exists, then it should be applied to land. Instead, the validity of the rule was challenged. Therefore it is appropriate to consider how the rule developed.

The starting point in explaining the rule is to consider the general approach to gifts taken by equity. Equity's approach to gifts was stated by Turner L.J. in his classic judgment in *Milroy v. Lord*.[7] There, the settlor sought to transfer shares in a bank to Lord to hold on trust for the plaintiffs. Transfer of the shares required entry in the books of the bank and no such entry had been made on the settlor's death. The Court of Appeal held that, therefore, the gift of the shares remained incomplete. In his judgment, Turner L.J. noted two points. First, he said:

> "I take the law of this Court to be well settled, that, in order to render a voluntary settlement valid and effectual, the settler must have done everything which, according to the nature of the property comprised in the settlement, was binding upon him. He may of course do this by actually transferring the property to the persons for whom he intends to provide, and the provision will then be effectual, and it will be equally effectual if he transfers the property to a trustee for the purposes of the settlement . . . but, in order to render the settlement binding, one or other of these modes must, as I understand the law of

---

[5] *Brown & Root Technology Ltd and another v. Sun Alliance and London Assurance Co Ltd* [1996] Ch. 51 at 65, *per* Judge Paul Baker Q.C. The absence of discretion by the third party frees the application of the rule to land from the difficulties caused in relation to shares by *Re Fry* [1946] Ch. 312. For a discussion of that case see L.A. Sheridan "Informal Gifts of Choses in Action (1955) 33 Canadian Bar Review 284; L. McKay, "Share Transfers and the Complete and Perfect Rule [1976] Conv. 139.

[6] See above n.2.

[7] See above n.2.

this Court, be resorted to, for there is no equity in this Court to perfect an imperfect gift".[8]

Secondly Turner L.J. noted that equity will not construe an imperfect transfer, which is intended to be direct to the donee, as a declaration of trust.[9]

The rule under discussion is derived from two cases in which *Milroy v. Lord* was distinguished. The cases coincidentally bear the same name, *Re Rose*,[10] and the rule is generally referred to as the rule in *Re Rose*.[11]

In *Re Rose* (1949), a testator bequeathed shares in a private company to Mr Hook "if such . . . shares have not been transferred to him previously to my death". During his life the testator executed a transfer of the shares to Mr Hook, but this was not registered by the company until after the testator's death. The Court of Appeal was asked whether the shares had been transferred to Mr Hook during the testator's life within the terms of the will. Jenkins J. (as he then was) considered the decision in *Milroy v. Lord* to be dependent upon the fact that the donor "had not done all in his power, according to the nature of the property given, to vest the legal interest in the property in the donee".[12] In effect, he interpreted Turner L.J.'s requirement for the donor to have done "everything . . . necessary to be done" as satisfied once the donor has done everything necessary *which is within his power*.[13] In Jenkins J.'s judgment, the crucial difference between the present case and *Milroy v. Lord* was that in the present case the donor had done all in his power by executing a transfer of the shares in accordance with the company's regulations. This was sufficient to complete the gift in equity even though legal title did not pass until recorded by the directors.[14] In contrast, the donor in *Milroy v. Lord* had not done everything in his power because

---

[8] See above n.2 at 1189.

[9] See above n.2 at 1190.

[10] *Re Rose, Midland Bank Executor and Trustee Co Ltd v. Rose* [1949] 1 Ch. 78; *Re Rose, Rose v. I.R.C.* [1952] 1 Ch. 499 (hereafter *Re Rose* (1949) and *Re Rose* (1952))

[11] The rule takes its name from *Re Rose* (1952).

[12] See above n.10 at 89.

[13] See also *Mascall v. Mascall* above n.2 at 128, *per* Browne-Wilkinson L.J.; the third construction of *Milroy v. Lord* discussed by L. McKay above n.5 at 140–141.

[14] *Re Rose* (1949) above n.10 at 89.

the document executed "was not the appropriate document to pass any interest in the property at all".[15]

This interpretation of *Milroy v. Lord* was followed by the Court of Appeal (including Jenkins L.J.) in *Re Rose* (1952). There, the Court of Appeal was asked whether a gift of shares in a private company took effect from the date of the donor's transfer or the date of registration by the directors.[16] The Court of Appeal held that in equity the gift was complete on the date of transfer. Unlike the earlier case, the Court analysed the position of the parties in the interim period between transfer and registration, during which time legal title remained vested in the donor. The Court considered that during this period the donor held the shares on trust for the donee.[17] The imposition of a trust appeared necessary because the effect of recognising the donee as entitled to the shares on the date of the transfer was to divide the legal and equitable title. Legal title remained with the donor until registration. The apparent need to impose a trust during this interim period provided the basis of Counsel's argument against treating the gift as complete on the date of transfer. Counsel argued, apparently consistent with Turner L.J.'s second observation in *Milroy v. Lord*,[18] that as the transfer was intended to operate as an absolute gift it could not be treated as a declaration of trust. In response, Evershed M.R. gave Turner L.J.'s judgment a restrictive interpretation. In Evershed M.R.'s view, Turner L.J. meant only that a document *which is not in the correct form* to effect a transfer cannot be treated as a declaration of trust. However, where the correct form has been used (and the donor has done all that is within his power) it is not inconsistent with *Milroy v. Lord* to impose a trust, for a limited period, to give effect to the transfer.[19]

---

[15] *ibid.* In *Re Rose* (1952) Evershed M.R. said (above n.10 at 509) the transfer in *Milroy v. Lord* was not in accordance with the regulations of the bank. The source of this statement was questioned in *Mascall v. Mascall* above n.2 at 124. However the significant point, which has not been disputed, is that in *Milroy v. Lord* the Court proceeded on the basis that the donor had not done all in his power to complete the gift.

[16] The significance was that registration, though not transfer, had occurred within five years of the donor's death. If registration was the date on which the gift took effect, then estate duty was payable.

[17] See above n.10 at 512, *per* Evershed M.R.; at 518, *per* Jenkins L.J.

[18] See above n.9 and text.

[19] In fact, as directors may refuse to register a transfer the trust could last indefinitely: Sarah Lowrie and Paul Todd "*Re Rose* Revisited" (1998) 57 C.L.J. 46 at 47.

In *Mascall v. Mascall*[20] the Court of Appeal confirmed the validity of the rule in *Re Rose* and accepted its application to land. There, the donor executed a transfer of the registered title to a house to the donee,[21] his son, and handed to his son the Land Certificate. Before the donee applied to be registered as proprietor a family dispute developed which resulted in the donor seeking to renege on the gift. The Court of Appeal held that in equity the gift was complete. The donor had done all within his power to vest the title in the donee and, pending registration, held the legal title on trust.

In *Westdeutsche Landesbank Girozentrale v. Islington L.B.C.*[22] Lord Browne-Wilkinson denied that the mere fact legal and equitable title is split requires the imposition of a trust.[23] This is contrary to the orthodox approach, illustrated by *Re Rose* (1952), and it is necessary to consider whether, in light of *Westdeutsche*, it is necessary to impose a trust. The question raises two issues, one of substance and one of terminology. The concept of a trust referred to by Lord Browne-Wilkinson arises where property is held by a trustee for a beneficiary in circumstances in which the trustee is under fiduciary obligations towards the beneficiary. The substantive issue is whether it is possible for legal and equitable title to be divided without the imposition of such obligations. It is submitted that there are circumstances in which this is appropriate, including the application of the rule in *Re Rose*. For example, in *Re Rose* (1952) the donor intended only to make a gift. It would not be appropriate to impose upon the donor fiduciary obligations towards the donee which would leave the donor susceptible to liability.[24] In the context of *Re Rose* (1952), this analysis is a more convincing explanation of the relationship between the rule in *Re Rose* and *Milroy v. Lord* than that given by the Court of Appeal. The transfer, intended to operate as an absolute gift, is not treated as a declaration of trust because the fiduciary obligations of trusteeship are not imposed. In the absence of a full discussion of the issue by Lord Browne-Wilkinson it may be difficult to identify when fiduciary obligations should not be imposed on the division of legal and equitable title. Sarah Lowrie and Paul Todd suggest that fiduciary

---

[20] See above n.2.
[21] The transfer was expressed to be for consideration but was in fact a gift. The reference to consideration, which was not paid, seems to have been an attempt to avoid capital gains tax. See, above n.2 at 122, *per* Lawton L.J.
[22] [1996] 2 All E.R. 961.
[23] See above n.22 at 989–990.
[24] Sarah Lowrie and Paul Todd above n.19 at 47.

obligations should not be imposed where there are good reasons for not doing so.[25] It seems consistent with the tenor of Lord Browne-Wilkinson's judgment to suggest that fiduciary obligations should not be imposed where there is no obligation in conscience for the legal owner to do more than recognise the equitable owner's entitlement.

Once accepted that legal and equitable title can be divided without the imposition of fiduciary obligations a subsidiary issue of terminology arises. Should such cases be described as involving a "trust"? This would be to use the concept of a trust broadly to describe any situation in which property is held for another.[26] For example, where the rule in *Re Rose* is applied, the donor is a trustee to the extent that he is obliged to hold the gift property for the benefit of the donee. It may be considered preferable to preserve the description "trust" for situations in which the usual obligations of trusteeship are imposed. However, in the context of the informal acquisition of rights it is advantageous to define the concept of a trust broadly. This point is illustrated in Part IV 1 of this chapter. Accepting this broad definition of a trust, the trust applied in the rule in *Re Rose* is constructive as it arises by operation of law.[27]

2. ELEMENTS OF A CLAIM

Re Rose (1949), *Re Rose* (1952) and *Mascall v. Mascall* all refer to the need for the donor to have done everything in his power to transfer the title. The clear and unequivocal intent evidenced by the donor executing the gift seems to remove objections to recognising the donee's entitlement. In *Mascall v. Mascall* the Court qualified this requirement, noting that the donor must only have done everything in his power "in the ordinary way of the transfer".[28] This was in response to an argument that the donor had not done everything in his power because he could have asked the Land Registry to register the transfer. Lawton L.J. considered this insufficient to defeat the gift as, in the ordinary way, it was the transferee's responsibility to apply for registration.

---

[25] See above n.19 at 47.
[26] Peter Birks, "Trusts Raised to Reverse Unjust Enrichment: The *Westdeutsche* Case" [1996] R.L.R. 3 at 12.
[27] Oakley, p. 318 On the concept of a trust and fiduciary obligations see also P. J. Millett, "Restitution and Constructive Trusts" (1998) 114 L.Q.R. 399 at 403–404.
[28] See above n.2 at 125, *per* Lawton L.J.

In registered land, the need for the donor to have done everything in his power means that the donor must have executed a transfer and provided the donee with access to the Land Certificate. Where the Land Certificate is held by a third party, it may be sufficient for the donor to authorise that party to produce the certificate.[29] It is essential for the donor to have provided access to the Land Certificate because in an ordinary transaction the transferee must present this to the Land Registrar for the transaction to be registered.[30] Therefore, unless access is provided the donor has not done everything in his power.[31]

3. SCOPE OF THE RULE

The rule in *Re Rose* applies only where completion of a gift requires action by a third party. In relation to land this restricts its application to gifts of registered titles. Formal requirements for all other gifts of land are wholly within the control of the parties. Under reforms introduced by the Land Registration Act 1997 the transfer by gift of an unregistered title may trigger compulsory first registration. The rule in *Re Rose* does not apply to such gifts as specific provision is made in the statute as regards the donee's rights from the time the transfer is executed. Under section 123A(3) of the Land Registration Act 1925 (introduced by the Land Registration Act 1997) the donee has two months from the date the transfer is executed to apply to be registered. During this interim period section 123A(4) of the Act provides for the transfer to operate to grant the legal estate. Hence, even before the donee applies to be registered, it is assumed that the gift is complete in law. If the donee fails to apply for registration within two months, then, under section 123A(5)(a) of the Act, the legal title reverts to the donor to hold on trust for the donee. This statutory trust produces a result analogous to the application of *Re Rose*.

---

[29] Alan Dowling, "Can Roses Survive on Registered Land?" (1999) 50 N.I.L.Q. 90 at 97.

[30] T.B.F. Ruoff and R.B. Roper *The Law and Practice of Registered Conveyancing* (6th ed., 1991), para. 3–25.

[31] *cf. Corin v. Patton* (1990) 169 C.L.R. 540 (High Court of Australia). There, the certificate of title to land, without which a transfer could not be registered, was held by a mortgagee. A gift of the land was considered incomplete as the donee had taken no action to procure production of the certificate. Mason C.J. and McHugh J. explained (at 560–561) that the gift failed because the donor "gave no authority for the mortgagee bank to hand the certificate of title to [the donee] for the purposes of registration".

The rule in *Re Rose* has no application to a transfer on sale. An uncompleted sale of land may be the source for the acquisition of proprietary rights under separate rules discussed in Chapter 5 (concerning the acquisition of rights derived from a specifically enforceable contract for sale of land or based on full payment of consideration). The acquisition of rights pursuant to a transfer on gift and a transfer on sale have a common foundation in equity looking to the future and pre-supposing the completion of a transaction. However, by providing consideration a purchaser of land may acquire rights at a time when action by the vendor remains necessary to complete the transfer. These rights are initially qualified, as dependent upon the availability of specific performance. When a transfer on sale has been executed, and therefore the only remaining act is registration, the position of a purchaser is analogous to that of a donee under *Re Rose*.[32]

The fact legal title remains vested in the donor does have practical significance. One illustration of this in the context of a transaction involving land[33] is provided by *Brown & Root Technology Ltd v. Sun Alliance and London Assurance Co Ltd*.[34] There, the tenant of commercial premises executed an assignment of the lease to its parent company. The assignment was not registered, and the assignor sought to terminate the lease by exercising a break clause.[35] The court was asked whether this was a valid exercise of the break clause. At first instance, Judge Paul Baker Q.C., using the rule in *Re Rose* as an analogy, considered that as the assignor had done all in its power to assign the lease the assignment was complete in equity. He concluded that this meant the assignor could not exercise the break clause. The Court of Appeal overruled this decision on the ground that exercise of a break clause is dependent solely upon legal

---

[32] The Land Registration Act 1925, s.123A applies equally to a transfer on sale and a transfer on gift which triggers compulsory first registration. There is no equivalent provision for the transfer of a registered title. Notwithstanding, pending registration of such a transfer, title is held on trust for the purchaser. See Chapter 5, n.2.

[33] This point was made in *Re Rose* (1952) above, n.10 in response to the hypothetical question: to whom should dividends be paid in the interim between equitable and legal completion of the gift? The Court explained that *vis-a-vis* the company, the donor, as registered holder of the shares, remained entitled. However, once paid, the dividends became property of the trust as part of the same gift. See 512–513, *per* Evershed M.R.; at 518, *per* Jenkins L.J.

[34] See above n.5 (at first instance); (1998) 75 P. & C.R. 223, CA.

[35] The break clause was expressly stated in the lease to be personal to the assignor and could not therefore be exercised by the assignee.

ownership. The Court of Appeal accepted that, *vis-à-vis* the parties to the assignment, the judge's analysis was sound:[36] *i.e.* in so far as relations between the parties to the assignment were concerned, the assignee was entitled to the land. However, *vis-à-vis* third parties the assignor, as holder of the legal title, remained entitled to the land.

III.   The second rule: where the donee is appointed as the donor's executor or administrator

If a gift of land remains incomplete on the donor's death, then the gift will generally fail. Upon the donor's death his property vests in his executors or (in the case of intestacy) administrators and equity will not assist a volunteer by requiring such persons to act to perfect the donee's title. However, there is one exceptional case in which the gift will be effective. If the donee is appointed as executor or administrator, then the donee does not need the assistance of equity to complete his title.[37] The donor's title to the land vests in the donee in his capacity as executor or administrator. This coincidental vesting of title in the donee is considered sufficient to perfect the gift.

1.   DEVELOPMENT OF THE RULE

This rule first developed from the different interpretations of common law and equity of the effect of a testator appointing his debtor as executor. The difficulty caused by such an appointment is that it prevents recovery of the debt. A debt is no more than the right to sue for money and the executor cannot bring an action against himself. In light of this, at common law the appointment was considered to extinguish the debt. As it was the testator's appointment of the debtor as executor which prevented recovery of the debt it was presumed the testator intended to extinguish the debt.[38] Equity

---

[36] See above, n.34 at 229. On the facts the analogy may not have been appropriate as the assignment may have been for consideration. Judge Paul Baker Q.C. noted only that "if there was any consideration the tenant has received it" (above n.5 at 65). If the assignment was for consideration, then the correct analogy is with the rules discussed in Chapter 5 concerned with uncompleted sales of land (which were referred to in the Court of Appeal by Mummery L.J.). However, this would not alter the outcome of the case.

[37] *James v. James* [1935] 1 Ch. 449 at 451, *per* Farwell J.

[38] See the explanation by Mason J. in the High Court of Australia in *Bone v. The Commissioner of Stamp Duties of New South Wales* (1974) 132 C.L.R. 38 at 53 (his decision was reversed on appeal on other grounds: [1977] A.C. 511).

does not generally take this view. Instead, equity presumes that a debtor appointed as executor has already paid the debt and therefore has available money representing the debt to pay to the beneficiaries under the will. However, equity acknowledges one exceptional case where the common law interpretation should prevail. In *Strong v. Bird*[39] it was held that the common law interpretation will prevail where the testator, during his life, did in fact intend to release the debt. This rule, known as the rule in *Strong v. Bird*, was subsequently held to apply outside the context of the release of a debt. It was held that where a testator, during his life, intended to transfer land (or other property) as a gift, and appointed the intended donee as executor, the appointment completed the gift.[40] Further, it was held that a debtor (or intended donee) who became appointed administrator when the creditor (or donor) died intestate would also benefit from the rule.

2. ELEMENTS OF A CLAIM

The application of the rule is subject to two requirements.[41] First, the donor must have intended to make an immediate[42] *inter vivos* gift of the land and that intention must have continued until his death. A strict interpretation of this requirement will ensure that the rule applies only when donative intent clearly subsisted at the time of the donor's death.[43] Secondly, the rule is dependent upon the coincidental vesting of the land in the intended donee upon his appointment as executor or administrator.[44] The application of the rule to administrators has been criticised.[45] It is inconsistent with the basis of the

---

[39] (1874) L.R. 18 Eq. 315.

[40] *Re Stewart* [1908] 2 Ch. 251.

[41] For a full discussion see Gilbert Kodilinye, "A Fresh Look at the Rule in *Strong v. Bird*" [1982] Conv. 14.

[42] Future gifts are excluded: *Simpson v. Simpson* [1992] 1 F.L.R. 601 at 623. Their exclusion is criticised by Underhill and Hayton, p. 139.

[43] See, *e.g. Re Gonin* [1979] 1 Ch. 16 at 39: no continuing intention to make a gift of land where the donor subsequently drew a cheque in favour of the donee representing the land.

[44] The gift is complete once title vests in the transferee, regardless of whether they subsequently prove the will. See, *e.g. Collier v. Calvert*, judgment July 22, 1996: application of *Strong v. Bird* not affected by subsequent removal of the transferee as executor under the Administration of Justice Act 1985, s.50.

[45] See, *e.g.* Walton J. in *Re Gonin* above n.43 at 34–35; Underhill and Hayton, p. 139 (who, p. 140, conditionally accept the extension on other grounds).

original common law rule that the appointment of a debtor as executor evidenced a presumed intent to release the debt. However, the common law rule is now able to prevail only where there is an *actual* intent to release a debt or to make a gift. It is the actual intent of the donor that is paramount. The vesting of land in the donee is important because it means that equity is not required to assist the volunteer to vest title. As there is actual, and not merely presumed intent, the means by which the land becomes vested in the donee should be irrelevant.[46]

3. NATURE OF THE RIGHT ACQUIRED

When the rule in *Strong v. Bird* applies, the donor's title to the land vests wholly in the donee who is absolutely entitled to the land. Unlike the rule in *Re Rose* there is no division of entitlement between the donor and donee and therefore no question of the imposition of a trust arises. It is thought that the donee remains vulnerable to claims to the land by creditors. This is because the common law rule recognised in *Strong v. Bird* gives no protection against creditors.[47] The reasoning, in relation to the release of a debt, is that as against the creditors the debtor is still treated as having in his hands money representing the debt. This reasoning does not apply where the rule is applied in relation to a gift. In that context, there is no question of the donor being treated as holding money which should have been paid by him to the donor. It is submitted that a gift completed by the rule in *Strong v. Bird* should be treated in the same way as any other *inter vivos* gift, and be capable of being set aside only under the same circumstances as other gifts.[48]

IV. The third rule: gifts made in contemplation of, and conditional upon, death

In both rules previously discussed in this chapter, the donor has intended an immediate transfer of land as a gift. In the final rule to be

---

[46] The application of the rule to administrators is supported by Kodilinye above n.41, p. 16–17.

[47] Meagher, Gummow and Lehane, para. 2907(f); Underhill and Hayton, p. 140; Parry and Clark, *The Law of Succession* (10th ed., 1996), p. 411.

[48] *e.g.* (in relation to creditors) under the powers in the Insolvency Act 1986, ss. 238–239, 339 and 423–425.

considered, the donor makes the gift in contemplation of death, with the intention that the gift should be complete (and therefore title be transferred) only upon his death. This type of gift is known as a *donatio mortis causa*. A *donatio mortis causa* enjoys a unique position as a gift made *inter vivos* but which takes effect only upon the donor's death. The consequence of this is that it may be seen as enabling proprietary rights to be acquired despite non-compliance with the usual formal requirements necessary either for a valid *inter vivos* gift or a valid testamentary gift.[49]

For there to be a valid *donatio mortis causa* it must be shown both that the elements of a claim are fulfilled and, more generally, that the property in question is capable of passing as such a gift. It is the latter requirement which seems to have caused most difficulty in the context of land and which will therefore be considered first.

1. Is Land Capable of Passing as a Donatio Mortis Causa?

As a *donatio mortis causa* becomes complete upon the donor's death, at that time his title is transferred to the donee. This does not cause difficulties where the subject of the *donatio mortis causa* is a chattel. The chattel will usually have been delivered to the donee at the time the gift was made[50] and no further action is necessary upon the donor's death to complete the donee's title. However, while a donor may deliver indicia of title to land,[51] this is insufficient to transfer title to land. Upon the donor's death, in the absence of a valid *inter vivos* transfer, title will not be transferred to the intended donee, but to the donor's executors or administrators. This does not represent an insurmountable obstacle to the application of a *donatio mortis causa* as recognition of the donee's entitlement could still be achieved by requiring the executors or administrators to hold the land on trust.[52] The difficulty with this solution is that section 53(1)(b) of the Law of Property Act 1925, which requires a declaration of trust of land to be evidenced in writing, will not have been complied with. Therefore, whether land may be the subject of a *donatio mortis causa* seems dependent upon finding a means of circumventing section 53(1)(b).

---

[49] Hanbury and Martin, p. 137.
[50] Delivery is a requirement of a *donatio mortis causa*. See below n.66 and text.
[51] See below n.66 and text.
[52] See Peter Sparkes, "Death-Bed Gifts of Land" (1992) 43 N.I.L.Q. 35 at 43. He explains that enforcement of a *donatio mortis causa* of property which does not pass at law by delivery involves the imposition of a trust.

Prior to the decision of the Court of Appeal in *Sen v. Headley*,[53] it was assumed that land could not be the subject of a *donatio mortis causa*. The difficulty in reconciling a *donatio mortis causa* of land with statutory formalities is one reason for the apparent exclusion of land. There was no direct authority in English law for the exclusion of land, but this view was supported by dicta in the House of Lords[54] and by decisions in Commonwealth jurisdictions.[55] In *Sen v. Headley*[56] the Court of Appeal held that land could be the subject of a *donatio mortis causa*. Nourse L.J., giving the judgment of the court, considered that section 53(2) of the Law of Property Act 1925 provided the solution to reconciling a *donatio mortis causa* of land with section 53(1)(b) of the Act. By virtue of section 53(2), section 53(1)(b) ". . . does not affect the creation or operation of . . . constructive trusts". By treating the trust necessary to give effect to the *donatio mortis causa* as a constructive trust, reliance could be placed on this exception.[57] Hence, upon the donor's death, his executors or administrators hold the land on constructive trust for the donee. The purpose of the trust in a *donatio mortis causa* is to facilitate the transfer of title to the donee in the absence of compliance with statutory formalities. The constructive trust is a useful mechanism to invoke to achieve the transfer of title because it is exempt from the formality requirements for the declaration of a trust of land.

Where a trust is used, a question does arise as to the timing of the gift. A gift by a *donatio mortis causa* is usually dated retrospectively to the time of the delivery.[58] This is an acceptable analysis where no action is required on the donor's death to complete the donee's title. Where a *donatio mortis causa* is dependent upon a trust, the trust cannot arise until property vests in the executors or administrators. In these circumstances it seems artificial to treat the gift as dating from

---

[53] [1991] Ch. 425.

[54] *Duffield v. Elwes* (1827) 1 Bli. N.S. 497; 4 E.R. 959.

[55] *e.g. Bayliss v. Public Trustee* (1988) 12 N.S.W.L.R. 540, discussed by C.E.F. Rickett, "No *Donatio Mortis Causa* of Real Property - A Rule in Search of a Justification?" [1989] Conv. 184.

[56] See above n.53.

[57] See above n.53 at 439–440, by reference to *Duffield v. Elwes*, above n.54. The application of a constructive trust in *Sen v. Headley* is criticised by Peter Sparkes, above n.52. He argues that a constructive trust should be imposed to give effect to a *donatio mortis causa* only where delivery is sufficient to effect a valid transfer of the equitable interest. This requirement would prevent a *donatio mortis causa* of land as mere delivery of indicia of title to land does not transfer the equitable title.

[58] *Re Korvine's Trust* [1921] 1 Ch. 343.

delivery. A further question arises as regards the timing of the trust. In *Westdeutsche* Lord Browne-Wilkinson considered that a trust cannot arise until the conscience of the trustee is affected.[59] At the time the property vests in them, the executors or administrators will not necessarily be aware of the circumstances giving rise to the *donatio mortis causa*. There are two ways in which this difficulty may be overcome. First, it may be sufficient to affect the executors' or administrators' conscience that they have received title in that capacity, without requiring knowledge of the *donatio mortis causa*. It is thought unlikely that this analysis will be accepted as the conscience of the trustees is not affected by the obligation owed to the donee. Secondly, it is submitted, the preferable way to overcome the difficulty is to accept the broad definition of the concept of a trust (adverted to above).[60] Upon the donor's death, the donee becomes entitled to the gift in equity. If it is accepted, as I have suggested it should be, that a trust arises whenever legal and equitable entitlement is divided, then the trust can date from that time. However, until the trustees are made aware of the circumstances giving rise to the *donatio mortis causa*, their conscience is not affected and they are under no fiduciary obligations towards the donee. On this analysis, while the *donatio mortis causa* dates from the time the land vests in the executors or administrators, fiduciary obligations do not arise until the trustees' conscience is affected by the obligation owed to the donee.

By transferring title to the donee, in a *donatio mortis causa*, in contrast to the other rules discussed in this chapter, equity intervenes to assist the donee. There seems no logical basis for recognising this exception to the maxim equity will not assist a volunteer. The correctness of the rule is best accepted as a concession to the donor in the special circumstances of impending death.[61] In *Sen v. Headley* Nourse L.J. explained:

> "Let it be agreed that the doctrine is anomalous. Anomalies do not justify anomalous exceptions. If due account is taken of the present state of the law in regard to mortgages and choses in action, it is apparent that to make a distinction in the case of land

---

[59] See above n.22 at 988.
[60] See above n.22 and text.
[61] Margaret Halliwell, "A Concession to Infirmity" [1991] Conv. 307; J.W.A. Thornely, "Laying Lord Eldon's Ghost: *Donatio Mortis Causa* of Land" [1991] C.L.J. 404 at 407.

would be to make just such an exception. A *donatio mortis causa* of land is neither more nor less anomalous than any other".[62]

It is submitted that there is one exceptional case where land may be the subject of a *donatio mortis causa* without equity's intervention to transfer title. If the donee is appointed executor or administrator, then, in that capacity, the donor's title will vest in the donee. This coincidental transfer of title removes the difficulties of reconciling a *donatio mortis causa* with section 53(1) of the Law of Property Act 1925. By analogy with the rule in *Strong v. Bird*[63] this transfer of title may be seen as sufficient to give effect to the gift.

2. ELEMENTS OF A CLAIM

Once it is accepted that land may be the subject of a *donatio mortis causa* it must be shown that the elements of a claim are fulfilled. There are three requirements which must be met.[64] First, the gift must be made in contemplation of death, which the donor believes to be impending.[65] Secondly, the donor must intend the gift to be conditional upon death. Until death title remains with the donor who may revoke the gift. Further, if the risk of impending death is removed, then the gift is revoked automatically. Thirdly the subject of the gift must be delivered to the donee during the donor's life.

The third requirement raises particular questions as to the application of *donatio mortis causa* to land and may still limit the types of right in land to which the rule applies.[66] For this requirement to be

---

[62] See above n.53 at 440.

[63] The rule in *Strong v. Bird* itself would not apply, the nature of the claim being different. In particular, *Strong v. Bird* is based on an intention to make an immediate *inter vivos* gift; not merely a gift conditional upon death.

[64] See the discussion in McGhee, *Snell's Equity* (30th ed., 2000), paras 20–02—20–09. The statement of these requirements in the preceding edition was approved in *Sen v. Headley* above n.53 at 431. Snell's Equity now treats the need to demonstrate that the property in question is capable of passing as a *donatio mortis causa* as a fourth requirement.

[65] *e.g.* as was the case in *Sen v. Headley* above n.53, because of illness (donor terminally ill with cancer).

[66] The difficulty in delivering land may be a further reason for the doubts as to the application of the doctrine (Hanbury and Martin, p. 139). The questions whether a thing is capable of delivery in compliance with this requirement and whether a thing is capable of being the subject of a *donatio mortis causa* may be merged: see J.W.A. Thornely above n.61 at 406.

fulfilled, the donor must deliver the gift to the donee with the intention of parting with dominion. The question to consider is how the need for delivery may be applied in relation to land. Where the gift is a chattel it is usual to deliver the thing itself. Where the gift is a chose in action it has long been accepted that this requirement may be fulfilled by delivery of the "indicia of title" to the chose in action.[67] In *Sen v. Headley*, the subject of the *donatio mortis causa* was unregistered land. By analogy with a chose in action, Nourse L.J. considered that delivery of the title deeds to land could be sufficient to fulfil this requirement as title deeds are the indicia of title to unregistered land.[68] On the facts of that case it was held the donor had constructively delivered the title deeds by slipping into the donee's handbag the only key to the locked box in which the deeds were kept.

While delivery of title deeds is, therefore, an essential element of a *donatio mortis causa* of land, the mere fact the title deeds have been delivered does not necessarily mean that the claim will succeed. It must be shown that in parting with the title deeds the donor has parted with dominion over the land itself. Nourse L.J. accepted the possibility of facts, "where there was a parting with dominion over the essential indicia of title to a chose in action but nevertheless a retention of dominion over the chose itself".[69] One example of such a case may be derived from the facts of *Sen v. Headley*. There, the donor retained possession of a set of keys to the house. This was not considered to affect the donee's claim because, at the time the gift was made, there was no practical possibility that the donor would return to the house.[70] This may suggest that if there had been a practical possibility of the donor returning to the house, then, by retaining a set of keys, he may have been held to have retained dominion over the house.

The need for delivery may still impose a practical limitation on the application of *donatio mortis causa* to land. The doctrine may apply to registered land only if accepted that delivery of the Land Certificate is sufficient.[71] Unlike title deeds in unregistered land, the Land Certificate is not the essential indica of title. Strictly, the Land Certificate is

---

[67] *Birch v. Treasury Solicitor* [1951] Ch. 298 at 308, *per* Evershed M.R.
[68] See above n.53 at 437–439.
[69] See above n.53 at 438.
[70] See above n.53 at 438–439.
[71] The position of registered land is considered by J.W.A. Thornely above n.61 at 407 and P.V. Baker, "Land as a *Donatio Mortis Causa*" (1993) 109 L.Q.R. 19 at 20.

only evidence of title and, in *Birch v. Treasury Solicitor*, Evershed M.R. (in the context of a chose in action) suggested that delivery of "mere evidence of title" would be insufficient.[72] However, the Land Certificate is generally treated as the "rough equivalent" to the title deeds.[73] Production of the Land Certificate is generally necessary for the transfer to be registered.[74] Moreover, it seems within the spirit of Nourse L.J.'s comments on the nature of the rule to accept delivery of a Land Certificate as sufficient. Accepting the rule as an anomalous, though legitimate concession, in the context of an impending death, it may be wrong to interpret the requirements in a manner which would make its application to land restricted and (in the present stage of completion of the land register) temporary.

Donatio mortis causa of a mortgage secured on land by delivery of the mortgage deeds[75] was accepted by the House of Lords in *Duffield v. Elwes*.[76] However, rights in land which are not represented by some indicia of title would seem unable to be the subject of a *donatio mortis causa* as this requirement could not be fulfilled. This would exclude, for example, most rights in land which are classified as equitable.[77]

3. NATURE OF THE RIGHT ACQUIRED

As has been seen, upon the donor's death title to his land will vest in his executors or administrators. Unless this is coincidentally the donee, the *donatio mortis causa* will take effect by the imposition of a constructive trust.[78] Therefore, initially the donee acquires an equitable proprietary right. This may seem inconsistent with Turner L.J.'s observation in *Milroy v. Lord* that an imperfect direct gift will not be treated as a declaration of trust.[79] However, as with the trust imposed

---

[72] Above n.67 at 308.

[73] Gray, p. 172.

[74] Ruoff and Roper above n.30.

[75] Whether delivery of the Charge Certificate in registered land would be sufficient raises the same issues as delivery of the Land Certificate.

[76] See above n.54, although denying the possibility of a *donatio mortis causa* of the land itself.

[77] *e.g.* beneficial rights acquired under the rules discussed in Chapter 6 seem excluded. Although claims to a *donatio mortis causa* are considered to be rare, this exclusion prevents a potentially practical (though perhaps considered undesirable) use of the rule by spouses or partners in relation to their beneficial shares in a family home.

[78] See above n.63 and text.

[79] See above n.9 and text.

on the application of the rule in *Re Rose*, this trust is merely a means of giving effect to the gift. The donee may terminate the trust by requiring a transfer of the donor's title by the executors or administrators. It seems that the right acquired by the donee remains vulnerable to claims by the donor's creditors, at least as a last resort where other assets are insufficient.[80] If a *donatio mortis causa* is correctly analysed as an *inter vivos* gift, dating from the time of delivery,[81] then it is submitted, as has been argued in relation to the rule in *Strong v. Bird*,[82] that the usual rules for *inter vivos* gifts should be applied.

V.   Transfers on trust

The discussion of the rules in this chapter has concentrated on transfers of land direct to a donee. It is generally accepted that the rules also apply where the transfer is made to trustees to hold on trust for the donee.[83] Once the transferee has acquired rights to the land which is the subject of the gift, he will hold the land on trust for the donee. Where the transferee's entitlement to the land is dependent upon the rule in *Re Rose* or a *donatio mortis causa* the donor's title will be held on trust for the transferee who will hold on sub-trust for the donee. A transfer of land to trustees raises the question of compliance with section 53(1)(b) of the Law of Property Act 1925. That section requires a declaration of trust of land to be evidenced in writing. The rules discussed in this chapter do not circumvent the need for the donor to comply with this requirement. If the trust subject to which the transferee is to hold the land is not evidenced in writing, then the donees may have to rely on the rule discussed in Chapter 3, which prevents the fraudulent reliance on non-compliance with statutory formalities, to prevent the trustee denying the trust.

---

[80] Snell, above n.64, para. 20–13; Parry and Clark above n.47, pp. 410–411.

[81] This is the current analysis, though its application where a trust is applied is doubted above n.58 and text. See Shân Warnock-Smith, "'*Donationes Mortis Causa*' and the Payment of Debts" [1978] Conv. 130.

[82] See above n.48 and text.

[83] *Re Rose* (1952) above n.10 concerned two transfers, one of which was on trust; the application of *Strong v. Bird* to such a transfer is generally based on *Re Ralli's Will Trusts* [1964] Ch. 288, but is not without question (see Kodilinye above n.41 at 20–22); a gift to trustees by a *donatio mortis causa* may be rare (Underhill and Hayton, pp. 129–130).

VI. Conclusion

In this chapter, three rules have been considered which, despite their disparate origin and requirements, share a common link. They identify circumstances in which giving effect to donative intent is considered paramount. It is not suggested that there is (or should be) a more general principle enabling rights to be acquired from incomplete gifts. Each of the rules discussed can be justified only in the limited context in which they apply. Recognition of a gift as complete when the donor has done all in his power may be accepted as a parallel to the rules discussed in Chapter 5 which enable rights to be acquired pursuant to an uncompleted sale of land. The rules identify a point in time when equity is prepared to pre-empt the completion of a transaction.[84] The coincidental vesting of title to land in the donee on the donor's death enables the gift to take effect where there is necessarily no prospect of it being revoked. There may be situations *inter vivos* where, a gift being intended, the land vests in the intended donee in another capacity. However, until the donor's death it remains possible for the gift to be revoked. A *donatio mortis causa* is more difficult to justify because, as has been seen, it is the only rule which requires equity's intervention to assist the volunteer. The justification for the rule may be bolstered as it is not unique in making special provision for the disposal of property on death. It may be seen in the context of concessions made for the provision for informal wills by soldiers and sailors.[85]

---

[84] Lowrie and Todd above n.19, p. 52.

[85] The Wills Act 1837, s.11 preserves a long-standing exception to the formality requirements for wills, enabling informal wills to be made by, "any soldier being in actual military service, or any marines or seaman being at sea". This exception, which relates to personal property, was extended to land by the Wills (Soldiers and Sailors) Act 1918, s.3.

Chapter 3.

To Prevent Statute Being Used as an Instrument of Fraud

I. Introduction

This chapter, together with Chapter 4 concerning transfers of land "subject to" a person's right, identifies circumstances in which proprietary rights are acquired as allowing reliance to be placed on statute would facilitate fraud. Some of the rules discussed in other chapters may be justified broadly as preventing fraudulent or inequitable conduct. This justification may be given, for example, for the doctrines of trust and estoppel discussed respectively in Chapters 6 and 7. However, it is only in this chapter, and exceptional circumstances in Chapter 4, that the sole justification for the acquisition of proprietary rights is the prevention of fraud. These cases apart, the acquisition of rights is dependent upon other factors, in particular, upon consideration or detriment being provided by the claimant.

Two basic factual situations may arise. First, a two party situation, where A transfers land to B (or to B and X) on an oral undertaking that A will retain rights in the land. For example, where A transfers a house to B who agrees that A should retain a life estate. The essence of the two party situation is that the transferor is intended to enjoy rights. Secondly a three party situation, where B undertakes (or B and X undertake) to hold the land in favour of C. Hence the person intended to enjoy rights is someone other than the transferor. For example, the transfer of a house to B to hold on trust for C. For convenience of analysis, the discussion in this Chapter separates these two factual situations. This division serves to highlight particular considerations that arise where the claimant of rights is a third party to the transfer. However, as will become apparent, not all cases involving fraud fall within such a clear division. In the cases in which the principle has been developed, legal title has been transferred to *B* with the intention that *A* or *C* enjoys an interest which is conventionally given effect under a trust. Section 53(1)(b) of the Law of Property Act 1925 requires a declaration of trust in relation to land to be ". . . manifested and proved by some writing signed by some person who is able to declare such trust. . .". Until this requirement is satisfied the trust remains valid but unenforceable.[1] As the trust is valid, problems do not generally arise if *B* does, in fact, hold the land subject to the trust. Difficulties arise in determining entitlement to the land if *B*, in reliance on the absence of writing, claims the land for himself.

The purpose of section 53(1)(b), as originally enacted in the Statute of Frauds 1677, is to prevent fraudulent claims to a trust. It is therefore logical to admit an exception to the requirement where it is used to facilitate rather than prevent fraud. However, it is not readily apparent that the denial of a trust should be classified as fraudulent. There is a danger that too broad an interpretation of fraud will be adopted. Such an interpretation could be used to enable the very thing the statute seeks to preclude; oral trusts of land. In light of this, to preserve the integrity of section 53(1)(b), it will be submitted in this chapter that the scope of the rule should be kept to a minimum. It will be seen that adopting this approach it is necessary to rely on the prevention of fraud only where the claimant is a volunteer. Further, that the prevention of fraud need not necessitate giving effect to the parties' informal agreement.

The application of the rule will first be discussed in the context of trusts. The general requirements of a claim will be explained and the two and three party situations will then be analysed in turn. Secondly it will be considered whether the principle may be applied in other factual circumstances.

II. Elements of a claim

1. USE OF STATUTE AS AN INSTRUMENT OF FRAUD

The concept of fraud is defined broadly in equity. It is seen as a general concept, encompassing actions considered abhorrent to good

---

[1] See T.G. Youdan, "Formalities for Trusts of Land, and the Doctrine in *Rochefoucauld v. Boustead*" (1984) 43 C.L.J. 306 at 320–322.

conscience.[2] Used in this broad manner, fraud is not restricted to circumstances in which there is an intention to cheat,[3] and is probably incapable of exhaustive definition.[4] Despite the elasticity of the concept, caution must be exercised in condemning conduct as fraudulent. It is well established that it is not fraud to rely on rights conferred by statute.[5] Hence to deny the existence of a trust because of non-compliance with statutory formalities is not necessarily fraudulent. The role of this rule should be to draw a workable distinction between fraudulent conduct and legitimate reliance on non-compliance with formal requirements.

In *Rochefoucauld v. Boustead*[6] the court considered fraud to arise where a transferee, who had agreed to hold land on trust, seeks to rely on non-compliance with statutory formalities to renege on the agreement. Lindley M.R. explained, ". . .it is a fraud on the part of a person to whom land is conveyed as a trustee, and who knows it was so conveyed, to deny the trust and claim the land himself".[7] The effect of fraud was considered to be to enable oral evidence of the trust to be admitted. However, it is difficult to reconcile this with the definition of fraud given by the Court.[8] The declaration of trust by the parties' agreement is the very thing which statute requires to be in writing. It cannot be shown that the agreement has been reneged upon until the existence of the agreement is established. This, in turn, can be ascertained only by admitting oral evidence. This circularity is apparent in Lindley L.J.'s judgment in *Rochefoucauld v. Boustead*. He seemed first to establish that the land had been transferred on trust and then to allow oral evidence of the trust to be admitted to prevent the transferee's fraudulent denial.

It is doubtful whether the mere denial of a trust on a transfer of land should be treated as constituting fraud. Applied broadly, *Rochefoucauld v. Boustead* has the effect that when land is transferred on trust, the trust is enforced as long as it is evidenced: in writing (within section 53(1)(b)); or orally. The effect of such a rule would be to reduce section 53(1)(b) to trusts declared by (current) holders of

---

[2] Meagher, Gummow and Lehane, para. 1208. See generally paras 1201–1211.
[3] *Nocton v. Lord Ashburton* [1914] A.C. 932 at 954.
[4] See, *e.g. Reddaway v. Banham* [1896] A.C. 199 at 221. There, Lord Macnaghten described fraud as "infinite in variety".
[5] *Midland Bank Trust Co Ltd v. Green* [1981] A.C. 513 at 531, *per* Lord Wilberforce.
[6] [1897] 1 Ch. 196.
[7] See above n.6 at 206.
[8] Youdan above n.1 at 325.

land. This would be a startling result for a rule purportedly based on the prevention of fraud. The underlying difficulty is in determining why the denial of an informal trust should, in some circumstances, be considered fraudulent. Writing in the context of secret trusts, Patricia Critchley suggests the fraud lies in the combination of the trustee's wrongdoing and the harm caused to the intended beneficiary and / or the testator.[9] Similarly, in relation to *Rochefoucauld v. Boustead*, it may be argued that the fraud lies in the combination of the trustee's wrongdoing and the harm to the transferor and, in a three party case, the beneficiary.[10] However, it seems that such a definition does no more than beg the question as to the nature of the underlying wrongdoing and harm, in light of non-compliance with statutory formalities. Other attempts have been made to rationalise the basis upon which equity acts. Youdan suggests the courts should balance the useful function of requiring compliance with formalities with the risk of injustice which insistence on this may cause.[11] However, he acknowledges that drawing this balance does not explain all situations in which the courts have intervened.[12]

Where the rule is applied, it is established that it is not necessary that the conveyance itself be obtained by fraud. In *Bannister v. Bannister* the judge at first instance found as fact that the conveyance had not been fraudulently obtained. In the Court of Appeal, Scott L.J. said that this did not prevent equity intervening when the transferee attempted to renege on the agreement. He explained that, "The fraud which brings the principle into play arises as soon as the absolute character of the conveyance is set up for the purpose of defeating the beneficial interest. . .".[13] The definition of fraud in *Rochefoucauld v. Boustead* is based on a denial of the trust by *B*, the

---

[9] Patricia Critchley, "Instruments of Fraud, Testamentary Dispositions, and the Doctrine of Secret Trusts" (1999) 115 L.Q.R. 631 at 648.

[10] Critchley suggests above n.9 at 653 that her discussion of fraud may be relevant in the context of *Rochefoucauld v. Boustead*.

[11] See above n.1 at 325.

[12] See Youdan's third hypothetical situation above n.1 at 327–328 and his subsequent discussion at 329–330. M.P. Thompson suggests that the situations in which this rule is applied are not based on one unified principle: M.P. Thompson, "Using Statutes as Instruments of Fraud" (1985) 36 N.I.L.Q. 358.

[13] [1948] 2 All E.R. 133 at 136.

original transferee.[14] A further question which has arisen is whether it is fraud for a subsequent purchaser from *B* to deny the trust. In *Hodgson v. Marks*,[15] at first instance, Ungoed-Thomas J. considered that it would be fraud for a subsequent purchaser to deny the trust, even if he purchased for value and without notice.[16] The Court of Appeal did not consider it necessary to decide this question as, in their judgment, the claimant had acquired rights by the application of other rules and those rights bound the purchaser as an overriding interest.[17] It is submitted that by selling the land *B* necessarily reneges on the agreement and thereby enables oral evidence to be admitted to establish that he held the land on trust. Whether the claimant's interest under this trust binds the purchaser should then be determined by reference to the usual rules of registered or unregistered land.[18]

2. TRANSFER OF LAND ON TRUST

Proprietary rights will be acquired only where the land has been transferred pursuant to an agreement to hold on trust.[19] It is not necessary for the technical language of a trust to have been used by the parties. All that is required is, "a stipulation under which some sufficiently defined beneficial interest in the property was to be taken by another".[20] The beneficial interest may be absolute[21] or it may be a

---

[14] It is unclear what the position would be if, *e.g.* the transfer is made to *B* and *X* and *B* alone agrees to the trust. The rules relating to testamentary secret trusts, which tend to be used as an analogy, are not appropriate here. Those rules depend in part on whether *B* knew of the trust at the time the will was executed and, furthermore, have been developed in a context where *B* and *X* are necessarily recipients of a gift. It is argued below that this rule need be applied only where the claimant is a donee (see below n.25 and n.32 and text). The consequence of this (at least in a two party situation) is that *B* and *X* are likely to be purchasers for value. Clearly, without knowledge of the trust, *X* cannot act fraudulently within the definition in *Rochefoucauld v. Boustead*, above n.6 and text.

[15] [1971] 1 Ch. 892.

[16] *ibid.* at 908–909.

[17] See above n.15 at 933. This aspect of the case is discussed below n.29 and text.

[18] See Ian Leeming, "Engines of Fraud and Occupational Hazards" [1971] Conv. 255 at 262; Underhill and Hayton, p. 227. If the purchaser agreed to recognise the claimant's rights, then the claimant may be protected by the application of the rule discussed in Chapter 4.

[19] Communication of the trust after completion of the conveyance is unlikely to be sufficient: Youdan above n.1 at 326–327.

[20] *Bannister v. Bannister* above n.13 at 136 *per* Scott L.J.

[21] *e.g. Rochefoucauld v. Boustead* above n.6.

lesser interest, such as a life interest.[22] However, proprietary rights will not be acquired if a person makes an oral declaration of trust in respect of land which he already owns. This may be seen as an illustration of legitimate reliance on non-compliance with formal requirements.[23]

III. Two party situation

The leading case, from which this rule has developed, is *Rochefoucauld v. Boustead*. There, the plaintiff owned land subject to a mortgage. The mortgage was sold and transferred to the defendant who had agreed to hold the land on trust for the plaintiff, subject to being reimbursed. The defendant subsequently denied that he had agreed to the trust.[24] The Court of Appeal was satisfied that the defendant had agreed to the trust and held that if formality requirements were not fulfilled,[25] then other evidence of the trust could be admitted to prevent the defendant's fraud. A key feature of the case is that the plaintiff had not provided consideration for the trust. The defendant had gratuitously agreed to assist the plaintiff who was unable herself to repay the mortgage. Therefore the sole justification for equity's intervention to recognise the trust was to prevent the defendant's fraud.

It is submitted that only where, as in *Rochefoucauld v. Boustead*, the claimant is a volunteer, is it necessary to enable the acquisition of proprietary rights to prevent the use of statute as an instrument of fraud. This may be illustrated by reference to two further cases in which the scope of this rule has been discussed. It will be seen that in these cases factors were present which would justify the acquisition of rights by the application of other rules. It is preferable to rely on alternative grounds of intervention when possible. This will help ensure that intervention based on the need to prevent fraud is narrowly construed.

---

[22] *e.g. Bannister v. Bannister* above n.13.

[23] See the discussion above n.5 and text.

[24] Although three parties were involved, in substance this was a two party case. The defendant had agreed with the plaintiff to take a transfer of land which would extinguish her existing interest (the equity of redemption) and to hold the land on trust for her. See W.A.J. Ford and W.A. Lee, *Principles of the Law of Trusts*, (2nd ed., 1990) para. 609.

[25] It is possible that the trust was in fact evidenced in writing: above n.6 at 207.

In *Bannister v. Bannister*[26] the defendant sold two cottages to the plaintiff on an oral understanding that the defendant could continue to occupy one of the cottages, rent free, for as long as she wished. The plaintiff sought to renege upon the agreement and evict the defendant. The Court of Appeal held that the effect of the agreement was to create a beneficial interest (a life interest) in the defendant's favour and that it would be fraudulent for the defendant to rely on the absence of writing to defeat this interest. Here, however, unlike in *Rochefoucauld v. Boustead*, the defendant had provided consideration for the agreement. The conveyance had been made at less than the market value of the cottages with vacant possession. The Court did not in fact place reliance on this, except as regards its interpretation of the nature of the defendant's interest.[27] However, in light of the defendant's consideration, the acquisition of proprietary rights could now be explained without relying solely on the need to prevent fraud. It may be interpreted, for example, as an agreement to share (successively) the beneficial interest enabling a claim based on a constructive trust of the type discussed in Chapter 6. Alternatively, as an assurance of rights on which the defendant relied to her detriment[28] (by transferring the land at an undervalue) within the estoppel doctrine discussed in Chapter 7.

In *Bannister v. Bannister*, although the transfer had been at an undervalue, the transferee had provided some consideration. Where no consideration is provided for a transfer of land the courts will readily create rights in favour of the transferor without the need to rely on the prevention of fraud. This is illustrated by *Hodgson v. Marks*.[29] There, the plaintiff executed a voluntary transfer of her home to Mr Evans, on an oral agreement that she retained the beneficial interest. The Court of Appeal was asked whether the plaintiff had rights binding on the defendant, who was a purchaser for value from Mr Evans. The court was satisfied that apart from any

---

[26] See above n.13.

[27] See above n.13 at 135–136. This is criticised by Youdan, above n.1 at 327–328. He notes that the fact the conveyance was at an undervalue affects the perception of injustice in determining whether the plaintiff should be able to rely on non-compliance with formalities. If the agreement had not been enforced, then the defendant would have been unjustly enriched by acquiring the land at an undervalue. See also M.P. Thompson, "Registration, Fraud and Notice" (1985) 44 C.L.J. 280 at 288.

[28] It was found as a fact that the defendant would not have transferred the land without the assurance.

[29] See above n.15.

argument based on fraud the plaintiff retained the beneficial interest following the transfer to Mr Evans.[30] The oral agreement, coupled with the plaintiff's detrimental reliance by executing the transfer was sufficient for a claim to a constructive trust of the type discussed in Chapter 6.[31]

IV. Three party situation

If *A* transfers land to *B* on an oral agreement that *C* should have a beneficial interest, then, as in the two party situation, equity will prevent *B* from fraudulently reneging on the agreement. While legal title remains vested in *B*, *B* will not be able to claim beneficial entitlement. In the context of a two party situation it has been seen that the acquisition of rights to prevent fraud is necessary only when the claimant is a volunteer. If the claimant has provided consideration, then he may acquire proprietary rights under other rules. Similarly, in a three party situation, if *C* has provided consideration, then other rules may operate in *C*'s favour. This is illustrated by *Du Boulay v. Raggett*.[32] There, the court enforced an informal agreement entered into between Mr Raggett and the claimants to the effect that Mr Raggett would sell to them parts of land he had successfully bid for at auction. The court was satisfied that it would be unconscionable for him to renege on the agreement. However, it was not necessary for the court to rely on the need to prevent fraud. The court gave an alternative ground for its decision based on the doctrine of part performance. Although that doctrine has how been abolished, it seems likely that the claimants could rely on other rules as the source of their rights. Mr Raggett assured the claimants that he would sell the land to them and the claimants had relied on this to their detriment by not bidding at the auction themselves. In these circumstances they may be able to claim rights based on Mr Raggett's assurance through the estoppel doctrine discussed in Chapter 7.

---

[30] See above n.15 at 933.

[31] Youdan, above n.1 at 326, n.4, acknowledges that the rule based on the need to prevent fraud is otiose in these circumstances. The case is discussed further in Chapter 6 Part II 3. As is seen in that discussion, in the absence of an agreement the mere fact the plaintiff did not intend a gift of the land would have been sufficient for her to claim a restitutionary resulting trust.

[32] (1989) 58 P. & C.R. 138.

However, in a three party situation, there is an additional factor to take into account. Where C has provided consideration, he may in fact have acquired rights against A (the transferor) rather than B (the transferee). If this is the case, then whether B is bound by those rights is a question of enforcement of an existing right on a transfer of title. This will be dependent upon the usual conveyancing rules of registered or unregistered land.

Where it is necessary to rely on the prevention of fraud, the question which has arisen is whether rights should be acquired by A or C. In a two party situation, intervention on behalf of A may be the only means of preventing fraud, despite the effect of this being to implement the parties' agreement. In a three party situation fraud can be prevented by intervening on behalf of the transferor, instead of the intended beneficiary. The inconclusive nature of the authorities is reflected in the different conclusions drawn from them by Youdan and Feltham. Youdan considers the authorities support C's claim,[33] while Feltham finds "no strong line of authority in C's favour".[34] As the claimant under this rule is necessarily a volunteer, there is no persuasive argument to do more than is necessary to prevent fraud. The risk of injustice to C is limited, as the effect of refusing to intervene in his favour will be no more than to deny a gift. Once fraud has been prevented by the acquisition of rights by A, the transferor and donor of the gift, A will have another opportunity to grant rights to C.

There are, however, two circumstances in which the court may be justified in conferring rights on C. First, there may be exceptional cases where intervention in C's favour is the only means of preventing fraud. This possibility is illustrated by the Court of Appeal decision in *Neale v. Willis*.[35] There, a husband wished to borrow money from his mother-in-law to help fund the purchase of a home. His mother-in-law gave him a loan pursuant to an agreement that the conveyance would be taken jointly with his wife. In fact, the husband took the conveyance in his sole name and, following the breakdown of the marriage, denied his wife had a beneficial interest.

---

[33] Above n.1 at 334. Oakley notes, p. 56 that, "no doubt has ever been cast on the ability of the third party to enforce the undertaking".

[34] J.D. Feltham, "Informal Trusts and Third Parties" [1987] Conv. 246 at 249. A's claim is also supported by Hanbury and Martin, p. 78 and Underhill and Hayton p. 227.

[35] (1968) 19 P. & C.R. 836.

The Court of Appeal held that the husband could not renege on his agreement and defeat his wife's interest. The wife had provided no consideration for her beneficial interest. Therefore, the only justification for the acquisition of rights by her was to prevent her husband's fraud.[36] The reason this case is exceptional is that the transferor was not a party to the agreement, which had not been entered into directly to obtain the conveyance of the land. Therefore it would not have been appropriate for the land to be held in the transferor's favour. Further, it would not have been appropriate for the land to be held in favour of the mother-in-law with whom the agreement had been entered. The agreement did not envisage that she, as a lender, should acquire rights in the house.[37] In these circumstances, it seems that intervention in favour of the wife was the only means of preventing fraud.[38]

Secondly, an assumption underlying the reasoning against C is that A will have another opportunity to grant rights to C. There are circumstances in which no such opportunity in practice arises. The clearest example is where A has died. On a strict view this (unlike the first situation) does not alter the reasoning against C. The purpose of the rule, of preventing fraud, is still achieved by vesting the beneficial interest in A's estate. However, a concession in favour of C may be justified in terms of giving effect to A's intentions as he has died in the belief the gift was effective.[39] Less certain is whether a concession

---

[36] If the money had been provided by the mother-in-law as a gift rather than a loan, then the case would now be decided on the basis of an agreement to share the beneficial interest, discussed in Chapter 6: cf. *Midland Bank Plc* v *Cooke* [1995] 4 All E.R. 562. That rule would also apply if, as may in fact have been the case (Feltham above n.34 at 249), money used to purchase the house was partly owned by the wife.

[37] cf. *Re Sharpe* [1980] 1 W.L.R. 219.

[38] Notwithstanding, the application of the rule in this case remains problematic. The fraudulent conduct in issue did not arise in the transaction in which the home was acquired, but in dealings to secure a loan to fund the purchase. It may be outside the scope of the rule to hold that reneging on an agreement entered into to secure one transaction (the loan) enables the court to impose a trust in relation to land acquired in a separate transaction.

[39] Feltham's strong argument against C's claim is written on the basis of a contest between "A who has changed his mind and C who is a mere volunteer", above n.34 at 248. His argument may be less persuasive where A has died, apparently in the belief the gift is complete. Underhill and Hayton, p. 227 support this concession in C's favour by an extension of the doctrine of testamentary secret trusts. An analysis of this may reveal circularity. Secret trusts arise where a gift of property made in a will is apparently absolute but, in fact, is intended to be held on a trust communicated separately to the transferee. It is unclear whether secret trusts

in C's favour should be extended to situations in which A is alive, but it would be impossible (or less attractive) for A to execute a gift in favour of C. For example, where the initial gift carried favourable tax consequences for A which would not arise on a newly executed gift.

V. Nature of the interest acquired

The effect of this rule is to prevent the transferee from reneging on an agreement to hold the land on trust. Therefore the claimant obtains a beneficial interest under a trust. The nature of the beneficial interest is dependent upon the agreement entered by the transferee. For example, the claimant may be solely entitled[40] or be entitled to a concurrent[41] or successive[42] interest. Prior to the Trusts of Land and Appointment of Trustees Act 1996, the effect of creating successive interests was to make the land settled land under the Settled Land Act 1925 and the claimant the tenant for life under that Act. As tenant for life, the claimant could require legal title to be conveyed to him and would have wide powers of management and sale. This result, which may have been contrary to the intentions of the parties,[43] is prevented by the 1996 Act. Successive interests are now regulated by that Act under which legal title and powers of management and sale are retained by the trustee.

There remains uncertainty as to the type of trust subject to which the land is held. There are two alternative interpretations. First, that equity enforces the express trust informally declared by the parties' agreement. Secondly that the express trust remains unenforceable but, by acting *in personam* against B, equity imposes a trust to ensure that B acts in accordance with conscience. The type of trust imposed

---

themselves avoid the requirement of s.53(1)(b) (as constructive trusts) or whether, in fact, secret trusts of land must comply with that provision. Oakley notes, p. 261 "the general view seems to be that no fully secret trust can ever fail for lack of writing, simply because of the maxim that a statute cannot be used as an instrument of fraud". However, if this rule is relied on, then, as has been argued, fraud may be prevented by the land being held in favour of the transferor (or testator) without the need to give effect to the trust.

[40] *Rochefoucauld v. Boustead* above n.6.

[41] *Neale v. Willis* above n.35.

[42] *Bannister v. Bannister* above n.13 although, as has been seen, above n.27 and text that case could now be decided by the application of other rules.

[43] See *Binions v. Evans* [1972] 1 Ch. 359 at 366, *per* Lord Denning M.R.

in such circumstances is generally interpreted as a constructive trust.[44] This question should not be seen wholly in isolation from the question whether, in the three party situation, C can enforce the trust. If it is the express trust which is enforced, then it is difficult to deny C's claim.[45] A solution based on constructive trust does not necessarily defeat C's claim but a constructive trust is more likely to operate in favour of A.[46] Considerations of conscience will prevent B from claiming beneficial entitlement without necessarily requiring B to give effect to the parties' agreement. The authorities are, again, inconclusive. In *Rochefoucauld v. Boustead* the court insisted that it was enforcing an express trust[47] while the decision in *Neale v. Willis* was based on a constructive trust.[48] It is submitted that the better view, which is also more consistent with denying C's ability to claim entitlement to the land, is that a constructive trust is imposed. This interpretation, as will now be seen, is more readily explained in terms of how the requirement for written evidence of the trust is overcome.

If the courts are enforcing the express trust, then the justification for giving effect to the trust despite non-compliance with section 53(1)(b) of the Law of Property Act 1925 must be explained. It may be argued that equity is prepared to enforce the trust, despite section 53(1)(b), because of its "utter detestation of fraud".[49] A comparison with the (now abolished)[50] doctrine of part performance may seem to support this analysis. That doctrine applied to contracts for sale of land which, like declarations of trust in relation to land, were unenforceable unless evidenced in writing.[51] When the requirements of the doctrine were met, the court could accept oral evidence of the contract and order specific performance despite the absence of written evidence. Under that doctrine it was clear that in ordering specific performance the court was enforcing the contract entered into by the parties despite non-compliance with statute.

However, to enforce the express trust would be to enable judge-made rules to override legislation. As Gbolahan Elias notes, the

---

[44] This may also be interpreted as a resulting trust. See, *e.g.* Underhill and Hayton, p. 225.

[45] But see Underhill and Hayton, p. 225–227. They treat the trust as express but do not support the third party's claim.

[46] Thompson above n.12 at 366; Youdan above n.1 at 334.

[47] See above n.6 at 208. However, that case involved a two party situation.

[48] See above n.35 at 839. This case also illustrates the possibility of a constructive trust being imposed in favour of C.

[49] Gray, p. 378.

[50] See below n.69 and text.

[51] Law of Property Act 1925, s.40(1) (now repealed).

suggestion that this is possible is "constitutionally suspect".[52] While the same criticism could have been directed against the doctrine of part performance, that doctrine was eventually legitimized by statute.[53] The court's insistence in *Rochefoucauld v. Boustead* that it was enforcing the express trust should be considered in the context of that case. If the trust was constructive, then the Statute of Limitations would have acted as a bar to the plaintiff's claim. The Statute did not affect the enforcement of an express trust. Therefore, to avoid the application of the Statute courts tended to treat trusts as express rather than constructive.[54]

If enforcing the express trust was the only means of preventing fraud, then the paramount need to do so may rebut these arguments. However, fraud may be prevented, and consistency with statute maintained, by a solution based on constructive trust. Section 53(2) of the Law of Property Act 1925 exempts constructive trusts from the requirement of writing. Hence, by imposing a constructive trust, section 53(1)(b) is respected.[55] Perhaps the most persuasive objection to the imposition of a constructive trust is that such trusts do not usually operate in favour of donees.[56] However, it may be more reasonable to expect judge-made law to admit an exceptional case than to allow judge-made law to override statute.

VI. Application of the principle to other factual situations

In the cases discussed so far, legal title has been transferred on an undertaking that *A* or *C* should enjoy a beneficial interest. Three

---

[52] Gbolahan Elias, *Explaining Constructive Trusts* (1990), p. 108. The same criticism may be directed against an analysis provided by Swadling "The Proprietary Effect of a Hire of Goods" in *Interests in Goods* (Palmer and McKendrick eds, 2nd ed. 1998), p. 512. He suggests the trust is express, as the effect of fraud is that the statute does not apply and the requirement of writing is removed. This is tantamount to suggesting that the courts can decide to dis-apply statute.

[53] Law of Property Act 1925, s.40(2). That section was repealed, and the doctrine of part performance abolished, by the Law of Property (Miscellaneous Provisions) Act 1989.

[54] See Thompson above n.12 at 366.

[55] See Youdan above n.1 at 324 and 333. Youdan doubts whether s.53(2) is intended to operate in these circumstances. However, reliance on the provision where an express trust fails for lack of form is supported by Russell L.J. in *Hodgson v. Marks* above n.15 at 933 (discussing resulting trusts).

[56] Gray, p. 379.

41

variations on this may arise. First, a subsisting beneficial interest may be transferred. Secondly, the agreement may relate to an interest, such as an easement, which is not a conventional beneficial interest. Thirdly the agreement may relate to an interest which is not a recognised proprietary right.

1. Transfer of a Subsisting Beneficial Interest

The same rule may be applied *mutatis mutandis* where a subsisting beneficial interest is transferred. Once there has been a valid transfer of the beneficial interest,[57] equity may prevent fraudulent reliance on the absence of writing as regards the agreement to hold on (sub) trust.[58]

2. Agreements Relating to Non-Beneficial Interests

The fraud committed by the transferee is the same regardless of the nature of the interest to be enjoyed by *A* or *C*. If the transferee takes pursuant to an agreement *C* will have an easement, then it seems as desirable to prevent the transferee from reneging on the agreement as where *C* is to enjoy beneficial entitlement. Two difficulties arise in applying the rule where the agreement relates to a non-beneficial interest.

First, the mechanism used by the court to prevent *B*'s fraud is the imposition of a constructive trust. The imposition of a trust is appropriate where *C* is intended to have a right to possession of the land. Where the agreement relates to an interest in land (by which is meant a right exercised over land possessed by someone else) the trust mechanism is not appropriate. Interests in land, which include easements and covenants, are not conventionally treated as "beneficial" interests under a trust. The courts have imposed constructive trusts to protect interests which do not conventionally exist under a trust.[59] However, although trust doctrine may be sufficiently flexible

---

[57] This must be in writing to comply with the Law of Property Act 1925, s.53(1)(c).

[58] *cf.* Graham Battersby, "Formalities for the Disposition of Equitable Interests Under a Trust" [1979] Conv. 17 at 37 point 2.

[59] *e.g. Lyus v. Prowsa Developments* [1982] 1 W.L.R. 1044. There, applying the rule discussed in Chapter 4, the court imposed a constructive trust to protect an estate contract.

to recognise any interest as an interest under a trust,[60] the effect of imposing a trust in relation to interests in land may be questioned. The constructive trust imposed will be a "trust of land" within the scope of the Trusts of Land and Appointment of Trustees Act 1996.[61] The rights and obligations created by that Act do not seem appropriate where the "beneficiary" is in fact, for example, a claimant to an easement. Where the interest is not a conventional beneficial interest it would be preferable to confer on the claimant[62] an equitable interest corresponding to the interest conferred by the agreement.[63] However, section 53(1)(a) of the Law of Property Act 1925 requires writing to create an interest in land. Without imposing a constructive trust (as permitted by section 53(2))[64] it is difficult to reconcile intervention with the formality requirement. Intervention could be justified only by reference to a general insistence that "fraud unravels everything"[65] and, as has been seen, reliance on such a proposition is not readily justified.[66]

The second difficulty is that the effect of non-compliance with section 53(1)(a) of the Law of Property Act 1925 differs from section 53(1)(b). Section 53(1)(a) requires writing to create an interest in land. Under section 53(1)(b) a declaration of trust of land need only be *evidenced* in writing. The significance of the distinction is that a declaration of trust which is not evidenced in writing is valid but unenforceable while non-compliance with section 53(1)(a) makes the agreement void.[67] *Rochefoucauld v. Boustead* establishes that a court may accept oral evidence to give effect to an agreement which would

---

[60] Underhill and Hayton note, p. 159: "All property real or personal. . . may be made the subject of a trust". A.J. Oakley, "The Licensee's Interest" (1972) 35 M.L.R. 551 at 557 envisages easements and covenants taking effect under a constructive trust.

[61] Trusts of Land and Appointment of Trustees Act 1996, ss.1(1)(a) and 1(2)(b).

[62] Where the agreement confers rights on *C*, these may be exceptional cases where intervention in *C*'s favour is the only means of preventing fraud. See above n.35 and text.

[63] *cf.* the effect of entering a specifically enforceable contract for sale of such an interest discussed in Chapter 5.

[64] The Law of Property Act 1925, s.52(2) provides generally that "This section" does not affect the operation of constructive trusts.

[65] See Lord Denning M.R. in the Court of Appeal in *Midland Bank Trusts Co. Ltd v. Green* [1980] Ch. 590 at 625 referring to his own judgment in *Lazarus Estates Ltd v. Beasley* [1956] 1 Q.B. 702. The decision of the House of Lords, reversing the Court of Appeal, does not place doubt on this general principle.

[66] See above n.52 and text.

[67] *cf.* the effect of non-compliance with the Law of Property Act 1925, s.53(1)(c).

otherwise be unenforceable. The question which needs to be considered is whether the principle can go further and enable the court to act pursuant to an agreement which is void.

A contrast may be made with the courts' treatment of oral contracts for sale of land. Under section 40(1) of the Law of Property Act 1925, such contracts, like oral declarations of trust of land, were valid but unenforceable. As has been seen,[68] the doctrine of part performance enabled the court to accept oral evidence of a contract and to order specific performance despite the absence of writing. Section 40(1) was repealed by the Law of Property (Miscellaneous Provisions) Act 1989. Under the 1989 Act, oral contracts for sale of land are now void and not merely unenforceable. As a consequence, it has been held that the court may no longer enforce the agreement by the application of part performance.[69] *Prima facie* this may suggest that the court cannot give effect to void agreements by the application of this rule. However, in the context of part performance the court is asked to order specific performance of the contract. That is, the court is asked to enforce the agreement actually entered into by the parties. If, under this rule, the court was asked, in substance, to order specific performance of the parties' agreement, then the fact the agreement is void would prevent the court's intervention. However, it is not necessary to analyse the application of this rule in terms of the court giving effect to the agreement entered into by the parties. The court intervenes to prevent fraud, and not to complete the parties' agreement. The effect of intervention will not necessarily produce a result which coincides with the agreement. In light of this, it is submitted that the court may be able to intervene to prevent a fraudulent attempt to renege on an agreement, even when the effect of non-compliance with formalities is to make the agreement void.[70]

3. AGREEMENTS RELATING TO NON-PROPRIETARY RIGHTS

The courts have not considered whether proprietary rights would be conferred to prevent a transferor from reneging on such an agreement. It is submitted that there is unlikely to be any practical scope

---

[68] See above n.50 and text.
[69] *United Bank of Kuwait v. Sahib* [1996] 3 W.L.R. 372. Whether part performance has in fact been abolished remains the subject of debate. The doctrine is considered further in Chapter 5.
[70] *cf.* Chapter 5, where it is argued that rights may be acquired pursuant to a void contract for sale of land where the purchaser has paid the consideration in full.

for the application of the rule in this context. As has been seen, this rule need be invoked only where the claimant is a donee. If the right conferred on the donee is not proprietary, then it will be no more than a bare licence. As such licences may be revoked with reasonable notice there seems no practical reason to require a transferor to recognise such a right.[71]

VII. Application of this rule in conjunction with the rules discussed in chapter 2

In Chapter 2, three rules were discussed which enable the acquisition of proprietary rights to give effect to an imperfect gift. It was noted that these rules may apply where there is a voluntary transfer of land to trustees to hold on trust for the donee.[72] The application of the rules discussed in that chapter enables the trustees to assert their entitlement to the land but does not circumvent the formal requirement in section 53(1)(b) of the Law of Property Act 1925 for the trust in favour of the donee to be evidenced in writing. If that requirement is not complied with, then the rule discussed in this chapter will prevent the trustees from fraudulently denying the trust. However, as the fraud has arisen in a three party situation, the prevention of fraud will not necessarily result in the acquisition of rights by the intended donee. Two of the rules discussed in Chapter 3, the rule in *Strong v. Bird* and a *donatio mortis causa*, apply only on the transferor's death. If the trustees' title is based on the application of one of these rules, then rights should be acquired by the donee. This is within the concession enabling the third party to claim rights where the transferor has died in the belief the gift was effective.[73] If the trustees' title is based on the rule in *Re Rose*, then the transferor may be surviving and fraud can be prevented by the creation of rights in favour of the transferor.

VIII. Conclusion

This chapter has considered circumstances in which proprietary rights are acquired to prevent a transferee fraudulently reneging on

---

[71] *cf.* the discussion in Chapter 4 of whether proprietary rights may be created where a purchaser takes subject to an existing contractual licence. Contractual licences, unlike bare licences, may be irrevocable.

[72] Chapter 2, Part V.

[73] See above n.39 and text.

an agreement pursuant to which land was transferred. It has been seen that intervention is not readily justifiable, as the broad interpretation adopted of fraud runs the risk of negating the purpose of the statutory formalities. It has been submitted that intervention to prevent fraud is, in any event, necessary only where the claimant is a volunteer. In other circumstances, it will be more appropriate to rely on other rules enabling the informal acquisition of rights. To the extent that rights are acquired by a volunteer, a parallel may be drawn with the rules discussed in Chapter 2, which enable the acquisition of rights derived from an imperfect gift. However, the basis of those rules is different. As has been seen, the rules in Chapter 2 identify circumstances where giving effect to the donor's intent becomes paramount. The donor's conduct therefore provides the motivation for intervention. In this chapter, the sole motivation is to prevent fraud, and the focus of the rule is the conduct of the transferee. Where the result of intervening to prevent fraud coincides with giving effect to the parties agreement, this should be seen as incidental.

Chapter 4.

Where a Purchaser Takes Land "Subject to" a Person's Rights

I. Introduction

The rule to be discussed in this chapter provides for the acquisition of rights where land is transferred "subject to" the claimant's rights. Proprietary rights are acquired by the claimant and enforced against the transferee despite the fact that, by statute, the transferee takes free from the claimant's rights. This rule is closely related to that discussed in Chapter 3, which provides for the acquisition of proprietary rights to prevent statute being used as an instrument of fraud. Indeed, traditionally the rules discussed in Chapters 3 and 4 are treated as an application of the same doctrine and are considered together. They are separated here because this rule is much less certain both in terms of the authorities on which it is based and as a matter of policy. In terms of the authority for the rule, it will be seen that its scope is heavily dependent on a minority judgment in one case and an *obiter* discussion in another. The legitimacy of the rule as a matter of policy may be questioned because of the distinct situation in which this rule applies. In Chapter 3, the court was asked to create in favour of the claimant rights which the claimant did not enjoy at the time of the transfer. In this chapter, the court is asked to create new rights as a means of enforcing rights which the claimant did enjoy at the time of the transfer. Both registered and unregistered land contain detailed rules to determine the enforceability of rights on a transfer of title. Given the existence of these rules, the question that arises is why parties are seeking instead to protect the claimant by the imposition of a "subject to" clause. It seems that there are two main reasons why the parties may attempt to do so, both of which raise questions of policy distinct from those arising in Chapter 3. First, the claimant's interest may be void against the transferee by the application of the statutory schemes. This may either be because of a failure to utilise the schemes or because, in any event, statute enables the transferee to override the claimant's interest. In the former situation, the court's intervention may undermine the integrity of those schemes.[1] In the latter, the court is asked to substitute the parties' assessment of when an interest should be enforceable for that provided by Parliament.[2] Secondly, the claimant's interest may be personal and therefore incapable of being enforced under the statutory rules. Here, the effect of the rule is to create a *proprietary* right to enforce a *personal* right. This raises the fundamental question of the distinction between the two types of right.[3]

II. Elements of a claim

The acquisition of proprietary rights under this rule is dependent on two express requirements. First, there must be a transfer of land "subject to" recognition of the claimant's rights. Secondly the parties must have intended the "subject to" clause to create new rights in the claimant's favour. Where these requirements are satisfied, it is considered to be fraud for the transferee to deny the claimant his rights. Therefore, to prevent this fraud, rights are conferred on the claimant which the claimant is able to enforce against the transferee. In the cases in which the rule has been applied, the claimant has been a third party to the transfer of land. As the claimant is able to enforce the rights there may be a further, implied, requirement. It may be necessary to show either that the claimant is not a volunteer or, if the claimant is, that enabling him to enforce the agreement is the only means of preventing fraud.

---

[1] Decisions in other contexts demonstrate the reluctance of the courts to assist claimants whose interests could have been made enforceable by registration. See, *e.g. Midland Bank Trust Co. Ltd v. Green* [1981] A.C. 513; *Lloyds Bank plc v. Carrick* [1996] 4 All E.R. 630.

[2] The dangers of this are illustrated by *Lyus v. Prowsa Developments Ltd* [1982] 1 W.L.R. 1044. There, by insisting a transferee remained "subject to" the claimant's rights the vendor-mortgagee risked breaching its duty to obtain the best price reasonably available (Charles Harpum, "Constructive Trusts and Registered Land" (1983) 42 C.L.J. 54 at 57) and adversely affecting any other creditors and claimants (Paul Jackson, "Estate Contracts, Estates and Registered Land" [1983] Conv. 64 at 67).

[3] See the discussion below, Part IV.

1. Transfer "subject to"

For this requirement to be satisfied the transferee must have acquired the land pursuant to an express agreement to hold it "subject to" rights in the claimant's favour. The agreement need not be included in the transfer. In *Lyus v. Prowsa Developments Ltd*[4] a clause contained in the contract for sale but not in the transfer itself was considered sufficient. In *Loke Yew v. Port Swettenham Rubber Co. Ltd*[5] the Privy Council accepted as sufficient a stipulation made outside the contract and transfer. Two further extensions to this have been suggested. In *Binions v. Evans* Lord Denning M.R. considered that a "subject to" clause could be implied.[6] In *Bahr v. Nicolay (No. 2)*, a decision of the High Court of Australia, Wilson and Toohay JJ. seemed to place reliance on an assurance of rights made subsequent to the transfer.[7] However, the definition of fraud, considered below,[8] places doubt on both extensions. In this context fraud is based on the purchaser reneging on a "positive stipulation" entered into to "acquire" land.[9]

2. Intention to Create New Rights

Once established that the purchaser has taken "subject to" the claimant's rights the purpose underlying the inclusion of the clause must be considered. In *Ashburn Anstalt v. Arnold* Fox L.J. made it clear that the mere inclusion of a "subject to" clause is not itself sufficient for a claimant to acquire rights. He explained that the importance of certainty of title prevents the court from intervening on the basis of slender materials.[10] For the court to intervene, it must be shown that the purpose of the clause was to create new rights in favour of the claimant. Two points need to be considered. First, why it is necessary

---

[4] See above n.2.
[5] [1913] A.C. 491.
[6] [1972] 1 Ch. 359 at 369. He suggested, in particular, that purchasers should impliedly take land subject to the rights of licensees in occupation. Commenting on the case, Hayton noted, [1972] Conv. 277 at 279 "this suggestion cannot be countenanced for it would be to let in by the back door contractual licences as property rights binding purchasers always".
[7] (1987–88) 164 C.L.R. 604 at 633; see Gray, p. 196.
[8] See below, Part II. 3.
[9] *Lyus v. Prowsa Developments Ltd* above n.2, p. 1054.
[10] [1989] 1 Ch. 1 at 25–26.

to show an intention to create new rights. Secondly, how to ascertain the purpose of a clause.

As has been seen, this rule applies where land is transferred "subject to" rights the claimant enjoyed at the time of the transfer. It is not necessary that the claimant's rights were enforceable against the vendor and capable under the statutory schemes of being enforceable against the transferee.[11] However, it seems clear that if the purpose of the clause is to enforce the claimant's existing rights against the transferee, then the clause will be ineffective. This rule does not operate to enforce the claimant's existing rights *directly* against the transferee. Instead, the claimant is able to enforce his rights *indirectly* by the acquisition of new rights. This analysis of the application of the rule is apparent from *Lyus v. Prowsa Developments Ltd.*[12] There, proprietary rights were acquired by claimants pursuant to a transfer of land "subject to" their estate contract. Dillon J. distinguished *Miles v. Bull (No. 2)*[13] where a transfer, "subject to" such rights of occupation as might subsist in favour of the wife" was held ineffective to enable the wife to enforce rights against the transferee. Dillon J. explained that there, "[t]he wife was to get no *fresh* rights".[14] The reason it is necessary to demonstrate an intention to create new rights may relate to why "subject to" clauses are used. As has been seen,[15] the fact parties are relying on such a clause suggests that either the claimant's existing rights are void against the transferee or his rights are incapable of enforcement against third parties. In these circumstances, to enforce those rights directly against the transferee would be a direct contravention of statute.

Ascertaining the purpose of a clause is a question of fact. Guidelines may be derived from the case law as to the factors the court will take into account, but these are no more than persuasive. Three factors in particular may indicate that the clause was intended to create new rights. First, where the vendor risks liability towards the claimant unless the claimant is able to enforce rights against the transferee.[16] Secondly, where the transferee pays less than the market

---

[11] In *Lyus v. Prowsa Developments Ltd* above n.2 the claimants' estate contract was not enforceable against the vendor-mortgagee. See Jackson above n.2 at 65.

[12] See above n.2.

[13] [1969] 3 All E.R. 1585.

[14] See above n.2 at 1054 (emphasis added). See also Oakley, p. 57.

[15] See above n.1 and text.

[16] In *Lyus v. Prowsa Developments Ltd* above n.2 at 1051 Dillon J. noted that in *Binions v. Evans*, "The provision that the cottage was sold subject to the defendant's rights was. . . imposed in some part for the protection of the vendors". See also *Ashburn Anstalt v. Arnold* above n.10 at 26.

value in return for recognising the claimant's rights.[17] Thirdly in *Lyus v. Prowsa Developments Ltd* it seems that the absence of any other reason for including the clause was persuasive in determining an intention the purchaser give effect to the claimants' rights.[18] Conversely, proprietary rights will not be acquired where the court is satisfied that the clause was included to protect the vendor from liability to the purchaser (rather than the claimant) for non-disclosure of a right which is in fact binding on the purchaser.[19]

3. FRAUD

Fraud in this context, as in the "instrument of fraud" doctrine discussed in Chapter 3, has been defined by reference to *Rochefoucauld v. Boustead*.[20] Both rules are concerned with a fraudulent attempt to rely on statutory rights. The fraud in Chapter 3 relates to reliance on the absence of a formal declaration of trust pursuant to which land was transferred. In reneging on a "subject to" clause, the purchaser relies on the fact the claimant's rights are not capable of being enforced against third parties, or an available means of ensuring enforcement has not been utilised. The classification of such conduct as fraudulent requires the same note of caution as that expressed in Chapter 3: there is a danger that too elastic a definition of fraud will be adopted. The role of this rule should be to identify the circumstances in which reliance on statutory rights is illegitimate. While it is possible to define the concept of fraud applied in "subject to" cases, this should not be read in isolation, but in the context of the other elements of a claim. It is only considered illegitimate to rely on statutory rights when fraud, of the nature defined, arises in combination with those other elements.

---

[17] In *Ashburn Anstalt v. Arnold*, above n.10 at 23 Fox L.J. relied on this to justify the decision in *Binions v. Evans*. Jonathan Hill, "Leases, Licences and Third Parties" (1988) 51 M.L.R. 226 at 232 suggests that this is now the only situation in which this rule will be applied.
[18] See above n.2 at 1053. See *Ashburn Anstalt v. Arnold* above n.10 at 24–25, *per* Fox L.J. "There was, therefore, no point in making the conveyance subject to the contract unless the parties intended the purchaser to give effect to the contract"; Harpum above n.2, p. 55.
[19] In *Lyus v. Prowsa Developments Ltd* above n.2 at 1051–1052 Dillon J. gave an example of a transfer subject to a restrictive covenant 60 or 90 years old. This is also how Dillon J. interpreted the subject to clause in *Miles v. Bull (No. 2)* above n.13.
[20] [1897] 1 Ch. 196.

The concept of fraud that is applied in "subject to" cases was explained by Dillon J. in *Lyus v. Prowsa Developments Ltd*. There, a mortgagee sold land to the first defendant (D1) "subject to" the plaintiffs' estate contract. The first defendant, in turn, sold the land to the second defendant (D2) pursuant to a similar agreement. The court held that both defendants were under an obligation to give effect to the plaintiffs' estate contract. D1 argued that under the rules of registered land, following the transfer to them, any rights acquired by the claimant by virtue of the "subject to" clause were not binding. Dillon J. noted that it is not fraud to rely on rights conferred by statute. However, he explained that: "the fraud on the part of the defendants. . .lies not just in relying on the legal rights conferred by an Act of Parliament, but in the first defendant reneging on a positive stipulation in favour of the plaintiffs in the bargain under which the first defendant acquired the land".[21] To prevent this fraud, the new rights acquired by the claimants by virtue of the "subject to" clause were enforceable despite the rules of registered land. The theoretical basis on which rights are enforced is that equity acts *in personam* against the transferee who "is directly bound in right of his own conscience".[22] However, in any event, the basis of D1's argument may be challenged. As rights are created by the transfer they should, in principle, bind the transferee. The transferee under a "subject to" clause should not be able to argue that he takes free from the rights thereby created any more than, in Chapter 3, a transferee of land on trust would be able to argue that the trust was void on the transfer.

4.   THE IMPLIED REQUIREMENT

In the cases in which this rule has been applied, its effect has been to enable a third party to a transfer of land to enforce an agreement

---

[21] See above n.2 at 1054. Contrast Harpum, "Purchasers With Notice of Unregistered Land Charges" (1981) 40 C.L.J. 213 at 216. He argues that fraud should be restricted to where the transferee induces the claimant not to register his interest. This, in any event, could found a claim to rights under the rule discussed in Chapter 7.

[22] Hayton, *Registered Land* (3rd ed., 1981), p. 19. Peter Bennett, "Registered Land and Good Faith" (1984) 47 M.L.R. 476 at 477–478, offers an alternative interpretation of the rule which would enable it to be seen as consistent with statute. He suggests that the interest acquired by the claimant could be analysed as arising a *scintilla temporis* following the transfer. There would be a *scintilla temporis* in which, consistent with statute, the land vested in the transferee free from the claimant's unprotected rights. However, *scintilla temporis* is considered to be an artificial doctrine and it has been rejected in other contexts: *Abbey National Building Society v. Cann* [1991] 1 A.C. 56.

reached between the vendor and purchaser. In Chapter 3, it was argued that where an agreement entered into between a vendor and transferee confers rights on third parties, the third party should be able to enforce the agreement only exceptionally where this is necessary to prevent fraud. When applying the rule in this chapter, the courts seem prepared to allow the third party to enforce the agreement even when this is not strictly necessary. This is demonstrated by *Lyus v. Prowsa Developments Ltd*. There, as has been seen, the court held that both the original transferee (D1) and a subsequent purchaser (D2) were under an obligation to give effect to the claimants' estate contract. C.T. Emery and B. Smythe note that, prior to the second sale, fraud could have been prevented without recourse to this rule. The mortgagee could have prevented fraud by enforcing the "subject to" agreement against D1. It was necessary to rely on this rule only following the sale to D2. However, they note that it is unclear whether the court considered the fact there had been a second sale to be decisive to the application of the rule.[23]

By enabling a third party to enforce the agreement the rule has been criticised as acting contrary to privity of contract.[24] Swadling suggests that in applying the rule the courts' real objection is to privity of contract and the (then) failure of English law to recognise the concept of a contract for the benefit of a third party.[25] He therefore argues that where a purchaser is bound, it is as a matter of contract law and not property law.[26] If Swadling's analysis is accepted, then the "subject to" rule would not be a means of enabling the acquisition of proprietary rights, but merely a means of enabling a claimant to enforce a contractual obligation against a purchaser of land. In light of the unease expressed as to the legitimacy of this rule, such an analysis is not without attraction. This is particularly so, as the enactment of the Contracts (Rights of "Third Parties") Act 1999

---

[23] C.T. Emery and B. Smythe, "The Imposition of Trusts by 'Subject to' Clauses" (1983) 133 N.L.J. 798 at 799. This point could also be made in relation to *Binions v. Evans*, above n.6. There, the cottage was still held by the original purchaser and therefore the agreement could have been enforced by the vendor.

[24] M.P. Thompson, "Registration, Fraud and Notice" (1985) 44 C.L.J. 280 at 288; Peter Sparkes, "Leasehold Terms and Contractual Licences" (1988) 104 L.Q.R. 175 at 178. In *Binions v. Evans* above n.6 at 368 Lord Denning M.R., explained this rule, by reference to the judgment of Lord Upjohn in *Beswick v. Beswick* [1968] A.C. 58, as an example of equity aiding the common law.

[25] Swadling, "The Proprietary Effect of a Hire of Goods" in *Interests in Goods* (Palmer and McKendrick eds., 2nd ed., 1998).

[26] See above n.25, p. 513.

provides for the enforcement of a contract by a third party for whose benefit the contract has been entered.[27] However, it is submitted that the analysis should not be accepted. In making his analysis, Swadling compares cases applying the "subject to" rule with a principle of maritime law derived from *De Mattos v. Gibson*.[28] That case provides that the purchaser of a ship with notice of a pre-existing charterparty can be restrained by the charterer from preventing the performance of the charterparty.[29] The basis of this rule is distinct from that applicable to a transfer "subject to" a claimant's rights. The *De Mattos* principle was developed by reference to *Tulk v. Moxhay*[30] and is based on the purchaser's notice of the pre-existing obligation. The principle applied to a transfer of land "subject to" a claimant's rights is explicitly founded on the fraud that results from reneging on a positive stipulation. In comparing the two principles, Swadling relies on the affirmation of *De Mattos* by the Privy Council in *The Strathcona*.[31] There, Lord Shaw emphasised that the purchaser did not merely have notice of the prevailing charterparty, but had agreed to recognise the obligation.[32] On its facts, therefore, the case was analogous to a transfer of land "subject to" the claimant's rights. However, the principle applied was still described by reference to *Tulk*, and to the obligations of a purchaser with notice, and not on the basis of fraud. It is submitted that the different basis of the principles of notice and fraud is vital. In cases in which the "subject to" principle has been applied, the mechanism used to confer proprietary rights has been the constructive trust. It is the presence of fraud in reneging on the stipulation that justifies the imposition of the trust.

However, the fact the courts are willing to intervene in favour of the claimant may indicate that there is a further, implied requirement to a claim. Intervention may be explained on the basis that, in the cases in which this rule has been applied, the claimants have not been mere volunteers. In *Binions v. Evans* and *Lyus v. Prowsa Developments Ltd* the claimants were seeking to enforce rights for which they had provided consideration. In *Binions v. Evans* there was a direct

---

[27] The effect of the Act is considered below, Part VI.

[28] (1859) 4 De G. & J. 276.

[29] The scope of the rule is considered by Alison Clarke, "*De Mattos v. Gibson* Again" [1992] L.M.C.L.Q. 448.

[30] (1848) 2 Ph. 774.

[31] *Lord Strathcona Steamship Co v. Dominion Coal Co* [1926] A.C. 108.

[32] See above n.31 at 116.

contractual nexus between the claimant and the vendor. *Lyus v. Prowsa Developments Ltd* suggests that a direct nexus is not necessary. In that case, there was no contractual nexus between the plaintiffs and the vendor-mortgagee, but the plaintiffs had paid consideration to the mortgagor.[33] It may be an implicit requirement in the third party's ability to enforce the agreement that the claimant is not a volunteer. However, by analogy with Chapter 3, the court may be justified in enabling the claimant to enforce the agreement regardless of whether he is a volunteer in exceptional cases where this is the only means of preventing fraud. Further, in the absence of a direct contractual nexus, this may be preferable as an explanation of the enforcement of the agreement in *Lyus v. Prowsa Developments Ltd*. As Emery and Smythe explain,[34] once there had been the sale to D2, enabling the claimants' to enforce the agreement became the only means of preventing fraud.

III. Scope of the rule

The scope of this rule remains uncertain but it is potentially extremely broad. The most striking feature is that the courts seem prepared to apply the rule where land is transferred "subject to" a right which is not recognised as proprietary. If the rule does apply in such a case, then, in this respect, it is the source of proprietary rights *sui generis*. It gives proprietary status to rights which, when created expressly, are personal.

In *Binions v. Evans*,[35] the plaintiffs purchased a cottage "subject to" the right to occupy the cottage for life which had been conferred on the defendant by the vendor. Notwithstanding, the plaintiffs sought to evict the defendant. In the Court of Appeal, all three judges agreed that as the plaintiffs had taken "subject to" the defendant's rights they could not evict her. However, they disagreed as to the nature of the defendant's rights. The majority (Megaw and Stephenson L.JJ.) considered that the defendant was a beneficiary under a trust governed by the Settled Land Act 1925.[36] Lord Denning M.R.

---

[33] J.D. Feltham, "Informal Trusts and Third Parties" [1987] Conv. 246 at 250 notes the claimant was not a "mere donee".

[34] See above n.23 at 799.

[35] See above n.6.

[36] Further, Megaw L.J. seems to have considered that the plaintiffs were bound by this trust. He said, above n.6 at 370 "The plaintiffs took with express notice of the agreement which constitutes, or gives rise to, the trust. They cannot turn the defendant out of the house against her will; for that would be a breach of the trust which binds them".

disagreed with this analysis. In his view, the vendor had conferred on the defendant a contractual licence.[37] He considered that the contractual licence was an equitable interest in the land enforceable against the plaintiffs as purchasers with notice. However, he said that even if the defendant did not obtain an equitable interest in the land on the creation of the licence, then "nevertheless it is quite plain that she obtained one afterwards when [the vendor] sold the cottage".[38] He explained: "Whenever the owner sells the land to a purchaser, and at the same time stipulates that he shall take it 'subject to' a contractual licence, I think it is plain that a court of equity will impose on the purchaser a constructive trust in favour of the beneficiary".[39] Hence, Lord Denning M.R. was prepared to impose a proprietary right, at the time of transfer, to protect the defendant's rights on the basis that those rights were personal. His judgment is not strong authority as it is a minority judgment. Subsequently, in *Ashburn Anstalt v. Arnold*,[40] the Court of Appeal considered, in an *obiter* discussion, that on the facts of *Binions v. Evans* it would have been appropriate to impose a constructive trust to protect the contractual licence.

The application of this rule to contractual licences, coupled with the ability of the claimant to enforce the agreement, gives rise to the possibility of this rule being used to facilitate the acquisition of proprietary rights to protect other personal rights.[41] If this is a correct application of the rule, then it provides a means to cut across the conventional division between personal and proprietary rights. Rights which are otherwise personal become proprietary "through the back door" by a transfer "subject to" those rights.[42] Opinion is divided as to whether such an application of the rule is desirable.[43] Considered in context, the cases concerned with contractual licences may not support the application of the rule to other personal rights. The cases should be seen in light of the debate as to whether contractual licences themselves should be recognised as proprietary. Prior to

---

[37] Above n.6 at 367.

[38] Above n.6 at 368.

[39] *ibid.*

[40] Above n.10 at 23.

[41] See, *e.g.* Harpum above n.2 at 56. He suggests this rule could be used to enable positive covenants to be enforced.

[42] Hill above n.17 at 232.

[43] A.J. Oakley, "Licences and Leases—A Return to Orthodoxy" (1988) 47 C.L.J. 353 at 355 supports the application of the rule in relation to contractual licences. Gray, p. 195 suggests the rule is "probably best limited to those rights which are generally accepted to be *proprietary* in quality" (emphasis included).

Ashburn Anstalt v. Arnold, the prevailing view seemed to be that a contractual licence conferred proprietary rights.[44] *Ashburn Anstalt v. Arnold* stands alone as a case where the court considered it may be appropriate to create proprietary rights to protect a contractual licence having first stated that such licences are personal.[45] However, the point was made only in an *obiter* discussion.

IV. Nature and enforceability of the right acquired

As in Chapter 3, the mechanism used by equity to prevent the transferor's fraud is the constructive trust.[46] The transferee is made trustee of the land and the claimant acquires an equitable, beneficial interest corresponding to the interest conferred by the agreement. For example, in *Lyus v. Prowsa Developments Ltd* a constructive trust was imposed under which the transferee was required to give effect to the claimants' estate contract. An estate contract is not a conventional beneficial interest and again, therefore, the question arises whether it is appropriate to impose a trust in relation to all interests.[47] It is submitted that here, as in Chapter 3, where the agreement relates to a non-beneficial proprietary interest it would be more appropriate for the claimant to acquire an equitable right corresponding to the interest referred to in the agreement.

The appropriateness of a constructive trust may also be questioned where the "subject to" rule is used to enforce personal rights. For example, M.P. Thompson notes the difficulty in analysing the ambit of a trust imposed to give effect to a contractual licence.[48] Swadling

---

[44] See, *e.g. Re Sharpe* [1980] 1 W.L.R. 219; *D.H.N. Food Distributors Ltd v. Tower Hamlets L.B.C.* [1976] 1 W.L.R. 852. In both cases the courts considered that a contractual licensee enjoyed proprietary rights under a constructive trust from the time the licence was created.

[45] Although, as has been noted, above n.39 and text, in *Binions v. Evans* Lord Denning M.R. was prepared to impose a trust to protect a contractual licence on the basis the licence was personal, he had in fact held that the creation of the licence conferred proprietary rights. Further, he was a strong advocate in favour of giving contractual licences proprietary status.

[46] In *Bahr v. Nicolay (No. 2)*, above n.7 at 618 Mason and Dawson JJ. considered the trust to be an express trust. This raises the same question of non-compliance with the Law of Property Act 1925, s.53(1)(b) as discussed in Chapter 3, Part V.

[47] This point is discussed in Chapter 3, Part VI. 2.

[48] M.P. Thompson, "Leases, Licences and the Demise of *Errington*" [1988] Conv. 201 at 206.

uses the difficulty in defining the ambit of such a trust as a means of doubting that a proprietary right is acquired. It is submitted that this argument is again based on a false analogy with the *De Mattos* principle as discussed in *The Strathcona*.[49] In the latter case, Lord Shaw considered that the purchaser of a ship with notice of a pre-existing charterparty held the ship on constructive trust for the charterer. As Swadling correctly argues, there could be no constructive trust because there is no property interest enjoyed by the charterers. The obligation imposed on the purchaser in respect of the charterparty did not detract from the purchaser's legal or equitable ownership.[50] Referring to the application of a constructive trust in *Binions v. Evans*, Swadling suggests that the same criticism applies.[51] An obligation to respect a contractual licence (which is not a proprietary right) does not detract from the purchaser's legal and equitable ownership of the cottage. However, as has been seen, for proprietary rights to be acquired pursuant to a "subject to" clause, it is essential that the parties intended to create *new* rights in favour of the claimant. The right held on trust is not the (personal) right the claimant had, but the new (proprietary) right imposed to prevent the purchaser's fraud. Where these new rights do not meet the characteristics of a recognised proprietary right, they constitute proprietary rights *sui generis*.

Once proprietary rights have been acquired by the claimant, the enforcement of those rights against subsequent purchasers should be dependent on the general rules of registered or unregistered land. This approach was not adopted in *Lyus v. Prowsa Developments Ltd.* There, the subsequent purchaser (D2) did not dispute that if a trust was imposed on the original transferee (D1), then they would hold on a "similar trust".[52] However, this was based on the fact that D2 had also entered into a "subject to" clause.[53]

V. Time at which the right is acquired

Although it is the transferee's fraud in reneging on the agreement which justifies the court's intervention, it seems that proprietary

---

[49] See above n.28 and text.
[50] See above n.25 pp. 499–500.
[51] See above n.25 p. 511.
[52] See above n.2 at 1048.
[53] Emery and Smythe, above n.23, at 800 doubt whether in fact this clause demonstrated an intention to enable the plaintiffs to enforce their rights against D2.

rights arise at the time of the transfer rather than the time of the fraud.[54] The time of transfer is the time at which the claimant's existing rights may become void by the application of rules of registered or unregistered land and therefore it is from that time that the claimant is dependent upon this rule for his rights. This may reveal a further difference between this rule and that discussed in Chapter 3, under which rights are acquired to prevent statute being used as an instrument of fraud. There, where there has been an informal declaration of trust, the claimant's interest may be valid following the transfer despite being unenforceable. Equity need intervene only at the point in time at which the trustee relies on the absence of formalities to fraudulently deny the trust.[55]

VI. Conclusion

The rule discussed in this chapter enables the court to enforce an agreement entered into by a transferee to hold land "subject to" the claimant's rights. It is closely related to the "instrument of fraud" rule discussed in Chapter 3, as both rules are based on the prevention of a particular form of fraudulent conduct. Notwithstanding, the rules differ in their effect. In Chapter 3, it was seen that the court does not enforce the parties' agreement, but intervenes only to the extent necessary to prevent fraud. By enforcing a "subject to" clause, the court gives effect to the parties agreement despite the fact the agreement may conflict with general rules of land law that determine what type of right binds a purchaser of land and in what circumstances.

The practical need to rely on this rule may be reduced by the Contracts (Rights of "Third Parties") Act 1999.[56] That Act enables a person who is not a party to a contract to enforce a term of the contract which expressly provides that he may, or that confers a

---

[54] See *Binions v. Evans* above n.6 at 368, *per* Lord Denning M.R. (cited above n.39 and text). It was because the interest arises at the time of transfer that its enforcement was questioned in *Lyus v. Prowsa Developments Ltd* above n.2.

[55] However Smith, p. 120 notes it is "extremely likely" that, in any event, the interest dates from the transfer.

[56] The Act applies to contracts entered into on or after May 11, 2000. Contracts entered between November 11, 1999 and May 11, 2000 may expressly provide for its application.

benefit on him.[57] Hence, where a "subject to" clause is interpreted as a valid contract between vendor and purchaser to create proprietary rights in favour of a third party claimant, the claimant may be able to enforce the contract. As the effect of the Act is to enable the enforcement of the parties' contract, there are at least two limitations on its application *in situ*. First, a contract to create proprietary rights must comply with section 2 of the Law of Property (Miscellaneous Provisions) Act 1989. If it does not, then there is no contract to enforce. Secondly the contract must be for the creation of a recognised proprietary right. A contractual licence expressly created is personal. The application of the 1999 Act in the context of a contractual licence would produce the result advocated by Swadling. The claimant would have only a contractual right enforceable against the purchaser.

---

[57] Contracts (Rights of "Third Parties") Act 1999, s.1.

Chapter 5.

Where there is an Uncompleted Sale[1]

I. Introduction

This chapter is concerned with the sale of a proprietary right in land which has not yet been completed. "Sale" is used in this chapter to denote both the transfer of an existing proprietary right (for example, the transfer of an existing freehold or leasehold estate) and the creation of a new proprietary right (for example, the creation of a lease, easement or mortgage in favour of the purchaser). Two situations will be considered in which the uncompleted sale itself becomes the source for the creation of proprietary rights. The basis for the creation of the rights is equity's maxim "equity regards as done that which ought to be done". If parties have entered into an agreement which "ought" to be executed, then equity treats the parties as though the agreement has been executed. In the first situation to be considered the agreement ought to be executed because the parties have entered into a specifically enforceable contract; in the second, because the purchaser has paid the consideration in full (and any other conditions of sale have been complied with).

The following discussion of the application of equity's maxim draws a distinction between the sale of different types of proprietary right in land. The primary distinction is that between the sale of 'legal rights' and 'equitable interests'. Legal rights are divided into legal estates and legal interests. The distinction between these is that legal estates (freehold and leasehold) confer a right to possession of

---

[1] This chapter is based on the author's earlier article, "Acquiring Property Rights from Uncompleted Sales of Land" (1998) 61 M.L.R. 486.

land, while legal interests, such as easements, are rights exercised over land which is possessed by someone else. Equitable interests is a generic term used to describe all proprietary rights which are classified as equitable, including, for example, beneficial interests under a trust and equitable easements.

II. The first situation: where there is a specifically enforceable contract

1. CONTRACTS FOR SALE OF LEGAL RIGHTS IN LAND

Where a sale of land is not completed by deed the sale is generally ineffective to convey or create a legal right.[2] However the absence of a deed prevents the agreement from having effect only as regards the legal title. If the parties have, notwithstanding, entered into a contract for sale which meets the requirements of specific performance, then equity will give effect to the parties' agreement. The fact that the contract is specifically enforceable means that it "ought" to be executed. Therefore, equity will treat the parties as though it has been executed and the purchaser will be entitled, in equity, to the right he has contracted to buy.[3] The application of the principle must initially be considered by reference to two distinct situations. The first situation concerns contracts to create a legal right or to assign an existing legal interest. The second is a contract for sale of an existing legal estate. This distinction is necessary because, until recently, it seemed that the consequence of applying the principle in each factual situation necessarily differed. The distinction between these situations is also made, in connection with the transfer of registered land, in section 123A of the Land Registration Act 1925.[4]

---

[2] Law of Property Act 1925, s.52(1). In registered land, (in relation to registered titles) legal title does not pass until the transfer is completed by registration. Therefore, the right acquired by the purchaser under the rule discussed in this part of this chapter continues until registration. *cf.* Peter Sparkes, *A New Land Law* (1999), p. 82 n.89, referring to this author's article above n.1. An exception arises for transfers that trigger compulsory first registration. The Land Registration Act 1925, s.123A assumes a transfer operates to pass legal title for a transitional period of two months. The right acquired under that provision by a purchaser who fails to apply for registration within the two month period is analogous to the right acquired by a purchaser under the rule discussed in this part.

[3] Rights may now be acquired by a third party who is able to enforce the contract under the Contracts (Rights of "Third Parties") Act 1999. If V enters a specifically enforceable contract with P, which confers rights on C, then the effect of treating the contract as executed is to confer rights on C.

[4] Introduced by the Land Registration Act 1997.

The classic illustration of the first situation is the Court of Appeal decision in *Walsh v. Lonsdale*.[5] There, Lonsdale entered into a specifically enforceable contract to grant a lease to Walsh. No deed was executed, with the result that the agreement was ineffective to create the legal lease the parties had intended. Notwithstanding, Walsh took possession of the premises and started paying rent, although he did not pay yearly in advance as required under the terms of the parties' agreement. Lonsdale levied distress for the unpaid rent and this was challenged by Walsh. The Court of Appeal considered that if, under the parties' agreement, the rent was payable, then distress could be levied. The Court considered that as the agreement was specifically enforceable the parties should be treated as though a lease had been created. To achieve this, the Court gave effect to the parties' agreement in equity by recognising their contract as creating an equitable lease. The uncompleted sale of the legal lease became the source for the creation of a lease in equity. Similarly, specifically enforceable contracts to create an interest in land are treated as creating the corresponding interest in equity. Hence, for example, a specifically enforceable contract to create a legal easement creates an equitable easement;[6] a specifically enforceable contract to create a legal mortgage creates an equitable mortgage.[7] In the same way, effect will be given to a specifically enforceable contract to transfer an existing legal interest.[8]

In *Chan v. Cresdon Proprietary Ltd*[9] the High Court of Australia emphasised that the equitable lease acquired by entering into a specifically enforceable contract is a different proprietary right from the lease the tenant has contracted to buy. There, the respondent agreed to grant a lease to S Ltd but no lease was formally executed. The appellant had agreed to act as guarantors for the performance by S Ltd of its obligations "under this lease". On the assumption that *Walsh v. Lonsdale* applied, the Court considered that the appellant had not guaranteed S Ltd's liability under the equitable lease thereby acquired. As the equitable lease was a separate right from the lease which S Ltd had contracted to buy, liability under the equitable lease was not liability "under *this* lease".

[5] (1882) 21 Ch.D. 9.
[6] *May v. Belleville* [1905] 2 Ch. 605.
[7] *National Provincial and Union Bank of England v. Charnley* [1924] 1 K.B. 431 at 440.
[8] See, *e.g.* in relation to the transfer of a mortgage, E.L.G. Tyler, *Fisher & Lightwood's Law of Mortgages* (9th ed., 1977), p. 253. However, not all legal interests are capable of being transferred independently of an estate in the land. See below n.31 and text.
[9] (1989) 168 C.L.R. 350.

In the second situation in which this principle applies, the division between the right acquired and the right the purchaser has contracted to buy is more apparent. This is in relation to a specifically enforceable contract for sale of an existing legal estate. The conveyance of a legal estate in land is comprised of two stages: the contract and the conveyance. Legal title does not pass until the conveyance. However, once the parties have entered into a specifically enforceable contract equity will treat the parties as though the contract has been executed. As with the first situation in which this principle applies, equity confers on the purchaser a right in the land corresponding to that which he has contracted to buy. The consequence of equity's intervention is to separate legal and equitable ownership of the estate transferred: legal title remains with the vendor while the purchaser is entitled to the estate in equity. Until recently, it was believed that the inevitable result of any division of legal and equitable entitlement to an estate is the creation of a trust. The effect of this in the context of a contract for sale of an existing legal estate is that the vendor is considered to become trustee of the land for the purchaser. The trust is generally treated as a type of constructive trust.[10] The most significant practical consequence of the imposition of a trust is that the vendor was considered necessarily to be placed under fiduciary obligations towards the purchaser as regards the management of the land.[11] However, the trust is perceived as being "of a highly unusual nature".[12] For example the vendor, who continues to have an interest in the land, remains in possession and receives profits derived from the land pending completion of the sale.[13] Following *Westdeutsche Landesbank Girozentrale v. Islington L.B.C.*,[14] it is no longer necessary to see the imposition of fiduciary obligations as the inevitable consequence of the division of legal and equitable entitlement. In Chapter 2 it was submitted that there are circumstances in which it is appropriate to accept that legal and equitable title is divided without the imposition of fiduciary obligations. However, adopting a broad definition, such

---

[10] Oakley, p. 275 describes it as "one of the oldest types of constructive trust, having been well established by 1651".

[11] The rights and responsibilities of the parties to the trust are discussed fully by Oakley, Ch. 6 and D.W.M. Waters, *The Constructive Trust: The Case for a New Approach in English Law* (1964), Ch. II.

[12] Oakley, p. 292.

[13] Oakley, p. 292.

[14] [1996] 2 All E.R. 961.

situations could still be described as involving a trust.[15] It may be more appropriate to treat the division of title that occurs by entering a specifically enforceable contract to sell a legal estate as not imposing fiduciary obligations on the vendor. This would provide conceptual coherence to the application of equity's maxim by ensuring that the consequence of intervention is the same in all situations in which the rule is applied. In all situations, the purchaser acquires an equitable interest corresponding to the right he has contracted to buy. Where this results in the division of legal and equitable title to an estate, a form of trust may be imposed, but the vendor will not necessarily be placed under any fiduciary obligation towards the purchaser.

2. CONTRACTS FOR SALE OF EQUITABLE INTERESTS IN LAND

In the situations discussed above, the parties have entered into a contract for sale of a legal right and effect has been given to the contract in equity. The next question to consider is whether the same principle applies where the contract for sale itself relates to an equitable interest. The application of the maxim to equitable interests was considered by Lord Radcliffe in *Oughtred v. I.R.C.*[16] in the context of a specifically enforceable contract for sale of the beneficial interest under a trust of shares in a private company. The application of the maxim to the facts of that case raised two novel questions. First, in the situations discussed above, parties have entered into a contract for sale of a legal right. For the purchaser to acquire the right he has contracted to buy, a deed is required. Conferring upon the purchaser the corresponding equitable interest does not circumvent the formal requirements relating to the interest the purchaser has contracted to buy. Section 53(1)(c) of the Law of Property Act 1925 requires the disposition of an equitable interest to be in writing. In *Oughtred* the contract in question, although specifically enforceable, was oral. Therefore, the application of the principle would circumvent the statutory requirement relating to the equitable interest the purchaser had contracted to buy. The contract in question related to a subsisting beneficial interest and therefore the application of the principle would also involve the imposition of a constructive sub-trust. Treating the parties as though the contract had been

---

[15] Chapter 2, Part II.1.
[16] [1960] A.C. 206.

executed would require the vendor to hold his beneficial interest on sub-trust for the purchaser. As a trust would be imposed, section 53(2) provided a possible statutory basis for circumventing section 53(1)(c). Section 53(2) provides that, "this section does not affect the creation or operation of. . . constructive trusts" although it was uncertain whether in fact this negated the need for writing. Secondly even if the court could reconcile the application of the principle with section 53, then, in addition, there were doubts whether the constructive trust imposed upon a vendor could operate as a sub-trust. The opposing views are reflected in comments on the decision in *Oughtred* by Waters and Oakley. Waters said, "the constructive trust, assuming as it does a division of legal and equitable interests, is irreconcilable with the sale of an equitable interest. . .".[17] Oakley, however, was satisfied that, "as a matter of principle there seems no reason why a constructive trust should not operate by way of sub-trust".[18]

Despite these difficulties, Lord Radcliffe, in a dissenting judgment, was satisfied that the principle does apply to contracts for sale of an equitable interest. The facts of *Oughtred* were that a number of shares in a private company were held on trust for Mrs Oughtred for life, remainder to her son absolutely. Mrs Oughtred and her son entered into an oral agreement under which he agreed to give up his reversionary interest in the shares (thus making his mother solely entitled to the beneficial interest) in consideration of which she would transfer to him other shares in the same company which she owned absolutely. Considering the effect of the oral agreement, Lord Radcliffe said the son: "created in his mother an equitable interest in his reversion since the subject-matter of the agreement was property of which specific performance would normally be decreed by the court. He thus became a trustee for her of that interest *sub modo*".[19] Hence on this analysis, Mrs Oughtred acquired a proprietary right in her son's beneficial interest by entering into a specifically enforceable contract. As the agreement ought to be executed, Lord Radcliffe would treat the parties as though it had been executed.[20] He

---

[17] Above n.11, p. 116.
[18] Oakley, p. 278.
[19] See above n.16 at 227.
[20] Lord Cohen, above n.16 at 230, also dissenting, agreed that the effect of the oral agreement was to make the son a trustee of the shares for his mother.

considered that section 53(2) enabled this constructive sub-trust to arise regardless of non-compliance with section 53(1)(c).[21]

In *Oughtred*, the question for the House of Lords was whether *ad valorem* stamp duty was payable on the transfer of the shares. Subsequent to the parties' oral agreement the sale was completed by the transfer of the legal title to the shares to Mrs Oughtred.[22] As the transaction had been completed the majority did not consider it necessary to separate the stages of the transaction to determine whether stamp duty was payable. Lord Jenkins noted that the interest acquired by entering a specifically enforceable contract: "has never (so far as I know) been held to prevent a subsequent transfer, in performance of the contract, of the property contracted to be sold from constituting for stamp duty purposes a transfer on sale of the property in question".[23] In light of this the majority did not consider it necessary to decide whether in fact there was a trust.[24] Therefore, while Lord Radcliffe dissented on the main question it was still possible to accept as correct his analysis of the effect of the parties' agreement. Subsequently, doubts as regards the intervention of equity in relation to a specifically enforceable contract for sale of equitable interests seem to have been removed by the Court of Appeal's endorsement of Lord Radcliffe's analysis in *Neville v. Wilson*.[25]

While *Oughtred* concerned personal property the statutory provisions in issue apply equally to land. Therefore, accepting as correct Lord Radcliffe's analysis, equity should treat a specifically enforceable contract for sale of an equitable interest in land as though it has been executed. Where the subject-matter of the contract is a beneficial interest this will be achieved by the imposition of a constructive sub-

---

[21] Lord Cohen did not adopt Lord Radcliffe's analysis of the agreement. Lord Cohen considered that there was no transfer of the son's beneficial interest and therefore no question of compliance with s.53(1)(c) arose. Instead, in his view, a new equitable interest was carved out of the son's beneficial interest and it was this new interest which the son held on trust. However, following *Neville v. Wilson* [1996] 3 W.L.R. 460 (on which see below n.25 and text) Lord Radcliffe's view appears definitive. See Patrick Milne, "*Oughtred* Revisited" (1997) 113 L.Q.R. 213 at 214.

[22] This aspect of the case is discussed fully below in Part III of this chapter.

[23] See above n.16 at 240.

[24] See above n.16 at 239–240, *per* Lord Jenkins (with whom Lord Keith agreed); at 233, *per* Lord Denning.

[25] See above n.21 at 471–472, *per* Nourse L.J. "we are of the opinion that the analysis of Lord Radcliffe, based on the proposition that a specifically enforceable agreement to assign an interest in property creates an equitable interest in the assignee, was undoubtedly correct".

trust. However the principle will no longer apply to an oral contract for sale of land. This is because, as will be seen, writing is now required for a contract for sale of land to be specifically enforceable. In relation to land, *Oughtred* and *Neville v. Wilson* remain significant where there is a written contract for sale of an equitable interest under a trust of land. In relation to such a contract, the cases establish that the constructive trust imposed may operate by way of sub-trust.

3. The Requirements of Specific Performance

A contract for sale of land will be specifically enforceable if three conditions are met. First, there must be a valid contract. Secondly, the purchaser must have provided consideration; specific performance is an equitable remedy and equity will not assist a volunteer. Thirdly the purchaser must not have acted unconscionably as such conduct precludes reliance on equity.

For a contract for sale of land to be valid two further conditions must be met. First, the formal statutory requirements must have been complied with. Contracts entered into before September 27, 1989 are governed by section 40 of the Law of Property Act 1925. That section provides that, "no action may be brought. . ." upon a contract for sale of land unless the contract is evidenced in writing. Under this provision, an oral contract for sale of land is not void but is unenforceable by action. If the purchaser does an act of part performance on the basis of the existence of the contract, then the contract becomes specifically enforceable. The contract may then be the source for the acquisition of proprietary rights in the same way as a specifically enforceable contract evidenced in writing. This is illustrated by *Lloyds Bank plc v. Carrick*.[26] There, Mrs Carrick entered into an oral contract to buy an existing lease from the vendor. She acted in part performance of the contract by paying the purchase moneys and moving in. Morritt L.J. explained that once the contract became specifically enforceable by virtue of Mrs Carrick's part performance equity would treat the parties as though the contract had been executed.[27] Mrs Carrick thereby became entitled, in equity, to the vendor's lease. The doctrine of part performance was developed by the courts and received statutory recognition in section

---

[26] [1996] 4 All E.R. 630.
[27] See above n.26 at 637.

40(2) of the Law of Property Act 1925. Following recommendations by the Law Commission section 40 was repealed, and the doctrine of part performance abolished, by the Law of Property (Miscellaneous Provisions) Act 1989.[28] Contracts entered into on or after September 27, 1989 must comply with the more stringent requirements of section 2(1) of that Act. That section provides, "a contract for the sale or other disposition of an interest in land can only be made in writing. . .". An oral contract is therefore void and can no longer be the source of rights under this principle.

The second requirement for a valid contract for sale of land is that the right the purchaser has contracted to buy must be, in substance, a recognised proprietary right. This principle cannot be used as the source for the acquisition of proprietary rights *sui generis*. For example, specific performance is not available for a contract to grant an easement which does not comply with the characteristics of an easement derived from *Re Ellenborough Park*,[29] or of a lease which is not expressed to be for a term certain.[30] An analogous requirement applies in relation to the transfer of an existing interest. Specific performance could not be ordered of a contract to assign an interest, where the interest in question can exist only appurtenant to an estate.[31]

4. THE NATURE OF THE PROPRIETARY RIGHT

The source of the proprietary right, as has been seen, is the specifically enforceable contract. To explain the nature of the proprietary right two issues must be addressed. First, the extent to which

---

[28] Law Com. No. 164, *Transfer of Land: Formalities for Contracts for Sale Etc. of Land*. In *Singh v. Beggs* (1996) 71 P. & C.R. 120 Neill L.J. doubted whether in fact part performance has been abolished. He said, at 122, "the doctrine is an equitable doctrine, and it may be that in certain circumstances the doctrine could be relied on". His judgment is criticised by S.J.A. Swann, "Part performance: back from the dead?" [1997] Conv. 293.

[29] [1956] Ch. 131. See Paul Jackson, *The Law of Easements and Profits* (1975), pp. 40–43.

[30] Peter Sparkes, "Certainty of Leasehold Terms" (1993) 109 L.Q.R. 93 at 103–104.

[31] *e.g.* an easement. See J. Gaunt and P. Morgan, *Gale on Easements* (16th ed., 1997), p. 79 "Inasmuch as an easement attaches to the dominant tenement in respect of which it is granted, it is obvious that an easement already in existence as a legal easement cannot be disposed of separately, and that there can be no question of creating an interest in an existing easement apart from the land to which it belongs". Contrast the position of profits à prendre. As they may exist in gross, the owner may "get the benefit. . . by selling or letting an interest in it": *Goodman v. Saltash* (1882) 7 App. Cas. 633 at 658, *per* Lord Blackburn.

the right acquired has a life of its own independent of the contract from which it is derived; secondly the dependence of the right on the availability of specific performance.

(a) An independent proprietary right?

The relationship between the proprietary right acquired by a purchaser under a specifically enforceable contract, and the underlying contract, has been considered in relation to the enforcement of the right against third parties. The question to be considered is whether the right acquired by application of this principle exists independently of the contract, to enable it to be enforced against third parties who are not bound by the contract. This has practical importance because it determines how the purchaser should protect rights acquired under this principle. It is also important in determining the nature of the right acquired. If the right cannot be enforced against third parties who are not bound by the contract, then it does not meet one of the defining characteristics of a proprietary right. The relationship between the right acquired and the contract has been discussed in relation to two areas. First, unregistered land in which the contractual source of the right may affect the rules governing its enforcement. Secondly the enforcement of covenants following the assignment of an equitable lease acquired by entering an agreement to create a lease.

Where parties have entered a specifically enforceable contract for sale of land the contract may be an "estate contract", itself a proprietary right in land.[32] The category of estate contracts may be sufficiently broad to include all contracts for sale of land. This means that parties entering a specifically enforceable contract for sale of land may thereby create two proprietary rights: the estate contract (which is created expressly) and the right acquired informally by equity treating the contract as executed. In unregistered land, certain types of estate contract are registrable as a Class C(iv) land charge and depend for their enforcement on registration. The enforcement of the type of right the purchaser has informally acquired may usually

---

[32] Simon Gardner, "Equity, Estate Contracts and the Judicature Acts: *Walsh v. Lonsdale* Revisited" (1987) 7 O.J.L.S. 60, n.26 notes the proposition an estate contract is proprietary is "so well known that it is difficult to find authority. . .".

be dependent upon registration under another class of land charge or under the doctrine of notice. Therefore, whether the informally created right is independent of the contract can be determined by considering how a purchaser should protect his interest. Is the registration of the contract essential or is it sufficient to use rules relating to the right informally acquired? In *Lloyds Bank plc v. Carrick*[33] the Court of Appeal did not give the interest informally acquired any life independent of the contract.

In *Carrick*, as has been seen, Mrs Carrick entered into a specifically enforceable contract to buy a lease from the vendor. She thereby acquired two proprietary rights. The contract for sale of the lease, as a contract to convey a legal estate, was within the category of estate contracts registrable as a Class C(iv) land charge. As the contract was specifically enforceable equity would treat the contract as executed. This divided legal and equitable entitlement to the lease and it was considered that the vendor held the lease on trust for Mrs Carrick.[34] Subsequently, the vendor granted a mortgage over the property as security for a loan from Lloyds Bank. Mrs Carrick had not registered her estate contract[35] with the result that it was void against Lloyds Bank. The question for the Court of Appeal was whether Mrs Carrick had any interest in the property "separate and distinct" from the contract which, if established, would bind the mortgagee under the doctrine of notice. The Court of Appeal held that Mrs Carrick could establish no interest independent of the contract.

In *Carrick*, it was not argued that the beneficial interest Mrs Carrick acquired by entering into the specifically enforceable contract was "separate and distinct" from the contract. It was accepted that this interest was void because of her failure to register the contract. If correct, then this has significance outside the factual context of the case. If the equitable interest acquired by Mrs Carrick by reason of the fact the contract for sale was specifically enforceable was void through her failure to register the *contract*, this challenges treating the

---

[33] See above n.26.
[34] The case was decided prior to *Westdeutsche*. However, as has been seen above n.15 and text, it may still be correct to describe the situation as giving rise to a trust even though the mere existence of a specifically enforceable contract may not impose upon the vendor any fiduciary duties.
[35] The contract was specifically enforceable through part performance. It was not disputed that such a contract is registrable as a Class C(iv) Land Charge although the point was perhaps not without doubt. See J.T. Farrand, *Emmet on Title* (19th ed., 1986), para. 19.008.

interest as proprietary. Enforceability against third parties is a defining characteristic of a proprietary right. If the interest acquired by a purchaser is not enforceable *per se*, independent of the contract, then it cannot be said to meet this characteristic. On this analysis the purchaser's right seems more akin to a licence. An analogy may be made with the licence attached to a profit à prendre, or other recognised proprietary right, to enable the exercise of the right. Such a licence, while itself not a proprietary right, may be enforced against third parties who are bound by the proprietary right.[36] However it is generally accepted that the interest acquired by the purchaser under a specifically enforceable contract is "a proprietary interest of a sort".[37] Although the point is not without controversy, it seems accepted in other situations in which the Land Charges Act is applicable that the interest acquired by entering a specifically enforceable contract exists independently from the contract. For example, a specifically enforceable contract to create a legal easement or mortgage is an estate contract registrable as a Class C(iv) land charge.[38] However it is accepted as sufficient for the holder to register the corresponding equitable interest acquired.[39] As these rights are derived from the same principle it is submitted that in all cases the interest acquired under a specifically enforceable contract should be recognised as a proprietary right independent from the contract.

The basis upon which rights acquired by entering a specifically enforceable contract are enforced against third parties has also been considered in relation to the assignment of an agreement to create a

---

[36] See Gray, p. 901. He explains "such a licence enjoys the perpetually binding effect attributed to the proprietary interest to which it is annexed".

[37] *Oughtred v. I.R.C.* above n.16 at 240, *per* Lord Jenkins.

[38] The Report of the Committee on Land Charges (the Roxburgh Committee), Cmnd. 9825 (1965) recognised that an equitable easement is registrable within Class C(iv). Contrast Lord Denning M.R. in *E.R. Ives Investment Ltd v. High* [1967] 2 Q.B. 379. He said, at p. 395 that an agreement for an easement is not registrable within Class C(iv). A contract to create a mortgage may be registrable within Class C(iv). Geoffrey Rowley, "Conveyancing and Equitable Charges" [1962] Conv. 445 at 446–449 argues against such registration. Where there has been a deposit of documents of title registration is contrary to the policy of the land charges scheme. See Megarry and Wade, para. 19—222; S.J. Bailey, "Land Charges and Notice" (1949) 10 C.L.J. 241 at 245; R.E. Megarry, "Priority After 1925 of Mortgages of a Legal Estate in Land" (1940) 7 C.L.J. 243 at 251.

[39] The Roxburgh Committee *ibid.* accepted that an agreement for an easement is registrable as a Class D(iii) land charge. A contract to create a mortgage may be registrable as a Class C(iii) land charge (Gray, p. 141) unless there has been a deposit of title deeds (Land Charges Act 1972, s.2(4)(iii)(a)).

lease.[40] The orthodox view was that the right assigned by the tenant under an equitable lease was a contract rather than an independent lease. The consequence of this was that the enforcement of the leasehold covenants by and against the assignee was based on rules governing the assignment of contracts. The benefit but not the burden of a contract can be assigned, with the result that the assignee obtained the benefit of the covenants but was not bound by their burden.[41] This was considered unsatisfactory and there was, "a strong current of a practical tendency to treat the agreement for a lease as a fully institutionalised proprietary interest. . .".[42] The new rules governing the enforcement of leasehold covenants on an assignment enacted in the Landlord and Tenant (Covenants) Act 1995 apply equally to leases and agreements for a lease.[43] Therefore, in this respect at least, the effect of statutory intervention is that the tenant seems to acquire a proprietary right independent of the contract.

(b) Dependence upon specific performance

Jessel M.R.'s judgment in *Walsh v. Lonsdale*[44] was broad enough to suggest that once a party asserts a right to specific performance he, "is to be treated as if this had already been decreed without the examination usually undertaken before that remedy is awarded".[45] In *Chan v. Cresdon Proprietary Ltd*,[46] however, the High Court of Australia emphasised the discretionary nature of specific performance. On the facts of the case, the Court considered it, "would be imprudent to assume that specific performance would be awarded as a matter of course".[47] The judgment serves to emphasise that to acquire rights under this principle it must be shown that specific performance is available; that is the basis upon which the contract

---

[40] See Gardner above, n.32 at 65–68; R.J. Smith, "The Running of Covenants in Equitable Leases and Equitable Assignments of Legal Leases" (1978) 37 C.L.J. 98.

[41] *Manchester Brewery Co v. Coombs* [1901] 2 Ch. 608; *Purchase v. Lichfield Brewery Co* [1915] 1 K.B. 184.

[42] Gardner above, n.32 at 68.

[43] "Assignment" is defined in the Landlord and Tenant (Covenants) Act 1995, s.28(1) as including an equitable assignment and a "tenancy" as including an agreement for a tenancy. The old rules continue to apply to tenancies created prior to January 1, 1996.

[44] See above n.5.

[45] This interpretation is given by Meagher, Gummow and Lehane, para. 237.

[46] See above n.9.

[47] See above n.9 at 255.

"ought" to be performed. Moreover, once acquired, the right remains qualified as dependent upon the continuing availability of specific performance. If specific performance ceases to be available (for example, through unconscionable conduct on the part of the purchaser), then the proprietary right ends. Gardner argues that continuing specific performance should not be a requirement. He notes that this injects into the right an element of precariousness contrary to Lord Wilberforce's classic definition of proprietary rights as enjoying, "some degree of permanence and continuity".[48]

III. The second situation: where the purchaser has paid the consideration in full

In the previous part of this chapter it has been seen that equity's maxim "equity regards as done that which ought to be done" operates when parties enter a specifically enforceable contract for sale of land. The availability of specific performance means that the contract "ought" to be executed and equity will treat the parties as though it has been executed. The effect of equity's intervention is that the purchaser acquires a proprietary right corresponding to the right he has contracted to buy. However, that right is precarious as dependent upon the continuing availability of specific performance.

For a contract to be specifically enforceable, it is necessary for the purchaser to have provided some consideration. The rights and obligations of the parties change when the purchaser has paid the consideration in full. This change may be illustrated by reference to the sale of a legal estate. On the conventional analysis, once full payment is made, the vendor ceases to have an interest in the land to protect. The vendor becomes a bare trustee of the land for the purchaser, and the purchaser is entitled to any benefit derived from the land.[49] It has been argued that, following *Westdeutsche*, it is no longer necessary to impose fiduciary obligations on the vendor by reason of the initial division of legal and equitable entitlement to the estate under a specifically enforceable contract. It is submitted that

---

[48] *National Provincial Bank v. Ainsworth* [1965] A.C. 1175 at 1248; Gardner above, n.32 at 64. More cautiously he doubts, at n.167, whether specific performance should be a requirement at all.

[49] Oakley, pp. 292–293.

the effect of full payment of consideration by the purchaser is now twofold. First, accepting the argument based on *Westdeutsche*, that it is at the point when full payment is made (and any other conditions of sale have been complied with) that it becomes appropriate to place the vendor under fiduciary obligations towards the purchaser. Secondly the purchaser's right is no longer dependent upon specific performance. This is significant because the absence of the need to rely on specific performance removes the element of precariousness that otherwise characterises the purchaser's right.[50] Before full payment of consideration, it is the availability of specific performance that enables the application of equity's maxim "equity regards as done that which ought to be done" by demonstrating that the contract "ought" to be performed. However, once the consideration has been paid, the fact of full payment itself provides a sufficient basis to assert that the contract "ought" to be performed.

The assumption underlying the preceding analysis is that the acquisition of rights by the purchaser is divided into two discrete stages. First, the parties enter a contract for sale of land at a future date. Once the purchaser provides consideration (for example, a deposit) rights are acquired based on the specifically enforceable contract. Secondly the purchaser pays the consideration in full. At this second stage, the nature of the purchaser's right is changed, as it ceases to be dependent on specific performance. As the purchaser's right is initially derived from the contract, the contract must be valid by complying with section 2(1) of the Law of Property (Miscellaneous Provisions) Act 1989. It is possible for the contract and conveyance to be simultaneous. It will be submitted that in such situations equity's intervention is not dependent upon the existence of a valid contract. The payment of consideration itself is a sufficient basis for holding that rights are acquired by the purchaser. Before the scope of a principle based on full payment of consideration is discussed, it is necessary to consider the courts' assessment of the effect of full payment of consideration.[51]

The leading case on the effect of full payment of consideration is *Oughtred v. I.R.C.* There, as has been seen,[52] Mrs Oughtred entered

---

[50] See above n.48 and text.
[51] It should be noted that the cases discussed were decided prior to *Westdeutsche*, and therefore on the basis that the vendor under a specifically enforceable contract owed fiduciary obligations towards the purchaser.
[52] See above n.19 and text.

into a specifically enforceable agreement to buy her son's beneficial interest in shares. Lord Radcliffe explained that the effect of entering into the agreement was to make the son a constructive trustee *sub modo* of his interest in favour of his mother. Subsequently, Mrs Oughtred paid the consideration in full to her son. The trustees of the shares then executed a deed of transfer vesting legal title to the shares in Mrs Oughtred. The House of Lords was asked whether this transfer of the legal title also conveyed to Mrs Oughtred the beneficial interest in the shares. If it did, then the deed of transfer would attract substantial stamp duty.[53] Lord Radcliffe explained that once Mrs Oughtred paid the consideration in full her son became: "in a full sense and without more the trustee of his interest for her. She was the effective owner of all outstanding equitable interests".[54] In Lord Radcliffe's judgment, the consequence of this trust was that Mrs Oughtred was entitled to the shares prior to the transfer of the legal title and therefore stamp duty was not payable. The trust to which Lord Radcliffe refers seems to be based on the fact Mrs Oughtred had paid the consideration in full. There is no suggestion that her interest in the shares remained qualified as dependent upon the continuing availability of specific performance. Instead, the effect of full payment was to transform the trust, from a trust *sub modo* to a trust "in a full sense and without more". However, the authority of Lord Radcliffe on this point remains doubtful. The support for his analysis by the Court of Appeal in *Neville v. Wilson* is limited to the acquisition of rights by entering a specifically enforceable contract.[55] Therefore, the first question to consider is whether other cases support the acquisition of rights based on payment of consideration.

1. AUTHORITY FOR THE PRINCIPLE

In *Tailby v. Official Receiver*[56] the House of Lords was asked whether an assignment of future book debts transferred the equitable interest to the assignee. It was established that such an assignment was effective if the subject-matter was sufficiently defined. The assignment in question extended to any business carried out by the assignor

---

[53] The deed would attract liability to *ad valorem* duty assessed at £663. If, however, the deed transferred only the bare legal title, then stamp duty would be just 50p.

[54] See above n.16 at 227–228.

[55] See above n.25.

[56] (1888) 13 App. Cas. 523.

during the period of the security which, it was argued, was too vague. The Court of Appeal had based its judgment on the non-availability of specific performance. The Court considered that since the agreement was not specifically enforceable the equitable interest did not pass.[57] In the House of Lords, Lord Macnaghten explained that specific performance was not relevant. He said that once the consideration has passed (and the scope of the parties' agreement was ascertained): "you have only to apply the principle that equity considers done that which ought to be done if that principle is applicable under the circumstances of the case. The doctrines relating to specific performance do not, I think, afford a test or measure of the rights created".[58] Hence, in Lord Macnaghten's view, once the consideration has been paid, equity considers that the agreement ought to be executed without reference to specific performance. Further support may be derived from the House of Lords decision in *Chinn v. Collins*.[59] There, Lord Wilberforce considered the effect of an assignment of the equitable interest in shares in a public company. It was clear that the contract was not specifically enforceable.[60] Notwithstanding, he accepted that, "as soon as there was an agreement for their sale accompanied or followed by payment of the price, the equitable title passed at once to the purchaser. . .".[61]

Oughtred, Tailby and *Chinn v. Collins* are all concerned with equitable interests in personal property. There is also support in the case law for the application of a principle based on payment of consideration to rights in land. The principle was applied in relation to an equitable interest in land in *DHN Food Distributors Ltd v. London Borough of Tower Hamlets*.[62] There, Goff and Shaw L.JJ. held that by virtue of payment of the purchase price DHN became entitled to the beneficial interest in business premises. No reference was made in

---

[57] (1887) 18 Q.B.D. 25 at 30–31, *per* Lindley L.J.

[58] See above n.56 at 547–548.

[59] [1981] A.C. 533.

[60] *ibid.*, at 548. This was argued on the basis that the relevant law was the law of Guernsey, where the trustees were resident, and the law of Guernsey does not recognise specific performance. In any event, in English law specific performance is not available in relation to shares in a public rather than a private company.

[61] *ibid.*

[62] [1976] 1 W.L.R. 852.

their judgments to specific performance.[63] In *Bridges v. Mees*[64] Harman J. applied the same principle to the transfer of a legal estate in land. There, the plaintiff had entered an oral agreement to buy land from the vendor following which, over a period of time, he paid the consideration. The vendor then sold the same piece of land to the defendant who became registered proprietor. Harman J. accepted the plaintiff's argument that the effect of paying the consideration was to make him the sole beneficial owner.[65] Subsequently, Harman J. seemed to treat the plaintiff as acquiring two distinct rights: the beneficial interest and the right to bring an action for specific performance to acquire the legal title.[66]

Against these cases is the Court of Appeal's decision in *Carrick*.[67] There, the court rejected an argument that a beneficial interest acquired by entering a specifically enforceable contract matured, and ceased to be dependent on the contract, once the purchase money was paid in full. The court considered that the only effect of payment of the consideration in full was to make the trust a bare trust by removing the beneficial interest of the vendor.[68] However, the possibility of acquiring rights based on payment of consideration was dismissed by the Court of Appeal without a full consideration of the earlier case law. The Court's reliance on the contract in that case may be explained by the fact Mrs Carrick's claim was based on part performance: the effect of part performance is to make a contract specifically enforceable.[69] Further, it is submitted that the Court's judgment was directed by other considerations, in particular the perceived need to uphold the integrity of the system of registration of land charges.[70]

---

[63] While one of three grounds for the decision in that case it was the main ground in the judgments of Goff and Shaw L.JJ. See D. Sugarman and Frank Webb, "'Three-in-One': Trusts, Licences and Veils" (1977) 93 L.Q.R. 170. Lord Denning M.R. above n.62 at 859 said of the argument that DHN were entitled to the beneficial interest "that may be right, but the President of the Lands Tribunal rejected it, and I am not prepared to say that he was wrong".

[64] [1957] 1 Ch. 475.

[65] See above n.64 at 484.

[66] See above n.64 at 486.

[67] See above n.26.

[68] See above n.26 at 638.

[69] See the discussion of *United Bank of Kuwait plc v. Sahib* [1996] 3 W.L.R. 472 below n.75 and text.

[70] See below n.94 and text.

2. THE SCOPE OF THE PRINCIPLE

The practical application to land of a principle based on payment of consideration may have been curtailed by section 2(1) of the Law of Property (Miscellaneous Provisions) Act 1989. That section requires a contract for sale of a legal right or equitable interest in land to be in writing. An oral agreement for the sale of land is void. If there is a written contract and payment of consideration, then it is almost inconceivable specific performance would not be available.[71] Therefore it would not be necessary to argue that the right has been acquired on the basis that the consideration has been paid in full. The fact of full payment would still be relevant in determining the nature of the purchaser's rights. It could still be argued (where there is a division of legal and equitable entitlement to an estate) that once payment is made, the vendor is placed under a fiduciary obligation towards the purchaser. Further, that in all cases, the purchaser's right ceases to be dependent on specific performance. However, if a principle based on payment of consideration is to have practical significance as a means of *acquiring* rights, then it will have to be shown that it can operate in the absence of a valid contract.

Whether the principle may apply in the absence of a valid contract has not been considered by the courts. In cases decided prior to the entry into force of the Law of Property (Miscellaneous Provisions) Act 1989 the question did not arise. Before the enactment of section 2(1) of that Act the absence of writing did not affect the validity of a contract but only its enforceability.[72] Therefore an oral contract followed by full payment of consideration would be valid. Notwithstanding, Lord Radcliffe's judgment in *Oughtred* may be sufficiently broad to support the application of the principle in such circumstances. While there was a valid contract in that case, it was the payment of consideration which made Mrs Oughtred the effective owner of her son's beneficial interest.[73] In contrast, in *Bridges v. Mees*, Harman J. did seem to place reliance on the existence of a contract. This is apparent in his discussion of the enforceability against third parties of the rights acquired by the purchaser. He explained the enforcement of the rights by reference to the enforcement of the

---

[71] Although specific performance will not be ordered if the purchaser has acted unconscionably.

[72] See the discussion above n.26 and text.

[73] See above n.52 and text.

contract.[74] However, in both *Oughtred* and *Bridges v. Mees* the parties had entered into an agreement for the future acquisition of rights by the purchaser. There was a clear distinction between the parties' agreements and the intended execution of the agreements by the transfer of the shares or land to the respective purchasers. Situations arise where there is no clear distinction between the agreement and the transfer. The events occur simultaneously, with full payment of consideration necessarily having been made. In such situations there should be no question of the existence of a valid contract for sale. The parties have not purported to enter into a contract for a future transfer, but have purported to execute a transaction. The purchaser's payment of consideration in the execution of an informal sale should be regarded as a sufficient basis for the acquisition of rights.

A factual situation which, it is submitted, should be analysed in the above manner, arose in *United Bank of Kuwait plc v. Sahib*.[75] There, Sonegal guaranteed to a bank the repayment of moneys provided to Mr Sahib. Sonegal paid its maximum liability under the guarantee (which is equivalent to the full payment of consideration) and Mr Sahib, who had undertaken to indemnify Sonegal, directed that the land certificate relating to a house was held to Sonegal's order. The Court of Appeal was asked whether this notional deposit of the land certificate was sufficient to create in favour of Sonegal an equitable mortgage. The argument that a mortgage had been created was based on the doctrine of part performance. Prior to the 1989 Act a "much criticised but well-established rule"[76] provided that a deposit of title deeds to land by way of security was sufficient to establish an equitable mortgage. The deposit of title deeds was considered to be a sufficient act of part performance for the court to accept oral evidence of the existence of a contract. Part performance also made the contract specifically enforceable with the result that equity treated the parties as though the contract had been executed. An equitable mortgage was therefore created under the principle discussed in Part II of this chapter. The Court of Appeal held that this method of creating a mortgage did not survive the 1989 Act. As the effect of part performance is to make the contract specifically enforceable, the doctrine necessarily presupposes the existence of a valid contract.[77]

---

[74] See above n.64 at 486–487. This approach is criticised above n.36 and text.
[75] See above n.69.
[76] See above n.69 at 377, *per* Peter Gibson L.J.
[77] See above n.69 at 381.

Following the 1989 Act, a contract for a mortgage can only be made in writing.[78]

It is submitted that a doctrine based on full payment of consideration could have been applied. Equity should have treated the parties as though the agreement for a mortgage had been executed. However this is not because, as the parties argued, there had been part performance. The parties in *Sahib* had not intended the formal execution of a mortgage in future. The direction as regards the holding of the land certificate demonstrated an agreement and simultaneous execution of a mortgage, against the background of full payment of consideration (by the mortgagee's payment of the maximum liability under the guarantee). It is on this basis that equity should have intervened. The parties' agreement "ought" to be regarded as executed because (in the parties' minds) it *had been* executed.

The question arises whether the acquisition of rights by full payment of the consideration in the absence of a valid contract can be reconciled with section 2(1) of the Law of Property (Miscellaneous Provisions) Act 1989. The basis for allowing such a principle to be applied may be found by analogy with proprietary estoppel. In making the recommendations which led to the 1989 Act, the Law Commission noted that, "any reform if unable to reduce the risk of injustice should at least not increase it". The Law Commission was satisfied that although part performance would not be available "there are a range of other possible remedies enabling justice to be achieved between the particular parties".[79] Reference was made in particular to the application of estoppel.[80] In *Sahib*, estoppel was not of assistance because the challenge to the creation of a mortgage was made by a third party to any estoppel.[81] In *Yaxley v. Gotts*[82] the question of how to reconcile a claim based on proprietary estoppel with section 2(1) was raised in the Court of Appeal. Section 2(5) of the Act provides that nothing in section 2, "affects the creation or operation of. . . constructive trusts". No exception is made for proprietary estoppel.

---

[78] See above n.69 at 380.
[79] See above n.28, para. 5.1.
[80] See above n.28, para. 5.2.
[81] The extent to which estoppel may replace part performance is considered by Lionel Bently and Paul Coughlan, "Informal Dealings With Land After Section 2" (1990) 10 L.S. 325 and Christine Davis, "Estoppel: An Adequate Substitute for Part Performance?" (1993) 13 O.J.L.S. 99.
[82] [1999] 3 W.L.R. 1217.

This may seem a glaring omission given the Law Commission's assertion that such a claim is available.[83] Further, in *Yaxley* the court accepted that estoppel cannot be invoked to render valid a transaction which the legislature has, on grounds of general public policy, enacted to be invalid.[84] Hence, any role given to estoppel had to be consistent with this public policy principle. The court ultimately left the position of estoppel unclear by deciding that the purchaser could rely on a claim based on constructive trust.[85] In doing so, the court relied on the similarity between a claim to an estoppel and to a constructive trust in the context of a joint enterprise for the acquisition of a home.[86] The court acknowledged that there are circumstances where an estoppel arises in which a claim to constructive trust could not be made.[87] For example, where a claim to estoppel is based on acquiescence (discussed in Chapter 7). Significantly, the court considered that in such cases no question of the application of section 2 is likely to arise.[88] The court's acceptance that the application of section 2 does not arise in the context of such claims implicitly demonstrates why section 2 should never apply to a claim to proprietary estoppel. Such a claim is based on the conduct or actions of the parties, not on a contract between the parties. As section 2 provides formality requirements for contracts, the need to comply with the provision should arise only when a claim is based on a contract. On this analysis, the absence of a reference to proprietary estoppel in section 2(5) is readily explicable. Proprietary estoppel is not excepted from section 2(1) because it is not necessary to do so.

Similarly, it is submitted that where the contract and transfer are simultaneous no question of compliance with section 2 should arise. The purchaser's claim to a proprietary right is not based on a contract for sale, but on the action of the parties in executing the transaction. In *Yaxley* Beldam L.J. noted it would be a "strange policy" that allowed relief to be claimed in the absence of an agreement, but

---

[83] The draft Bill published with the Law Commission's Report contained a provision parallel to s.2(5) with no express exception for proprietary estoppel (clause 1(3)). In light of the Law Commission's comments, this would imply that the Commission did not consider such an exception to be necessary.

[84] See above n.82 at 1224, referring to *Halsbury's Laws of England* (reissue 4th ed.) vol. 16 para. 962.

[85] Roger J. Smith, "Oral Contracts for the Sale of Land: Estoppels and Constructive Trusts" (2000) 116 L.Q.R. 11 at 13.

[86] See above n.82 at 1227.

[87] See above n.82 at 1242.

[88] See above n.82 at 1242; Smith above n.85 at 13.

denied relief to a claimant who had relied on a clear promise.[89] *A fortiori* it would be a strange policy to deny relief for the invalidity of a contract where, by their actions, the parties have in fact executed a transfer.

IV. Relationship with other means of acquiring proprietary rights

The factual circumstances surrounding an uncompleted sale may meet the requirements of other means of acquiring proprietary rights in land without a formal grant. However, in *Lloyds Bank plc v. Carrick*[90] the Court of Appeal held that the acquisition of rights by entering a specifically enforceable contract acted as a bar to asserting rights based on an agreement to share the beneficial ownership or estoppel.[91] There, as has been seen,[92] the interest acquired by Mrs Carrick by entering into a specifically enforceable contract was void against Lloyds Bank as she had not registered the contract as a Class C(iv) land charge. The Court of Appeal rejected her argument that she had also acquired rights under these other principles which, not being registrable, were binding on the bank as a purchaser with constructive notice. Following the Court's judgment, the acquisition of rights under a specifically enforceable contract is mutually exclusive from these other principles. A purchaser who, for example, satisfies the elements of a claim to the acquisition of rights based on an agreement to share the beneficial ownership is prevented from relying on that principle if he has entered a specifically enforceable contract for sale. In *Carrick* the relationship between the principles arose in relation to the enforcement of rights against a third party. However, a bar on reliance on other principles may also affect the nature of the purchaser's right as between the original parties. The ability to claim rights based on an agreement to share the beneficial ownership would, for example, enable the purchaser to avoid the precarious nature of a right based on specific performance.[93]

The scope of the Court's decision in *Carrick* is uncertain. The judgment may be explained as a policy decision to uphold the system

---

[89] See above n.82 at 1242.
[90] See above n.26.
[91] The acquisition of rights under those principles is discussed in Chapters 6 and 7.
[92] See above n.35 and text.
[93] See above n.48 and text.

of registration of land charges.[94] Ultimately Mrs Carrick lost, "because she failed to do that which Parliament has ordained must be done if her interest is to prevail over that of the bank, namely register the estate contract".[95] The Court's reasoning in this respect may be criticised. It is doubtful that the system would be undermined by recognising that Mrs Carrick had acquired rights, in addition to her estate contract, which are outside the land charges scheme.[96] In any event, outside that factual context the desire to treat the principles as mutually exclusive may not be as strong. However, it would clearly be unsatisfactory to treat them as mutually exclusive for some purposes but not for others.

Carrick prevents reliance on these other principles only where a purchaser has acquired rights under a contract. If rights are acquired without a valid contract under the principle discussed in Part III of this chapter, then there may again be cases in which the requirements of other principles are met. The overlap may not be substantial. As has been seen, there are situations in which a claim based on estoppel is not appropriate.[97] No practical problems will be caused by an overlap with the acquisition of proprietary rights by an agreement to share beneficial ownership. Where there is an overlap, the nature of the purchaser's rights will be the same under the different principles; the purchaser will be absolutely entitled to a beneficial interest.[98] The enforcement of the interest against third parties will be based on the same rules. In particular, as rights have been acquired without a valid contract there is no question of enforcement being based on registration of an estate contract. Further, a beneficial interest acquired by payment of consideration may not have the same transitional quality as one based on a specifically enforceable contract. Where such an informal sale has been made it may not be anticipated by the parties that the agreement will be formally executed.

---

[94] See Patricia Ferguson, "Estate Contracts, Constructive Trusts and the Land Charges Act" (1996) 112 L.Q.R. 549 at 549–550.

[95] See above n.26 at 639, *per* Morritt L.J.

[96] As the Court of Appeal seemed prepared to do in *E.R. Ives Investment Ltd v. High* above n.38. See also Ferguson above n.94 at 552.

[97] See above n.81 and text.

[98] Under both principles, the trustee will be under fiduciary obligations to the claimant. In relation to a claim based on full payment of consideration, it has been argued above n.71 and text, that it is appropriate to impose such obligations when consideration has been paid in full.

The result of the decision in *Carrick* may be that a purchaser with a contract is in a worse position than one without.[99] An ability to rely on other principles may also reduce considerably the need to rely on the acquisition of rights based on contract. Where reliance on contract results in the division of legal and equitable entitlement to an estate, the purchaser may almost invariably satisfy the elements of a claim to a proprietary right based on an agreement to share the beneficial ownership.[1] In other situations (for example, contracts to create easements and mortgages) the purchaser may be able to establish proprietary estoppel. Notwithstanding, it is submitted that in this respect the decision is correct. Precluding reliance on these principles may be justified by reference to the role of the acquisition of rights based on contract. Where parties have entered a contract for sale it may usually be anticipated that there will ultimately be a formal grant of rights. The purpose of enabling the purchaser to derive rights from the contract is to determine the rights and responsibilities of the parties in the period leading to the completion of the formal grant. The rights informally acquired are therefore transitional in nature subsisting, for example, during the inevitable delay between contract and conveyance. In contrast rights acquired under the other principles may be expected to be enduring. In particular, in relation to the acquisition of rights by an agreement to share the beneficial ownership, the rights may arise precisely because of a failure, at the formal completion of a sale, to record a "purchaser" who has provided consideration as holder of the legal title.

V. Conclusion

In this chapter it has been seen that a sale of land, which has not been completed, may be the source for the acquisition of proprietary rights by the purchaser. The right acquired is an equitable interest which

---

[99] In *Carrick* above n.26 at 639 the Court of Appeal acknowledged that Mrs Carrick may have been in a better position without a contract. She may then have been able to assert a common intention constructive trust which would have bound the bank. More generally, the dependence on specific performance may be a disadvantage.

[1] As purchase money will have been paid to make the contract specifically enforceable a claim may be made to a resulting or constructive trust of the type discussed in Chapter 6.

corresponds to the interest the purchaser has agreed to buy. In the principle discussed in Part II of this chapter the right is acquired because the purchaser has entered a specifically enforceable contract for sale. In Part III it was suggested that a right may also be acquired by a purchaser who pays the consideration in full in the absence of a valid contract. Even if this wider principle is not accepted as a means of acquiring rights, then the fact the consideration has been paid may still affect the nature of the purchaser's rights in important respects. The right may cease to be qualified as dependent upon the continuing availability of specific performance and, where there is a trust, fiduciary obligations may be imposed on the trustee. The legitimacy of drawing legal consequences from the fact consideration has been paid in full may not be universally accepted. It could be seen as rewarding the imprudent (or those acting without the benefit of proper advice) and not the cautious who, although ready and able to pay, choose not to do so without the certainty provided by compliance with formal requirements. However, there are two alternative ways of justifying drawing legal consequences from full payment, in both of which such a distinction seems acceptable. Intervention may be seen as purely a reaction to the *fait accompli* that payment has been made. Equity ensures that a vendor who has accepted payment is not able to deny rights. Alternatively, intervention may be seen as offering purchasers a choice. In paying the purchase price, the purchaser elects to rely on the equitable interest thereby acquired.

Chapter 6.

Where there is an Agreement to Share the Beneficial Interest or Conferring a Beneficial Interest is Necessary to Prevent Unjust Enrichment

I. Introduction

The rules to be discussed in this chapter are concerned with determining beneficial entitlement to land. Beneficial ownership is initially ascertained by a series of *prima facie* presumptions. *Prima facie*, equity follows law and therefore beneficial entitlement is enjoyed by the holders of the legal title. If legal title to land is vested in *A*, then *A* alone is entitled beneficially. If legal title is vested in *A* and *B*, then those parties are entitled to the beneficial interest as joint tenants. A challenge to these presumptions may arise in two ways. First, in both cases a claim to beneficial entitlement may be made by a non-legal owner, *C*. Secondly, in the context of legal co-ownership, a co-owner may challenge the presumption of equitable joint tenancy. The challenge to the presumptions may be supported by a formally declared trust. Such a trust is unenforceable unless its declaration is evidenced in writing, signed by the settlor, in compliance with section 53(1)(b) of the Law of Property Act 1925. The rules to be discussed in this chapter enable a beneficial interest to be established in the absence of a formally declared trust. These rules are not the exhaustive means available to establish a beneficial interest. For example, a beneficial interest may also be established by a unilateral assurance of rights, by application of the estoppel doctrine discussed in Chapter 7. In this chapter, the beneficial interest arises either because the parties have agreed to share beneficially (the agreement may be express or inferred) or because conferring a beneficial interest is necessary to prevent unjust enrichment. Both rules are discussed in this chapter because of their close relationship. The rules evolved, to an extent, through the same body of case law and raise the same questions of policy. Further, the same factual situation may result in the application of either rule. For the operation of these rules to be appreciated it is necessary to consider their application in light of the justification for enabling a beneficial interest to be established in the absence of a formally declared trust, and the context in which claims may arise.

The legal justification is provided by section 53(2) of the Law of Property Act 1925. As has been seen in relation to other rules discussed in this book, that subsection ensures that the formal requirement in section 53(1)(b) "does not affect the creation or operation of resulting, implied or constructive trusts". Hence, beneficial interests may be established informally where their recognition is supported by those trust doctrines. However, the real justification lies beyond section 53(2). Peter J. Clarke explains that formality rules for dealings with land are imposed for a purpose, "to promote certainty and to ensure that individuals realise both when they are gaining benefits and accepting burdens with respect to a property with which they are involved".[1] The justification for enforcing formality rules is removed where they would frustrate rather than achieve these objectives.[2] A claim based on the rules to be discussed in this chapter is the basis upon which family members may attempt to establish a proprietary right in their home. In this context, it is not realistic to require parties' expectations as to acquiring an interest, or undertaking the burden of trusteeship, to be formally declared. The parties' expectations are more likely to be found in their course of conduct throughout their relationship. The doctrines of trust in section 53(2) are the legal tools available to give effect to the parties' expectations when a failure to do so would frustrate the purpose of the formality requirements

In the family home context, there are two principal situations in which disputes as to entitlement to land are likely to arise.[3] The first concerns the breakdown of a relationship which has involved joint occupation of a home or, during the course of which, land has been acquired by, or transferred between, the parties. Typically cases

---

[1] Peter J. Clarke, "The Family Home: Intention and Agreement" (1992) 22 Fam. Law 72.
[2] *ibid.*
[3] Graham Moffat, *Trust Law Text and Materials* (2nd ed., 1994), pp. 441–442.

within this category involve the breakdown of an emotional relationship between unmarried partners, but disputes also arise in other family contexts. For example, on the breakdown of an arrangement between parents and adult children which has involved the acquisition of a home. The rules do not apply, however, in the context of a marital relationship. The distribution of property on divorce is subject to a separate regime.[4] Secondly where an encumbrancer, such as a mortgagee, asserts a right over a family home and the claimant seeks to establish a prior, and binding, beneficial interest. Where a question of beneficial entitlement is raised there are at least three alternative views as to what intervention by the court should achieve. Each view may be given effect by the imposition of one of the trust types referred to in section 53(2).

The first possible approach is for the courts to seek to determine what the parties' respective entitlement to (or ownership of) the property is. In adopting this approach the courts have required the claimant to establish an agreement (express or inferred) to share beneficial entitlement and detrimental reliance on that agreement. The claimant's share has then been quantified by reference to his or her detriment. There are a number of difficulties with this approach. For example, the search for an agreement may in fact be unrealistic. It may be difficult to quantify a claimant's share accurately where the detriment is otherwise than in the form of a financial contribution. Overall, the approach is perceived as being market-based and as a consequence it has, in practice, tended to operate to the disadvantage of female claimants.[5]

Secondly, the court may determine the claimant's entitlement by application of the doctrine of unjust enrichment. The courts' response to unjust enrichment is to provide restitution of the benefit enjoyed by (*in casu*) the legal owner as a result of the claimant's contribution. The result of applying this approach may be the same as the first: the claimant may acquire a beneficial interest which corresponds to his or her expenditure. The approaches differ in how this result is achieved. In the first approach, the claimant's contribution is used to quantify the claimant's share once he or she has established an entitlement to a beneficial interest. That entitlement is

---

[4] For a discussion of the distribution of property on divorce, see John Dewar, *Law and the Family* (1989), Chapter 8.

[5] Moffat above n.3, pp. 443–449; Kate Green, "Thinking Land Law Differently: Section 70(1)(g) and the Giving of Meanings" (1995) 3 Fem. L.S. 131 at 143–146.

based on the agreement to share the beneficial interest and the claimant's detrimental reliance on the agreement. In the second approach, the claimant's contribution is the justification for intervention. The court intervenes as the holder of the legal title would otherwise be unjustly enriched at the claimant's expense.

The difficulties in adopting a restitutionary approach lie in the nature of the interest acquired and the timing of that interest. Restitution need not result in the acquisition of a proprietary right. In particular, in English law the normal rule is that a proprietary right is not acquired where the enrichment is in the form of services rendered rather than a monetary payment.[6] Hence this type of claim will not assist a claimant where the dispute as to beneficial entitlement arises following a claim to the property by an encumbrancer, such as a mortgagee.

Any interest which is acquired by unjust enrichment dates from the time the enrichment became unjust. This limits the effectiveness of a restitutionary approach where the unjust factor does not arise simultaneously with the claimant's contribution. For example, it could be argued that a detriment was made on the basis of an assumption the claimant would continue to live in a house.[7] The enrichment would become unjust only on the failure of that assumption. Any interest acquired would therefore date from the breakdown of the relationship (the failure of the assumption), rather than the date of the enrichment.[8] Even where a proprietary interest is acquired this would not assist the claimant in a dispute with an encumbrancer whose interest pre-dates the failure of the assumption. Further, if the relationship (and therefore the assumption) are

---

[6] English courts do not usually confer proprietary rights as a remedy for unjust enrichment where such rights did not previously exist. However, where a claimant has improved land it is possible that a lien (a proprietary security interest) may be acquired: Andrew Tettenborn, *Law of Restitution in England and Ireland* (2nd ed., 1996), p. 45.

[7] Tettenborn above n.6, p. 109. He gives the following example: "you pay for the construction of a 'granny flat' in my house with a view to your residing with me there for the rest of your life, but the relationship between us later breaks down".

[8] *cf. Westdeutsche Landesbank Girozentrale v. Islington L.B.C.* [1996] 2 All E.R. 961 at 991. There, Lord Browne-Wilkinson considers when a trust arises where, *e.g.* a transfer for value is made under a contract the consideration for which subsequently fails. He explains that it would be, "incompatible with the basic premise on which all trust law is built, *viz* that the conscience of the trustee is affected" to treat the trust as arising on the date the money was paid. He notes that: "Unless and until the trustee is aware of the factors which give rise to the supposed trust, there is nothing which can affect his conscience".

subsisting at the time of the encumbrancer's claim, then no interest will have been acquired by unjust enrichment. In light of these difficulties, an approach based on unjust enrichment may be appropriate only in relatively rare cases where the unjust factor arises simultaneously with the claimant's contribution and confers a proprietary right.

Thirdly the courts could adopt a form of redistributive justice and allocate beneficial entitlement as it considers appropriate in light of the parties' conduct. Objections to this approach may arise, in particular, in view of the two different situations in which disputes are likely to arise. An approach which seems 'fair' in a dispute between the home sharers may not be appropriate where the action involves an encumbrancer.[9] To the extent that the encumbrancer may be a mortgagee or creditor, redistributive justice will have an adverse impact on commercial certainty and the value of domestic property as security. An approach based entirely on redistributive justice has been rejected by the courts. In *Springette v. Defoe* Dillon L.J. commented, "The court does not as yet sit, as under a palm tree, to exercise a general discretion to do what the man in the street, on a general overview of the case, might regard as fair".[10]

It will be seen in this chapter that the basis upon which claims are currently determined combines all three approaches. If a claim to a beneficial interest is based on an agreement to share, the court applies the first approach to establish whether, in fact, an agreement has been reached. Once the agreement is established, the courts adopt a flexible approach to the quantification of that interest which accords with a form of redistributive justice. In the absence of an agreement, a beneficial interest may still be acquired by a claimant who has made a financial contribution to the acquisition of land. Where a financial contribution has been made, and the circumstances reveal neither an agreement to share nor an intention to make a gift of the contribution, the claimant will acquire a share in proportion to his or her contribution. This approach, it will be submitted, is based on unjust enrichment.

---

[9] In *Midland Bank plc v. Dobson* [1986] 1 F.L.R. 171 at 174 Fox L.J. noted the need to treat with caution an assertion by parties as to an agreement to share beneficial ownership, of which there is no contemporary evidence, and which accommodates a current need to defeat a creditor.
[10] [1992] 2 F.L.R. 388 at 393.

II. Where the beneficial interest is conferred to prevent unjust enrichment

1. THE RESTITUTIONARY RESULTING TRUST

As has been seen,[11] *prima facie* beneficial ownership is enjoyed by the holder of the legal title. Where legal title is co-owned the parties are entitled to the beneficial interest as joint tenants. In the absence of an expressly declared trust, and save in two exceptional categories of case, these presumptions are readily rebutted by a claimant *C*, who is not a legal owner but has provided purchase moneys, or where the legal co-owners contributed to the acquisition unequally. In *Dyer v. Dyer* Eyre C.B. explained: "The clear result of all the cases, without a single exception, is that the trust of a legal estate whether freehold, copyhold, or leasehold, whether taken in the names of the purchaser and others jointly, or in the name of others without that of the purchaser, whether in one name or several, whether jointly or successive, results to the man who advances the purchase money".[12] Where the claimant is not a legal owner, the presumption then becomes that *C* has a beneficial interest in proportion to his or her contribution and the onus is placed on the holder of the legal title to displace this presumption. Where legal co-owners have contributed unequally their beneficial shares are presumed to reflect their respective contributions within a tenancy in common. These propositions are well established and it is generally accepted that the acquisition of a beneficial interest by *C*, or of unequal shares by legal co-owners, is based on a resulting trust. However the basis upon which the trust is imposed has been doubted. For simplicity, this question will now be discussed by reference to a claimant, *C* who is not a legal owner. The same principles apply *mutatis mutandis* to a claim by a legal co-owner. It will be submitted, accepting an argument advanced by Birks,[13] that the trust imposed is a response to unjust enrichment.

Birks suggested that the resulting trust is restitutionary in an attempt to provide synergy between the law of restitution and

---

[11] See the Introduction to this chapter.

[12] (1788) 2 Cox 92 at 93; 30 E.R. 42 at 43. For a modern example, see *Springette v. Defoe* above n.10.

[13] Birks, "Restitution and Resulting Trusts" in *Equity and Contemporary Legal Developments* (Goldstein ed., 1992). See also Robert Chambers, *Resulting Trusts* (1997), Ch. 4.

resulting trusts. His argument may be explained by reference to the following example. Say *C*, intending to treat her children equally, transfers a house into the name of her daughter *A*. *C* has forgotten that she has already transferred other property to *A*.[14] Traditionally, restitution and resulting trust analyse this situation differently. Following the transfer to *A*, equity presumes a resulting trust and the onus is placed on *A* to rebut this presumption (by establishing that a gift was intended). Restitution, however, places the onus on *C* to demonstrate that *A*'s enrichment is unjust (in this example, on the basis that the gift was made in the mistaken belief *C* would thereby treat her children equally). Birks suggests that this conflict of approach can be resolved by analysing the claim to restitution on the principles underlying the trust.[15] The resulting trust presumed on the transfer is a response to the unjust enrichment. While Birks focused on mistaken gifts and failure of consideration he suggested, further, that "[t]he partnership between restitutionary obligations and the resulting trust may, it seems, turn out to operate over a considerable number of causes of action within the field of substantive unjust enrichment".[16] Birks explains that in the majority of those causes of action the unjust factor may be defined, "at a rather high level of generality, that the plaintiff did not intend or did not fully and freely intend that the defendant should have the enrichment in question in the events which have happened".[17]

William Swadling notes the assumption underlying Birks' argu-ment is that the presumption of resulting trust is rebutted only by positive evidence of an intention to make a gift.[18] Stated conversely, the trust arises from a presumption that *C* did not intend a gift. Swadling rejects Birks' thesis on the basis that the presumption of resulting trust is rebutted by, "*any* evidence which is inconsistent with the presumption that the transferee is to be a trustee".[19] On Swadling's analysis, the resulting trust is not based on unjust enrichment, but on a presumption that the parties intended there to be a trust.[20] Proof of the unjust factor would also demonstrate that

---

[14] This example is based on *Lady Hood of Avalon v. Mackinnon* [1909] 1 Ch. 476 discussed by Birks above n.13, pp. 340–341.
[15] See above n.13, pp. 343–347.
[16] See above n.13, p. 371.
[17] *ibid.*
[18] William Swadling, "A New Role for Resulting Trusts?" (1996) 16 L.S. 110 at 111.
[19] *ibid.*
[20] The different interpretations of the presumption of resulting trust adopted by Birks and Swadling are explained by Swadling above n.18 at 116–117.

the parties did not intend there to be a trust and would, therefore, rebut the presumption of trust.[21] Applied to the example above, proof that the transfer to A was made by mistake (and therefore that A has been unjustly enriched) is inconsistent with the presumption that the parties intended A to be a trustee and therefore rebuts the presumption of resulting trust. In *Westdeutsche*[22] the House of Lords expressed agreement with Swadling's analysis.

However, it is submitted that Swadling's analysis is flawed in its assumption that proof of an unjust factor is *necessarily* inconsistent with the imposition of a trust. His analysis does not prevent unjust enrichment being the source of the acquisition of a beneficial interest by a claimant, C who has contributed to the purchase of land transferred into A's name. The difference between this situation and the example discussed above lies in the factor which makes the enrichment unjust. In the case, for example, of a mistaken gift, the unjust factor is inconsistent with a presumption that the parties intended there to be a trust because the transfer was made and received "with the intention that the [land transferred] should become the absolute property of [the transferee]".[23] However, in the case of C, who has contributed to the purchase of land in A's name, the only factor that makes the enrichment unjust is the broad explanation given by Birks; namely that C did not intend A to be enriched.[24] There was never an intention that the land should become the absolute property of A. The only evidence of intent is the intent not to make a gift to A of C's contribution. This is wholly consistent with requiring A to hold on trust for C in proportion to C's contribution. Further, as A was never intended to benefit, the unjust factor arises simultaneously with the transfer.[25] Hence from the time of the transfer C has a proprietary right which protects C

---

[21] See above n.18 at 111–112.

[22] See above n.8.

[23] *Westdeutsche* above n.8 at 911, *per* Lord Browne-Wilkinson.

[24] See above n.17 and text.

[25] *Quaere* whether this is consistent with Lord Browne-Wilkinson's comment in *Westdeutsche* above n.8 that a trust arises only when the conscience of the trustee is affected. One possible explanation is that A's conscience is affected merely by receipt of property to which he is not in fact entitled: see, *e.g. Re Diplock* [1948] 1 Ch. 465 at 488 and 503. Hence, where the was never an intent that A should benefit absolutely (rather than an initial intent that A should benefit which is subsequently vitiated) A's conscience is affected from the time of the transfer. However, on Lord Browne-Wilkinson's analysis, A's conscience may not be affected until he has knowledge of the obligation owed to the claimant.

against subsequent encumbrances.[26] Therefore, it is submitted that where a claimant contributes to the purchase of land in the name of another restitution provides the appropriate approach for intervention by the court. This analysis epitomises a market based approach in which it is presumed that people do not intend gifts. Gray describes the acquisition of an interest by resulting trust as, "outstanding evidence of what Woodhouse J. once termed the 'solid tug of money'[27]. . . [I]n our money conscious world it is scarcely conceivable that [C] should have intended to confer a gratuitous benefit on [A]".[28]

2. The 'Inferred Agreement' Constructive Trust and its Relationship With the Resulting Trust

An analysis of the resulting trust as based on the absence of an intention to make a gift, enables a distinction to be drawn between the resulting trust and another type of trust applicable in the same factual situation; the inferred agreement constructive trust. That type of constructive trust arises where the court infers from the conduct of the parties, evidence of an agreement to share the beneficial interest. In *Lloyds Bank plc v. Rosset* Lord Bridge considered it extremely doubtful whether anything less than direct contributions to the purchase would be sufficient to infer such an agreement.[29] Hence, where a claimant has contributed to the acquisition of land, that contribution may be analysed as conferring proprietary rights in either one of two ways; under a resulting trust or an inferred agreement constructive trust. The practical difference between the two types of trust lies in the extent of the beneficial interest acquired. The claimant to a resulting trust, as has been seen, acquires a beneficial share in proportion to his or her contribution. Where a constructive trust is established the court applies a broad brush approach to quantifying the claimant's share, which may enable the acquisition of a share greater than the contribution made.[30] As both trusts are based on a direct contribution, the question to consider is how to determine which trust to apply.

---

[26] *cf.* above n.8 and text.
[27] *Hofman v. Hofman* [1965] N.Z.L.R. 795.
[28] Gray, p. 396, reference provided.
[29] [1991] 1 A.C. 107 at 132–133.
[30] See Part III. 3 of this chapter below.

Where a claimant has made a direct contribution to the acquisition of land, the circumstances surrounding that contribution must be taken into account. In some cases it may be possible to establish no more than the absence of an intention to make a gift. This is most likely to be the case where the transaction is considered commercial in nature. *Springette v. Defoe*[31] may be explained on this basis. There, a house was purchased in the joint names of Springette and Defoe. On the basis of the parties' respective contributions to the acquisition the court considered the house to be held on resulting trust, under which Springette had a 75 per cent beneficial share and Defoe the remaining 25 per cent. Defoe had sought to establish a 50 per cent share based on express discussions as to beneficial ownership.[32] His claim failed as it was established in the parties' evidence that no actual agreement had in fact been reached. The court did not discuss the doctrine of inferred agreement constructive trust. Subsequently, in *Midland Bank plc v. Cooke*,[33] Waite L.J. explained why the resulting trust was appropriate. He emphasised the context of the transaction in *Springette v. Defoe*. The case concerned the, "part-pooling of resources by a middle aged couple already established in life whose house-purchasing arrangements were clearly regarded by the court as having the same formality as if they had been the subject of a joint venture or commercial partnership".[34] However, Waite L.J. refused to treat the case as establishing in principle that the absence of an express agreement precludes the court from inferring an agreement.[35] The circumstances in which a contribution is made may enable the court to infer an intention to share the beneficial interest. This was the basis upon which contributions were construed in *Cooke*, where the claimant's contribution was her half share of a wedding gift used as a deposit on a home. Further, this may usually be the appropriate analysis where the contribution is made towards the purchase of a shared home in the context of an emotional relationship.[36] This distinction between the two trust types is consistent with the

---

[31] See above n.10.
[32] This aspect of the case is discussed below n.84 and text.
[33] [1995] 4 All E.R. 562.
[34] See above n.33 at 575.
[35] *ibid.*
[36] In *Lloyds Bank v. Rosset* above n.29 Lord Bridge considered *Pettitt v. Pettitt* [1970] A.C. 777 and *Gissing v. Gissing* [1971] A.C. 886 to be examples of claims based on the inferred agreement constructive trust. Both cases involved a claim to a share in a home by a spouse.

judgment of the Court of Appeal in *Drake v. Whipp*.[37] Peter Gibson
L.J., giving the judgment of the Court, indicated that a resulting trust
could not arise where there was an agreement to share (including an
agreement inferred from direct contributions) upon which the
claimant had relied to her or his detriment.[38] The imposition of a
resulting trust is precluded by the existence of an agreement to share.

In *Springette v. Defoe* Dillon L.J. took as a starting point the
presumption of resulting trust and considered whether that initial
presumption was rebutted by evidence of constructive trust. The
suggestion the resulting trust can be rebutted by a constructive trust
is described by Moffat as "puzzling".[39] It is submitted that the initial
inquiry whether there is a resulting or constructive trust should be
seen as delimiting the scope of those trust types and not as one trust
rebutting a presumption of the other. If, for example, the court
concludes that a party's contribution gives rise to an inferred
agreement constructive trust,[40] then that should be taken to indicate
that there never was a resulting trust.[41] As has been seen, the two
types of trust represent different inferences drawn from the fact a
contribution has been made. There is an inherent inconsistency in
treating circumstances surrounding a contribution initially as disclos-
ing no more than the absence of an intention to make a gift and
subsequently as evidence of an intention to share beneficially.

In practice, where a claimant seeks to establish a proportionate
share, it may not seem necessary to state whether the share is based
on resulting trust or inferred agreement constructive trust. On either
basis the claimant acquires a beneficial interest which dates from the
time of the contribution. However, as *Tinsley v. Milligan*[42] illustrates
there are circumstances in which it is not possible to establish an
agreement to share. There the claimant, Milligan, had contributed to
the purchase of a house which was transferred into the sole name of
her lesbian partner, Tinsley. The purpose of transferring the house

---

[37] [1996] 1 F.L.R. 826.
[38] *ibid.* at 828–829.
[39] See above n.3, p. 464.
[40] Or, as was argued in *Springette v. Defoe* above n.10, an express agreement constructive
trust.
[41] See further *Drake v. Whipp* above n.37 at 828–829. Peter Gibson L.J. explained that
the principle of resulting trust "could not apply" if the elements of a claim to
constructive trust were present. He did not suggest that the constructive trust
displaced an initial presumption of resulting trust.
[42] [1993] 3 W.L.R. 126. See also *Lowson v. Coombes* [1999] 2 W.L.R. 720.

into Tinsley's name was to facilitate social security fraud by both parties. Following the breakdown of the relationship, Tinsley claimed to be the sole beneficial owner. The House of Lords was asked whether the fraud underlying the transaction prevented Milligan from asserting a beneficial share based on her contributions. Lord Browne-Wilkinson noted that in argument in the case no distinction had been drawn between the resulting trust and the inferred agreement constructive trust.[43] However, he explained that the presumption of resulting trust was crucial to the case.[44] The majority of the House of Lords[45] held that the underlying illegality did not prevent Milligan from asserting her share. This was on the basis that as Milligan's interest was presumed from the fact of her contribution she did not have to rely on the illegality.[46] It seems clear, however, that the same conclusion could not be reached by application of the inferred agreement constructive trust. To rely on that doctrine, Milligan would have to establish that by virtue of her contribution an agreement to share the beneficial interest could be inferred. This would necessarily have entailed relying on the purpose of the transfer into Tinsley's sole name and, therefore, on the illegality.[47]

3. Cases Where no Presumption of Resulting Trust can be Made

In two exceptional categories of case, no presumption of resulting trust is made in favour of C. In these situations, beneficial ownership is initially considered to be enjoyed by the holders of the legal title despite C's contribution. The burden of proof is reversed and the

---

[43] See above n.42 at 148.

[44] *ibid.*

[45] Lords Browne-Wilkinson, Jauncey and Lowry. Lord Goff delivered a dissenting judgment with which Lord Keith agreed.

[46] See above n.42 at 148.

[47] Despite acknowledging the presumption of resulting trust as crucial, Lord Browne-Wilkinson did not clearly separate the two trust doctrines throughout his judgment. He explained, above n.42 at 153 "Miss Milligan established a resulting trust by showing that she had contributed to the purchase price of the house *and* that there was a common understanding between her and Miss Tinsley that they owned the house equally" (emphasis added). However, any common understanding between the parties was necessarily tainted by the parties' illegal purpose and could not be relied upon. Lord Jauncey at 144, referred to the trust as based on the "agreement" title should be in Tinsley's name. However, he did not distinguish between the types of trust but referred to Lord Diplock's general description of non-express trusts in *Gissing v. Gissing* above n.36. Lord Lowry described Milligan's trust as resulting from the "fact" of her contribution.

onus is placed on *C* to establish that he or she did not intend to confer a benefit on the legal owner. The first, and least certain situation, is a statutory exception provided by section 60(3) of the Law of Property Act 1925. That section provides, "In a voluntary conveyance a resulting trust for the grantor shall not be implied merely by reason that the property is not expressed to be conveyed for the use or benefit of the grantee".

This seems to state that a presumption of resulting trust will not be made where *C* makes a gratuitous transfer of land to a grantee. However, the effect of section 60(3) is unclear.[48] It provides only that a presumption of trust will not be drawn *"merely"* because the conveyance is not expressed as being for the grantee's benefit. Section 60(3) does not prevent *C* demonstrating that a trust does in fact exist. Further, the provision does not explain the effect of removing the application of the presumption. As has been seen,[49] the presumption of resulting trust reflects a reluctance to presume that a gift was intended. Section 60(3) is drafted in neutral terms. It does not expressly replace the presumption of trust with a presumption of gift.[50] However, this must in fact be its effect.[51] It is submitted that, save as affected by section 60(3), the same principles apply whether *C* executes a voluntary transfer to *A* of land *C* currently owned, or purchases land in *A*'s name. This retains the distinction, explained above,[52] between the resulting and constructive trust. Where *C* purchases land in *A*'s name, the burden of proof is on *A* to show a gift was intended. In the absence of donative intent, there will at least be a resulting trust in favour of *C*. If there is an agreement *C* should be beneficial owner, there will be a constructive trust. Due to section 60(3), where *C* executes a voluntary transfer the burden of proof lies with *C* instead of *A*. Again, the circumstances surrounding the transaction must be taken into account. If the circumstances demonstrate that a gift was not intended, then a resulting trust should be imposed in *C*'s favour. If the circumstances show, further, that the

---

[48] See, *e.g.* Smith, p. 114.

[49] See above n.28 and text.

[50] *cf.* the presumption of advancement.

[51] There is a voluntary conveyance and no presumption of trust, *ergo* the land must be treated as a gift. In light of this, it may not have been considered necessary to expressly provide a presumption of gift in s.60(3). However, the neutrality of the provision, in contrast to the presumption of advancement, may suggest that the burden of proof under s.60(3) is more readily discharged.

[52] See above n.30 and text.

parties intended there to be a trust, then a constructive trust should be imposed. This approach may be illustrated by reference to *Hodgson v. Marks*.[53]

In *Hodgson v. Marks*, Hodgson executed a voluntary transfer of her home to her lodger, Mr Evans. The transfer was made on an oral agreement that Hodgson would remain beneficial owner. Despite this agreement, Mr Evans sold the house to Marks. The Court of Appeal held that Hodgson had a beneficial interest in the house which bound Marks as an overriding interest under section 70(1)(g) of the Land Registration Act 1925. There is little doubt that the recognition of a beneficial interest in favour of Hodgson was correct. Mr Evans had provided no consideration for the transfer and it was clear that the parties did not intend him to take beneficially. The difficulty lies in how to reconcile this conclusion with sections 53(1)(b) and 60(3) of the Law of Property Act 1925. It was clear from section 53(1)(b) that the parties' oral declaration of trust was not enforceable. Section 60(3) would seem to prevent the implication of a resulting trust merely because the property was not expressed to be conveyed for Mr Evans' benefit. Notwithstanding, the Court of Appeal considered that the trust in favour of Hodgson was a resulting trust. The Court did not consider the effect of section 60(3). Russell L.J., giving the judgment of the court, commented that the court was not concerned with the question whether the presumption of resulting trust applies on a voluntary transfer.[54] Russell L.J. imposed a resulting trust on the basis, "the evidence is clear that the transfer was not intended to operate as a gift".[55] He explained: "If an attempted express trust fails, that seems to be just the occasion for implication of a resulting trust, whether the failure be due to uncertainty, or perpetuity, or lack of form".[56] Birks considers Hodgson's interest is correctly seen as arising under a resulting trust. He notes: "The key to the resulting trust [in *Hodgson v. Marks*] is that Mrs Hodgson, without invoking the presumption [of resulting trust], showed by evidence that the transfer was not a beneficial gift to Mr Evans".[57] However, it is submitted that Hodgson's beneficial interest

---

[53] [1971] 1 Ch. 892.
[54] See above n.53 at 933.
[55] *ibid.*
[56] *ibid.*
[57] See above n.13, p. 364. Contrast Birks' earlier analysis of the case in *An Introduction to the Law of Restitution* (revised ed., 1989) p. 61–64.

should in fact be seen as based on a constructive trust. The parties had agreed that Hodgson should remain beneficial owner. Counsel argued that the parties' unenforceable express trust precluded the implication of a resulting trust. Russell L.J. rejected this. He noted: "It would be a strange outcome if [Hodgson] were to lose her beneficial interest because her evidence had not been confined to negativing a gift but had additionally moved into a field forbidden by section 53(1)(c) for lack of writing".[58] However, the fact there was an oral agreement meant that the circumstances surrounding the transfer did not merely demonstrate the absence of an intention to make a gift. Hodgson could establish an agreement to share the beneficial interest upon which she had relied to her detriment.[59] These circumstances are more appropriate for the imposition of a constructive trust.[60]

The second situation in which no presumption of resulting trust is drawn in favour of C is where the courts apply a presumption of gift or advancement. Whether this presumption will be applied is dependent solely upon the relationship between C and the legal owner. In the context of certain relationships, the court draws an initial presumption that C intended to make a gift. The onus is then placed on C to establish that a gift was not intended. Only where C discharges this burden of proof is a resulting trust imposed. The range of relationships in which the presumption of advancement applies was well established by the early twentieth century. Its application is based on beliefs, which are now out-dated, of relationships within which there was a moral obligation for C to provide for the legal owner. The presumption applies, principally, to transfers from a father to his child (but not from a mother to her child or from a child to either parent) and from a husband to his wife (but not from a wife to her husband). The applicability of the presumption to modern transactions was doubted by the House of Lords in *Pettitt v. Pettitt*[61] in the context of a claim to a beneficial interest by a husband to property held by his wife. The House of Lords noted the change in the social environment since the presumptions were established, in particular the growth in home-ownership in the period post World War II.[62] Lord Diplock explained:

---

[58] See above n.53 at 933.
[59] By executing the transfer.
[60] On the facts of that case, an express agreement constructive trust.
[61] See above n.36.
[62] See the comments above n.36 by Lord Reid at 793; Lord Hodson at 811; Lord Diplock at 824.

"It would, in my view, be an abuse of the legal technique for ascertaining or imputing intention to apply to transactions between the post-war generation of married couples 'presumptions' which are based upon inferences of fact which an earlier generation of judges drew as the most likely intentions of earlier generations of spouses belonging to the propertied classes of a different social era".[63]

Subsequently, in *Gissing v. Gissing*, Lord Diplock summarised the view of the majority of the House in *Pettitt*[64] as being that:

"even if the 'presumption of advancement' as between husband and wife still survived today, it could seldom have any decisive part to play in disputes between living spouses in which some evidence would be available in addition to the mere fact that the husband had provided part of the purchase price of property conveyed into the name of the wife".[65]

Despite these criticisms the application of the presumption of advancement was accepted by the House of Lords in *Tinsley v. Milligan*.[66] There, as has been seen,[67] property acquired by the joint contributions of a lesbian couple was transferred into Tinsley's sole name in order to facilitate the parties' social security fraud. Following the breakdown of the relationship, Milligan was able to establish a beneficial interest based on the presumption of resulting trust. The relationship between the parties in that case was not one to which the presumption of advancement applied. Lord Browne-Wilkinson acknowledged, *obiter*, that if the presumption of advancement applied, then the outcome of the case would have been different. This can be illustrated by reference to an example of land acquired by the joint contributions of a father and son which is transferred into the son's sole name to facilitate social security fraud. Following a family breakdown, the father seeks to establish a beneficial share. As the presumption of advancement applies, it is presumed that the father

---

[63] See above n.36 at 824. Lord Diplock's criticism was directed at both the presumptions of advancement and of resulting trust.

[64] Lord Upjohn above n.36 at 813 considered the presumptions to "remain as useful as ever in solving questions of title".

[65] See above n.36 at 907.

[66] See above n.42.

[67] See above n.42 and text.

intended to make a gift to his son and the onus is on the father to establish that a gift was not intended. It is likely that the father will be prevented from discharging this burden of proof as doing so would probably require reliance on the illegal purpose.

Tinsley therefore serves both as an indication that the presumption of advancement remains applicable and to illustrate its likely impact. In light of the earlier criticism of the presumption, in relationships to which it applies the courts may require little evidence to discharge the burden of proof. The presumption will have greatest impact in the context of illegality where the claimant is prevented from making a claim to beneficial entitlement which requires reliance upon the purpose of the transaction. As Margaret Halliwell notes, the consequence of *Tinsley* is that, "[l]ike cases will no longer be treated alike".[68] In the example above, if the land is transferred into the father's name, then the son could establish his beneficial interest as there is no presumption of advancement in a transfer from a child to his parent. Clearly, in both cases the inequity is the same.[69]

The doctrine of presumed resulting trust discussed in this section enables the acquisition of a beneficial interest in proportion to the claimant's contribution. It is a restitutionary response whereby the courts, in the absence of an intention to make a gift, ensure that the legal owner is not unjustly enriched at *C*'s expense. In the majority of cases, the absence of donative intent is presumed. However, in the exceptional cases discussed above, the initial onus is placed on *C* to establish that a gift was not intended. A response based on unjust enrichment is inherently limited to conferring a share in proportion to *C*'s contribution: that is the extent to which the legal owner would otherwise be unjustly enriched. The approach of the courts, and the trust doctrine applied, is different where *C* is able to establish an agreement to share the beneficial ownership. These claims will now be considered.

III. Where there is an agreement to share the beneficial interest

To acquire a beneficial interest on the basis of an agreement to share all three requirements must be met. First, it must be established that

---

[68] Margaret Halliwell, "Equitable Proprietary Claims and Dishonest Claimants: A Resolution?" [1994] Conv. 62 at 66.
[69] *ibid.*

the parties in fact reached an agreement: "The court cannot devise arrangements which the parties never made".[70] However, the agreement itself is no more than a, "merely voluntary declaration of trust and unenforceable for want of writing" by application of section 53(1)(b) of the Law of Property Act 1925.[71] Therefore, secondly, it must also be established that the claimant has acted to his or her detriment. It is the claimant's detriment which brings into operation the saving provisions of section 53(2).[72] Thirdly there must be a causative link between the agreement and the detriment. In *Midland Bank v. Dobson* Fox L.J. explained the detriment must be made, "in pursuance of the agreement".[73] The second and third requirements may be discussed collectively as the need for the claimant to demonstrate detrimental reliance.

The agreement upon which the claim is based may be express or may be inferred by the parties' conduct.[74] In either case, the other elements of a claim must also be satisfied. However, where a claim is based on an inferred agreement, the requirements tend to be merged: the conduct of the parties from which an agreement is inferred also represents the claimant's detrimental reliance. Due to the significance attached to the parties' conduct in such a case, the type of conduct from which an agreement will be inferred has been interpreted restrictively. Once the elements of a claim have been satisfied, the court adopts a uniform approach to the quantification of the beneficial interest regardless of whether the agreement is express or inferred. This part of this chapter will first consider how a beneficial interest may be established on the basis of an express and inferred agreement. The approach of the courts to the quantification of that interest will then be discussed.

1. Establishing a Beneficial Interest Where There is an Express Agreement

(a) Establishing the agreement

In *Rosset* Lord Bridge explained that a claimant to a beneficial interest based on an express agreement must establish an "agreement,

---

[70] *Gissing v. Gissing* above n.36 at 898, *per* Lord Morris.
[71] *Gissing v. Gissing* above n.36 at 905, *per* Lord Diplock. See also *Midland Bank v. Dobson* above n.9 at 175.
[72] *Midland Bank v. Dobson* above n.9 at 175.
[73] *ibid.*
[74] See, *e.g.* the explanations of the agreement in *Gissing v. Gissing* above n.36 at 905–906 and *Lloyds Bank plc v. Rosset* above n.29 at 132–133.

arrangement or understanding reached between [the parties] that the property is to be shared beneficially".[75] Further, he explained that this could be established only by, "evidence of express discussions between the partners, however imperfectly remembered and however imprecise their terms may have been".[76] The agreement must usually have been entered prior to the acquisition of the land but "exceptionally" a later agreement is sufficient.[77] On the facts of that case, the House of Lords held that discussions which had taken place prior to the acquisition did not establish an agreement to share beneficial ownership.

Lord Bridge's formula has been criticised both in relation to the time and nature of the agreement envisaged. The need for the agreement to exist prior to acquisition, strictly applied, would prevent the acquisition of a beneficial interest by one partner who moves into a house already owned by the other partner.[78] Further, Lord Bridge did not offer any guidance as to when circumstances would be considered "exceptional" to enable reliance on a later agreement. The nature of the agreement seems, *prima facie*, wholly unrealistic. A couple setting up home together are unlikely to discuss their respective beneficial interests.[79] The requirement has been seen as exerting "a tight stranglehold over the development of any rational law of family property in England".[80] However, Clarke suggests that an agreement between the parties, as a result of legal advice given on

---

[75] See above n.29 at 132.

[76] *ibid.*

[77] *ibid.*

[78] Clarke above n.1 at 74. However, see *Stokes v. Anderson* [1991] 1 F.L.R. 391. The claim in that case related to a home previously owned jointly by the claimant's partner, Mr Stokes and his former wife. On the breakdown of the Stokes' marriage, Mr Stokes had agreed to buy his wife's half share. Nourse L.J., at 398, considered that although the factual background was an unusual feature of the case it did not have "any determinative effect on its outcome". A trust in the claimant's favour could attach immediately to Mr Stokes' original half share and subsequently to the other half once this had been transferred to Mr Stokes. Ultimately, the claimant was awarded a 25% share, said by the court to represent half of that half of the beneficial interest the claimant had contributed towards acquiring from Mr Stokes' former wife. In *Hammond v. Mitchell* [1991] 1 W.L.R. 1127, the court relied on a post-acquisition assurance without commenting on Lord Bridge's requirement.

[79] See, *e.g. Pettitt v. Pettitt* above n.36 at 810, *per* Lord Hodson: "The conception of a normal married couple spending the long winter evenings hammering out agreements about their possessions appears grotesque".

[80] Gray, p. 421.

the purchase of a house, may in fact be the norm.[81] Further, it is clear from the terms of Lord Bridge's judgment that the express agreement may be fairly informal. Lord Bridge's description of an agreement based on imperfectly remembered discussions of imprecise terms demonstrates that what must be established falls well below the usual requirements of a formal contract.[82] In light of the informal nature an agreement may take, in *Hammond v. Mitchell* Waite J. considered the effect of the requirement to be that:

> "the tenderest exchanges of a common law courtship may assume an unforeseen significance many years later when they are brought under equity's microscope and subjected to an analysis under which many thousands of pounds of value may be liable to turn on fine questions as to whether the relevant words were spoken in earnest or in dalliance and with or without representational intent".[83]

Although the agreement may be informal, the need to establish an agreement does require some communication between the parties. This is demonstrated by the Court of Appeal decision in *Springette v. Defoe*. There, it was found as fact that the parties in question each held the same, uncommunicated, belief that the beneficial interest in their house was enjoyed equally. This was considered insufficient to establish an agreement. Steyn L.J. commented: "Our trust law does not allow property rights to be affected by telepathy".[84] It is not enough that each party "happened at the same time to have been thinking on the same lines in his or her uncommunicated thoughts, while neither had any knowledge of the thinking of the other".[85]

---

[81] See above n.1 at 74. Contrast the view expressed by Sir Christopher Slade in *Springette v. Defoe* above n.10 at 396: "All too frequently the courts of this country still have to consider cases where, despite many prior judicial warnings given to their legal advisers, the parties to the transfer of the legal estate in property into joint names have failed either to include in the form of transfer a declaration of trust. . . or to reach any explicit agreement defining such shares".

[82] Clarke above n.1 at 74.

[83] See above n.78 at 1139.

[84] See above n.10 at 394. See Nicola Glover and Paul Todd, "Inferring Share of Interest in Home: *Midland Bank v. Cooke* [1995] 4 Web J.C.L.I. They suggest that "communication does not necessarily mean talking. . . If the evidence showed that the parties really were capable of communicating by telepathy, there is no obvious reason why the law should not allow this method of communication to be used to create beneficial interests".

[85] See above n.10 at 393.

The informal nature the agreement may take is epitomised by Lord Bridge's approval in *Rosset* of *Eves v. Eves*[86] and *Grant v. Edwards*[87] as "outstanding examples" of successful claims based on an express agreement.[88] In both cases, the requirement for an express agreement was satisfied by the fact the legal owner (the male partner) had given his cohabitee an "excuse" for acquiring a house in his sole name. In *Eves v. Eves* Mr Eves had told the claimant that but for the fact she was under 21 (and therefore, at the time of the conveyance in question, incapable of holding legal title)[89] the house in question would have been purchased in the parties' joint names. In fact the claimant was 21 by the date of completion. Further, Mr Eves admitted in evidence that he had used her age as an excuse and always intended the house to be in his sole name.[90] In *Grant v. Edwards* the claimant was told by her partner that she would not be made joint legal owner as this may prejudice her ongoing divorce proceedings.[91] It was found that in fact the legal owner had no intention of making the claimant joint legal owner once those proceedings were complete.[92] The excuses given in these cases were explained by Lord Bridge to be evidence of express discussions within his formula on the basis that the claimants, "had been clearly led by the male partner to believe, when they set up home together, that the property would belong to them jointly".[93]

The courts' reliance on "excuses" as evidence of an agreement has been criticised.[94] It is necessarily based on an interpretation of the excuse as a concealed acknowledgement the claimant has an interest rather than as a softened way of denying one.[95] This interpretation may not be justified, particularly where the excuse is objectively

---

[86] [1975] 1 W.L.R. 1338.

[87] [1986] 1 Ch. 638.

[88] See above n.29 at 133.

[89] The Law of Property Act 1925, s.1(6) provides "A legal estate is not capable. . . of being held by an infant". Prior to 1970, this operated to exclude persons under 21.

[90] See above n.86 at 1340.

[91] See above n.87 at 643.

[92] *ibid.*

[93] See above n.29 at 133.

[94] See, *e.g.* Clarke above n.1 at 74–75; Gardner, "Rethinking Family Property" (1993) 109 L.Q.R. 263 at 265 and 282.

[95] Gardner, *ibid.* He illustrates this point by example: "If I give an excuse for rejecting an invitation to what I expect to be a dull party, it does not mean that I thereby agree to come: on the contrary, it means that I do not agree to come, but for one reason or another find it hard to say so outright".

valid.[96] The basis upon which excuses are accepted as evidence of discussions suggests that even a valid excuse could satisfy this requirement. The claimant is still led to believe that but for the excuse given she would have a proprietary right. However, the factual background to *Rosset* suggests there may be circumstances in which an objectively valid excuse will be accepted as a softened denial of an interest. There, funds used to acquire the house in question had been obtained from the husband's family trust on condition the house was placed in his sole name. If this had been given to Mrs Rosset as an "excuse" for her husband's sole ownership,[97] then it seems likely the court would still have held that no agreement had been reached. Lord Bridge explained that: "If Mr and Mrs Rosset had ever thought about it, they must have realised that the creation of a trust giving Mrs Rosset [a beneficial share] would have been nothing less than a subterfuge to circumvent the stipulation which the Swiss trustee insisted on as a condition of releasing the funds".[98] In these circumstances, the court would have required "very cogent evidence" of an agreement.[99]

In both *Eves v. Eves* and *Grant v. Edwards* the excuses given suggested that but for the factors stated the claimant would immediately have a proprietary interest. *Hammond v. Mitchell*[1] suggests that an agreement of an immediate interest is not necessary. There, the agreement was based on discussions between the parties both prior and subsequent to the purchase of a house. Prior to the purchase, Hammond told Mitchell the house would be in his sole name because he had tax problems and was going through a divorce.[2] Subsequently, he had said to Mitchell, "Don't worry about the future because when we are married it will be half yours anyway and I'll always look after you and [our son]".[3] The former excuses may justify the finding of an agreement. As with the earlier cases they suggested that but for those factors Mitchell would have an immediate interest. The latter, however, seems no more than an assurance of

---

[96] *e.g.* a 17-year-old claimant who has been told she is not joint legal owner because her age prevents her from holding legal title.

[97] Although it appears that the trustee's stipulation was the reason for Mr Rosset's sole ownership it is not apparent that he led Mrs Rosset to believe that but for the stipulation she would have and interest.

[98] See above n.29 at 128.

[99] *ibid.*

[1] See above n.78.

[2] See above n.78 at 1131.

[3] *ibid.*

future rights to arise on an event (the parties' marriage) which never in fact took place.[4]

The overall effect of the "excuse" cases seems to be that only an outright denial of an interest will prevent a finding of evidence of express discussions. Ultimately, the difficulty in interpreting excuses may be seen as an illustration of the generally unrealistic nature of the requirement of an express agreement. In the context of cases in which claims arise property dealings are unlikely to be clearly articulated.

(b) Detrimental reliance

In *Rosset*, Lord Bridge explained that once an express agreement has been established the claimant need only demonstrate that he or she, "has acted to his or her detriment or significantly altered his or her position in reliance on the agreement".[5] Whether there has been a detrimental reliance is a question of fact. However, there is a general requirement that acts by the claimant must be "referable" to the agreement. This requirement is unlikely to present difficulties as the courts have indicated that once the agreement is established this will be inferred.[6] Further, it is possible to identify to some extent forms of detriment that will, in principle, be sufficient. Conduct which would be sufficient for the courts to imply an agreement is, *a fortiori*, a sufficient detriment in reliance on an express agreement.[7] In *Rosset* Lord Bridge agreed that the conduct of the claimants in *Eves v. Eves* and *Grant v. Edwards* was a sufficient detriment. In *Grant* the claimant had used her income to pay general household expenses. This was considered to be an indirect contribution to the mortgage because her partner's income was insufficient to meet the household expenses in

---

[4] Glover and Todd above n.84. See also Anna Lawson, "Acquiring a Beneficial Interest in the Family Home" [1992] Conv. 218 at 221. She also notes at 220, that while the court in *Hammond v. Mitchell* treated the excuses as an agreement, they are more accurately "evidence" of an agreement. Gardner above n.94 at 267 treats *Eves v. Eves* and *Grant v. Edwards* as involving beliefs as to the future and considers there is no requirement in the authorities that the claimant believe she has an immediate interest.

[5] See above n.29 at 132.

[6] *Grant v. Edwards* above n.87 at 657

[7] It is apparent from Lord Bridge's judgment in *Rosset* above n.29 at 132–133 that a stricter standard is imposed when the parties' conduct is used as evidence of an agreement.

addition to the mortgage. By paying the other expenses, the claimant therefore enabled her partner to use his income to pay the mortgage. In *Eves* the claimant, Miss Eves, did not make any financial contribution but contributed practically to improvements made to the home. Lord Denning detailed her contribution:

> "She did a great deal of work to the house and garden. She did much more than many wives would do. She stripped the wall paper in the hall. She painted woodwork in the lounge and kitchen. She painted the kitchen cabinets. She painted the brickwork in the front of the house. She broke up the concrete in the front garden. She carried the pieces to a skip. She, with him, demolished a shed and put up a new shed. She prepared the front garden for turfing. To add to it all, they had their second child".[8]

For such practical assistance to be accepted as detriment the work performed must be of more than a merely ephemeral nature. In *Pettitt* Lord Diplock commented: "It is common enough nowadays for husbands and wives to decorate and to make improvements in the family home themselves, with no other intention than to indulge in what is now a popular hobby, and to make the home pleasanter for their common use and enjoyment".[9] Such activities have no affect on proprietary ownership.[10] In *Rosset* Lord Bridge doubted whether Mrs Rosset's assistance in renovations to the house in question would have been a sufficient detriment even if an express agreement had been established. At first instance, the judge described the extent of her work as, "valuable"[11] and Mrs Rosset herself as possessing skill in the planning, renovation and decoration of the house, "over and above that acquired by most housewives".[12] Despite this, Lord Bridge suggested that in financial terms her contribution to the acquisition of the house was, "so trifling as to be almost de minimis".[13]

---

[8] See above n.86 at 1340.

[9] See above n.36 at 826.

[10] *Pettitt* involved a claim to a beneficial interest based on an implied agreement. However, Lord Diplock's comments are sufficiently broad to indicate that such activities could not affect proprietary ownership even where there is an express agreement.

[11] See above n.29 at 130 cited in Lord Bridge's judgment.

[12] See above n.29 at 129 cited in Lord Bridge's judgment.

[13] See above n.29 at 131. *cf.* Lord Hodson's comment in *Pettitt* above n.36 at 807 that general decorating is insufficient to constitute a detriment even where it does enhance the value of the house.

In *Grant v. Edwards* and *Eves v. Eves* the claimants' detriment had a clear financial value either in money (*Grant*) or in money's worth (*Eves*).[14] In *Hammond v. Mitchell*[15] the court accepted as sufficient, a detriment which is not readily quantifiable in financial terms. There, the claimant, Mitchell, and her partner, Hammond, shared an enjoyment of trading and bargain hunting. Hammond, and to a lesser extent Mitchell,[16] engaged in a number of commercial ventures with varying degrees of success. Mitchell's detriment was found in the fact that, "she gave her full support on two occasions to speculative ventures which, had they turned out unfavourably, might have involved the entire bungalow [the property in which she was held to have an interest] being sold up to repay the bank an indebtedness to which the house and land were all committed up to the hilt".[17] It seems that the nature of Mitchell's support was principally moral: the ventures had been discussed with Mitchell who shared Hammond's excitement at the deals and had encouraged and supported his involvement.[18] Mitchell also provided some practical assistance in dealing with inquiries and supervising work at a factory.[19] Treating Mitchell's moral support as a detriment involves circularity. *Prima facie* Mitchell did not have an interest in the home. It is difficult to see on what basis her support for a venture which risked the loss of the home could thereby confer an interest.[20] Mitchell's practical assistance may have been a relevant detriment by analogy with the physical detriment of Miss Eves. Although Mitchell's efforts were not directed at the bungalow, they were directed at business activities the success of which was essential to avoid foreclosure by the bank on loans secured on the bungalow. However, it seems unlikely that Mitchell's practical efforts were sufficiently extensive, particularly in light of Lord Bridge's restrictive approach to physical labour in *Rosset*.

The courts have also indicated that certain forms of conduct will not, in principle, be accepted as a detriment. In particular, it seems

---

[14] Moffat comments above n.3 at 455 that Miss Eves' labour was the sort that might otherwise have to be paid for.

[15] See above n.78.

[16] It seems that income generated by Mitchell's independent business activities was spent on, *inter alia*, clothing, items for the house and family "treats": such expenditure would not in itself constitute a relevant detriment.

[17] See above n.78 at 1137, *per* Waite J.

[18] See above n.78 at 1133.

[19] See above n.78 at 1133–1134.

[20] Lawson above n.4 at 222.

clear that general domestic activities, such as caring for children, shopping and cooking etc do not affect proprietary rights.[21]

Whether the claimant's conduct constitutes detrimental reliance seems to depend on the context in which, and by whom, the acts are performed. In *Grant v. Edwards*, Nourse L.J. defined the conduct required of a claimant as, "conduct on which the woman could not reasonably have been expected to embark unless she was to have an interest in the house".[22] Browne-Wilkinson V.-C. suggested, more broadly, that anything done by the claimant which related to the "joint lives" of the parties would be a sufficient detriment.[23] However, he expressly acknowledged this comment to be *obiter*.[24] The converse of Nourse L.J.'s formula is that anything the claimant could reasonably have been expected to do regardless of proprietary ownership will not constitute a relevant detriment. In *Midland Bank plc v. Dobson*[25] the Court of Appeal held that the claimant's contributions towards household expenses and towards ordinary periodic decorating were not acts of detrimental reliance. Instead, the court considered that she contributed towards expenses merely, "because she thought the expenditure appropriate"[26] and decorated because, "it was the sort of work members of a family do".[27] Similarly, in *Button v. Button* Lord Denning M.R. explained that husbands and wives should not acquire beneficial shares by doing the sort of things husbands and wives may be expected to do for the benefit of the family.[28]

The essence of the courts approach, in the absence of a clear financial contribution, is to look for conduct beyond that which may be expected of someone in the claimant's position. Hence in *Eves*, in upholding Miss Eves' claim, Lord Denning M.R. described her acts as, "more than many wives would do".[29] In contrast, doubting whether Mrs Rosset's acts would have been a sufficient detriment, Lord Bridge described her conduct as, "the most natural thing in the

---

[21] See, *e.g. Pettitt* above n.36 at 826.

[22] See above n.87 at 648.

[23] See above n.87 at 657.

[24] *ibid.* Moffat suggests above n.3 at 455 there is an echo of the joint lives doctrine in *Hammond v. Mitchell* above n.78.

[25] See above n.9.

[26] See above n.9 at 176, *per* Fox L.J.

[27] See above n.9 at 177, *per* Fox L.J.

[28] [1968] 1 W.L.R. 457 at 461–462 cited with approval in *Pettitt* above n.36 by Lord Reid at 796 and Lord Hodson at 807.

[29] See above n.86 at 1340.

world for any wife".[30] The danger with this approach is that conduct
tends to be genderised. Conduct by a male partner may be dismissed
as no more than he could be expected to do for the benefit of the
family: the same conduct by a female claimant, because it is not
considered "normal" or "usual" for that gender, is seen as conduct
she could not be expected to perform unless to acquire an interest.
For example, Anne Bottomley suggests that by emphasising Miss
Eves' conduct as more than a woman would normally undertake
Lord Denning treated as a detriment acts which were in fact
minimal.[31] Flynn and Lawson[32] provide a similar analysis of *Wayling v.
Jones*.[33] That case concerned a claim by Wayling to an hotel owned by
his homosexual partner. Flynn and Lawson suggest that, as a man,
activities carried out by Wayling in the domestic sphere had a
visibility (and contributed to establishing a detriment) which would
not be found in the same activities carried out by a woman.[34] The
same view may explain the decision in *Hammond v. Mitchell*. It seems
conceivable that Mitchell's moral support for Hammond's business
ventures had a visibility because of her shared enjoyment of the
masculine-based commercial sphere. In this context it is particularly
notable that Mitchell's detriment was identified specifically in her
support for ventures which ran the risk of losing the home. Her
willingness to run that risk for commercial motives is in sharp
contrast with the "expected" ideological norm[35] of a woman's
attachment to her home.

Although in the cases discussed above an assessment of detriment
by reference to "normal" gender roles worked to the advantage of the

---

[30] See above n.29 at 131.

[31] Anne Bottomley, "Self and Subjectives: Languages of Claim in Property Law"
(1993) 20 Journal of Law & Society 56 at 69, n.10.

[32] Flynn and Lawson, "Gender, Sexuality and the Doctrine of Detrimental reliance"
(1995) 3 Fem. L.S. 105.

[33] (1995) 69 P. & C.R. 170. The claim in that case was based on an assurance of rights
(discussed in Chapter 7) rather than an agreement to share beneficial ownership.
The need for a detrimental reliance is common to both rules and Flynn and
Lawson's discussion assumes the same standard of proof is applicable. Whether this
is the case seems open to debate (see, *e.g.* Patricia Ferguson's discussion of the
possibly different evidentiary requirements of the concepts: "Constructive Trusts—
A Note of Caution" (1993) 109 L.Q.R. 114 at 115–120). On a cautious approach, it
cannot be said with certainty that Wayling's conduct would have been considered to
establish detrimental reliance if his claim was based on an agreement to share
beneficially.

[34] See above n.32 at 118–119.

[35] See, *e.g.* Rosemary Auchmuty, *Gender Perspectives in Property Law* paper presented at
the S.P.T.L. conference 1994.

claimants, the approach is open to criticism on a number of counts. First, it is clearly discriminatory. Whether a form of conduct is accepted as detriment may ultimately be dependent upon the gender of the claimant. Secondly the approach should lead to the rejection of the majority of claims. By definition, a claimant's conduct will consist predominantly of acts which he or she may be expected to perform. Thirdly, commenting on *Wayling v. Jones*, Flynn and Lawson suggest that the success of Wayling's claim undermined the integrity of the parties' relationship.[36] Wayling's domestic activities were treated as a detriment because the boundaries of "normal" conduct are formulated by reference to roles expected in a heterosexual relationship.

Perhaps the most significant effect of the courts' assessment of detriment by gender roles is the consequent rejection of domestic activities as constituting a detriment. Combined with the judicial preference for a financial detriment, the effect has been to discriminate against female applicants. This form of discrimination has been subject to particular criticism as the case law developed at a time when women's access to employment was limited and social pressure encouraged them to adopt the role of housewife and mother. This criticism is summarised by Rosemary Auchmuty:

> "What Land Law did in these fifty years [to 1994] was to set up conditions for acquiring a share in the home which most women could not meet. The law insisted on financial contribution, but denied access to well-paid jobs, or any job at all, with which to make the contribution. The law enforced social norms which forced women to stay at home and depend on their husbands, but when relationships ended it took away women's homes for the simple reason that they had not made themselves independent of their husbands. The law assumed, and judges often stated, that housework and childcare were women's work, but took it completely for granted, assigning it no economic value. The law went along with the ideology that the home was women's 'sphere', that women were society's 'home-makers'; and then turned them out of the homes they had made".[37]

As will be seen,[38] the impact of this discrimination has at least been lessened by the courts' approach to quantifying beneficial shares.

---

[36] See above n.32 at 121.

[37] See above n.35. For a fuller account of gender perspectives in this area of law see generally, Flynn and Lawson above n.32; Bottomley above n.31; Moffat above n.3, Ch. 12, pp. 443–446.

[38] Part III 3 of this chapter.

2. Establishing a Beneficial Interest Where the Agreement is Inferred

Where there is no evidence of an express agreement between the parties the court may be prepared to imply that an agreement was in fact reached. In their acceptance of inferred agreements, the courts recognise that it may not be realistic to expect parties entering a relationship to discuss their respective rights in their home. The existence of an agreement may instead be indicated by (and inferred from) their conduct.[39] The courts have emphasised that there is a distinction between inferring from the parties' conduct that an agreement was probably made and implying an agreement where there is no evidence to support one.[40] Ultimately, however, the courts' willingness routinely to find an agreement by certain types of conduct seems at odds with the basic proposition in *Gissing* that courts cannot invent agreements.[41] A claim based on an inferred agreement is subject to the same requirements as one based on an express agreement. Hence, for the agreement to be established, the conduct of the claimant must be referable to an agreement which existed at the time the property was acquired. As the agreement is based on the parties' conduct, this requirement means that it is the parties' conduct up to the time of the acquisition that is relevant. For an agreement to be based on conduct subsequent to the acquisition the conduct must be explicable only on the basis that an agreement did in fact exist at the earlier time.[42]

The conduct from which an agreement may be inferred was defined restrictively by Lord Bridge in *Rosset*. He said: "[D]irect contributions to the purchase price by the partner who is not the legal owner, whether initially or by payment of mortgage instalments, will readily justify the inference necessary for the creation of a constructive trust. But, as I read the authorities, it is at least extremely doubtful whether anything less will do".[43] This statement is not necessarily an accurate reflection of the position established by the authorities at the time of the decision in *Rosset*.[44] As Ferguson

---

[39] *Gissing* above n.36 at 906.
[40] See, *e.g. Gissing* above n.36 at 897.
[41] Gardner above n.94 at 264.
[42] *Gissing* above n.36 at 906.
[43] See above n.29 at 133.
[44] See below n.52 and text.

notes,[45] it is arguable that Lord Bridge was over-concise and, due to the brevity of his judgment (in particular the absence of a full discussion of the earlier authorities), it is difficult to assess whether he intended to change the law.[46]

An initial contribution to the purchase price arises most clearly where the claimant has contributed towards the initial deposit and legal expenses. Such a contribution may also be established where the claimant's status as tenant has enabled property to be purchased at a price below its market value.[47] The claimant's contribution in such a case is calculated as the difference between the market value of the property and the price paid. The courts' treatment of contributions to the mortgage *pari passu* with initial contributions is a recognition of the, "economic realities of the transaction".[48] For the parties, the economic reality is that a home is purchased over a number of years by payment of the instalments. Therefore, their contributions to the instalments is as much an indication of an agreement at the time of acquisition as their conduct in relation to the initial deposit. The mere fact a claimant has contributed towards the mortgage will not necessarily mean that an agreement will be inferred. In *Gissing* Lord Diplock suggested that an agreement will be inferred where the claimant has made, "regular and substantial contributions".[49] Viscount Dilhorne said that the payment of a single instalment by a wife while her husband was abroad would not indicate the existence of an agreement.[50] Ultimately, whether an agreement will be inferred is dependent upon the facts of each case.[51]

In *Rosset*, Lord Bridge referred only to "direct" contributions to mortgage instalments as sufficient conduct to infer an agreement. In *Gissing* the House of Lords accepted in principle that an agreement

---

[45] See above n.33 at 116.

[46] Moffat suggests above n.3 at 465–466 that the exclusion of indirect contributions may have been a means by which Lord Bridge sought to draw a clear distinction between claims based on express and inferred agreements.

[47] See, *e.g. Marsh v. von Sternberg* [1986] 1 F.L.R. 526. There, Bush J. explained at 531, that it is possible to infer that as part of the parties' agreement they regarded the discount as a contribution by the qualifying tenant. Bush J.'s analysis was approved by Staughton L.J. in *Evans v. Hayward* [1995] 2 F.L.R. 511. Contrast *Springette v. Defoe* above n.10 where in the context of a resulting trust a discount was treated as an actual contribution.

[48] *Gissing* above n.36 at 906, *per* Lord Diplock.

[49] See above n.36 at 908.

[50] See above n.36 at 900.

[51] *Gissing* above n.36 at 907.

could also be inferred where the claimant contributed to the mortgage indirectly by paying other household expenses.[52] Lord Reid could see no good reason for distinguishing the types of contribution. He noted, further, that the distinction would be "unworkable" where resources are pooled into a joint account from which the mortgage and other expenses are paid.[53] Subsequently, in *Burns v. Burns*,[54] Fox L.J. said he did not doubt a claimant would succeed where, by spending her income on household expenses, she enabled her partner to pay the mortgage.[55] In both *Gissing* and *Burns* the claimants failed. However, in neither case were the claimants' earnings necessary to enable the mortgage to be paid. In *Hall v. Hall*,[56] a beneficial interest was successfully established in the absence of an express agreement where the claimant's partner conceded that the house could not have been acquired without the claimant's income. Lord Denning M.R. referred generally to the claimant acquiring a share through her contributions to the "joint household".[57] In *Burns*, Fox L.J. explained *Hall* as a case in which the claimant, through the pooled income of the parties, had contributed directly or indirectly to the mortgage. However any doubt, following *Rosset*, as to whether a claim based on indirect contributions could still be made seem to have been removed by *Ivin v. Blake*.[58] There, the Court of Appeal applied (*inter alia*) *Rosset* to reject a claim for a beneficial interest on the basis that the claimant had contributed only indirectly to the purchase of the house. The exclusion of indirect contributions is difficult to justify. Where the legal owner's income is insufficient to pay both the mortgage and other household expenses the economic reality is that both parties' incomes are necessary for the house to be acquired. Once this is established, a claim to beneficial ownership should not be dependent upon the precise manner in which the parties organise

---

[52] See above n.36 at 896–897, *per* Lord Reid at 903, *per* Lord Pearson and 908 *per* Lord Diplock (although Lord Diplock's comments are confined to claimants who have made an initial contribution).

[53] See above n.36 at 896. See also the comments by Lord Pearson at 903 and Lord Diplock at 906–908. Clarke comments above n.1 at 75, that as a result of this distinction the "prudent" (and it may be added, better-educated) partner will insist on paying part of the mortgage and let the legal owner buy groceries etc.

[54] [1984] 1 Ch. 317.

[55] See above n.54 at 330.

[56] (1982) 3 F.L.R. 379.

[57] See above n.54 at 381.

[58] (1994) 67 P. & C.R. 263. The decision is criticised by Anna Lawson, "Direct and Indirect Contributions to the Purchase Price of a Home" [1996] Conv. 462.

their finances. As Moffat notes,[59] logically the same argument could be applied to non-financial forms of indirect contribution to mortgage instalments. For example, where a claimant's domestic labour, such as child care, enables the legal owner to pay the mortgage by obviating the need to pay for child care. The courts have generally refused to see domestic labour as conduct from which an agreement to share beneficial ownership can be inferred.[60] The possibility of applying the same argument to these types of conduct may explain the courts' restrictive approach to indirect financial contributions. The exclusion of all indirect contributions does provide a degree of certainty.

3. QUANTIFYING BENEFICIAL INTERESTS

Where a claimant has established a beneficial interest (whether on the basis of an express or implied agreement) the next question for the court is how that interest should be quantified. This was described in *Eves* by Brightman J. as, "the most difficult part of the case" and as a question to which there is "no ready answer".[61] Until relatively recently the quantification of beneficial interests had been subject to little discussion in the courts.[62] The issue is yet to be considered authoritatively by the House of Lords as in all three cases in which the House has discussed the principles applicable to claims based on an agreement to share the beneficial interest[63] the claimant has failed to establish an interest.

As has been seen,[64] where a beneficial interest is established by a resulting trust that interest is necessarily quantified by reference to the mathematical value of the claimant's contribution: that is the extent to which the legal owner would otherwise be unjustly enriched. A strict mathematical approach is not necessarily appropriate where the interest is established by an agreement to share. There would, in any event, be practical difficulties in adopting such an approach. For example, the moral support which formed the basis of

---

[59] See above n.3 at 465.
[60] See, *e.g.* the discussion by Fox L.J. in *Burns v. Burns* above n.54 at 330–332.
[61] Above n.86, 1345.
[62] See the almost cursory treatment of the issue in, *e.g. Eves* above n.86 at 1342, *per* Lord Denning M.R. and in *Hammond v. Mitchell* above n.78, by Waite J.
[63] *Pettitt* above n.36, *Gissing* above n.36 and *Rosset* above n.29.
[64] Part II of this chapter.

the claimant's interest in *Hammond* is not readily given a financial value. In *Gissing*, in an *obiter* discussion, Lord Diplock treated the question of quantification as dependent upon the parties' agreement. He suggested that where the parties have not expressly agreed how the claimant's interest is to be quantified, then an agreement may be inferred from their conduct. Lord Diplock explained:

> "the court must first do its best to discover from the conduct of the spouses whether any inference can reasonably be drawn as to the probable common understanding about the amount of the share of the contributing spouse upon which each must have acted in doing what each did, even though that understanding was never expressly stated by one spouse to the other or even consciously formulated in words by either of them independently".[65]

Lord Diplock's explanation of when an agreement as to quantification may be inferred mirrored his discussion of how to establish an inferred agreement to share beneficial ownership.[66] Hence, on his approach, quantification, as with the establishment of a beneficial interest, is based on the parties' agreement. In both stages of the inquiry, whether an agreement can be inferred is based on a broadly comparable assessment. However, the consequence of failing to establish an agreement as to quantification could not mirror the effect of failing to establish an agreement to share. Once the claim to a beneficial interest has been established, some interest must be awarded. Lord Diplock considered that in the absence of an (express or inferred) agreement as to quantification the court should resort to the maxim, "equality is equity" and award equal shares.[67] Subsequently, although the courts in some cases have sought to rely on the parties' agreement, a different standard has been applied to inferring an agreement as to quantification than to inferring agreements to share. As will now be seen, the courts' approach to quantification cannot fully be explained as giving effect to the parties' agreement. The courts' approach will be considered first in relation to express agreement cases, as it is the approach developed in this context which is now applied generally.

---

[65] See above n.36 at 908.
[66] See Lord Diplock's discussion above n.36 at 906.
[67] See above n.36 at 908.

Prior to *Stokes v. Anderson*,[68] there was little discussion in the case law of how agreements as to quantification could be inferred. In inferring an agreement in *Grant v. Edwards*, Nourse L.J. relied, in particular, on the fact that money paid by insurers following a fire at the house in question was paid into a joint bank account.[69] In *Gissing* Lord Diplock considered the possible inferences which could be drawn from payments towards mortgage instalments.[70] Further, the courts did not consistently refer to the parties' intentions. In *Eves*, Lord Denning M.R. awarded the claimant a 25 per cent beneficial interest without explanation as to how this conclusion was reached.[71] In *Stokes v. Anderson* Nourse L.J. explained how the parties' agreement was to be inferred. He explained that, "all payments made and acts done by the claimant are to be treated as illuminating the common intention as to the extent of the beneficial interest".[72] There, the claimant was awarded a 25 per cent beneficial interest which had an approximate value of £30,000.[73] Her claim to a beneficial interest was established by express discussions, upon which she had acted to her detriment by making a direct financial contribution to the acquisition of £12,000. Nourse L.J. did not consider it necessary to look beyond those contributions to establish her interest. However, in adopting a broad approach to quantification, he took account of all the claimant's other acts. He referred, in particular, to money she had paid towards the cost of an extension and to her, "decorating of the house and working on the grounds".[74] Hence, Nourse L.J. specifically took into account acts which did not constitute the claimant's "detriment". Further, it is at least extremely doubtful whether some of these acts could have constituted a relevant detriment.[75] Nourse L.J. considered that his approach, incidentally, brought the doctrine of constructive trusts closer to proprietary

---

[68] [1991] 1 F.L.R. 391.

[69] See above n.87 at 650–651.

[70] See above n.36 at 907–909. See also Peter Sparkes, "The Quantification of Beneficial Interests: Problems arising from Contributions to Deposits, Mortgage Advances and Mortgage Instalments" (1991) 11 O.J.L.S. 39.

[71] See above n.86 at 1342. The only indication Lord Denning M.R. gave as to how he reached this figure was that he considered 50% too much. Brightman J. at 1346, also concluded the claimant was entitled to 25% without explanation and "without great confidence".

[72] See above n.68 at 400.

[73] The value of the property is discussed by the court above n.68 at 400–401.

[74] See above n.68 at 397 and 401.

[75] See, *e.g.* the discussion in Part III 1(b) of this chapter.

estoppel.[76] Similarly, in *Grant*, Browne-Wilkinson V.-C had drawn on proprietary estoppel to provide guidance for quantifying beneficial interests.[77] Hence, while Lord Diplock drew on how an interest is established to quantify that interest, subsequent courts have sought guidance instead from another principle which enables the informal acquisition of rights in land. However, proprietary estoppel can offer only limited guidance. As will be seen in Chapter 7, the remedy awarded when an estoppel is established is not limited to a beneficial interest.[78] The comparison seems useful only at a general level of developing a flexible approach towards quantification.

In *Midland Bank plc v. Cooke*[79] the Court of Appeal extended Nourse L.J.'s broad approach to claims based on an inferred agreement to share.[80] There the claimant, Mrs Cooke, established a beneficial interest in her matrimonial home enforceable against mortgages granted by her husband. An agreement to share was inferred by the claimant's contribution to the initial deposit. That contribution arose as the husband's parents had paid the deposit as a joint wedding gift: Mrs Cooke was attributed with contributing half of that gift. Waite L.J. explained the approach the courts should take to quantifying beneficial interests as follows:

> "the duty of the judge is to undertake a survey of the whole course of dealing between the parties relevant to their ownership and occupation of the property and their sharing of its burdens and advantages. That scrutiny will not confine itself to the limited range of acts of direct contribution of the sort that are needed to found a beneficial interest in the first place. It will take into consideration all conduct which throws light on the question what shares are intended".[81]

In this statement, Waite L.J. expressly acknowledges that conduct which could not found a beneficial interest may, notwithstanding, be taken into account in quantifying an interest. Applied to the facts, by reference to the conduct of the parties Waite L.J. considered: "One

---

[76] See above n.68 at 399.
[77] See above n.87 at 657.
[78] Chapter 7, Part IV.
[79] See above n.33.
[80] Although *Stokes* was not discussed by the court. See Philip Wylie, "Computing Shares in the Family Home" [1995] Fam. Law 633 at 635.
[81] See above n.33 at 574.

could hardly have a clearer example of a couple who had agreed to share everything equally".[82] He therefore awarded Mrs Cooke a 50 per cent beneficial share.

This broad approach to quantifying beneficial interests has received some support.[83] It gives value to activities, such as those within the domestic and child care spheres, which cannot be relied upon to establish an inferred agreement to share or as a relevant detriment. Such factors may now affect proprietary ownership at the later stage of quantifying an interest which has been established. Taking into account such factors mitigates criticism of the principles discussed in this chapter as operating against female claimants.[84] However, it seems illogical to enable factors which cannot create beneficial entitlement to determine the extent of an interest. This can be illustrated by reference to *Cooke*. There, as has been seen, Mrs Cooke's interest was quantified as 50 per cent because the course of dealings between her and her husband was considered to infer an agreement to, "share everything equally".[85] However, Mrs Cooke was able to establish an interest only on the basis that (fortuitously) the initial deposit was a joint wedding gift. Therefore, she had made a direct contribution to the purchase (of approximately 6 per cent of the purchase price) from which an agreement to share could be inferred. If, for example, the deposit had been provided by Mr Cooke alone, then Mrs Cooke would not have obtained any interest. Further, the decision may have an impact on the extent to which residential property is considered adequate security for a loan. It will be difficult for mortgagees, at the time a loan is agreed, to determine what inferences may be drawn from the parties' conduct over a period of time. However, in this respect it is perhaps necessary to consider *Cooke* in a broader context. The policy of the court is to enable mortgagees to protect themselves against claims by beneficiaries (and therefore ensure family property can provide adequate security) by obtaining the beneficiary's informed consent to the

---

[82] See above n.33 at 576.
[83] Simon Gardner, "Fin de Siècle Chez *Gissing v. Gissing*" (1996) 112 L.Q.R. 378 at 382 considers the approach to have "a good claim to prevail". Alison Dunn, "Whipping up Resulting and Constructive Trusts" [1997] Conv. 467 at 472 cautiously welcomes the approach as enabling a responsive approach without detracting from the certainty and adherence to principle required by *Rosset*. Contrast the criticism of *Cooke* by Martin Dixon, "A Case Too Far?" [1997] Conv. 66.
[84] See above n.29 and text.
[85] See above n.33 at 376.

transaction under the principles now stemming from *Barclays Bank v. O'Brien*.[86] In *Cooke*, the mortgagee was bound by Mrs Cooke's interest as her consent to the loan was obtained through her husband's undue influence. Seen in the broader context, the combined effect of *Cooke* and *O'Brien* is to give the court greater flexibility in disputes between the parties without adversely affecting the commercial value of domestic property as security.[87]

In adopting a broad approach to quantification the courts have purported to base their decision on an agreement between the parties inferred from their conduct. The difficulty with this claim is that decisions have not been fully reasoned. The courts have explained that quantification is dependent upon the parties' agreement, and that in inferring an agreement the whole course of conduct between the parties should be taken into account. However, the courts have not explained how inferences are drawn. Mark Powlowski suggests that in using domestic services to alter proprietary rights the courts are reverting back to a doctrine of family assets.[88] That doctrine, which enabled property acquired by the joint efforts of a family (specifically a married couple) to be treated as belonging to the family equally, has long been rejected.[89] Other recent cases are also indicative of a form of family assets doctrine. For example, there seems to be a willingness on the part of the courts to award equal shares in a matrimonial home.[90] In *Cooke* Waite L.J. indicated that he had relied, to some extent, on the fact the parties were married.[91] Notwithstanding, the

---

[86] [1994] 1 A.C. 180.

[87] *cf.* the two principal situations in which a claim to a beneficial interest may be made outlined above n.3 and text. See the policy of "give and take" identified by John Dewar, "Land, Law, and the Family Home" in *Land Law: Themes and Perspectives* (Bright and Dewar eds., 1998), p. 327 and pp. 333–334. He suggests the courts have increased the possibility of establishing a share in the family home (give) but have simultaneously developed techniques to ensure those shares do not affect third parties (take).

[88] Mark Powlowski, "*Midland Bank plc v. Cooke*—A New Heresy?" [1996] Fam. Law 484 at 486. See also Patrick O'Hagan, "Quantifying Interests Under Resulting Trusts" (1997) 60 M.L.R. 420 at 425.

[89] *Pettitt v. Pettitt* above, n.36; *Gissing v. Gissing* above, n.36.

[90] In *McHardy and Sons Ltd v. Warren* [1994] 2 F.L.R. 338 at 340 Dillon L.J. considered the, "irresistible conclusion" where a parent pays the deposit of a matrimonial home as a gift is that the couple should share the home equally.

[91] He noted, above n.33 at 576: "When to all that [*i.e.* the course of conduct between the parties] there is added the fact (still an important one) that this was a couple who had chosen to introduce into their relationship the additional commitment which marriage involves, the conclusion becomes inescapable that their presumed intention was to share the beneficial interest in the property in equal shares".

doctrine of family assets is not an adequate explanation of the courts' approach. There is not yet an inference or presumption of equal ownership which characterised that doctrine.[92] It is submitted that the courts are engaged in a form of redistributive justice. In relation to *Cooke*, Gardner surmises that Waite L.J. drew an inference from the parties' conduct based on an agreement which may have been reached if parties in the position of Mr and Mrs Cooke had addressed their minds to the issue of quantification.[93] That is, while purporting to infer an agreement from the parties' conduct, the court in fact inferred an agreement which it considered the parties should have reached. This is a form of reasoning which, in *Gissing*, the House of Lords insisted could not be used to infer an agreement to share.[94] The courts' initial inquiry remains directed at the question "Whose is this?" Not "To whom shall this be given?"[95] However, once this question has been answered, the courts now, "divine a share which, on the facts of each case, accords with justice and good conscience".[96]

IV. Conclusion

Where parties enter an agreement to share a beneficial interest, such an interest may be acquired notwithstanding the absence of a formally declared trust. A beneficial interest will also be imposed to prevent the unjust enrichment of the legal owner that would otherwise result where the claimant has made a financial contribution to the acquisition of land. In both cases, the acquisition of the beneficial interest is justified in legal terms by the doctrines of resulting and constructive trust which, by section 53(2) of the Law of Property Act 1925, are not subject to formality requirements. The resulting trust, as has been seen, is a response to unjust enrichment.

---

[92] See, *e.g.* the discussion of the doctrine of family assets by Lord Denning M.R. in the Court of Appeal in *Gissing v. Gissing* [1969] 2 Ch. 85 at 93.

[93] See above n.83 at 381.

[94] See, *e.g.* Lord Morris above n.36 at 898: "The court does not decide how the parties might have ordered their affairs: it only finds how they did".

[95] *Pettitt v. Pettitt* above n.36 at 798, *per* Lord Morris.

[96] Michael Haley, commenting on *Clough v. Killey* March 7, 1996 (unreported) and *Drake v. Whipp* above n.37 (1996) 18 J.S.W.F.L. 481 at 486. Contrast *Mortgage Corporation Ltd v. Shaire*, judgment 25 February 2000. There, Neuberger J. doubted that, in quantifying beneficial shares, the courts have a "roving commission".

The constructive trust may be broadly seen as a means of preventing a form of fraud.[97] In Chapter 3 it was noted that only in the rule discussed in that chapter, (under which rights are acquired to prevent the use of statute for fraud) and exceptionally that discussed in Chapter 4, (where land is transferred "subject to" a person's right) is intervention by the courts justified solely in terms of the prevention of fraud. In contrast to a claimant within those rules, the claimant to a constructive trust will necessarily have acted to his or her detriment. In *Gissing*, Lord Diplock explained,[98] that the fraud in the context of a constructive trust arises by virtue of the fact the claimant has been induced to act to his or her detriment by the (constructive) trustee in the belief he was thereby acquiring a beneficial interest. Hence, intervention is justified by the fact a detriment has been provided.

The challenge for the courts has been to delimit the boundaries of a constructive trust. That boundary seems to lie between inferring from the parties' conduct an agreement to share and implying an agreement the parties did not in fact reach. The difficulty with this, is that in the context in which claims arise clear evidence of the parties' agreement may be as improbable as a formally declared trust. Current case law indicates the re-introduction of an element of discretion at the stage of quantifying beneficial shares which have been found to exist. The question remains whether, in light of this development, the initial insistence on compliance with the *Rosset* criteria can be logically retained.[99]

---

[97] *Gissing* above n.36 at 905.
[98] See above n.36 at 905.
[99] See Gardner above n.83 at 382.

Chapter 7.

Where There has Been a Unilateral Assurance of Rights

I. Introduction

The rule to be discussed in this chapter applies where an owner of land represents to a claimant that the claimant has (or will acquire) an interest in the representor's land. In this chapter, the claimant is referred to as *C* and the land owner (or representor) as *LO*. The rule prevents, or estops, *LO* from reneging on the assurance of rights where, as a result of *C* acting in reliance on the assurance, it would be unconscionable for *LO* to do so. This species of estoppel is referred to as proprietary estoppel. It has been described by the Law Commission as, "one of the principal vehicles for accommodating the informal creation of proprietary rights".[1]

The rule operates in two distinct stages. In the first stage an "equity" arises in favour of *C*. The equity arises when *LO* seeks, unconscionably, to renege on an assurance of rights he has made. Secondly the equity is satisfied by a court, in the exercise of its discretion, awarding *C* a remedy. At the first stage, *C* acquires an "inchoate equity". As will be seen,[2] it remains uncertain whether the inchoate equity is itself a proprietary right, enforceable by *C* not only against *LO* but also against a subsequent purchaser of *LO*'s title to the land. The remedy awarded by the court at the second stage may or may not be a proprietary right. Hence, subject to the status of the inchoate equity, this rule is not invariably the source of proprietary

---

[1] Law Com. No. 254 *Land Registration for the Twenty-First Century*, para. 3.33.
[2] Part III below.

rights. However, the breadth of remedies available means that estoppel has the potential to be used to circumvent any formality requirement for the express grant of a legal or equitable interest in land, including an express declaration of trust. Where a proprietary right is awarded, the court may require the representor formally to execute the grant of the right. Hence, while the right is acquired informally by estoppel, there may subsequently be a formal grant.

The justification for conferring proprietary rights on C is dependent upon when such rights are acquired. If the inchoate equity is proprietary, then the justification is tied to the reason LO is estopped from reneging on the assurance of rights. LO is estopped on the ground that it would be unconscionable to renege on the assurance. To the extent that unconscionable conduct is the justification, a comparison may be made with the rule discussed in Chapter 3. That rule provides for the acquisition of proprietary rights where it would be fraudulent to rely on non-compliance with statutory formalities. However, in the context of estoppel, unconscionability alone does not create the proprietary right. It is also necessary to establish that C acted to his or her detriment. If, however, a proprietary right is acquired (if at all) only when awarded as a remedy, then the justification must also take into account the purpose underlying the court's choice of remedy. That purpose, as will be seen, remains subject to debate.[3]

This chapter will first explain the requirements that must be satisfied for an estoppel to arise. Each of the two stages in which the doctrine operates, and the nature of the right acquired by C, will then be discussed. Consideration will also be given to the relationship between this and other species of estoppel, and with other principles which may be applied to similar factual situations. In the latter context it will be seen that the distinguishing element of an estoppel claim within this chapter is that it is based on a unilateral assurance of rights. It is the absence of a need to demonstrate mutuality which separates estoppel from other means of informal acquisition applicable to similar situations.[4]

II. Elements of a claim

The elements of a claim under the modern doctrine of estoppel stem from the judgment of Oliver J. in *Taylors Fashions Ltd v. Liverpool*

---

[3] See below Part IV.
[4] See below Part V.

Victoria Trustees Co.[5] The importance of the case lies in Oliver J.'s assertion of a broad approach and his rejection of an earlier approach by Fry J. which had, for one hundred years, restricted the development of proprietary estoppel. Oliver J.'s judgment needs to be considered in context of the historical development of the rule.

Historically, proprietary estoppel was applied in three distinct categories of case.[6] First, where an informal gift of land was made. In this category, the estoppel operated as an exception to the general rule that equity will not perfect an imperfect gift. That rule, and its other exceptions, are the subject of Chapter 2. Estoppel is distinguished from the rules discussed in that chapter as it may perfect a gift only where the donee, the claimant to estoppel, has acted to his or her detriment. Secondly, where *LO* encouraged *C* to believe that he would acquire rights in *LO*'s land. These are referred to as "common expectation" cases as both *LO* and the claimant believe that *C* will acquire an interest in the land. Thirdly where *LO* acquiesced in *C*'s mistaken belief that *C* had rights in the land. These are classified as cases of "unilateral mistake"; *C* alone is mistaken as to his rights. The development of the doctrine was hindered by a failure to distinguish clearly between the requirements of the second and third categories.

The requirements of the second and third categories are derived, respectively, from the judgments of Lord Kingsdown (common expectation) and Lord Cranworth L.C. (unilateral mistake) in *Ramsden v. Dyson*.[7] Lord Kingsdown envisaged an estoppel arising where both *C* and *LO* have fostered an expectation that *C* will acquire rights.[8] Lord Cranworth L.C., in contrast, referred to a situation in which *C* alone is mistaken as to his rights and *LO*, aware of the true position, perceives *C*'s mistake but abstains from setting him right.[9] The distinction between the two categories therefore relates to *LO*'s knowledge. In unilateral mistake cases only, it is essential for *LO* to be aware of the true position. This distinction affects how the assurance of rights may be established. In a case involving a unilateral mistake, the assurance is usually provided

---

[5] [1982] 1 Q.B. 133.
[6] For a discussion of these, see Mark Powlowski, *The Doctrine of Proprietary Estoppel* (1996), Chapter 6.
[7] (1866) L.R. 1 H.L. 129.
[8] See above n.7 at 170, considered in *Taylors Fashions* by Oliver J. above n.5 at 147.
[9] See above n.7 at 140–141.

passively by *LO*'s acquiescence. *LO* is aware of his own rights, and that *C* is acting in a mistaken belief as to his (*C*'s) rights, but fails to advise *C* as to the true position. In cases of common expectation, where both parties are mistaken as to their rights, the assurance must be derived from some active encouragement by *LO* of *C*'s actions. Mere acquiescence will not give rise to an assurance of rights where *LO* is not aware both of his own rights and of *C*'s mistaken belief.

In *Willmott v. Barber*,[10] *C* argued that *LO*'s acquiescence gave rise to an estoppel in circumstances in which both parties were in fact mistaken as to their rights. There, *C* had been granted an option to purchase land by a tenant but was not aware that, under the terms of the lease, the tenant required his landlord's consent to assign. *C* argued the landlord was obliged to give consent as he had acquiesced in *C*'s expenditure of money on the land acting in the mistaken belief the tenant was able to assign. Fry J. dismissed the claim (correctly) on the basis that, in the absence of knowledge of the true position by the landlord, his acquiescence could not generate an estoppel. However, in dismissing the claim on this basis, Fry J. purported to give a general formulation of estoppel in terms of five probanda. He explained:

> "A man is not to be deprived of his legal rights unless he has acted in such a way as would make it fraudulent for him to set up those rights. What, then, are the elements or requisites necessary to constitute fraud of that description? In the first place the plaintiff must have made a mistake as to his legal rights. Secondly, the plaintiff must have expended some money or must have done some act (not necessarily upon the defendant's land) on the faith of his mistaken belief. Thirdly, the defendant, the possessor of the legal right, must know of the existence of his own right which is inconsistent with the right claimed by the plaintiff. If he does not know of it he is in the same position as the plaintiff, and the doctrine of acquiescence is founded upon conduct with a knowledge of your legal rights. Fourthly, the defendant, the possessor of the legal right, must know of the plaintiff's mistaken belief of his rights. If he does not, there is nothing which calls upon him to assert his own rights. Lastly, the defendant, the possessor of the legal right, must have encouraged the plaintiff in his expenditure of money

---

[10] (1880) 15 Ch. D. 96.

or in the other acts which he has done, either directly or by abstaining from asserting his legal right. . . in my judgment, nothing short of this will do".[11]

The difficulty with this formulation is that it reflects a situation in which C alone is mistaken as to his rights. This is apparent, in particular, in the third and fourth probandum, which refer to the representor's knowledge of his own rights, and of C's mistake. Fry J.'s probanda do not expressly acknowledge that estoppel can arise in cases, (like the one before the court) in which both parties are mistaken as to their rights. Presented as a general formulation for estoppel, Fry J.'s probanda seem to preclude such claims. This apparent exclusion of common expectation claims seems to be a consequence of the manner in which Fry J. approached the case. He considered the claim only from the point of view of a claim based on acquiescence. Acquiescence is most likely to generate an estoppel in a case of unilateral mistake. Fry J. did not consider the case from its other perspective: as a claim to estoppel where, as envisaged by Lord Kingsdown in *Ramsden v. Dyson*, both parties are mistaken as to their rights. Considered from this point of view, the claim to estoppel would fail, not because the landlord was unaware of the true position, (as, by definition, in a case of common expectation the representor is not aware of the true position) but because the landlord had not actively encouraged C. In a common expectation case the assurance must be derived from LO's active encouragement of C. The apparent exclusion of common expectation cases endured until the application of estoppel was reconsidered by Oliver J. in *Taylors Fashions*.

In *Taylors Fashions*, C argued that their landlord, the defendants, were estopped from denying that they were bound by an option to renew C's lease of business premises. The option had been granted by the defendants' predecessors in title and had not been registered as a land charge as it was believed such options were not registerable. Following the assignment of the freehold to the defendants, C expended money on the premises in the belief, shared by the defendants, that the option remained valid. Subsequently, (in an unconnected action) it was established that an option to renew a lease was in fact registerable as a land charge. As a result, C's option was void against the defendants for non-registration at the time of the

---

[11] See above n.10 at 105–106.

assignment. *C* argued that, through their acquiescence in *C*'s expenditure, the defendants were estopped from relying on the non-registration. The defendants' acquiescence had created an assurance of rights, upon which *C* had relied to their detriment. As with *Willmott v. Barber*, the case concerned a claim to estoppel by acquiescence in circumstances in which both parties were mistaken as to their rights: at the time of *C*'s expenditure, both believed the option to be valid. The defendants argued, by reference to the probanda, that as they were not aware of their rights, their acquiescence could not generate an assurance.[12] Although the claim to estoppel failed, Oliver J. did not apply the probanda. Instead, he explained:

> "the application of [estoppel]. . . requires a very much broader approach which is directed rather at ascertaining whether, in particular individual circumstances, it would be unconscionable for a party to be permitted to deny that which, knowingly, or unknowingly, he has allowed or encouraged another to assume to his detriment than to inquiring whether the circumstances can be fitted within the confines of some preconceived formula serving as a universal yardstick for every form of unconscionable behaviour. So regarded, knowledge of the true position by the party alleged to be estopped, becomes merely one of the relevant factors - it may even be a determining factor in certain cases - in the overall inquiry".[13]

The defendants' lack of knowledge of the true position was relevant, because in the absence of such knowledge, their acquiescence did not create an assurance of rights.[14] The defendants could be under no duty to communicate that which they did not know: that the option was void for non-registration. The significance of the case is that, unlike the probanda, Oliver J.'s broad formulation does not reject the possibility of estoppel arising where *LO* is unaware of the true position. It was clear from Oliver J.'s judgment that such a claim could succeed where *LO* actively encouraged *C*'s actions. This reopened the possibility of estoppel being established in a case historically classified as involving a common expectation.

---

[12] See above n.5 at 144–147.
[13] See above n.5 at 151–152.
[14] See above n.5 at 147.

Oliver J.'s approach has subsequently been approved by the Court of Appeal and Privy Council.[15] In the context of the broad approach, the key elements of a claim are that there has been an assurance of rights, upon which C has relied to his detriment. Each of these elements will now be considered.

1. ASSURANCE OF RIGHTS

(a) The nature of the assurance

C must have been given an assurance he has, or will acquire, rights in the representor's land. The assurance must usually have been made by the title holder against whom the estoppel is claimed.[16] It is not necessary for the assurance to be precise as to the nature of the rights conferred on C. In *Plimmer v. Mayor of Wellington*,[17] Sir Arthur Hobhouse noted that a claim need not fail, "merely on the ground that the interest to be secured has not been expressly indicated".[18] This is because it is for the court to decide what interest is in fact acquired by C.[19] However, it is necessary for C to have been given an assurance of rights in LO's land. A general assurance that LO will support C will not give rise to an estoppel. Proprietary estoppel can be used to restrict only LO's exercise of proprietary rights and a general assurance of support is not sufficiently linked to the use of property.[20] Hence, in *Coombes v. Smith*[21] a general assurance LO would, "always provide [C] with a roof over her head" was insufficient to establish an estoppel.[22] There, C had moved into a house owned by the defendant in the expectation (which was never

---

[15] *Habib Bank Ltd v. Habib Bank A.G. Zurich* [1981] 1 W.L.R. 1265, CA; *Lloyds Bank plc v. Carrick* [1996] 4 All E.R. 630, CA; *Lim Teng Huan v. Ang Swee Chuan* [1992] 1 W.L.R. 113, PC. Contrast the application of Fry J.'s probanda by Roch L.J. (with whom Hirst L.J. agreed) in *Matharu v. Matharu* (1994) 68 P. & C.R. 93.

[16] In *Matharu v. Matharu* above, n.15 in exceptional circumstances, a representation made by the title owner's son was accepted. The court took into account the cultural context, in which anything said by the son was considered to have the authority of his father.

[17] (1884) 9 A.C. 699.

[18] See above n.17 at 713.

[19] See above n.17 at 714.

[20] Sean Wilken and Theresa Villiers, *Waiver, Variation and Estoppel* (1998), pp. 307–308.

[21] [1986] 1 W.L.R. 808.

[22] See above n.21 at 818.

fulfilled) that the defendant would live with her. That case also suggests that assurances of rights made in the context of an on-going relationship may be insufficient to form the basis of a claim to estoppel, unless it is clear C's rights are not conditional upon the continuance of the relationship. The court considered that, in any event, the claim would fail as there was no assurance that C would continue to enjoy rights on the breakdown of the parties' relationship.[23] In this respect, the court distinguished *Pascoe v. Turner*.[24] There, a claim to estoppel was successfully made where C had been assured, at the termination of a relationship, that a house and its contents were hers. This was considered to assure C of rights in the house regardless of the fact the parties' relationship had ended.

Estoppel may also be established where C is assured that he will acquire rights in the future, even where the rights are conditional. Further, it may not be necessary for the land in which the right is to be acquired to be specified. These principles are illustrated by cases in which C has argued that she was given an assurance she would inherit land on LO's death. In *Re Basham*,[25] C's stepfather, Mr Basham, had encouraged her to believe that she would inherit his entire estate on his death. Mr Basham died intestate and C claimed to be entitled to his property through the doctrine of estoppel. C's claim was treated as a claim to an assurance of future rights (on Mr Basham's death) in non-specific property (his entire estate). The assurance may also in fact have been conditional upon C working for Mr Basham. Although not expressly analysed as such by the court, the court noted C had commented to her husband that she, "had worked all her life for her parents, and if she didn't she wouldn't get what she had been promised".[26] The court held that there was no authority limiting estoppel to assurances of existing rights.[27] The court considered that the appropriate mechanism to give effect to an assurance of future rights was a constructive trust. Therefore, Mr Basham was considered to hold his estate on constructive trust for C.[28] The reasoning in *Re Basham*, in particular the application of a constructive trust, has been criticised. The imposition of a trust is

---

[23] *ibid.*
[24] [1979] 1 W.L.R. 431. See *Coombes v. Smith* above n.21 at 818–819.
[25] [1986] 1 W.L.R. 1498.
[26] See above n.25 at 1503.
[27] See above n.25 at 1509.
[28] See above n.25 at 1504.

inconsistent with the courts' general discretion as to the remedy awarded in an estoppel claim.[29] Moreover, to the extent that the imposition of a trust restricts the representor's use of property during his life, it may exceed C's expectations and therefore conflict with the general principle that the fulfilment of those expectations is the maximum remedy available.[30] It is also arguable whether in fact the claim in *Re Basham* was correctly analysed as being to non-specific property and whether estoppel encompasses such claims. Wilken and Villiers analyse the case as a claim to specific property to be selected by a triggering event (Mr Basham's death).[31] Once the triggering event occurred, the subject of the claim (his estate at that time) could be identified. Hence, *Re Basham* may indicate that while the assurance of rights need not relate to specific property, the property must be ascertained at the time the claim is made. *Layton v. Martin*[32] may go further and prevent a claim to estoppel unless the assurance relates to specific property. There, Scott J. considered estoppel was:

> "concerned with the question whether an owner of property can, by insisting on his strict legal rights, therein, defeat an expectation of an interest in that property. . . The question does not arise otherwise than in connection with some asset in respect of which it has been represented, or is alleged to have been represented, that the claimant is to have some interest".[33]

However, the claim in that case would have failed, in any event, as LO had assured C generally that C would be financially secure.[34]

Notwithstanding the criticism directed at the reasoning in *Re Basham*, the application of estoppel to assurances of future rights has been accepted. Estoppel was successfully claimed in such circumstances in *Wayling v. Jones*.[35] There, C had been assured by his

---

[29] Jill Martin, "Estoppel and the Ubiquitous Constructive Trust" [1987] Conv. 211 at 213. The courts' general remedial discretion is discussed below, Part IV.

[30] Wilken and Villiers above n.20, pp. 313–314. In *Re Basham* above n.25 at 1505 the court indicated that Mr Basham would have been prevented from dealing with his property during his life in a manner calculated to defeat the trust. The role of C's expectation in determining the remedy is considered below Part IV 1.

[31] See above n.20, p. 314.

[32] [1986] 2 F.L.R. 227.

[33] See above n.32 at 238.

[34] See above n.20 and text; Wilken and Villiers above n.20, p. 313. The case was not cited in *Re Basham* above n.25.

[35] (1993) 69 P. & C.R. 170.

homosexual partner, Jones, that he (C) would inherit Jones' business. Jones had successively owned a series of businesses and had, on at least two occasions, executed a will in favour of C in relation to the business then owned. However, Jones failed to change his will following the final change of business before his death. The Court of Appeal upheld C's claim to the proceeds of sale of the business by estoppel. The court's judgment is concerned primarily with the question of reliance; there is no discussion of the status of assurances of future rights, and no suggestion that Jones held the business on constructive trust for C. Further, the question of non-specific property did not arise as C had been assured he would inherit the particular business Jones owned at his death.[36]

The circumstances in which an assurance of future rights can be used to claim estoppel has been considered in two recent cases and is of general importance as to the nature of an assurance in estoppel claims. The question that has troubled the courts is when an assurance of future rights, which is inherently revocable, should be able to form the basis of an estoppel claim. In the first case, *Taylor v. Dickens*,[37] Judge Weeks took an unduly technical approach. He sought to distinguish between cases in which a will is executed but then revoked, and those (including *Re Basham* and *Wayling v. Jones*) in which no will is executed. In the former case, according to Judge Weeks, a claim to estoppel will succeed only if established that LO assured C the will would not be revoked. This approach was widely criticised,[38] and was overturned in *Gillett v. Holt*.[39]

In *Gillett v. Holt*, Holt had promised to bequeath his farm to C. He executed a will to that effect, but following the breakdown in relations with C, Holt revoked his will. The Court of Appeal considered the inherent revocability of a testamentary disposition to be irrelevant in determining whether an assurance is made.[40] The significant factor is whether, in all the circumstances, the assurance is, "more than a mere statement of present (revocable) intention, and is

---

[36] See above n.35 at 172. Jones had assured C that he would change his will to refer to the new business.

[37] [1998] 1 F.L.R. 806.

[38] See, *e.g.* M.P. Thompson, "Emasculating Estoppel" [1998] Conv. 210; W.J. Swadling [1998] R.L.R. 220. In *Gillett v. Holt* [2000] 2 All E.R. 289 at 303, these criticisms were considered well founded.

[39] See above n.38. However, the court noted that the actual result in *Taylor v. Dickens* may be justified on other grounds.

[40] See above n.38 at 304.

tantamount to a promise".[41] On the facts, the claim to estoppel succeeded. The assurances had been made over a long period of time, usually in the company of family, and in some instances were "completely unambiguous".[42] However, it is unclear from whose perspective the assessment of the assurance is to be made. Giving the judgment of the court, Robert Walker L.J. initially states, "the assurances given on this occasion were intended to be relied on, and were in fact relied on".[43] This suggests the relevant inquiry is from the point of view of LO. Did LO intend the assurance to be more than a statement of present intent? Subsequently, Robert Walker L.J. notes, "it is the other party's detrimental reliance on the promise which makes it irrevocable".[44] The question arises how to assess a situation in which LO intends to make merely a statement of current intent, but this is relied upon by C in the belief an assurance had been made. From *Gillett v. Holt*, it seems the answer will depend on whether, in all the circumstances, it would be unconscionable for LO to renege on the statement, or whether C acted entirely, "with his eyes open".[45]

The need to establish more than a statement of present intent may imply a more general requirement about the nature of the assurance. It is in this respect that cases considering assurances of future rights are of wider significance to estoppel claims. The cases illustrate that the assurance C will acquire rights must not be conditional upon a formal grant of the rights.[46] A statement of present intent does not suffice, as it is no more than an indication of a subsequent grant, or of the likely terms of a will. The need for an assurance that rights will be acquired irrespective of a formal grant is also illustrated in claims to estoppel in another context; claims arising from pre-contractual relationships.

Pre-contractual negotiations do not usually provide an assurance of rights as the parties' expectation is that rights will not be acquired unless negotiations conclude with their formal execution. For an estoppel to arise, it must be established that there was in fact an assurance rights would be acquired irrespective of formal execution.[47]

---

[41] *ibid.*
[42] *ibid.*
[43] *ibid.*
[44] See above n.38 at 305.
[45] See above n.38 at 304.
[46] Martin Dixon, "Estoppel: A Panacea for all Wills?" [1999] Conv. 46 at 50 commenting on the first instance decision in *Gillett v. Holt*.
[47] *J.T. Developments Ltd v. Quinn* (1991) 62 P. & C.R. 33 at 46–47.

Estoppel was successfully claimed in the context of pre-contractual negotiations in *Crabb v. Arun D.C.*[48] There, the Council had reached an agreement in principle to grant a right of way to C.[49] The Court of Appeal did not discuss the nature of pre-contractual negotiations, but considered that, on the facts of the case, the subsequent conduct of the Council had led C to believe he would have a right of way.[50] The nature of pre-contractual negotiations was discussed in another successful claim in *J.T. Developments v. Quinn.*[51] There, C were told, in the course of negotiations, that their landlord was prepared to grant them a new lease of business premises. The Court of Appeal, (Glidewell L.J. dissenting) accepted the finding of fact by the judge at first instance that there had been a firm assurance C would be granted a tenancy regardless of the outcome of negotiations. However, in upholding C's claim, the court emphasised that it, "should always have in mind the fact that the parties to such negotiations normally do not intend to affect the legal relationship between them until the actual agreement is made".[52] The question for the court was whether C had been given an assurance they would have a new lease, "*before anything further was done towards the agreeing or granting of a new lease, and without any further acts on the part of the landlord*".[53] These cases may be contrasted with the Privy Council decision in *A.G. of Hong Kong v. Humphreys Estate (Queen's Gardens) Ltd.*[54] There, the plaintiffs had agreed "subject to contract" to grant C leases of a number of flats. No leases were in fact granted and C's claim to estoppel failed. The Privy Council considered that while an agreement expressly made "subject to contract" did not preclude a claim to estoppel,[55] the plaintiffs had not indicated, "expressly or by implication that they had surrendered their right to change their

---

[48] [1976] 1 Ch. 179.
[49] This explanation of the agreement was given by the judge at first instance, noted by the Court of Appeal above n.48 at 189.
[50] See above n.48 at 189.
[51] See above n.47.
[52] See above n.47 at 47.
[53] See above n.47 at 49, emphasis included.
[54] [1987] 1 A.C. 114.
[55] Lord Templeman noted above n.54 at 127–128: "It is possible but unlikely that in circumstances at present unforeseeable a party to negotiations set out in a document expressed to be 'subject to contract' would be able to satisfy the court that. . . some form of estoppel had arisen to prevent both parties from refusing to proceed with the transactions envisaged by the document". *cf. Salvation Army Trustee Co Ltd v. West Yorkshire M.C.C.* (1981) 41 P. & C.R. 179.

mind and to withdraw".[56] In *Gillett v. Holt*, Robert Walker L.J. explained the case, "as an example of a purchaser taking the risk, with his eyes open, of going into possession and spending money while his purchase remains expressly subject to contract".[57]

(b) Establishing the assurance

Hence, it is established that for a claim to estoppel to succeed there must be an assurance C has or will acquire rights in land without a formal grant. The next issue to consider is how the assurance can be made. The assurance may be made actively, by words or conduct, or passively, by acquiescence while C acts in the mistaken belief he has or will acquire rights. *Pascoe v. Turner*[58] illustrates an active assurance. There, LO told C, "the house is yours and everything in it".[59] In *Inwards v. Baker*[60] LO suggested that C, his son, who was considering buying land to build a bungalow, "put the bungalow on my land and make the bungalow a little bigger".[61] This was a clear assurance C would have some rights, even though the nature of the rights was not specified.[62] Relatively weak evidence of an active assurance may be sufficient, particularly where it is maintained over a period of time.[63] In *Greasley v. Cooke*,[64] C, who had lived for over 40 years in the house which was the subject of her claim to estoppel, had been encouraged to believe that the house would be her home for the rest of her life.[65] Her claim succeeded. Lord Denning M.R. explained that statements made to her were, "calculated to influence her - so as to put her mind at rest - so that she should not worry about being turned out".[66] *Crabb v. Arun D.C.*[67] illustrates that LO's conduct may be interpreted as an assurance of rights. There, in finding an assurance had been made, the court emphasised the conduct of the Council which had erected gates at a point it had indicated C would have a right of way.[68]

---

[56] See above n.54 at 124.
[57] See above n.38 at 304.
[58] See above n.24.
[59] See above n.24 at 434.
[60] [1965] 2 Q.B. 29.
[61] See above n.60 at 35.
[62] Mark Howard and Jonathan Hill, "The Informal Creation of Interests in Land" (1995) 15 L.S. 356 at 366.
[63] Howard and Hill above n. 62 at 366.
[64] [1980] 1 W.L.R. 1306.
[65] See above n.64 at 1309.
[66] See above n.64 at 1311.
[67] See above n.48.
[68] See above n.48 at 189.

The courts are more cautious in claims to an assurance of rights derived from *LO*'s acquiescence. It seems likely, even within the context of Oliver J.'s broad approach to estoppel, that acquiescence can generate an assurance of rights only where *LO* is aware *C* is acting in a mistaken belief he has or will acquire rights.[69] The effect of this may be that acquiescence will create an assurance of rights only in cases historically classified as involving a unilateral mistake. More controversial is whether acquiescence may also create an assurance in cases of *misprediction* rather than mistake. These are cases in which *C* is aware that he does not have rights but runs the risk that rights will be granted. As in cases of mistake, *LO*, aware of the true position, knowingly stands by while *C* acts to his detriment. *Ramsden v. Dyson* has been interpreted as an example of such a case. There, *C*, who were tenants at will, built houses on their landlord's land in the belief they would thereby be granted a long lease. Birks notes that *C* were not acting under a mistaken belief.[70] *C* knew they were tenants at will but mispredicted that by building a house they would become entitled to a long lease. *C*'s claim failed because the landlord did not know of their misprediction. The House of Lords accepted that if the landlord had known, then the claim would have succeeded. This may be considered to imply that acquiescence in *C*'s misprediction can create an assurance of rights.[71] However, it is submitted that it is doubtful *Ramsden v. Dyson* establishes that a misprediction can create an assurance of rights. Given the courts' reluctance to derive an assurance from *LO*'s failure to inform *C* of a mistake, it seems unlikely one could be derived from failing to inform a risk-taker that he has miscalculated the risk. Even if an assurance of rights is found, a claim to estoppel may still fail on the ground it is not unconscionable to assert legal rights against a person who has mispredicted the effect of their actions.[72]

---

[69] In *Taylors Fashions* above n.5 at 152 Oliver J. acknowledged that the representor's knowledge may be a determining factor in some cases. As has been seen above n.14 and text, no assurance was derived from *LO*'s acquiescence in that case as they were not aware of the true position.

[70] Birks, *Introduction to the Law of Restitution* 1989 (revised ed.) pp. 277–279.

[71] Birks suggests the House of Lord's decision establishes that if the landlord had known of *C*'s misprediction, then *C* would have had a claim to restitution. This requires only a finding that *LO* would otherwise be unjustly enriched. It does not require *LO*'s inaction to be construed as giving an assurance of rights.

[72] Birks' argument a landowner with knowledge of a misprediction is "unjustly" enriched is criticised by, *e.g.* Burrows, *The Law of Restitution*, (1993), pp. 315–320. In response to the criticism, see Birks, "In Defence of Free Acceptance" in *Essays on the Law of Restitution* (Burrows ed., 1991). The significance of unconscionability in estoppel actions is considered below Part II 4.

In situations in which, in principle, acquiescence could create an assurance, the claim may still fail if *LO*'s failure to intervene is explicable on another basis. In *Williams v. Coleman*[73] the Court of Appeal considered that *LO*, who was a disabled, middle-aged widow, may have acquiesced in *C*'s occupation of her land merely because "she was not disposed to make a fuss" or "wanted to avoid trouble". *C*'s claim to estoppel therefore failed. A successful claim to estoppel by acquiescence was made in *Salvation Army Trustee Co Ltd v. West Yorkshire M.C.C.*[74] There, *C* had constructed a new hall in the mistaken belief their old hall was to be compulsorily purchased as part of a road widening scheme. The road widening was postponed and *C*'s land was not in fact required. Woolf J. considered that the defendant authority had stood by when it knew or ought to have known *C* continued to incur expenditure acting under a mistaken belief.[75] He considered that the authority's "conscious silence"[76] was sufficient to create an assurance of rights.

2. RELIANCE

Once established that there has been an assurance of rights, it must be shown that *C* relied on the assurance to his detriment. The elements are connected as the quality of the assurance may influence the finding of reliance.[77] The element of reliance is, in essence, a test of causation.[78] Reliance, "demonstrates that it was the legal owner's assurance which caused the estoppel claimant to act to his detriment or change his position".[79] *C*'s claim will fail if there is an insufficient connection between the assurance and *C*'s acts. In *Coombes v. Smith*,[80] *C*'s claim to estoppel would have failed on this requirement even if she had been able to establish an assurance of rights. Jonathan Parker Q.C., considered, *obiter*, that *C*'s acts in leaving her husband to move into a house provided by the defendant, and having the defendant's child, were not in reliance on any assurance of rights. He explained,

---

[73] June 27, 1984.
[74] See above n.55.
[75] See above n.55 at 196.
[76] *ibid.*
[77] *Gillett v. Holt* above n.38 at 301.
[78] Wilken and Villiers above n.20, p. 260.
[79] Powlowski above n.6, p. 43.
[80] See above n.21.

"it would be wholly unreal, to put it mildly, to find. . . that [C] allowed herself to become pregnant by the defendant in reliance on some mistaken belief as to her legal rights. She allowed herself to become pregnant because she wished to live with the defendant and to bear his child".[81] Further, that C moved into the defendant's house, "because she preferred to have a relationship with, and a child by, the defendant rather than continuing to live with her husband".[82]

Despite the need for some causative link, it is not necessary for the assurance to be the sole motive for C's actions. In Re Basham Edward Nugee Q.C. commented: "I am satisfied that *one reason* why [C] did so much for the deceased was her belief that. . .he would leave his estate to her on his death."[83] In *Amalgamated Investment & Property Co Ltd v. Texas Commerce International Bank Ltd*[84] Robert Goff J. considered reliance required C's conduct to be "influenced" by the assurance.[85] In this respect, he added, "it is, in my judgment, no bar to a conclusion that the other party's conduct was so influenced, that his conduct did not derive its origin only from the encouragement or representation of the first party".[86] By reference to Robert Goff J.'s judgment, Balcombe L.J. in *Wayling v. Jones*, explained: "The promises relied upon do not have to be the sole inducement for the conduct: it is sufficient if they are an inducement".[87]

It is not always necessary for C to prove reliance. In *Greasley v. Cooke* Lord Denning M.R. held that the burden was on LO to prove that C did not rely on the assurance.[88] Edward Nugee Q.C. indicated that he would have applied this in *Re Basham*. He considered that if the evidence in that case had not established reliance, then C would still succeed in the absence of proof that she did not rely on the assurance.[89] The circumstances in which reliance will be presumed were considered by Jonathan Parker Q.C. in *Coombes v. Smith*. He

---

[81] See above n.21 at 820.
[82] See above n.21 at 820.
[83] See above n.25 at 1507 (emphasis added).
[84] [1982] 1 Q.B. 84.
[85] See above n.84 at 104.
[86] *ibid.*
[87] See above n.35 at 173. In explaining the requirements for estoppel, Balcombe L.J. drew on cases involving constructive trusts arising (under the rule discussed in Chapter 6) from an agreement to share beneficial ownership. His judgment has been criticised as the requirements for detrimental reliance under estoppel may not be identical. See Powlowski, above n.6, p. 48.
[88] See above n.64 at 1311.
[89] See above n.25 at 1507.

explained the presumption applies where, "following assurances made by the other party, the claimant has adopted a course of conduct which is prejudicial or otherwise detrimental to her".[90] In *Wayling v. Jones* Balcombe L.J. suggested that the course of conduct in question must be, "of such a nature that inducement may be inferred".[91] In light of this, reliance may not be presumed if the acts used to establish detriment are of such a nature they may have been performed regardless of the assurance.[92] Balcombe L.J.'s formulation may mark a shift in emphasis in determining the application of the presumption.[93] Lord Denning M.R.'s formulation of the presumption in *Greasley v. Cooke* emphasises *LO*'s intention. He considered the presumption to apply where the assurance is, "calculated to influence" *C*.[94] Balcombe L.J.'s formulation, in contrast, focuses instead on the nature of *C*'s conduct.[95] One danger with this approach is that the courts' judgment as to whether an act would have been performed regardless of the assurance (and therefore the courts' decision on the application of the presumption) may be influenced by the gender of the claimant.[96]

Where reliance is presumed, the next question to consider is how the representor can rebut the presumption. This was discussed in *Wayling v. Jones*, where *C*'s claim to estoppel had failed at first instance on the ground he had not relied on the assurance. *C* had acknowledged in the course of his evidence that if no assurance of rights had been made, he would have followed the same course of conduct.[97] The Court of Appeal held that this was insufficient to discharge *LO*'s burden of proof. The court considered that to discharge the burden, *LO* must establish that *C* would have acted the same way if the assurance of rights, once made, had been retracted.[98] *C* had said in evidence that in those circumstances he would have left and therefore his claim to estoppel succeeded. Wilken and Villiers criticise this approach. They suggest it is sufficient for the representor

---

[90] See above n.21 at 821.
[91] See above n.35 at 173.
[92] Wilken and Villiers above n.20, p. 262.
[93] Christine J. Davis, "Estoppel - Reliance and Remedy" [1995] Conv. 409 at 411–412.
[94] See above n.64 at 1311–1312.
[95] Wilken and Villiers above n.20 p. 262.
[96] See the discussion of gender in relation to detrimental reliance in Chapter 6, Part III 1(b).
[97] See above n.35 at 174.
[98] See above n.35 at 175.

to establish that C acted in the way he did for some reason other than the assurance of rights.[99] As has been seen, the courts do not require the assurance to be the sole factor inducing C's conduct. Therefore, even if Wilken and Villiers' approach is adopted, it would seem necessary to prove that the assurance was not one of the factors that motivated C's actions.

3. DETRIMENT

It must be shown that in relying on the assurance C acted to his detriment.[1] In *Gillett v. Holt*, Robert Walker L.J. noted that the elements are "intertwined".[2] In the absence of detriment by C it will not be considered unconscionable for the representor to renege on the assurance.[3] This requirement may be more accurately described as a need for C to "change his position" in reliance on the assurance.[4] This formulation was adopted, for example, by Edward Nugee Q.C. in *Re Basham*.[5] The reference to change of position emphasises that C's acts need not themselves be onerous. The detriment will arise, as a result of C's change of position, if LO reneges on the assurance.[6] The detriment must usually be suffered personally by C. However, in *Matharu v. Matharu*[7] the court considered that C had suffered a detriment by her husband spending money on the house which was the subject of her claim to estoppel. This constituted a detriment to C because it meant her husband had less money available to benefit her and their children.[8] Further, in *Re Basham* the court referred to the activities of C's husband as well as those of C personally.[9]

The burden of establishing detriment lies with C.[10] It is uncertain whether a detriment in fact requires a "net loss". Such an approach

---

[99] See above n.20, pp. 262–263.

[1] See, *e.g. Sledmore v. Dalby* (1996) 72 P. & C. R. 196 at 197. Hobhouse L.J. explained the detriment must be, "distinct [from the assurance and reliance] and substantial".

[2] See above n.38 at 301.

[3] However, as will be seen below, Part II 4 the mere fact C has acted to his detriment may not make it unconscionable for the representor to renege on the assurance.

[4] Wilken and Villiers above n.20, p. 265.

[5] See above n.25 at 1504. See also, *e.g. E.R. Ives Investment Ltd v. High* [1967] 2 Q.B. 379 at 405, *per* Winn L.J., "where estoppel applies [C] . . . has, ex hypothesi, suffered a past detriment or other change of position".

[6] Wilken and Villiers above n.20, p. 265.

[7] See above n.15.

[8] See above n.15 at 102. This is criticised by Mary Welstead, "Proprietary Estoppel - A Flexible Familial Equity" [1995] Conv. 61 at 64.

[9] See above n.25 at 1505.

[10] *Coombes v. Smith* above n.21 at 821.

has been recognised,[11] and is illustrated by *Sledmore v. Dalby*.[12] There, in assessing *C*'s detriment, the court took into account that *C* had enjoyed the benefit of 18 years' rent free accommodation.[13] Upholding the estoppel claim in *Re Basham*, Edward Nugee Q.C. noted that *C* had not received any "commensurate reward" for services she had provided to *LO*.[14] Whether this approach should still be adopted is doubtful following *Gillett v. Holt*.[15] There, the Court of Appeal emphasised that detriment is not a narrow and technical concept, and was critical of attempts to balance advantages and disadvantages.[16] However, the main concern of the court in relation to detriment was perhaps to ensure due account is taken of non-financial activities. It may be that although a net loss (or net detriment) must still be shown, in assessing whether this is the case, due account must be made of non-financial factors. Subject to the possible overriding requirement of a net loss, the courts have adopted a flexible approach to finding a detriment. In particular, a sufficient detriment in the context of a claim to estoppel may be established by actions falling short of what would be accepted as a detriment in the context of a claim to a constructive trust based on an agreement to share beneficial ownership under the rule discussed in Chapter 6. The courts' more generous approach within this rule may be explicable on the basis that the court retains a discretion as to the remedy obtained by *C*.[17]

In *Pascoe v. Turner*,[18] the detriment comprised financial expenditure by *C* on *LO*'s land, through carrying out redecoration, improvements and repairs. A financial detriment was also apparent in *Inwards v. Baker*[19] where *C* had built a house on *LO*'s land. However, it is established that the detriment need not be financial, nor be directly related to the land. For example, the court has accepted as sufficient detriment a decision to abandon divorce proceedings,[20] leaving a job

---

[11] Wilken and Villiers above n.20, p. 277.
[12] See above n.1.
[13] *C*'s claim did not fail for failing to demonstrate a detriment, but the court considered the minimum equity required to satisfy his claim had expired. The court's approach to the remedy in that case is considered below n.24 and text.
[14] See above n.25 at 1505.
[15] See above n.38.
[16] See above n.38 at 308–310.
[17] Welstead above n.8 at 65.
[18] See above n.24.
[19] See above n.60.
[20] *Matharu v. Matharu* above n.15. It is difficult to accept this as a detriment, not least because the proceedings could have been recommenced at any time. See Welstead above n.8 at 64.

and home to move closer to *LO*,[21] and personal services provided to
LO and his family. In *Gillett v. Holt* the Court of Appeal seemed to
consider generally how *C*'s actions (and omissions) over a long
period of time were influenced by his relationship with *LO*.[22] The
extent to which personal services may constitute a detriment is
particularly controversial. In *Greasley v. Cooke*[23] *C* had initially moved
into the house which was the subject of her claim as a paid maid, to
care for the family of a widower. She had subsequently stopped
receiving a wage and had cohabited with one of the widower's (adult)
children. Detriment was found in the care she had provided for the
children, one of whom was mentally ill, and consequently, in giving
up the possibility of a career outside the home.[24] Similarly, in *Re
Basham* acts which cumulatively established detriment included the
care *C* and her husband had provided for *C*'s stepfather and the fact
the couple had refrained from moving away for new employment.
Despite these decisions, it is unlikely that care provided in the
context of a familial or on-going emotional relationship will be
accepted as detriment. In *Re Basham* Edward Nugee Q.C. noted that
there was no blood relationship between *C* and *LO*.[25] Further, *C*'s
acts were considered to go beyond those expected through natural
love and affection. In any event, it was clear that, "there was no great
love and affection between [*C*'s] husband and the deceased, and that
he was only willing to pay for meals that [*C*] provided for the
deceased and to work as he did in the garden of the cottage because
of the expectation that the deceased's estate would in due course pass
to [*C*]".[26] In *Coombes v. Smith*[27] *C* argued she had acted to her
detriment by, *inter alia*, bearing *LO*'s child, caring for the child,
looking after the house he had provided and refraining from seeking
employment. Jonathan Parker Q.C. considered, *obiter*, that no detriment was established. *C* had acted, "as occupier of the property, as
the defendant's mistress, and as [their child's] mother, in the context
of a continuing relationship with the defendant".[28] *C*'s omission to
seek employment was considered to be a benefit, rather than a

---

[21] *Jones (A.E.) v. Jones (F.W.)* [1977] 1 W.L.R. 438.
[22] See the discussion of detriment by the court above n.38 at 307–311.
[23] See above n.64.
[24] See above n.64 at 1312.
[25] See above n.25 at 1505.
[26] See above n.25 at 1505–1506.
[27] See above n.21.
[28] See above n.21 at 820.

detriment, as *LO* had been content to support her.[29] However, the court has on occasion indicated a broader approach to detriment which suggests that even services provided in the context of a relationship may be sufficient. In *Wayling v. Jones*, services provided by *C* to his homosexual partner as, "companion and chauffeur"[30] in the context of their on-going relationship were considered a detriment. However that case, as was seen in Chapter 6, may be explicable on the basis of the courts' apparent tendency to assess detriment by reference to gender expectations.[31] Further, *C* had, in addition, provided detriment outside the domestic sphere by assisting *LO* in his business ventures.

4. THE ROLE OF UNCONSCIONABILITY[32]

The modern doctrine of estoppel is considered to be founded on the need to prevent unconscionability.[33] In *Taylors Fashions* Oliver J. suggested the authorities support, "a much wider equitable jurisdiction [than that contended by the defendants] to interfere in cases where the assertion of strict legal rights is found by the court to be unconscionable".[34] Applying this approach, he considered the question for the court was, "whether, in all the circumstances of the case, it was unconscionable for the defendants to seek to deny that which, at the material time, everybody shared".[35] On a number of occasions the courts have emphasised that there is no jurisdiction to intervene to prevent *LO* asserting his legal rights unless it would be unconscionable for him to do so. In *Crabb v. Arun D.C.* for example, Scarman L.J. explained: "The court therefore cannot find an equity established unless it is prepared to go as far as to say that it would be unconscionable and unjust to allow the defendants to set up their undoubted rights against the claim being made by the plaintiff".[36]

---

[29] See above n.21 at 820–821.
[30] See above n.35 at 171.
[31] Chapter 6 Part III 1(b).
[32] Some of the ideas expressed in this part were first presented by the author as a paper at the International Workshop on Estoppel, August 23–25, 1999, Universitiy Malaya.
[33] See, *e.g.* Margaret Halliwell, "Estoppel: Unconscionability as a Cause of Action" (1994) 14 L.S. 15.
[34] See above n.5 at 147.
[35] See above n.5 at 155.
[36] See above n.48 at 195. See also, *e.g. Inwards v. Baker* above, n.60 at 35; *Ives v. High* above n.5 at 394–395; *Taylor v. Dickens* above n.37 at 821.

However, the precise role of unconscionability remains uncertain. There are at least three different roles that could be attributed to the requirement. These different roles will now be considered and it will be submitted that unconscionability should be seen as an over-arching requirement to a claim.[37]

The first, and broadest possible role for unconscionability, is that it establishes an estoppel independently from the need to demonstrate an assurance and detrimental reliance.[38] Although this approach has received academic support,[39] the prevailing judicial opinion is against it. In *Taylor v. Dickens*[40] an argument by *C* that there is a wide equitable jurisdiction for the court to intervene where it would be unconscionable for legal rights to be asserted was treated by Judge Weeks with "undisguised hostility".[41] He considered that if such a jurisdiction existed, "one might as well. . . issue every civil judge with a portable palm tree".[42]

Secondly, in *Sledmore v. Dalby*[43] the Court of Appeal seemed to treat estoppel as arising without considering whether it was uncon-scionable for *LO* to assert her legal rights. Instead, unconscionability was taken into account in the context of ascertaining the appropriate remedy. This suggests that unconscionability is not in fact a consid-eration in establishing a claim to estoppel, but only in determining the appropriate remedy once a claim has been established. However this approach runs contrary to the general statement in *Crabb* that an estoppel cannot be established unless it is unconscionable for legal rights to be asserted.[44] Patrick Milne has argued that in *Sledmore* the

---

[37] Unconscionability is used in the context of estoppel to create rights. This is conceptually different to another context in which the concept is used; to vitiate an existing contractual agreement. The use of unconscionability in the latter context is discussed by Nicholas Bamforth, "Unconscionability as a Vitiating Factor" [1995] L.M.C.L.Q. 538, who, at 542, acknowledges that unconscionability serves a different function in the two contexts. However, the possible roles for unconscionability discussed here in relation to estoppel do mirror some of the possibilities discussed by Bamforth.

[38] *cf.* Bamforth's first sense in which unconscionability is applied above n.37 at 539–540. This is the role Bamforth attributes the concept in the context of vitiating an existing contract.

[39] Thompson above n.38; Halliwell above n.33.

[40] See above n.37.

[41] Thompson above n.38 at 213.

[42] See above n.37 at 50.

[43] See above at n.1.

[44] See above n.36 and text.

absence of unconscionability should have been used to prevent the estoppel arising.[45]

The third, and it is submitted the correct role for unconscionability, is that it is an over-arching requirement. It may be accurate to describe it as a fourth element to a claim, to be established in addition to an assurance and detrimental reliance.[46] However, it is over-arching because it also permeates the other three elements. The basis of attributing this role to unconscionability is the judgment in *Gillett v. Holt*.[47] There, the Court of Appeal emphasised the need in proprietary estoppel claims to consider issues "in the round".[48] To divide a claim into specific requirements is convenient, but it is also essential to take a holistic approach and to make an overall assessment of the claim. Hence, for example, an inquiry whether a statement by *LO* constitutes an assurance may be linked to whether it would be unconscionable for *LO* to renege on the statement. However, in assessing unconscionability, the court may also take into account factors that are not directly concerned with establishing an assurance or detrimental reliance. Wilken and Villiers suggest that once those three elements are established, "the court will take into account 'all the circumstances of the case' to ascertain whether it would be unconscionable to deny the claimant a remedy".[49] In *Gillett v. Holt*, at first instance, Carnwath J. related unconscionability to *LO*'s knowledge. He suggested that, "normally it is the promisor's knowledge of the detriment being suffered in reliance on his promise which makes it 'unconscionable' for him to go back on it".[50]

Accepting unconscionability as an over-arching requirement does not mean that it will be explicitly addressed in every case. In *Crabb*, Scarman L.J. said that to determine whether it would be unconscionable for *LO* to assert his rights required a consideration of Fry J.'s probanda.[51] By reference to this, Patrick Milne suggests that satisfaction of the probanda, "not only establishes that there has been detrimental reliance on a belief encouraged by a person with an

---

[45] Patrick Milne, "Proprietary Estoppel and the Element of Unconscionable Conduct" [1997] C.L.J. 34 at 36.

[46] *cf.* Bamforth's third sense in which unconscionability is applied above n.37 at 540–541.

[47] See above n.38.

[48] See above n.38 at 301.

[49] See above n.20, p. 244 (footnote omitted).

[50] [1998] 3 All E.R. 917 at 929.

[51] See above n.48 at 195.

inconsistent legal right, it also proves that the assertion of the legal right involved would be unconscionable".[52] In contrast he considers that when the *Taylors Fashions* approach is applied, unconscionability is expressly an issue.[53] However, the cases do not fit neatly within this distinction. For example, unconscionability was not discussed in *Re Basham*,[54] although the court's approach broadly corresponds with *Taylors Fashions* and, further, the judge noted that the probanda were not satisfied.[55] The better view may be that, regardless of the approach adopted, unless unconscionability is expressly discussed it is implicit that the court considered it unconscionable for *LO* to renege on the assurance. This is the basis upon which the judgment in *Re Basham* has been treated.[56]

III. Nature of the inchoate equity

Once the elements of a claim to estoppel are established, *C* can prevent *LO* from asserting his rights. Proprietary estoppel can be used as a sword as well as a shield[57] and therefore the estoppel claimant can invoke the estoppel in court either offensively or defensively. The court will then decide on the appropriate remedy to satisfy the estoppel. In the transitional period between the estoppel arising and the award of a remedy by a court, *C* has an inchoate equity. This equity arises, at the latest, from the date it becomes unconscionable for *LO* to renege on the assurance.[58] In this part of the chapter the nature of this inchoate equity is discussed. The issue to be addressed is whether the equity is a personal interest, enforceable only by *C* against *LO*; or is proprietary, enforceable against a subsequent purchaser of *LO*'s title.

The inchoate equity does not seem fully to comply with Lord Wilberforce's classic definition of proprietary rights as being, "definable, identifiable by third parties, capable in its nature of assumption

---

[52] Patrick Milne, "Proprietary Estoppel in a Procrustean Bed" (1995) 58 M.L.R. 412 at 412–413.

[53] *ibid.*

[54] See above n.25.

[55] See above n.25 at 1508.

[56] *Gillett v. Holt* (at first instance) above n.50 at 928. The Court of Appeal, above n.38 at 302 noted that *Re Basham* had been cited twice in that court without its correctness being challenged.

[57] *Crabb v. Arun D.C.* above n.48.

[58] *Lim v. Ang* [1992] 1 W.L.R. 113 at 118.

by third parties, and have some degree of permanence or stability".[59] The equity is transitional, in so far as it exists only until the grant of a remedy by the court. In this respect, it may be said to lack the requirements of "permanence and stability". It is ill-defined, as the remedy awarded to satisfy the equity remains uncertain until determined by the court. The absence of these characteristics may make the inchoate equity incapable in its nature of binding third parties. For *C* to inform a purchaser that he or she has such an equity, "gives notice of a right so imprecise, so incapable of definition, so impossible of measurement in legal phraseology or terms of money"[60] that the consequence of recognising the inchoate equity as proprietary would almost certainly be to paralyse any dealings with the land. Notwithstanding, there is a trend towards recognising the equity as enjoying some degree of proprietary status.[61] The Law Commission has provisionally recommended that the equity be treated as proprietary for the purposes of registered conveyancing.[62] The equity has in fact been enforced against persons other than the original *LO*. However, as will now be seen, it is unclear from the authorities whether such enforcement has been based on acceptance of the equity as proprietary.

In *Inwards v. Baker*,[63] the inchoate equity was held to bind *LO*'s successors in title who had inherited the land under his will. Lord Denning M.R. suggested, *obiter*, that "any purchaser who took with notice would clearly be bound by the equity".[64] *Inwards* was applied in *Jones (A.E.) v. Jones (F.W.)*.[65] The equity has also been enforced against an *inter vivos* donee. In *Voyce v. Voyce*[66] the Court of Appeal considered a donee to be in no better position than *LO*.[67] Dillon L.J.'s judgment may be seen as indicating, further, that only a purchaser for value without notice would be protected.[68] In *Sledmore v. Dalby*[69] *LO* had assigned land which was subject to an inchoate

---

[59] *National Provincial Bank v. Ainsworth* [1965] A.C. 1175 at 1248.
[60] *Ainsworth* above n.59 at 1234, *per* Lord Upjohn, explaining why the deserted wife's equity should not be considered proprietary.
[61] Mark Powlowski, "Proprietary Estoppel—Satisfying the Equity" (1997) 113 L.Q.R. 232 at 234.
[62] See above n.1 at para. 3.36.
[63] See above n.60.
[64] See above n.60 at 37.
[65] See above n.21.
[66] (1991) 62 P. & C.R. 290.
[67] See above n.66 at 296.
[68] *ibid.*
[69] See above n.1.

equity to his wife. Roch L.J. considered that the wife, the appellant, "was not a purchaser for value nor was she a purchaser without notice of the respondent's equity. Consequently the conveyance [to her] had no effect on the respondent's equity and the freehold acquired by the appellant was subject to it".[70] However, Powlowski notes that the basis upon which the estoppel bound the wife in that case is not entirely clear.[71] He suggests that it is apparent from findings at first instance by the Recorder that the appellant was bound by the equity because she had knowledge of, and had acquiesced in, the assurances of rights made by her husband. Through this, her own conscience was affected by the equity.[72] Aside from donees, the equity was enforced against *LO*'s trustee in bankruptcy in *Re Sharpe*.[73] The court based its reasoning on the estoppel claimant holding an irrevocable licence which gave rise to a constructive trust. This use of the constructive trust was based on authorities subsequently reconsidered in *Ashburn Anstalt v. Arnold*.[74] In light of that case, it is unlikely that the reasoning in *Re Sharpe* could be applied today. However, it will be seen below that it may still be possible on appropriate facts to impose a constructive trust to protect an estoppel claimant.[75]

The enforceability of an inchoate equity against a purchaser for value was considered in *Ives v. High*. There, *C* had agreed with *LO* that the foundation of *LO*'s flats could encroach upon *C*'s land, in return for which *LO* would allow *C* a right of access across the yard of the flats. The flats had subsequently been sold and P, the current owner, sought to deny *C* a right of way. Lord Denning M.R. considered that *C* had an equity which, as it was not registerable as a land charge, bound the purchaser as a purchaser with notice.[76] Both Danckwerts and Winn L.JJ., by reference to *Inwards v. Baker*, considered the purchaser to be bound by *C*'s claim to estoppel. In *Ives*, the purchaser had actual notice of the equity. There is no modern authority which directly addresses the enforcement of the equity against a purchaser with constructive notice.[77] Subsequent

---

[70] See above n.1 at 201.
[71] See above n.61 at 233.
[72] See above n.61 at 234.
[73] [1980] 1 W.L.R. 219.
[74] [1989] Ch. 1.
[75] See below n.87 and text.
[76] See above n.5 at 394–396.
[77] However, the possibility of such enforcement is accepted in pre-1926 authorities. See Simon Baughen, "Estoppels Over Land and Third Parties: An Open Question?" (1994) 14 L.S. 147 at 148–151.

courts have taken divergent views on the effect of *Ives v. High*. In *Lloyds Bank plc v. Carrick* Morritt L.J. suggested that, in the light of *Ives*, it would be difficult to argue against the enforcement of an equity.[78] However, the question of enforcement did not have to be decided and the issue was not discussed. In contrast, in *United Bank of Kuwait plc v. Sahib*,[79] Peter Gibson L.J. considered that *Ives* (together with other cases to which he was referred which did not involve an estoppel) did not come near to establishing the enforceability of an equity against an independent third party whose own conscience was not affected.[80] He considered that a claimant to estoppel has no proprietary right in the land unless and until the court declares what right the claimant has.[81]

In light of these authorities, the enforceability of an inchoate equity against purchasers remains uncertain. There are no strong authorities in favour of enforcement. *Inwards v. Baker*, which was relied upon in *Ives*, did not itself involve a purchaser. In *Ives*, estoppel was discussed together with the principle of benefit and burden and the latter principle may be a more satisfactory explanation of the case.[82] The absence of enforceability against purchasers would seem to confirm that the inchoate equity is not a proprietary right. In light of other respects in which the equity falls short of Lord Wilberforce's criteria,[83] the nature of the inchoate equity is so uncertain that categorization as proprietary seems inappropriate. It may be necessary, or at least more desirable, to be able to explain those cases in which the equity has been enforced against third parties in a manner which does not require the equity to be classified as a proprietary right.

One possibility is that the equity, although not a fully-fledged proprietary interest, is within the category of "mere equities". Mere equities, although not capable themselves of binding purchasers, may

---

[78] See above n.15 at 642.

[79] [1996] 3 W.L.R. 372.

[80] See above n.79 at 386.

[81] *ibid.* See also *Birmingham Midshires Mortgage Services Ltd v. Sabherwal*, judgment December 17, 1999. Although the proprietary status of an estoppel is not expressly discussed, Martin Dixon suggests that in its rejection of one of the arguments in the case the judgment, "supports the view that 'estoppels' are not rights in themselves, but merely a means of gaining rights": "Overreaching and the Trusts of Land and Appointment of Trustees Act 1996" [2000] Conv. 267 at 273.

[82] *cf. Sahib* above n.79 at 386. The principle of benefit and burden as applied in the case is discussed in Chapter 8, Part IV.

[83] See above n.59 and text.

do so if ancillary to or dependent upon an equitable interest.[84] Simon Baughen suggests the inchoate equity may be seen as ancillary to whatever interest the court grants the estoppel claimant.[85] Hence, if a court awards the claimant a proprietary right, then the claimant's inchoate equity could (retrospectively) bind purchasers. The difficulty with this solution is that the remedy awarded dates from the court's judgment. There is a logical difficulty in treating the inchoate equity as "ancillary" to an interest granted subsequent to the acquisition of the equity. Notwithstanding the artificiality of the analysis, it is supported by Wilken and Villiers as the most logical way to explain why the inchoate equity can bind third parties despite its ill-defined and uncertain nature.[86]

A further possibility, where it would constitute a form of fraud for the purchaser to deny the inchoate equity, would be to impose a constructive trust under the doctrine explained in *Ashburn Anstalt v. Arnold*.[87] The purchaser would then be required to hold the land on trust for the estoppel claimant. The circumstances in which such a constructive trust may be imposed are considered in Chapter 4. However, as was seen in that chapter, it remains uncertain whether a trust could be imposed to protect personal rights.[88] If it is not possible to do so and if, as has been argued, the inchoate equity is not itself proprietary, *Ashburn* could not be applied. In any event, the rule is restricted in its application to situations where land is transferred "subject to" (in this context) the estoppel claimant's rights.

To conclude, it is unlikely that the inchoate equity is proprietary.[89] Its enforcement, in some cases, against third parties may be explained by classifying the equity as a "mere equity" or by the imposition of a constructive trust. If the inchoate equity is a mere equity, it remains to consider how enforcement against third parties will be determined

---

[84] *National Provincial Bank v. Ainsworth* above n.59 at 1234.

[85] See above n.77 at 154.

[86] See above n.20, p. 298.

[87] See above n.74. See Patricia Critchley, "A Via Media for Estoppel and Third Parties" [1998] Conv. 502.

[88] Chapter 4, Part IV.

[89] The personal status of the inchoate equity has been assumed in the context of a debate on the relationship between estoppel and constructive trusts. See Patricia Ferguson, "Constructive Trusts—A Note of Caution" (1993) 109 L.Q.R. 114 at 126–127; David Hayton, "Constructive Trusts of Homes—A Bold Approach" (1993) 109 L.Q.R. 485 at 487–488; Lord Browne-Wilkinson, "Constructive Trusts and Unjust Enrichment" (1996) 10 T.L.I. 98 at 100.

in the context of unregistered and registered conveyancing.[90] In unregistered land, the enforceability of a claim to estoppel is governed by the doctrine of notice.[91] As a mere equity, however, the purchaser of an equitable interest without notice would also be protected.[92] In registered land, the claim may be protected as a minor interest or, in the absence of such protection, may be an overriding interest under section 70(1)(g) of the Land Registration Act 1925 if the claimant is in actual occupation.[93]

IV. Granting a remedy to satisfy the estoppel

The remedy awarded to the estoppel claimant is at the courts' discretion.[94] A variety of remedies have been awarded, including: the grant of *LO*'s legal title;[95] a right to reside for as long as *C* wishes,[96] or for life,[97] or until a loan is repaid[98] and monetary compensation.[99] In *Matharu v. Matharu*[1] the court did not grant *C* any rights but merely enabled her to use her estoppel to resist a claim for possession. The decision has been criticised as it left uncertain the nature of *C*'s rights and left her in a continuing relationship with *LO*, her father-in-law, with whom relations were strained.[2] In light of the

---

[90] For discussion of this, see Graham Battersby, "Informal Transactions in Land, Estoppel and Registration" (1995) 58 M.L.R. 637 at 640–643; T. Bailey, "Estoppel and Registration of Title" [1983] Conv. 99.

[91] *Ives v. High* above n.5.

[92] Battersby above n.90 at 642.

[93] Wilken and Villiers above n.20, p. 296 suggest that in *Lloyds Bank plc v. Rosset* [1991] 1 A.C. 107 and *Abbey National Building Society v. Cann* [1991] 1 A.C. 56 the House of Lords assumed, *sub silentio*, that a claim to estoppel was capable of binding under the Land Registration Act 1925, s.70(1)(g). The Law Commission has approved protecting the equity as a minor or overriding interest, though in the context of recommending the equity is recognised as an interest in registered land: see above n.1 at paras 3.33–3.36.

[94] See, *e.g.* Lord Denning M.R.'s statements of the courts' discretion in *Crabb v. Arun D.C.* above n.48 at 189 and *Greasley v. Cooke* above n.64 at 1312; *Griffith v. Williams* [1978] 2 E.G.L.R. 121 at 122, *per* Goff L.J. For a detailed discussion of the meaning of discretion in this context see Simon Gardner, "The Remedial Discretion in Proprietary Estoppel" (1999) 115 L.Q.R. 438.

[95] *Pascoe v. Turner* above n.24.

[96] *Greasley v. Cooke* above n.64.

[97] *Inwards v. Baker* above n.60.

[98] *Re Sharpe* above n.73.

[99] *Dodsworth v. Dodsworth* (1973) 228 E.G. 1115.

[1] See above n.15.

[2] See Walstead above n.8 at 66–67. Contrast *Pascoe v. Turner* above n.24 and *Gillett v Holt* above n.38, in which the courts were sensitive to the need to provide the parties with a "clean break" see the discussion below, n.22 and text.

155

range of remedies available, two issues arise for discussion. First, the purpose of the remedy, or the considerations underlying the courts' exercise of remedial discretion. Secondly, the status of the remedy: in what circumstances is a proprietary right acquired?

1. THE PURPOSE OF THE REMEDY

It may be considered undesirable for the court's remedial discretion to be completely unfettered. Clearly, the principles used to guide the courts' exercise of discretion should reflect the purpose of estoppel.[3] Two alternative views of how the court should determine the appropriate remedy have been advanced. Each offers a different view of the purpose of estoppel. One view is that estoppel should do no more than prevent harm being suffered by C. On this approach, the appropriate remedy is one that reflects C's reliance loss.[4] The alternative view is that the remedy should fulfil C's expectations. This necessarily implies that the purpose of estoppel is to give effect to the assurance of rights.[5] The opposing views may suggest a different outcome to the same case, as is illustrated by *Pascoe v. Turner*.[6] There, as has been seen, C incurred expenditure on LO's land following an assurance that the house was hers. Following the reliance loss approach, the most appropriate remedy may have been to award C financial compensation to the extent of her expenditure. On the facts, however, the court fulfilled C's expectations by requiring LO to convey his legal title to her.

Neither reliance loss nor fulfilment of expectations offers a satisfactory explanation for the remedy awarded in all claims to estoppel. A reliance based approach may be reflected in Scarman L.J.'s suggestion that the court should confer upon C the, "minimum equity to do justice".[7] However Scarman L.J. did not necessarily intend such an interpretation.[8] The approach does not seem consistent with the remedy in *Pascoe v. Turner*.[9] Further, restitution may be

---

[3] Andrew Robertson, "Reliance and Expectation in Estoppel Remedies" (1998) 18 L.S. 360 at 362.

[4] This approach is supported by, *e.g.* Robertson above n.3. Wilken and Villiers above n.20, p. 281 suggest the approach has "significant support".

[5] Robertson above n.3 at 362.

[6] See above n.24.

[7] See *Crabb v. Arun D.C.* above n.48 at 198.

[8] Elizabeth Cooke, "Estoppel and the Protection of Expectations" (1997) 17 L.S. 258 at 265–266.

[9] However, see Robertson above n.3 at 367. He suggests that even on a reliance loss approach this result may in fact have been achieved.

considered the more appropriate mechanism for claimants who wish to recover their reliance loss. It has been suggested that adopting a reliance loss theory as the usual response to estoppel may create inconsistencies between restitution and estoppel.[10] It would result in the courts awarding restitution in some cases on the basis of an express claim and in others on the basis of a claim to estoppel.[11] Cooke argues that with few exceptions the courts have in fact consistently protected *C*'s expectations.[12] Stephen Moriarty indicates that, "[f]or the most part. . . a remedy will be selected which best gives effect to what the person was told he could have".[13] The primary difficulty with accepting the expectation approach is that the "policy of informality"[14] it reflects would enable estoppel routinely to be used to circumvent formality requirements for the grant of a proprietary right. It seems unlikely that such a *carte blanche* for informal creation could be accepted. It would, in particular, seem to obviate the requirement of a written contract to dispose of an interest in land.[15] A general approach based on expectations would also seem to replace the courts' remedial discretion with a decision as to how to give effect to the promise.[16] A practical difficulty with the approach is that, as has been seen, the assurance of rights need not be precise.[17] It may therefore be far from clear what *C* expected.

The better view, it is submitted, is that while the court looks towards *C*'s expectation as the maximum that may be awarded[18] that expectation is one of a number of factors taken into account in determining the appropriate remedy.[19] M.P. Thompson has argued

---

[10] Cooke above n.8 at 281–282. Her argument is disputed by Robertson above n.3 at 364.

[11] Cooke above n.8 at 281–282.

[12] Cooke above n.8. She considers at 258–259, that while the protection of expectations is not automatic, it is the courts' "preference and the norm".

[13] Stephen Moriarty, "Licences and Land Law: Legal Principles and Public Policies" (1984) 100 L.Q.R. 376 at 388.

[14] Moriarty above n.13 at 398.

[15] Graham Battersby, "Contractual and Estoppel Licences as Proprietary Interests in Land" [1991] Conv. 36 at 38. The relationship between estoppel and contractual formalities is discussed in Chapter 5, Part III 2.

[16] *cf.* Smith, p. 167. Gardner argues above n.94 at 443 that this exercise does not involve the exercise of a discretion.

[17] See above Part II 1.(a).

[18] *Carrick* above n.15 at 641.

[19] For an alternative view, see Gardner above n.94 at 452–460 and 466. He suggests that the current approach of the courts is to award the expectation unless it is impracticable to do so, or on the occurrence of a number of specific factors (*e.g.* misconduct by either party). In the latter case, Gardner suggests that the remedy may exceed the expectation.

that inequitable conduct by either party is "one factor amongst many" the court may consider.[20] In *Crabb v. Arun D.C.*, in awarding C a right of way without requiring him to compensate LO, the court noted that LO's actions had rendered C's land landlocked for six years.[21] In *Pascoe v. Turner* it was clear from LO's conduct that he would use any means available to evict C. In light of this, in deciding to award C legal title in preference to a licence, Cumming-Bruce L.J., giving the judgment of the court, referred to the need to protect C "against the future manifestations of [LO's] ruthlessness".[22] Similarly, in *Gillett v. Holt* the remedy was influenced by a desire to free C from LO's Company (in which C and his wife were shareholders) and from LO personally. In *Pascoe v. Turner*, the court also took into account that although C's detriment was fairly small, it represented a significant proportion of her wealth.[23] When the assurance of rights was made, C was a widow in her 50's and had arranged her affairs on the basis that the house and its contents were hers. In *Sledmore v. Dalby* the court went further and balanced the competing needs and resources of C and LO to determine that C's equity was extinguished.[24] The decision has been criticised by J.E. Adams, who argues that events which occur after the equity has arisen should not affect the remedy.[25] In particular, he notes that the effect of the decision is to create a "floating equity", the appropriate remedy for which would have been different dependent upon the time the question of remedying the estoppel was considered.[26] The case has been seen as indicating the courts' acceptance of a reliance loss approach to remedies.[27] It does, at least, indicate that the "proportionality" of the remedy is one factor for the courts' consideration.[28]

2. The Status of the Remedy: Personal or Proprietary?

Once the court has granted a remedy, the nature of C's rights is dependent upon the orthodox classification of the remedy awarded.

---

[20] M.P. Thompson, "Estoppel and Clean Hands" [1986] Conv. 406 at 414.

[21] See above n.48 at 189, *per* Lord Denning M.R., at 192, *per* Lawton L.J. and at 199, *per* Scarman L.J.

[22] See above n.24 at 438–439.

[23] See above n.24 at 438.

[24] See above n.1 at 204–205.

[25] J.E. Adams, "Is Equitable Estoppel a Wasting Asset?" [1997] Conv. 458 at 463. See also Powlowski above n.61 at 235–236.

[26] See above n.25 at 463.

[27] Wilken and Villiers above n.20, p. 284; Powlowski above n.61 at 236–237.

[28] Powlowski above n.61 at 236.

Hence, only when the court awards *C* a proprietary right is a proprietary right acquired. If a personal right is awarded, then the right does not obtain any special status merely through being derived from the estoppel. At the stage of the grant of a remedy, estoppel is a means by which orthodox proprietary rights may be acquired and is not a source for the acquisition of proprietary rights *sui generis*.

For a period of time it seemed in fact that estoppel could generate new types of proprietary rights. This was a result of cases, in particular *Inwards v. Baker* and *Ives v. High*, in which licensees who had established an estoppel were able to enforce their interest against third parties. While these cases arose in the context of enforcing an inchoate equity, they were considered to indicate the development of a species of licence, the "estoppel licence" which was a proprietary right in land. Such cases may be explained on the basis that at the time they were decided, the status of another type of licence, the contractual licence, was uncertain.[29] Following *Ashburn Anstalt v. Arnold*,[30] which confirmed that contractual licences are personal interests, it is considered that a licence derived from an estoppel could not bind a third party.[31]

Where a proprietary right is awarded, the enforcement of that right against third parties is dependent upon the usual conveyancing principles applicable to that type of right.[32] The court may usually require *LO* formally to grant the right awarded. Until the right is granted, in unregistered land the court's order should be entered on the register of writs and orders affecting land maintained under section 6 of the Land Charges Act 1972. In registered land, the benefit of the court order is a minor interest, or may be protected as an overriding interest under section 70(1)(g) of the Land Registration Act 1925 where *C* is in actual occupation.[33]

---

[29] Although see P.N. Todd, "Estoppel Licences and Third Party Rights" [1981] Conv. 347 at 353. He suggests it was because of indications that the contractual licence was personal that the courts began to use an estoppel reasoning for the enforcement of licences.

[30] See above n.74.

[31] Battersby above n.15 at 39–47. The relationship between estoppel and contractual licences is considered below Part V 1.

[32] Battersby above n.90 at 640–643; T. Bailey, "Estoppel and Registration of Title" [1983] Conv. 99.

[33] Battersby above n.90 at 643.

V.   Distinguishing estoppel from other principles

1. ESTOPPEL, CONTRACTUAL LICENCES AND CONSTRUCTIVE TRUSTS

The elements of a claim to estoppel are closely related to circumstances in which the courts may hold that a contractual licence (based
on offer, acceptance and consideration) or constructive trust (of the
type discussed in Chapter 6, requiring an agreement and detrimental
reliance) has been created. Some factual situations could be open to
any of these three interpretations. For example, a claimant in
occupation may have a licence, a beneficial interest or an inchoate
equity. In other situations, the overlap is more likely to arise between
two of the principles. For example, a claim to a right of way may
involve a contractual licence or an estoppel but is unlikely to give rise
to a constructive trust.[34] There are significant practical differences
between the three principles, as a result of which the choice of which
to apply may be crucial. It is clear since *Ashburn Anstalt v. Arnold*[35] that
an interpretation of *C*'s claim as giving rise to a contractual licence
confers a personal interest. Although both constructive trust and
estoppel may create proprietary rights, the time at which the rights
arise, and their nature, differ. This, in turn, can have consequences
for the enforcement of the right against third parties. The constructive trust invariably confers upon *C* a beneficial interest arising
at the time the elements of a claim were fulfilled. In contrast, as has
been seen,[36] once the elements of a claim to estoppel are fulfilled, *C*
has only an inchoate equity which, it has been argued, is not
proprietary. In an estoppel claim, *C* will not invariably acquire a
proprietary right and, where such a right is awarded by the court, it
exists only from the date of the court's order.

The close relationship between contractual licence and estoppel
was the focus of debate when it seemed possible that although
contractual licences were personal, there was a species of "estoppel
licence" which was proprietary. Given the similarities in the circumstances giving rise to licences and estoppels, it was considered
undesirable to afford each a different status.[37] As has been seen,[38] the

---

[34] However, contrast Smith, p. 180.
[35] See above n.74.
[36] See above Part III.
[37] The relationship between licences and estoppel is discussed by Moriarty, above n.13;
Adrian Briggs, "Licences: Back to Basics" [1981] Conv. 212; P.N. Todd above n.29;
Jonathan Hill, "Leases, Licences and Third Parties" (1988) 51 M.L.R. 226.
[38] See above n.31 and text.

concept of an "estoppel licence" binding third parties was probably misconceived. Notwithstanding, the ability to distinguish between licences and estoppels remains important. The relationship between the elements of a claim to estoppel and to a constructive trust has led to suggestions, both academic[39] and judicial,[40] that those two principles are, at least in some contexts, now indistinguishable.

It is submitted that the defining characteristic of estoppel, and the element of a claim which distinguishes it both from contractual licences and constructive trusts, is that it is based on a *unilateral* assurance of rights. In relation to contractual licences, this distinction is reflected in two respects. First, a licence derived from a contract is necessarily founded on consensus. As Briggs notes: "The essence of a contract is that one person makes an offer which another accepts so that a set of terms is agreed to create and govern a consensual legal relationship".[41] Secondly, the need for consideration to support the contract differs from the detrimental reliance necessary for an estoppel as consideration must be requested.[42]

The constructive trust, as was seen in Chapter 6, is based on an agreement to share beneficial ownership. A unilateral assurance could not give rise to a constructive trust of the type discussed in that chapter. Smith notes that the presence or absence of mutuality may identify the "paradigm" constructive trust and estoppel cases.[43] It is increasingly being accepted that there is an area of overlap between

---

[39] David Hayton, "Equitable Rights of Cohabitees" [1990] Conv. 270. His view was doubted by Ferguson above n.89. Hayton responded above n.89.

[40] *Grant v. Edwards* [1986] Ch. 638 at 656–657, *per* Browne-Wilkinson L.J. Although his consideration of the relationship between the principles was guarded, he subsequently noted extra-judicially above n.89 at 100 that, "in any case where the elements necessary to found a . . . constructive trust are present so are the elements necessary to found a proprietary estoppel". See also *Mollo v. Mollo*, judgment October 8, 1999. Hunter Q.C., giving judgment, commented: "The authorities indicate that common-intention constructive trust and proprietary estoppel are similar doctrines which are often indistinguishable in practice". Further, *Carrick* above n.15 at 640 where Morritt L.J. commented that it is a "matter of some doubt" whether the two principles differ.

[41] See above n.37 at 215.

[42] Moriarty above n.13 at 393. However, he argued that it is "absurd" to use this as the basis for distinguishing personal and proprietary rights.

[43] Smith, p. 179. See also Hayton above n.39 at 271. He acknowledges the bilateral nature of a constructive trust and unilateral nature of estoppel as part of the conventional distinction.

the constructive trust and proprietary estoppel. In *Yaxley v. Gotts*,[44] Robert Walker L.J. considered, that "in the area of a joint enterprise for the acquisition of land. . . the two concepts coincide".[45] It is submitted that given the practical differences between the two concepts, in particular the differences in the right acquired by the claimant, it is desirable for a strict distinction to be maintained. There is a danger that a liberal application of estoppel will be used as a substitute for dealing with underlying shortcomings. In the context of a joint enterprise for the acquisition of land, the merging of estoppel and constructive trusts may result from the absence of a fully considered and coherent method for regulating the rights of homesharers; an issue currently being addressed by the Law Commission.[46] In light of this deficit, estoppel has come to be seen as a less artificial and more flexible means of dealing with disputes than the constructive trust. As estoppel has the potential to apply to a wide range of circumstances, there is a danger that a concession made to the application of the principle in the context of the joint application of land will produce undesirable results in another context. This is particularly the case where, for example, a broad approach to estoppel in a familial context is subsequently applied in a commercial context. It is acknowledged that the distinction between a unilateral assurance and an agreement may be difficult to draw. The task is made more difficult by the broad interpretation of "agreement" adopted in the constructive trust context.[47] However, drawing a working distinction between constructive trusts and estoppel may be no more difficult than distinguishing a licence from an estoppel. Referring to the latter distinction, Briggs commented, "although it may be felt hard to draw

---

[44] [1999] 3 W.L.R. 1217. In *Birmingham Midshires Mortgage Services Ltd v. Sabherwal*, above n.81 the Court of Appeal considered that in the context of the family home, judicial comments about the relationship between estoppel and constructive trusts applied equally to resulting trusts. It is submitted that it is incorrect to draw a parallel between the two trust types, given the restitutionary basis of the resulting trust (discussed in Chapter 6 Part II). The relationship between estoppel and restitution is discussed below, Part V 2.

[45] See above n.44 at 1227. He also acknowledged that there are circumstances in which an estoppel can be claimed where a constructive trust could not be established.

[46] Noted in Law Com. No. 239, Thirtieth Annual Report, paras 6.7–6.12.

[47] See Chapter 6, Part III 1 (a). Conversely, it may be argued that circumstances in which the court has apparently strained to find an agreement may be more appropriately seen as involving an assurance of rights. Drawing a clear distinction between constructive trusts and estoppel would therefore provide an opportunity for a rationalisation of existing case law.

a clear dividing line, clear lines are the stuff of which law is made, and hard cases make good lawyers".[48]

2. ESTOPPEL AND RESTITUTION[49]

Restitution, like estoppel, can be a response to unconscionable conduct.[50] While estoppel prevents a person from reneging on an assurance of rights where it would be unconscionable to do so, restitution provides a response to unjust enrichment. Not every instance of unconscionability reveals an unjust enrichment. For example, as Birks explains,[51] in *Crabb v. Arun D.C.* it was unconscionable for the Council to renege on their assurance of rights even though it had not been enriched by *C*'s detriment. However, there are cases in which a claim to estoppel also establishes that *LO* has been unjustly enriched at *C*'s expense. For example, where *C* acts on an assurance that if he builds a house on *LO*'s land, the land will be given to *C*.[52] *LO* may be estopped from reneging on the assurance as, following *C*'s detrimental reliance, it would be unconscionable for him to do so. However, if *LO* reneges on the assurance, then he may also be considered to be unjustly enriched at *C*'s expense. Whether *C*'s claim is treated as being to an estoppel or to lie in unjust enrichment will have an impact on the remedy awarded. If *C*'s claim lies in unjust enrichment, then he will obtain restitution of the (financial) amount by which *LO* would otherwise be unjustly enriched. If *C*'s claim is to an estoppel, then the remedy lies in the court's discretion. Given this difference in outcome, when should *C* be restricted to restitution?

Birks considers the dividing line lies between acquiescence and encouragement. His view is that restitution is the only appropriate

---

[48] See above n.37 at 216 (footnote omitted).
[49] Some of the ideas expressed in this part were first presented at the Conference referred to above n.32.
[50] While restitution for subtractive unjust enrichment is typically founded on the claimant's vitiated consent, unjust enrichment for undue influence (though *cf.* Birks and N.Y. Chin, "On the Nature of Undue Influence" in *Good Faith and Fault in Contract Law* J. Beatson and D. Friedmann (eds. 1995), Chapter 3) and, more controversially, free acceptance, are concerned with the defendant's unconscionable behaviour. The defendant's unconscionable behaviour also forms the basis of restitution for wrongs (*e.g.* breach of confidence and breach of a fiduciary relationship).
[51] See above n.70 at 292.
[52] *cf. Inwards v. Baker* above n.60.

response to acquiescence. He says: "There is a difference between inducing and not undeceiving".[53] Taken to its conclusion, Birks' approach would require claims to estoppel historically classified as involving a unilateral mistake to be restricted to restitution.[54] However, it is established that acquiescence can generate an assurance of rights in a unilateral mistake case where LO is aware that C is acting in a mistaken belief as to his rights, and fails to inform C.[55] It is submitted that C should be able to claim an estoppel whenever the unconscionability arises in the context of a unilateral assurance of rights and detrimental reliance, regardless of whether C has been induced or merely has not been undeceived. Where estoppel is available, C may choose, notwithstanding, to seek only restitution.[56] However, where unconscionability arises (in the form of an unjust enrichment) in the absence of the other elements to an estoppel, no such choice is available and C's only course of action is to seek restitution. The dividing line may be illustrated by a comparison of the effect of LO's acquiescence in C's unilateral mistake and in C's misprediction (the context in which Birks drew his distinction). A misprediction arises where C, although aware that he has no rights, or only limited rights, builds on LO's land in the hope that rights will be granted. Birks analyses two situations as involving a misprediction.[57] In the first, LO is aware of C's misprediction and acquiesces. In the second, LO actively encourages C's misprediction, by assuring C that rights will be granted.[58] Applying Birks' view, in the first situation, as C is relying on LO's acquiescence, he is restricted to a claim to restitution. In the second, as there is active encouragement, C can claim estoppel. However, the distinction between the two situations can be explained on the basis that only in the second has LO made an assurance of rights. As has been seen,[59] acquiescence generates an assurance only where C is mistaken as to his rights. It is at least doubtful whether acquiescence in C's

---

[53] See above n.70, p. 291.
[54] Since, as has been seen, above Part II 1(b) acquiescence can only give rise to an estoppel in a unilateral mistake case.
[55] *Ramsden v. Dyson* above n.7. In *Taylors Fashions* above n.5 at 152, Oliver J. acknowledged that knowledge of the true position by LO can be a determining factor.
[56] *cf. Hussey v. Palmer* [1972] 1 W.L.R. 1286.
[57] See above n.70, p. 277–279.
[58] Birks above n.70, p. 279, analyses *Inwards v. Baker* above n.60 in this way.
[59] See above Part II 1(b).

misprediction could generate an assurance. Where *LO* acquiesces in *C*'s misprediction, he may be unjustly enriched, but in the absence of an assurance there is no basis upon which he can be estopped from asserting his rights against *C*.

3. DIFFERENT SPECIES OF ESTOPPEL

The species of estoppel discussed in this chapter is generally referred to as proprietary estoppel. This classification, and the relationship between this and other types of estoppel, remains open to debate. Proprietary estoppel has also been referred to as equitable estoppel, although the latter term may also be used jointly or independently to describe promissory estoppel. In *Amalgamated Investment & Property Co Ltd v. Texas Commerce International Bank Ltd*,[60] Robert Goff J. considered proprietary estoppel to be "an amalgam of doubtful utility"[61] difficult to accept as a defined category.

Regardless of how it is classified, the estoppel established when the elements of a claim discussed in this chapter are met differs in important respects from other species of estoppel. It is the only form which can be used offensively as a cause of action and which enables substantively the informal acquisition of rights in land.[62] Two other types of estoppel can, or have been attributed as being able to, confer proprietary rights. The first, estoppel by deed, applies where there has been a formal grant of rights at a time when in fact the grantor did not hold title to the land granted. The estoppel prevents the grantor from denying the grant. If the grantor subsequently acquires title, then the estoppel is "fed" and the defective grant is corrected. Until such time, the grantee acquires an estate or interest by estoppel which binds all except the true owner.[63] Hence, although proprietary rights are acquired, there has in fact been compliance with formalities. The second type of estoppel, estoppel by representation, is an evidential doctrine which prevents a party to litigation denying the truth of facts as represented by them.[64] In *Hopgood v. Brown*[65] estoppel

---

[60] See above n.84.
[61] See above n.84 at 103. See generally his discussion of the classification of estoppels at 103–104.
[62] Wilken and Villiers above n.20, p. 104–108.
[63] The application of this principle in property transactions is discussed by Wilken and Villiers above n.20, pp. 235–242.
[64] The application of this principle in property transactions is discussed by Wilken and Villiers above n.20, pp. 181–183.
[65] [1955] 1 W.L.R. 213.

by representation was apparently used to confer proprietary rights on the claimant. There, the owner of land represented to the defendant that the boundary between their properties would lie where the defendant built a garage. In fact, the position of the garage did not reflect the original boundary. The plaintiff, a subsequent purchaser of the land, was held bound by the representation. Hence it seems that by invoking the estoppel by representation the defendant acquired title to the disputed boundary. Wilken and Villiers[66] argue that the estoppel could do no more than prevent the representor from contradicting the representation. On the basis of earlier authorities, it could not strip the representor of property rights. The correctness of the decision may be accepted, but by analysing the case as in 'fact involving a claim to proprietary estoppel.

VI. Conclusion

In this chapter it has been seen that proprietary rights may be acquired where *LO* has made an assurance of rights and, following *C*'s detrimental reliance, it would be unconscionable to renege on the assurance. Proprietary rights will not be acquired in every instance of estoppel. It has been seen that the inchoate equity generated by the estoppel is not proprietary, although it may in some circumstances be enforceable against a third party to the estoppel. Hence, whether a proprietary right is acquired rests on the discretion of the court in the grant of a remedy.

One final limitation on the application of estoppel should be noted. In *Carrick*[67] the Court of Appeal considered the existence of a valid contact for sale of land precluded the application of estoppel. The court therefore prevented a claimant who had failed to register her contract as a Class C(iv) land charge from claiming rights based on estoppel. The decision illustrates that estoppel is a means of creating rights, not of enforcing existing rights against third parties. The court did not discuss *Ives v. High* in relation to this issue. There, Danckwerts and Winn L.JJ. applied estoppel where a contract was void for non-registration. However, as has been noted, that case may be more readily explained by application of the principle of benefit and burden.[68]

---

[66] See above n.20, pp. 181–183.
[67] See above n.15.
[68] See above n.82 and text.

Chapter 8.

Where a Person has Accepted the Benefit of an Agreement Which has a Corresponding Burden

I. Introduction

The principle discussed in this chapter requires a person who has accepted the benefit of an agreement to comply with a corresponding burden. It is, in essence, a principle based on fairness which reflects such common adages as, "You can't have it both ways" or, "You can't eat your cake and have it too".[1] The factual circumstances giving rise to a claim within this chapter and Chapter 9 (which concerns the principle of non-derogation from grant) differ from other chapters in this book. In other chapters, a person claims a proprietary right because, for example, there has been an agreement or assurance that he has the right. In Chapters 8 and 9, proprietary rights are acquired as a consequence of the fact that a particular right is being enjoyed. In both chapters, the informal acquisition of rights reflects the requirements of common honesty arising from the enjoyment of a right. Chapter 8 concerns the requirements of common honesty of the person enjoying the right. In Chapter 9 attention is directed at the grantor of a right.

The principle of benefit and burden has taken two forms: conditional benefit and burden and the pure principle of benefit and burden. The dividing line between these two forms is uncertain. The House of Lords has rejected what it perceived to be the pure principle but approved a decision which had previously been analysed

---

[1] *Tito v. Waddell (No. 2)* [1977] Ch. 106 at 289, *per* Megarry V.-C.

as within the pure principle.[2] Questions remain as regards the scope and effect of the principle which was accepted by the House of Lords. Judicial and academic response has been mixed.[3] Criticism centres around the uncertain and potentially broad scope of a principle based on benefit and burden. There are two main situations in which the principle is applied, in both of which it acts contrary to established rules.[4] First, where the burden of the agreement to be enforced is not a recognised proprietary right. In particular, the principle has been used as a means for enforcing positive covenants.[5] Secondly where the agreement creates a recognised proprietary right but that right is unenforceable by application of the statutory schemes determining the enforcement of interests on a transfer of title.[6]

In this chapter, the development of the principle of benefit and burden will be considered first, followed by a discussion of the requirements which must be met for its application. It will then be seen that, despite the uncertainties, when the principle is applied it operates to enable the acquisition of a proprietary right, the content of which reflects the burden of the agreement.

II. Development of the principle

The principle of benefit and burden developed in two distinct categories of case in which the courts held that a person who had enjoyed the benefit of an agreement was bound by a burden imposed by the same agreement. In the first category of case the benefit and

---

[2] See the discussion below n.22 and text.

[3] In *Tito* above n.1 at 295 Megarry V.-C. was persuaded to support the principle by the fundamental concept of fairness it represents. Most criticism has been directed against the pure principle. See, in particular, the judgment of Brooking J. (with whose comments O'Bryan and Nicholson JJ. agreed) in *Government Insurance Office (N.S.W.) v. K.A. Reed Services Pty. Ltd* [1988] V.R. 829 (Supreme Court of Victoria). Gray, pp. 1135–1136, though commenting only briefly, seems to express more general doubts about the role of the principle.

[4] See generally the judgment of Brooking J. in *Reed* above n.3 at 831–841. Although directed primarily against the pure principle some of his criticisms, including his discussion (at 834–837) of the impact of the principle on the established law relating to covenants affecting land, are equally relevant to conditional benefits and burdens. The case is discussed by Bruce Ziff, "Positive Covenants Running with Land: A Castaway on Ocean Island?" (1989) 27 Alberta Law Review 354 at 361–364.

[5] See, *e.g. Halsall v. Brizell* [1957] 1 Ch. 169, and *Tito* above n.1.

[6] See, *e.g. E.R. Ives Investment Ltd v. High* [1967] 2 Q.B. 379.

burden were seen as intrinsically linked, to the extent that the agreement was analysed as conferring only a qualified right. The right granted (the benefit) was qualified by the need to comply with the burden. In the second category the courts applied a principle, derived from a rule relating to the construction of deeds, that a person who takes the benefit of an agreement must accept a burden contained in the same agreement.

The first category may be illustrated by two cases concerning the grant of mining rights: *Aspden v. Sedden (No 2)*[7] and *Urban District Council of Westhoughton v. Wigan Coal & Iron Co Ltd*.[8] In both cases, the grant of mining rights was coupled with a requirement that compensation be paid for damage caused to buildings on the mined land. The courts analysed the mining rights granted as qualified by the obligation to pay compensation. In *Aspden v. Sedden*, the parties had entered into an agreement which was construed as conferring a right to mine in such a way as to damage buildings. Bramwell B. referred to this right as being coupled with a "corresponding duty" to compensate and as "subject to" the obligation to compensate.[9] In *Urban District Council of Westhoughton v. Wigan Coal & Iron Co Ltd* Swinfen Eady M.R. explained, "the defendants are not entitled to insist upon their right to occasion subsidence [by mining] while at the same time failing to observe the terms upon which alone that right was granted to them [payment of compensation]".[10] He noted, further, "the defendants do not possess the right which they claimed—namely, to let down the plaintiffs' land and buildings without being under any obligation whatever to the plaintiffs for so doing".[11]

The second category stems from the judgment of Upjohn J. in *Halsall v. Brizell*.[12] There, a number of home-owners had entered a covenant to contribute towards the maintenance of, *inter alia*, roads and sewers which were held on trust for them. The amount of the contribution was to be determined each year at a meeting. Pursuant to a resolution made at a meeting, the defendants were asked to make

---

[7] (1876) 1 Ex. D. 496.
[8] [1919] 1 Ch. 159. This case, together with *Aspden*, is discussed in *Tito* above n.1 at 296–299 and by E.P. Aughterson, "Enforcement of Positive Burdens—A New Viability" [1985] Conv. 12 at 17–20.
[9] See above n.7 at 503. The Court of Appeal dismissed an appeal against his judgment.
[10] See above n.8 at 168.
[11] *ibid.*
[12] See above n.5.

additional payments in relation to a house divided into flats. The defendants successfully challenged this resolution as *ultra vires* the meeting. However, in his judgment, Upjohn J. also considered whether the covenant was enforceable at all against the defendants, who were not original parties to the deed. This part of his judgment, although *obiter*, provides the foundation for this second category. Counsel conceded that a person who takes the benefit of a deed must also accept the burden.[13] Relying on this concession as a statement of general principle,[14] Upjohn J. explained, "the defendants here cannot. . . take advantage of the trusts concerning user of the roads contained in the deed and the other benefits created by it without undertaking the obligations thereunder".[15] Upjohn J.'s reasoning is different from that adopted in the first category of case. He did not construe the covenant as granting only a qualified right to use the roads etc, subject to contributing towards their maintenance. He considered that the defendants were bound to accept the burden of the covenant solely because they enjoyed the benefit it conferred. This difference in reasoning is significant as it provides a much broader scope for the application of a principle based on benefit and burden.

Prior to the decision in *Rhone v. Stephens*[16] these two categories of case were treated as separate forms of the principle of benefit and burden. In *Tito v. Waddell (No. 2)*[17] Megarry V.-C. treated the first category as illustrations of a principle of conditional benefit and burden. He considered that principle to apply where an instrument confers, "only a conditional or qualified right, the condition or qualification being that certain restrictions shall be observed or certain burdens assumed".[18] The second category was described by Megarry V.-C. as the, "pure principle of benefit and burden," distinguished from the first category by the independence of the benefit from the burden.[19] In *Rhone*, Lord Templeman stated the pure principle broadly as providing that, "any party deriving any benefit from a conveyance must accept any burden in the same

---

[13] See above n.5 at 180.
[14] The authority referred to by Counsel does not support Upjohn J.'s general principle: see *Tito* above n.1 at 294–95.
[15] See above n.5 at 183.
[16] [1994] 2 A.C. 310.
[17] See above n.1.
[18] See above n.1 at 290.
[19] *ibid.*

conveyance".[20] On this interpretation, he rejected the pure principle.[21] However, he approved the decision in *Halsall* which he interpreted as an illustration of conditional benefit and burden. He explained: "Conditions can be attached to the exercise of a power in express terms or by implication. *Halsall* was just such a case and I have no difficulty in whole-heartedly agreeing with the decision".[22] Following Lord Templeman's judgment, there is now a single principle of benefit and burden applied by the courts. That principle, which may be referred to as conditional or corresponding benefit and burden, comprises the first category of case previously recognised and Lord Templeman's redefined second category. Applying Lord Templeman's analysis, the difference between the two categories may be explained in terms of express and implied conditions. Where an agreement (within the first category) grants a qualified right the burden may be described as an express condition. The second category is now restricted to agreements in which benefits and burdens which are *prima facie* independent are construed as conditional. The burden of such an agreement may be described as an implied condition. In rejecting what he perceived to be the pure principle, Lord Templeman rejected the application of the principle of benefit and burden where the benefit is neither expressly nor impliedly conditional upon the burden.[23] In light of Lord Templeman's judgment on the scope of the principle, the circumstances in which it may apply can now be discussed.

---

[20] See above n.16 at 322. See also the annotation of *Halsall* by R.E.M. Note (1957) 73 L.Q.R. 154 at 155. He defines the doctrine applied in that case as, "any person who takes a benefit under a deed must submit to the burdens imposed by that deed".

[21] See above n.16 at 322.

[22] *ibid.*

[23] See Nigel P. Gravells, "Enforcement of Positive Covenants Affecting Freehold Land" (1994) 110 L.Q.R. 346 at 349. He suggests that, on one interpretation, Lord Templeman did not reject the pure principle but was instead, "simply reiterating the indisputable proposition that there must be limits to any pure principle". On this view, agreements within the second category could be described as applications of a redefined pure principle. Similarly, the language of pure principle is used by Christine J. Davis, "The Principle of Benefit and Burden" (1998) 57 C.L.J. 522 at 537–544. However, as Gravells acknowledges, ultimately the categorisations and its terminology may not be important. John Snape, "The Burden of Positive Covenants" [1994] Conv. 477 at 481 suggests that the pure principle may still apply outside the context of a conveyance.

III. Requirements of the principle

For the principle of benefit and burden to apply it must first be established that an agreement has been entered which contains a benefit and burden. There is no particular form the agreement must take. In *Halsall* the agreement was contained in a deed while in *E.R. Ives Investment Ltd v. High*[24] the principle was applied to an oral agreement. However, the benefit and burden must be contained in the same agreement. In *Law Debenture Trust Corp plc v. Ural Caspian Oil Corp Ltd*[25] the court rejected an argument that a transfer of shares by shareholders in a number of companies was subject to a burden contained in a separate agreement entered between the transferee and the plaintiff, acting as trustee for the shareholders.[26] Once shown the parties have entered into an agreement two further requirements must be fulfilled. It must be shown that the benefit and burden are conditional (in the manner in which Lord Templeman explained in *Rhone*) and that the person against whom the burden is enforced has enjoyed the benefit.

1. CONDITIONAL BENEFIT AND BURDEN

For this requirement to be fulfilled it must either be shown that the agreement granted a qualified right, (in Lord Templeman's analysis, that the burden is an express condition of the right) or that the burden was an implied condition of the right.

Whether an agreement grants only a qualified right is a question of construction. The courts' interpretation of the agreements in *Aspden v. Sedden* and *Urban District Council of Westhoughton v. Wigan Coal & Iron Co Ltd* as the grant of qualified rights,[27] may be contrasted with *Radstock Co-operative and Industrial Society Ltd v. Norton-Radstock Urban District Council*.[28] There, a council had been granted the right to lay and maintain a sewer in an agreement in which they covenanted to

---

[24] See above n.6.

[25] [1993] 2 All E.R. 355.

[26] *ibid.* at 364–365. The transferee had covenanted to pay to the plaintiff any compensation received in respect of the companies' assets which had been confiscated during the Bolshevik revolution. The transferee had subsequently sold the shares without requiring the purchaser to enter a similar covenant.

[27] See above n.7 and text.

[28] [1968] 1 Ch. 605.

make good any damage. The Court of Appeal held, without a full discussion of the two earlier cases, that the covenant did not qualify the right to lay and maintain the sewer.[29] Agreements are construed as a whole and the mere fact the benefit and burden appear as separate covenants does not prevent the agreement being construed as the grant of a qualified right.[30] However, where the benefit and burden appear separately it may be more satisfactory to treat the case as involving an implied condition.[31]

If an agreement is not construed as the grant of expressly qualified rights, then it must be shown that the burden is an implied condition of the right conferred. This is the basis upon which Lord Templeman approved the decision in *Halsall*. Lord Templeman considered that the agreement in *Rhone* was outside the scope of the principle he approved. Therefore it is necessary to consider how the agreement in *Rhone* differed from that in *Halsall*. In *Rhone*, the agreement in question had been entered into on the conveyance of a cottage. The cottage shared a roof with a house and, prior to the conveyance, the properties had been in common ownership. The agreement had the effect of conferring mutual easements of support, in addition to which the owner of the house undertook to keep in repair the shared roof. Following sales of both properties the House of Lords considered whether the current owner of the house was bound by the obligation to repair the roof. The judgment is concerned primarily with the question whether the burden of a positive covenant may run with the land under the rule in *Tulk v. Moxhay*. Lord Templeman confirmed the exclusion of positive covenants from that rule and rejected an alternative argument based on the principle of benefit and burden. In light of Lord Templeman's judgment, it seems that the difference between *Halsall* and *Rhone* is the "relevance" of the burden to the benefit.[32] Unless the criterion of relevance is satisfied the

---

[29] Harman L.J. *ibid.* at 628 and Russell L.J. at 632, referred to *Westhoughton* without explaining how the case differed. At first instance, Ungoed-Thomas J. noted that the agreement in *Westhoughton* was, "very differently worded": [1967] 1 Ch. 1094 at 1120. He also noted that the Council was not dependent upon the agreement for use of the sewer as, by statute, the Council was vested with fee simple title to the sewer. If the right could be claimed without reference to the agreement, then on that ground the principle of benefit and burden should not be applied: see below n.37 and text.

[30] *Chamber Colliery v. Twyerould* (1893), noted [1915] 1 Ch. 268. See the discussion by Megarry V.-C. in *Tito* above n.1 at 297–298.

[31] *cf.* Aughterson above n.8 at 19.

[32] Lord Templeman said above n.16 at 322: "The condition must be relevant to the exercise of the right".

exercise of the right will not be considered conditional upon acceptance of the burden. Lord Templeman explained that: "In *Halsall v. Brizell* there were reciprocal benefits and burdens enjoyed by the users of the roads and sewers".[33] In *Rhone*, however, Lord Templeman considered that while there were reciprocal benefits and burdens of support the obligation to repair the roof was an "independent provision".[34] The different interpretations of *Halsall* by Lord Templeman and Megarry V.-C.[35] suggest that it is difficult to ascertain the circumstances in which the burden will be considered relevant to the benefit.[36]

2. ENJOYMENT OF THE BENEFIT

The reasoning underlying the principle of benefit and burden is that a person who has enjoyed the benefit of the agreement by exercising the right conferred is bound by the condition subject to which that right was granted. It is implicit in this reasoning that the exercise of the right is attributable to the agreement.[37] In *Thamesmead Town Ltd v. Allotey*[38] the Court of Appeal considered that the fact a benefit had been enjoyed incidentally was insufficient. There, a transfer of land contained no right to use landscaped and communal areas and therefore there could be no obligation to contribute to the maintenance of those areas. Similarly, there would be no basis for the application of the principle if the right could be claimed without reference to the agreement under which the condition is imposed. Therefore the existence of an alternative source of the right should prevent the application of the principle. In *Halsall*, Upjohn J. noted

---

[33] See above n.16 at 322.

[34] *ibid*. Although the requirement of reciprocity was fulfilled, the principle of benefit and burden would not apply to the easements of support because of the absence of choice: see below n.41 and text.

[35] See above n.22 and text.

[36] In *Rhone*, Lord Templeman did not discuss the agreement in *Tito* which required land to be replanted on completion of phosphate mining. While Lord Templeman rejected the principle applied in that case, it may be argued that the facts fall within the narrower principle which he approved. The obligation to replant may be considered as "relevant" to the right to mine as was the obligation to contribute towards maintenance to the right to use the roads etc. in *Halsall*.

[37] The person who has enjoyed the benefit must also have some connection with the agreement. This may extend beyond the original parties and their successors but will exclude "mere strangers": *Tito* above n.1 at 303, *per* Megarry V.-C.

[38] [1998] 37 E.G. 161.

that the defendants had no right to use the roads "apart from the deeds".[39] The only basis upon which the defendants could use the road was by reference to the deed, which imposed the obligation to contribute towards the cost of maintenance. In *Westhoughton*, Swinfen Eady M.R. explained the decision in *Aspden v. Sedden* in similar terms. He noted, "The ground of the decision was that the defendants were trespassers, and wrongdoers unless they could justify under their deed, and they could only do that upon the terms of the deed, paying compensation".[40] It is implicit in this that the defendants had no alternative source of the acquisition of the right.

The mere fact the benefit of an agreement has been enjoyed is insufficient for the application of the principle. There must have been, at least in theory, an opportunity to choose whether to accept the benefit.[41] This element of choice was a further basis upon which Lord Templeman distinguished *Halsall* from *Rhone*. Lord Templeman explained that in *Halsall*, "the defendant could, at least in theory, choose between enjoying the right and paying his proportion of the cost or alternatively giving up the right and saving his money".[42] In contrast, in *Rhone* the defendant, "could not in theory or in practice" be deprived of the benefit of the rights of support for failing to discharge the burden of repairing the roof.[43] Whether this distinction is realistic has been doubted.[44] Notwithstanding, the importance of the requirement was emphasised by the Court of Appeal in *Thamesmead Town Ltd v. Allotey*.[45] There, the court rejected an argument that merely by taking title to land a person became bound by the burden, even if he chose not to enjoy the benefit. The reason for the requirement may relate to the circumstances in which this principle is applied. As has been seen, the principle may be applied

---

[39] See above n.5 at 182. See also H.W.R. Wade, "Real Property—Positive Covenant—Deed—Perpetuity" [1957] C.L.J. 35 at 36. Commenting on *Halsall*, he notes: "One limit to the application of this doctrine is patent. It can apply only where the owner of the burdened land is seeking to exercise some privilege to which he would otherwise have no right".

[40] See above n.8 at 171–172.

[41] Louise Tee, "A Roof Too Far" [1994] C.L.J. 446 at 447–448 suggests that it is uncertain whether Lord Templeman considered this element of choice to be necessary or whether he was still considering the question of relevance. However, as Snape notes above n.23 at 482 contemporary comment on *Halsall* stressed this element of the decision.

[42] See above n.16 at 322.

[43] *ibid.*

[44] Gravells above n.23 at 350; Snape above n.23 at 482.

[45] See above n.38.

where an agreement imposes a burden, such as a positive covenant, which is not a recognised proprietary right. Wade suggests that the element of choice counters an argument that the effect of the principle is to annex novel burdens to land.[46] The element of choice means that the principle does not result in the burden of the agreement automatically running with the land. By choosing to enjoy the benefit of the agreement the burden, which is not otherwise enforceable, is tacitly accepted.

Once established that a person has chosen to enjoy the benefit of an agreement, the next question to consider is the extent to which the burden must be complied with. The benefit and burden may be continuing; for example, the right to use a road subject to periodic contributions to the cost of maintenance. Where this is the case, a person must comply with the burden for the duration the benefit is enjoyed.[47] Alternatively the benefit or burden may be unitary, requiring compliance only once. The agreement in *Tito* contained a unitary burden; the agreement imposed an obligation to replant land on completion of mining. Megarry V.-C. considered that if the burden is unitary and the benefit has been enjoyed by more than one person, then the person deriving the benefit at the time the burden arises must comply in full. Megarry V.-C. qualified this by providing that the benefit enjoyed must be "real and substantial" and not merely "technical".[48] It may be difficult to assess whether real and substantial benefit has been enjoyed.[49] The principle of benefit and burden is founded on a concept of fairness and, in essence, the

---

[46] See above n.39 at 37.

[47] See, *e.g. Ives v. High* above n.6 at 394, *per* Lord Denning: "So long as they take that benefit, they must shoulder the burden". In *Montague v. Long* (1972) 24 P. & C.R. 240 at 247, Graham J. explained the plaintiffs were under an obligation to accept the burden of an agreement (maintaining a bridge) while they enjoyed the benefit (use of the bridge) but could not be compelled to maintain the bridge if they no longer wished to use it.

[48] See above n.1 at 305. On this basis the burden of one set of agreements (referred to as the 1913 agreements) was not enforceable. It is implicit in Megarry V.-C.'s judgment that the burden would have to be complied with in full or not at all. A person can not be liable for a proportion of the burden relative to the extent to which they have enjoyed the benefit. However, Megarry V.-C. did suggest above n.1 at 308, that implied rights of indemnity may develop. It would seem to be a corollary of his judgment that the obligation to comply with the burden falls on the last person who does enjoy a "real and substantial" benefit. Snape above n.23 at 482, suggests the need to demonstrate a "real and substantial" benefit arose only in relation to the pure principle of benefit and burden.

[49] Aughterson above n.8 at 16.

question to consider is whether it would be "fair" to require compliance with the burden.[50]

IV. Effect of the principle

The key question is whether the principle of benefit and burden imposes merely a personal obligation,[51] or operates to create a proprietary right, mirroring in its substance the burden of the agreement. The effect of the principle is to ensure compliance with the burden of an agreement by a person who would not otherwise be bound through, for example, a relationship of privity of contract or privity of estate. It is generally considered that the burden of the agreement is passed[52] though this analysis is not universal.[53] As has been noted, the element of choice precludes the burden being annexed to the land to run automatically.[54] However, the existence of choice does not preclude a conclusion that the burden passes because it is a proprietary right: it is still "capable" of binding third parties to the agreement.

The strongest suggestion that proprietary rights are created is the judgment of Lord Denning M.R. in *Ives v. High*. There, the defendant had agreed with the developer of some flats that the foundations could encroach upon his land, in return for which he was given a right of way across the yard of the flats. The Court of Appeal was asked whether the defendant had rights binding against the plaintiffs, who were subsequent purchasers of the flats. The land in question was unregistered and, in his judgment, Lord Denning

---

[50] In giving the "real and substantial" test, Megarry V.-C. above n.1 at 305 emphasised that the benefit and burden principle is a "broad principle of justice".

[51] As is suggested, though without a discussion of the issue, by Davis above n.23 at 547.

[52] See, *e.g.* Megarry and Wade, para. 16.024.

[53] See clause 19(1)(b) of the draft Bill annexed to Law Com. No. 127, *Transfer of Land: The Law of Positive and Restrictive Covenants*. That clause abolishes, "any rule of law or equity . . . by virtue of which the benefit or burden of a covenant which touches and concerns the land may pass to a person other than the original covenantor or covenantee". The Law Commission explains, para. 24.32 that if enacted, this clause will not affect the principle of benefit and burden. The basis of this conclusion is that the principle does not operate to pass the burden of a covenant, but, "determines the consequences incurred by a particular person at a particular time if he fails to comply with it".

[54] See above n.46 and text.

first considered the position of the parties "apart from" the effect of the rules relating to the registration of land charges. Lord Denning considered that by the application of the principle of benefit and burden the defendant acquired a right of way.[55] Enjoyment of the benefit of the original agreement (the trespass on the defendant's land) was conditional on the burden (allowing the defendant a right of way). Lord Denning then considered the impact of the Land Charges Act. It is clear from his judgment that if the right acquired by the defendant was registrable, then it would be void for non-registration.[56] This is regardless of the fact the plaintiffs continued to enjoy the benefit of the agreement. Hence, Lord Denning treated the agreement as creating an (equitable) proprietary right by the application of the principle of benefit and burden. This right arose as between the original parties to the agreement.[57] It was binding against the plaintiffs because they enjoyed the benefit of the agreement and, as the right was not registrable as a land charge, the right was enforceable against the plaintiffs as purchasers with notice.[58] Both elements were essential: the plaintiffs enjoyed the benefit of the agreement and the right acquired by the principle of benefit and burden was enforceable under the applicable rules for determining the enforceability of interests in land.[59]

---

[55] Danckwerts L.J. above n.6 at 400, described the defendant as enjoying "equitable rights" and Winn L.J., at 405, considered the defendant had an "equity, which amounted to an equitable easement". Lord Denning at 394 explained: "The right arises out of the agreement of November 2, 1949, and the subsequent action taken on it: on the principle that 'he who takes the benefit must accept the burden'". His judgment is criticised by Graham Battersby, "Informal Transactions in Land, Estoppel and Registration" (1995) 58 M.L.R. 637 at 646 for not appreciating Counsel's argument that the principle of benefit and burden applied only because the agreement was void.

[56] See above n.6 at 395.

[57] Lord Denning explained above n.6 at 394: "When adjoining owners of land make an agreement to secure continuing rights and benefits for each of them in or over the land of the other, neither of them can take the benefit of the agreement and throw over the burden of it. This applies not only to the original parties, but also to their successors".

[58] Both Danckwerts L.J. above n.6 at 400, and Winn L.J. at 405, also seemed to rely on the doctrine of notice as the basis upon which the plaintiffs were bound by the right.

[59] If the principle of benefit and burden was applicable only when the agreement became void (see Battersby above n.55), then it would not apply between the original parties. Counsel conceded that the agreement became void on a sale by the original owners of the flat to the plaintiff's predecessors in title. Following that sale, by the application of the principle of benefit and burden, the defendant acquired a proprietary right. The question of enforcement of that right against a third party would have arisen for the first time on the sale to the plaintiffs.

There are two basis upon which a conclusion proprietary rights are acquired may be challenged. First, in a discussion of *Ives v. High*, Graham Battersby notes the precarious nature of the right acquired by application of the principle of benefit and burden as dependent upon each successor accepting the benefit of the agreement. Is the right too precarious to be considered proprietary? Battersby suggests that at any time the element of precariousness could be removed by the defendant registering his right of way. However, registration will not be possible in all situations. Further, the right of way Battersby envisages being registered is the right created by the original agreement. The possibility of registering the right is based on a combination of the principles of benefit and burden and proprietary estoppel.[60] On Battersby's analysis, the effect of a successor enjoying the benefit of an agreement is twofold: he is both bound by the burden and estopped from relying on the defendant's failure to register the right. Even if this argument is accepted,[61] it could assist only where, as in *Ives v. High*, the agreement envisaged the creation of a recognised proprietary right. In any event, registration does not remove the precarious nature of the right acquired by the principle of benefit and burden. The registration proposed by Battersby removes the precarious nature of the defendant's right only by "resurrecting" the original agreement and thereby preventing the need for the defendant to continue to rely on the principle of benefit and burden. Accepting the dependence of the right on enjoyment of the benefit of the agreement, it is uncertain how precarious the right is. Battersby notes that either each purchaser has a "once and for all" opportunity to repudiate the agreement (by not accepting the benefit) or the agreement may be repudiated at any time.[62] It is submitted that, on either analysis, the right could still be recognised as proprietary. An analogy may be made with the right acquired by entering an uncompleted sale of land. As was seen in Chapter 5, although the requirement has been criticised, such a right (until the purchase money has been paid in full) is dependent upon the continued availability of specific performance.[63] Equally, it seems a right could

---

[60] Battersby above n.55 at 649. Battersby at 646, criticises Lord Denning's view that the original agreement was not registrable.

[61] Smith, p. 175 n.161, says Battersby's attempt to link *Ives v. High* with proprietary estoppel, "appears somewhat tenuous".

[62] See above n.55 at 649. Battersby prefers the "once and for all" approach.

[63] Chapter 5, Part II 4(b).

be recognised as proprietary despite being dependent upon the continued enjoyment of a benefit. The right acquired under the principle of benefit and burden is different from that derived from a specifically enforceable contract in one important respect. The right derived from a specifically enforceable contract may be transitional in nature as it is anticipated that the contract will be executed. Subject to Battersby's argument, the principle of benefit and burden may remain the basis of the right. However, the dependence on the continued enjoyment of the benefit is an inherent characteristic of the principle. Any right acquired should exist only while the benefit of the agreement is enjoyed.

A further question that arises is whether the right created by the principle of benefit and burden ends if any successor does not accept the benefit. It is submitted that this is not necessarily the case, and that the enforcement of the right may instead only be suspended. As has been seen, the enforcement of the right is dependent upon two factors; acceptance of the benefit and on the right acquired binding the purchaser under the applicable rule for determining the enforcement of rights. Assume (as in *Ives v. High*) that the applicable rule is the doctrine of notice. Following the creation of a right by the principle of benefit and burden, the land is sold to *P1*, who has notice of the right (the burden), but chooses not to accept the benefit. The right, though *capable* of binding *P1*, is not in fact enforceable against him. *P1* then sells the land to *P2*, who has notice of the right and does accept the benefit. There seems no reason why the right (the burden) should not be enforceable against *P2*.

The second basis on which the proprietary nature of the right may be challenged is that the right has, on occasion, been described as a "mere equity".[64] Mere equities are not generally considered to be proprietary rights. 'Snell's Equity' describes them as, "not a right of property but a right, usually of a procedural nature, which is ancillary to some right of property, and which limits or qualifies it in some way".[65] The right acquired by application of the principle of benefit

---

[64] Jill E. Martin, *Hanbury & Maudsley Modern Equity* (13th ed., 1989) 870 (this view is not repeated in subsequent editions) *Poster v. Slough Estates Ltd* [1969] 1 Ch. 495 at 506.

[65] John McGhee, *Snell's Equity* (30th ed., 2000) para. 2–05. See further Ann R. Everton, "'Equitable Interests' and 'Equities'—in Search of a Pattern" [1976] Conv. 209 at 210–211. She notes that while there is basic agreement mere equities are not rights of property, questions arise as to whether a particular mere equity is, "possessed of a sufficiently proprietary flavour as to be capable of binding third parties".

and burden does not seem to meet this description. As the principle may enable the enforcement of rights not recognised as proprietary, the right can not be described in all cases as being ancillary to a proprietary right. There may exist a separate category of equities, comprising rights, "whose nature is different from conventional equitable interests".[66] In *National Provincial Bank Ltd v. Ainsworth* Lord Upjohn described such an equity, not ancillary to a proprietary right, as an equity "naked and alone".[67] He considered that such an equity was a personal interest incapable of binding purchasers.[68] In light of this, if the principle of benefit and burden gives rise to a mere equity, then a new equity must arise each time a successor enjoys the benefit of an agreement. The equity would enable the enforcement of the agreement against that particular successor. Such an analysis is inconsistent with that adopted by Lord Denning in *Ives v. High*. As has been seen, he considered that a right was acquired by the application of the principle of benefit and burden as between the original parties to the agreement. That right was enforceable against the successors both because they enjoyed the benefit of the agreement and the right was enforceable against them as purchasers with notice. In the factual context of that case, the right created by the parties' agreement was a recognised proprietary right; a right of way. Therefore, if Lord Denning treated the right acquired by the principle of benefit and burden as a mere equity, then notwithstanding it may still have been enforceable against successors as a mere equity ancillary to a proprietary right. However, the application of the principle should have the same effect regardless of the right envisaged by the parties' agreement. Moreover, Lord Denning did not seem to treat the right acquired by the principle as a mere equity.[69] He treated the right acquired by the principle as a type of equitable right of way. This is apparent from his discussion of the types of equitable easement registrable as land charges.[70] If the right acquired was not an equitable easement, then it could have been excluded from the class of registrable land charges without further discussion.

---

[66] Smith, p. 26.
[67] [1965] A.C. 1175 at 1238.
[68] *ibid*.
[69] Contrast the interpretation of Lord Denning's judgment by Cross J. in *Poster v. Slough Estates Ltd* above n.64 at 506.
[70] See above n.6 at 395–396.

Therefore, it is submitted that when the principle of benefit and burden is applied, its effect is to provide for the acquisition of a proprietary right which, in its substance, mirrors the burden of the agreement. The right is within the general definition of proprietary rights as being sufficiently stable and capable in its nature of binding third parties.[71] The right should be treated as dating from the time the benefit of the agreement is first accepted. Where the burden of the agreement does not meet the characteristics of a recognised proprietary right (for example, where the parties' agreement relates to a positive obligation) the right acquired is a proprietary right *sui generis*. Where a recognised proprietary right is acquired, the question arises as to the classification of that right. In *Ives v. High* Lord Denning considered that the right acquired was a type of equitable easement. However, the principle of benefit and burden is not based on the intervention of equity and, as a result, there is no reason for it to be restricted to the acquisition of equitable interests. In *Tito*, commenting on Lord Denning's classification of the right in *Ives v. High*, Megarry V.-C. noted that, "whether rights in land in England are legal or equitable depends to a considerable extent on the peculiarities of English land law".[72] It is possible that the right acquired may, on appropriate facts, be classified as legal. This would be the case, for example, where the principle is applied in the context of an agreement which is entered by deed.[73]

V. Conclusion

In this chapter it has been argued that where a person accepts the benefit of an agreement which has a corresponding burden, proprietary rights are created to ensure compliance with the burden. The principle of corresponding benefit and burden seems able to overcome not only the formal requirements for the creation of proprietary rights but other established rules of land law. In *Halsall*, Upjohn J. considered the defendant bound to accept the burden of an agreement notwithstanding the provisions of the agreement in

---

[71] *cf.* the definition given by Lord Wilberforce above n.67 at 1248.
[72] See above n.1 at 308.
[73] An analogy may be made with the status of easements impliedly granted on the transfer of legal title. Such easements, as they are implied into the transfer of legal title, are themselves legal. See Chapter 9, Part III.

question infringed the rule against perpetuities.[74] Apart from cases in which the burden is an express condition of the right, authority for the principle, at least until recently, remained far from clear. The principle rests on the *obiter* comments of Upjohn J. in *Halsall* and the approval of that decision, without a full discussion of the principle, by Lord Templeman in *Rhone*. The judgment of Megarry V.-C. in *Tito*, which contains the most comprehensive consideration of the principle by an English court, must be treated with caution following Lord Templeman's rejection of the principle applied by Megarry V.-C. The discussion of the principle in *Ives v. High*, which was not considered in *Rhone*, is to some extent obscured by the joint application in that case of the principles of benefit and burden and proprietary estoppel. Despite this unstable basis, the principle seems to be accepted as established. As a matter of law, its legitimacy is strengthened by its application (although failing on the facts) by the Court of Appeal in *Thamesmead Town Ltd v. Allotey*.[75]

In *Government Insurance Office (N.S.W.) v. K.V. Reed Services Pty. Ltd* Brooking J., in the Supreme Court of Victoria, described the general proposition that he who takes the benefit of a transaction must accept the burden as, "not a rule or doctrine, but rather a maxim, based on a notion of what is fair, which might underlie particular rules or doctrines of law or equity capable of being stated in more specific terms".[76] The principle approved by Lord Templeman, enabling the acquisition of proprietary rights, may come to be accepted as one aspect of a broader principle of benefit and burden.[77]

---

[74] See above n.5 at 182–183. Whether the principle is an exception to the rule against perpetuities is not without question. See Snape above n.23 at 482.

[75] See above n.38.

[76] See above n.3 at 831.

[77] For a discussion of the more general principle, see Davis above n.23.

Chapter 9.

To Prevent a Person Derogating from his Grant

I. Introduction

In Chapter 8 it was seen that a person who has enjoyed the benefit of an agreement may be required to accept a corresponding burden. Requiring acceptance of the burden was justified as it ensured that the conduct of the recipient of the benefit reached a general standard of fairness. The primary concern of the rule to be considered in this chapter is to ensure that a standard of fairness is met by the grantor of a proprietary right.[1] The rule imposes a duty on the grantor not to act in a manner inconsistent with the grant. The duty imposed is enforceable not only against the original grantor but also against his successors in title. Hence, the effect of imposing the duty is that the grantee acquires proprietary rights to protect the right originally granted.

The rule is referred to as the rule against derogation from grant. It is a well established rule which has been described as being, "as old, I will not say as the hills, but as old as the Year Books, and a great deal older".[2] The rule reflects the basic notion of common honesty that: "A grantor having given a thing with one hand, is not to take away the means of enjoying it with the other".[3] The challenge for the

---

[1] A "similar and equally binding duty" has been imposed on grantees: *Lyttleton Times Co Ltd v. Warners Ltd* [1907] A.C. 476 at 481, *per* Lord Loreburn L.C.; *Johnston & Sons Ltd v. Holland* [1988] 1 E.G.L.R. 264 at 268.
[2] *Birmingham, Dudley and District Banking Co v. Ross* (1887) 38 Ch. D. 295 at 312, *per* Bowen L.J.
[3] *ibid.* at 313.

courts has been to delimit the scope of the rule in a manner which reflects this underlying notion without imposing too onerous a duty on the grantor and, as the rule enables the acquisition of proprietary rights, consequently over-burdening the land. In *Harmer v. Jumbil (Nigeria) Tin Areas Ltd* Younger L.J. explained: "The rule is clear but the difficulty is, as always, in its application".[4] Although the basic rule is well established it continues to develop "step by cautious step"[5] and, as will be seen in this chapter, its scope remains uncertain in key respects.

For the rule against derogation from grant to apply, two requirements must be met. First, there must be a grant of rights in land for a particular purpose. Secondly the grantor must own land neighbouring the land which is the subject matter of the grant. If these requirements are met, then the grantor is under a duty not to use the neighbouring land in such a way as to derogate from the grant. The general rule will be discussed in Part II of this chapter. The discussion will first consider when the requirements are met. The scope and effect of the duty will then be explained. In addition to the general rule, there are a number of specific rules derived from non-derogation from grant. These rules, which are subject to their own requirements, will be discussed in Part III.

II. The general rule

1. THE REQUIREMENTS

(a) Grant of rights in land for a particular purpose

As the duty imposed is a duty not to derogate from the "grant" it must first be established that there has been a grant of rights. The difficulty in establishing this is that "grant" is not a term of art. The term has been interpreted in several different ways in different contexts and there is no definitive interpretation of the term in relation to non-derogation from grant. Two possible interpretations illustrate the difficulty.

---

[4] [1921] 1 Ch. 200 at 226.
[5] *Chartered Trust plc v. Davies* [1997] 2 E.G.L.R. 83 at 85, *per* Henry L.J.

The first and narrower interpretation is given in *Touchstone:* "But the word being taken more strictly and properly, it is the grant, conveyance, or gift, by writing, of such an incorporeal thing as lieth in grant, and not in livery, and cannot be . . . granted by word without deed".[6] On this interpretation, an interest is granted only where a deed is necessary for its creation. If this interpretation applies, then the duty not to derogate will arise only in relation to those legal rights which, by section 52(1) of the Law of Property Act 1925, must be created by deed.[7] If the essential requirement is the use of a deed on the facts, then the duty not to derogate may also apply to protect equitable interests where such interests have been created by deed. For example, the grant by deed of a lease in registered land where the lease remains equitable for non-registration. However, this interpretation would preclude the application of the rule to the majority of equitable interests which are not created by deed. It would also exclude rights acquired under most of the rules discussed in this book which arise in the absence of a deed.[8]

The second interpretation is derived from the decision of the Court of Appeal in *City Permanent Building Society v. Miller.*[9] That case suggests that any interest which has been created is "granted" (whether legal or equitable, created expressly or informally) to the exclusion of interests which there is only an agreement to create. In that case, the court considered whether an equitable lease acquired (under the rule in Chapter 5) by entering a specifically enforceable contract to create a lease was an overriding interest under section 70(1)(k) of the Land Registration Act 1925. That section protects "leases *granted* for a term not exceeding twenty-one years".[10] Jenkins L.J. said this necessarily meant that the lease must have been created and not merely agreed to be created.[11] If this interpretation is applied, then non-derogation from grant could not apply to protect interests

---

[6] E.G. Atherley, *Shepard's Touchstone of Common Assurances,* (8th ed., 1826) p. 228.

[7] Conversely, the rule would not apply to those legal rights for which a deed is not necessary, *e.g.* a legal lease not exceeding three years: Law of Property Act 1925, ss.52(2)(d) and 54(2).

[8] The principal exception, where there may be the informal acquisition of rights following the execution of a deed, is in relation to the transfer or creation of a registered title. Title will not be complete until registration. Pending registration, title will be held on trust for the transferee. See Chapter 5, n.2 (transfer on sale) and the rule in *Re Rose*, Chapter 2, Part II (transfer on gift).

[9] [1952] 1 Ch. 840.

[10] Emphasis added.

[11] See above n.9 at 853.

acquired by entering a specifically enforceable contract. The exclusion of the rule would be justified on the basis that in such a case rights are not "granted" but are merely agreed to be granted.[12] However the court's reasoning would not exclude the application of non-derogation to other interests informally created. The court's reasoning in *Miller* is entrenched in the basis on which rights are acquired by entering a specifically enforceable contract. As was seen in Chapter 5, the acquisition of rights by entering a specifically enforceable contract is based on equity looking to the future. As a specifically enforceable contract ought to be executed, equity treats the parties as though the contract has been executed. In *Miller*, in its interpretation of the phrase "leases granted", the court relied on the distinction between the position of the parties in law (an executory contract to create a lease) and in equity (an executed contract). This reasoning would not be appropriate where, for example, rights are acquired on the basis of an (executed) agreement to share beneficial ownership under the doctrine of constructive trust discussed in Chapter 6.

In applying non-derogation from grant the courts have indicated a broad interpretation. In *Johnston & Sons Ltd v. Holland*[13] the rule was applied in the context of a reservation. When an estate is created or transferred and the vendor reserves for himself an easement, the reservation is construed as though, following the creation or transfer, the purchaser granted (or "re-granted") the easement to the vendor. Through the re-grant, the purchaser becomes the nominal grantor of the easement. In *Johnston*, a landlord granted a lease of premises to a tenant but reserved for herself the right to use a wall for advertising. The tenant, who was the nominal grantor, was held to be under a duty not to derogate. In applying the duty, Nicholls L.J. emphasised that he was relying on the, "broad, common sense rationale" of non-derogation from grant, and not the, "highly technical conveyancing notion" of a re-grant.[14] He referred to the possibility that a grantee may be under a duty not to derogate from the grantor's use of land retained. However, he acknowledged that the interpretation of the reservation as a re-grant would achieve the same result.[15]

A broad interpretation of grant is also suggested by other decisions. In *North Eastern Railway v. Elliot*[16] the House of Lords considered that

---

[12] Non-derogation from grant could apply only on the actual grant of the interest by performance of the contract.
[13] See above n.1.
[14] See above n.1 at 268.
[15] *ibid.*
[16] (1861) 10 H.L.C. 333; 11 E.R. 1055.

a vendor under a compulsory sale of land was under the same duty not to use land retained to the prejudice of the sale as he would be on a voluntary sale. The application of non-derogation to a compulsory sale must now be doubted in light of the subsequent decision of the House of Lords in *Sovmots Investments Ltd v. Secretary of State for the Environment*.[17] There, the House of Lords refused to apply one of the specific rules derived from non-derogation from grant, the rule in *Wheeldon v. Burrows*,[18] to a compulsory purchase. The House of Lords relied on the fact the rule is derived from non-derogation to deny its application. This clearly implies that the House of Lords did not consider the general rule applicable to a compulsory sale.[19] In *Borman v. Griffith*[20] the court applied the rule in *Wheeldon v. Burrows* to a lease acquired by entering a specifically enforceable contract. The court considered that as the contract was specifically enforceable the lessee should enjoy the same rights to which he would be entitled on the actual grant of the lease. This interpretation is in direct conflict with the definition of grant derived from *City Permanent Building Society v. Miller*. As the decision in *Borman v. Griffith* is based on the rule in *Wheeldon v. Burrows* the case is not authority for the application of the general rule of non-derogation to a contract to create a right. However, the decision is closer in context than *City Permanent Building Society v. Miller* and the reasoning seems equally applicable to the general rule. Further, it is consistent with the underlying notion of common honesty for the courts to take a broad interpretation of grant rather than restricting the application of the rule by reference to a technical definition.

Once established that rights have been granted, the purpose of the grant must be identified. The purpose is important as it operates to delimit the grantor's duty; there will be a derogation from grant only where the grantor's acts interfere with the purpose of the grant. Without this limitation the duty imposed could become too onerous. In *Browne v. Flower*, Parker J. explained:

---

[17] [1977] 2 W.L.R. 951.
[18] (1879) 12 Ch. D. 31. The rule is discussed in Part III 3 of this chapter.
[19] See above n.17 at 958, *per* Lord Wilberforce: "The rule [in *Wheeldon v. Burrows*] is a rule of intention, based on the proposition that a man may not derogate from his grant . . . To apply this to a case where a public authority is taking from an owner his land without his will is to stand the rule on its head: it means substituting for the intention of a reasonable voluntary grantor the unilateral, opposed, intention of the acquirer". *North Eastern Railway v. Elliot* was not referred to.
[20] [1930] 1 Ch. 493.

"It is quite reasonable for a purchaser to assume that a vendor who sells land for a particular purpose will not do anything to prevent its being used for that purpose, but it would be utterly unreasonable to assume that the vendor was undertaking restrictive obligations which would prevent his using land retained by him for any lawful purpose whatsoever merely because his so doing might affect the amenities of the property he had sold".[21]

Despite the importance of the purpose of the grant there is relatively little discussion in the case law of how it is to be identified. This may suggest that in practice the courts have had little difficulty in defining the purpose. In *Harmer v. Jumbil* the purpose was expressed by the parties in the terms of the grant. There, a lease was granted with the express purpose the land was to be used for the storage of explosives. Younger L.J. explained that this was the "only authorised user" of the premises.[22] In addition, it may be necessary to define the purpose only in broad terms. In *Browne v. Flower* the purpose of the grant of a lease of a flat was defined generally as "residential purposes".[23] Hence actions by the grantor which interfered with that use could, *prima facie*, be a derogation from grant.[24] In defining the purpose, the court considers the circumstances surrounding the grant.[25] In *Chartered Trust plc v. Davies*,[26] the landlord of a small shopping arcade had granted leases of individual units within the arcade to various business tenants, including Mr Davies. By looking at the circumstances surrounding the grant of the lease to Mr Davies, the court identified the purpose of the grant as the lease of a unit within the arcade; not merely as a separate and individual unit. This was important as it ensured that the landlord was under a duty not to derogate from the grant in the management of the arcade as a whole. If the grantee's use of the land is unusually sensitive for the purpose

---

[21] [1911] 1 Ch. 219 at 227.

[22] See above n.4 at 225. See also *Johnston v. Holland* above n.1 where use of a wall was reserved specifically for the purposes of advertising.

[23] The lease prohibited use of the flat other than as a dwelling house.

[24] On the facts, the court held there had been no derogation from grant: see below n.50 and text.

[25] This approach mirrors that taken by the courts prior to the Trusts of Land and Appointment of Trustees Act 1996 in identifying the secondary or collateral purpose of a trust for sale. To identify the purpose, the court looked at "the trust itself or the circumstances in which it was made": *Jones v. Challenger* [1961] 1 Q.B. 176 at 181, *per* Devlin L.J.

[26] See above n.5.

in question, then the sensitive use will not be part of the purpose unless known to the grantor at the time of the grant. This is illustrated by *Robinson v. Kilvert*.[27] There, a lease was granted of a warehouse to be used for paper. Unknown to the landlord, some of the paper stored by the tenant was more sensitive than ordinary paper. It was held that actions of the landlord which damaged the tenant's paper, but would not have damaged ordinary paper, were not in derogation from the grant. The purpose of the grant did not incorporate the tenant's unusually sensitive use.

(b) Grantor owns neighbouring land

The duty not to derogate applies only where the grantor owns land neighbouring the land which forms the subject matter of the grant. The duty applies in relation to the grantor's activities on the neighbouring land and not to activities on the land granted.[28] Two reasons may explain this limitation. First, it is consistent with the view that non-derogation from grant operates to create a servitude. It imposes a burden on neighbouring land owned by the grantor (the servient land) to protect rights granted on the dominant land.[29] Secondly other means may be available to control the activities of the grantor on the land which is the subject matter of the grant. For example, on the grant of a lease, the implied covenant to permit quiet enjoyment prevents the landlord from interfering with the tenant's possession of the land.[30] In this respect, restricting non-derogation to neighbouring land assists in delimiting its relationship with other rules.[31]

It is not necessary for the neighbouring land to be physically contiguous to the land which is the subject matter of the grant. Although the issue has not been discussed in detail in the case law, in *Romulus Trading Co Ltd v. Comet Properties Ltd*[32] the lands in question

---

[27] (1889) 41 Ch. D. 88. See also *Aldin v. Latimar Clark, Muirhead & Co* [1894] 2 Ch. 437 at 444.
[28] *O'Cedar Ltd v. Slough Trading Co Ltd* [1927] 2 K.B. 123 at 129; D.W. Elliott, "Non-Derogation from Grant" (1964) 80 L.Q.R. 244 at 250.
[29] See the discussion below n.75 and text.
[30] The covenant is explained by P.F. Smith, *Evans and Smith: The Law of Landlord and Tenant* (5th ed., 1997), pp. 101–104.
[31] However, the relationship between non-derogation and quiet enjoyment is unclear: Elliott above n.28 at 273–276. Activities by a landlord on adjoining premises may be a breach of the tenant's quiet enjoyment: *Evans and Smith*, above n.30 at 103.
[32] [1996] 2 E.G.L.R. 70.

191

were not in fact contiguous.[33] The claim in that case failed on the ground that the grantor's actions did not in fact amount to a derogation,[34] but there was no suggestion that the rule was not, *prima facie*, applicable to the lands in question. An analogy may be made with the degree of proximity between the dominant and servient tenements required for an easement or restrictive covenant.[35] The duty will apply only when the grantor has a proprietary right in the adjoining land which is sufficient to support the right claimed.[36]

Prior to the decision of the Court of Appeal in *Johnston v. Holland*,[37] it seems to have been assumed that non-derogation affected the grantor's activities only on neighbouring land owned by him at the time of the grant. It had not been decided "or even suggested"[38] that the rule could also affect the grantor's activities on land acquired after the grant. The conveyancing history out of which *Johnston v. Holland* arose is complicated, but the essential facts can be shortly stated. The grantor of advertising rights assigned to a company, Johnston & Sons Ltd, the lease out of which the rights had been granted. The company also owned a car lot which adjoined the land over which the advertising rights were exercised. In the course of an on-going dispute with the holder of the advertising rights, Miss Holland, the company erected its own advertising hoarding on the car lot with the sole purpose of obscuring Miss Holland's advertisements.[39] The company, as the grantor's successor to the lease, was under the same duty as the grantor not to derogate from the grant.[40] The question for the court was whether this duty affected the company's activities on

---

[33] The neighbouring land is described in the head note as "nearby", and by Garland J. *ibid* at 72, as "virtually next door" to the subject of the grant.

[34] This aspect of the case is discussed below n.67 and text.

[35] See the discussion (in relation to easements) by Paul Jackson, *The Law of Easements and Profits* (1978), pp. 11–14.

[36] See, *e.g. Quicke v. Chapman* [1903] 1 Ch. 659 where non-derogation was not applied in relation to a grantor with only a licence in adjoining land.

[37] See above n.1.

[38] *Johnston v. Holland* above n.1 at 267, *per* Nicholls L.J. In *Quicke v. Chapman* above n.36 the court refused to apply non-derogation to a grantor who held a licence at the time of the grant but would subsequently obtain a proprietary right. The court's judgment focused on the question whether the grantor, as a licensee, was bound by the duty not to derogate but it seems implicit in the decision that the duty did not apply where a proprietary right was acquired subsequent to the grant. The case was not considered in *Johnston v. Holland*.

[39] The company's actions were clearly motivated by spite and it is unclear how far this influenced the court's decision. "Hill and Redman's, *Law of Landlord and Tenant*, para. 998 n.7 suggest caution in relying on the case.

[40] See below n.77 and text.

the car lot. The answer would be in the affirmative only if the original grantor would have been under the duty not to derogate in relation to the car lot. As the grantor did not own the car lot at the time of the grant, this depended, in turn, on whether the duty applied to after acquired land. The court acknowledged that Miss Holland was at risk that a stranger to the grant would acquire the car lot and obscure her advertisements. A stranger would be under no duty to protect Miss Holland's rights.[41] However, the court held that non-derogation was not limited to activities of the grantor on land owned at the time of the grant. Activities by the grantor on after acquired land could be a derogation from the grant notwithstanding the same activities by a stranger would give rise to no cause of action. In reaching this decision, Nicholls L.J. emphasised the rationale of common honesty underlying the rule. Where a grantor's use of land derogates from his grant he should not be in a better position merely because the land was acquired after the grant.[42]

In *Johnston*, the grantor did own some neighbouring land at the date of the grant in respect of which the duty not to derogate could have been applied. The question for the court was whether the duty could also be applied to new land acquired subsequent to the grant. The court considered, further, that the rule could apply to a grantor who owned no land at the time of the grant but subsequently acquired some. However, Nicholls L.J. added one note of caution. He stated that when at the time of the grant the grantor neither owns neighbouring land nor plans to acquire any, it would require a, "very exceptional case" to establish a derogation.[43]

The grantor's neighbouring land need not be a different physical piece of land to that in which rights have been granted. The requirement is also satisfied where the grantor retains an estate in the land granted, as where a landlord grants a lease. The landlord is under a duty not to derogate from the lease regardless of whether he owns a neighbouring piece of land.[44] The application of the rule is justified on the basis that the landlord's reversionary interest is the "neighbouring land".[45] The practical effect of applying the rule is that

---

[41] See above n.1 at 266.

[42] See the illustration discussed by Nicholls L.J. above n.1 at 268.

[43] *ibid*. The reason it would be difficult to establish a derogation from grant in such a case is considered below n.55 and text.

[44] Hill and Redman, above n.39, para. 998, seem to assume ownership of neighbouring land is not essential in the context of the grant of a lease.

[45] See the discussion, in the context of the grant by a tenant of a subtenancy, by N. Hopkins, "Surrender as an Assignment and the Protection of Third Parties" [1996] Conv. 284 at 287.

the landlord is placed under a duty not to derogate from the grant in the management of the lease.

2. Scope of the Duty

Once the requirements of non-derogation are met, the grantor is under a duty not to use the neighbouring land in a manner which makes the land granted, "unfit or materially less fit" for its purpose.[46] It is irrelevant whether the actions complained of are carried out directly by the grantor, or by a third party acting as the "natural result of the grantor's conduct".[47] Hence, a grantor will be in derogation by authorising a third party to use neighbouring land for a purpose which interferes with the grant.[48] In *Harmer v. Jumbil* and *Johnston v. Holland* the actions complained of wholly defeated the purpose of the grant,[49] but it seems that such an extreme interference is not necessary. However, actions which merely interfere with the grantor's comfort are not a derogation from the grant. This is illustrated by *Browne v. Flower*, where a lease had been granted for residential purposes. Subsequent to the grant, the grantor permitted the construction of a staircase which overlooked the tenant's flat. To retain privacy, the tenant would have to curtain the windows. This would reduce the level of light in the flat and thereby interfere with the tenant's comfort. Against this background, the tenant argued that the construction of the staircase was a derogation from the grant of the flat. Rejecting the tenant's argument, the court held that the flat had not been rendered unfit or materially less fit to be used as a residence. Parker J. explained: "The two rooms in question can be and are still in fact used for the same purpose for which they were used prior to the erection of the staircase. It is only the comfort of the persons so using the rooms that is interfered with by what has been done".[50] Parker J. considered that to hold this interference to be

---

[46] *Browne v. Flower* above n.21 at 226, *per* Parker J.
[47] Elliott above n.28 at 251.
[48] See, *e.g. Harmer v. Jumbil* above n.4. There, the acts which caused the derogation were carried out by the grantor's tenants of neighbouring land using the land for the purposes of their lease.
[49] In *Harmer v. Jumbil* above n.4 at 225, Younger L.J. explained that the grantor's actions made the only authorised use of the land a statutory offence. In *Johnston v. Holland* above n.1 it was clear that the grantor's actions wholly frustrated the grantee's exercise of her rights.
[50] See above n.21.

a derogation from the grant would extend the rule to an unreasonable extent.

Not every act by a grantor which makes the land granted unfit for its purpose is a derogation from grant. The scope of the grantor's duty is defined variously by reference to what was in the "reasonable contemplation"[51] of the parties at the time of the grant, or as what was "necessarily implicit"[52] in the grant. In *Harmer v. Jumbil* Younger L.J. warned that without such a limitation on the scope of the duty, "that which was imposed in the interest of fair dealing might, in unscrupulous hands, become a justification for oppression, or an instrument of extortion".[53] He advised that the duty must be construed "fairly, even strictly, if not narrowly".[54] The scope of the duty can be illustrated by reference to an example given by Nicholls L.J. in *Johnston v. Holland*. There, as has been seen,[55] the company derogated from the grant of advertising rights by erecting its own advertising hoarding on adjoining land acquired subsequent to the grant. The court considered it necessarily implicit in the grant that the grantor would not take over the advertising site himself. In contrast, Nicholls L.J. said that there would have been no derogation if the company had constructed a building on the land which, coincidentally, obstructed the grantee's advertisements. Clearly the land granted would still have been rendered unfit for its purpose. However, it was not considered necessarily implicit in the grant that the grantor would not build on any land acquired after the grant in any way which would obstruct the advertisements.

The assessment to be made is what was within the contemplation of the parties at the time of the grant, not the later time of the alleged derogation. It was on this basis that in *Johnston v. Holland* Nicholls L.J. suggested it would be difficult to establish a derogation by action on land acquired after the grant when, at the time of the grant, the grantor owned no neighbouring land. Although in principle the rule could apply, it would have to be shown as necessarily implicit at the time of the grant that the grantor would not do the act complained of if he subsequently acquired land. In assessing what was within the contemplation of the parties at the time of the grant, the court takes

---

[51] *Port v. Griffith* [1938] 1 All E.R. 295 at 300, *per* Luxmoore J.
[52] *Johnston v. Holland* above n.1 at 268.
[53] See above n.4 at 226.
[54] *ibid.*
[55] See above n.37 and text.

into account the state of the law of non-derogation at that time. In *Romulus* the tenant of business premises argued that his landlord had derogated from the grant by granting a lease of neighbouring premises for a similar business. At the time of the grant in question, it was established by case law that the grant of premises for a particular trade did not imply a monopoly over that trade in relation to neighbouring property held by the grantor.[56] The plaintiffs' argument for implying a monopoly was based largely on developments in non-derogation which post-dated their grant. Hence assessed at the time of the grant, with reference to the prevailing state of the law, it would not have been in the reasonable contemplation of the grantor that neighbouring premises could not be let to a competitor.[57]

Once established that the grantor's acts have made the land unfit or materially less fit, and that it was implicit that the grantor would not act in the manner complained of, the nature of the interference is irrelevant. In the majority of cases there is likely to be a physical interference with the land granted. This was the case, for example, in *Johnston v. Holland* where the company's hoarding physically obstructed the grantee's advertisements. However, in *Harmer v. Jumbil* Younger L.J. explained:

> "the obligation imposed may, I think, be infinitely varied in kind, regard being had to the paramount purpose to serve which it is imposed. If, for instance, the purpose of a grant would in a particular case be frustrated by some act of the lessor on his own land which, while involving no physical interference with the enjoyment of the demised property, would yet be completely effective to stop or render unlawful its continued user for the purpose for which alone it was let, I can see no reason at all in principle why . . . that act should not be prohibited".[58]

There, a lease of land had been granted to be used for the storage of explosives. The grantor's successor in title[59] subsequently allowed

---

[56] *Port v. Griffith* above n.51.

[57] See above n.32 at 74.

[58] See above n.4 at 226. Younger L.J. said that a non-physical interference which frustrated the use of the land was a derogation from grant. However, there is no reason why a non-physical interference which makes the land materially less fit should not also be a derogation. The language used by Younger L.J. reflects the facts of the case, where the only permitted use of the land was frustrated.

[59] Successors in title are subject to the same duty as the original grantor: see below n.77 and text.

buildings to be constructed on neighbouring land which, due to their proximity, made continued use of the land to store explosives a statutory offence. Hence, without any physical interference, the land granted was made unfit for its purpose. The Court of Appeal held that there had been a derogation from the grant.

In the majority of cases the duty imposed on the grantor has been restrictive in nature: a duty to refrain from acting in a manner which derogates from the grant. However, in *Davies*[60] the Court of Appeal held the grantor to have derogated from the grant by failing to act. The duty not to derogate from the grant was therefore seen as extending to a duty to take positive steps to protect the grant. *Davies*, as has been seen,[61] concerned the grant of a lease of a unit within a shopping arcade. The unit was used by the tenant's daughter, Miss Davies, to establish a "niche" shop selling puzzles and executive toys. The arcade was not the anticipated success. The landlord subsequently granted a lease of another unit to a pawnbroker who conducted his business in such a way as to cause a nuisance to Miss Davies. Miss Davies did not take action against the pawnbroker,[62] but argued instead that the landlord's failure to end the nuisance was a derogation from grant. The Court noted that the landlord had recognised in the lease that the enjoyment of the tenancy depended in part on its actions in letting and controlling the other units and the common parts.[63] This placed the landlord under a duty to act to end the nuisance. Failing to act was a derogation from the grant as it interfered with the purpose of the lease: it interfered with the tenant's enjoyment of the unit as a unit within the arcade.[64] It is clear from the court's judgment that non-derogation does not invariably require positive action by the grantor. Such action is required only where, as in that case, the circumstances surrounding the grant establish that the grantor was under a duty to act.

In *Davies*, the loss suffered by the grantee was economic. However, the interference by the grantor which caused the loss was the grantor's failure to end the nuisance. It was the nuisance which made

---

[60] See above n.5.
[61] See above n.26 and text.
[62] The Court of Appeal noted, above n.5 at 88, that litigation is too expensive and uncertain for the tenant's willingness to take action to be her only protection. Miss Davies had not initiated any proceedings but raised the landlord's derogation in defence in an action for arrears of rent.
[63] See above n.5 at 85.
[64] See above n.26 and text.

the land unfit or materially less fit for its purpose.[65] One question which has arisen is whether there can be a derogation from grant when the interference itself, not merely the loss caused by the interference, is economic. In *Romulus*[66] it was argued that non-derogation should not only prohibit acts which make land unfit or materially less fit for its purpose, but also acts which cause the grantee "any substantial economic disadvantage".[67] There, the plaintiffs had been granted a lease of business premises for the purposes of banking, including the provision of safes and safe deposit boxes. The landlord subsequently granted a lease of nearby premises to another tenant to be used for substantially the same purpose. The plaintiffs argued that this subsequent lease was a derogation from their grant. In essence, the plaintiffs argued that by granting a lease to them for a particular trade, the landlord impliedly granted them a monopoly of that trade in respect of other property the landlord owned.[68] This argument had been rejected previously in *Port v. Griffith*.[69] Further, in *O'Cedar* it had been held that action by a grantor which substantially increased the cost to the grantee of using the land for its intended purpose was not a derogation from grant.[70] However, in *Romulus*, the plaintiffs argued that non-derogation had developed since those earlier decisions. They relied on two cases which suggested an economic disadvantage was sufficient[71] and, more generally, on other respects in which the scope of non-derogation had been extended in cases such as *Johnston v. Holland*. Garland J. rejected the plaintiffs'

---

[65] See H.W. Wilkinson, "Nuisance by a tenant as a derogation from grant" (1998) 148 N.L.J. 57 at 58.

[66] See above n.32.

[67] See above n.32 at 72, *per* Garland J.

[68] See above n.32 at 73, referring to an argument made by Danckwerts as counsel in *Port v. Griffith* above n.51 at 296.

[69] See above n.51.

[70] See above n.28. The grantor's actions had increased the cost of the grantee's insurance.

[71] *Molton Builders v. City of Westminster* (1975) 30 P. & C.R. 182; *British Leyland Motor Corporation Ltd v. Armstrong Patents Co Ltd* [1986] A.C. 577. In the former, Lord Denning said at 186, that the grantor must not do anything which "substantially deprives" the grantee of the benefit of the grant. However, Lord Denning also referred to the need to show that the premises had become, "unfit or materially less fit". The latter case concerned the application of non-derogation from grant outside the context of land. The House of Lords held that a car manufacturer could not rely on their copyright to prohibit the manufacture of spare parts as this would derogate from car owners' rights to repair their vehicles in the most economical way. In *Romulus*, Garland J. was not prepared to apply in the context of land the same broad economic test applied in that case.

arguments and confirmed that a mere economic disadvantage is not a derogation from grant.[72]

In *Romulus*, the grantee sought to extend the scope of non-derogation and substitute the test of whether premises are unfit or materially less fit with one based on economic disadvantage. As has been seen,[73] once it is established that the grantor's acts have made the land unfit or materially less fit for its purpose the nature of the interference is generally irrelevant. Therefore it is submitted that, notwithstanding the decision in *Romulus*, an economic interference which makes the premises unfit or materially less fit (rather than merely constituting an economic disadvantage) could be a derogation. This view is supported by comments made in *O'Cedar*. There, the court rejected an argument that action by the grantor which increased the cost of the grantee's insurance was a derogation. However, Branson J. noted that: "If there had been evidence to show that the action of the [grantor] had rendered it impossible in a commercial sense to insure these buildings at all. . .different considerations might well apply".[74]

3. Giving Effect to the Duty: the Acquisition of Proprietary Rights

The duty not to derogate is given effect by conferring upon the grantee proprietary rights defined by reference to the scope of the duty. The grantee therefore informally acquires a proprietary right to protect the right which has been granted. The right acquired has been described variously as a specie of servitude[75] and as an obligation.[76] The essence of a servitude is that it is a right which benefits one piece of land, the dominant tenement, while imposing a burden on another, the servient tenement. The right acquired by

---

[72] Garland J. explained above n.32 at 72 the basic question for him was whether *Port v. Griffith* above n.51 remained good law. He affirmed that decision partly because he felt constrained by authority and partly, "because of the great element of uncertainty which a more liberal approach would necessarily involve"; at 74.

[73] See above n.58 and text.

[74] See above n.28 at 127.

[75] It is described as a servitude by Elliott above n.28 at 250, and Jackson above n.35 at 2.

[76] See, *e.g.* the description of the doctrine in *Browne v. Flower* above n.21 at 225, *per* Parker J. and *Harmer v. Jumbil* above n.4 at 220, *per* Lord Sterndale M.R. at 225, *per* Warrington L.J. and at 226, *per* Younger L.J. as imposing implied obligations.

non-derogation benefits the grantee's land (the dominant tenement) and imposes a burden on the grantor's neighbouring land (the servient tenement). To this extent it is convenient to use the language of servitude in discussing the right. However, in applying the rule, the courts are more persuaded by the requirements of common honesty than with the technical definition of a servitude. As will be seen, the rule may apply in situations where it would not be possible to rely on established servitudes such as easements and restrictive covenants. As with established specie of servitudes the benefit and burden of the right acquired by non-derogation passes to successors in title to the dominant and servient lands.[77] Megarry and Wade suggest that, "the grantee and his successors in title have a proprietary interest of a special kind against the grantor's land, into whosesoever hands it may pass".[78] However, it is submitted that this broad statement needs to be qualified. Where the right acquired has the characteristics of a recognised proprietary right, enforceability should be determined by the usual rules applicable to that type of right. The broad statement in Megarry and Wade is based on *Johnston v. Holland* in which the right acquired did not in fact correspond with a recognised right. Where the right acquired does not correspond with a recognised proprietary right, there remain practical difficulties in determining the basis upon which the grantor's successors in title are bound. It seems neither practical nor desirable, for example, to require every grantee to protect the right acquired by non-derogation by entry on the register. Such practical difficulties, despite their importance, were not discussed in *Johnston v. Holland*.

It is possible that in the majority of the cases the scope of the duty not to derogate conforms with the characteristics of an easement[79]; that is, the requirements of the duty could have been expressly agreed by creating an easement in favour of the grantee. In those cases, by the application of non-derogation, the grantee is considered to acquire an easement. By enforcing the easement against the grantor's successors they are bound not to derogate from the grant. However, on a number of occasions the courts have stated that the doctrine is not merely a means of acquiring easements. In *Browne v. Flower*, in a judgment which has been relied upon in a number of cases,[80] Parker J explained:

---

[77] See, *e.g. Johnston v. Holland* above n.1 where the parties to the action were the successors in title to the original grantor and grantee.

[78] Mergarry and Wade para. 18–076.

[79] Elliott above n.28 at 245.

[80] See, *e.g. Harmer v. Jumbil* above n.4 and *Johnston v. Holland* above n.1.

"But the implications usually explained by the maxim that no one can derogate from his own grant do not stop short with easements. Under certain circumstances there will be implied on the part of the grantor or lessor obligations which restrict the user of the land retained by him further than can be explained by the implication of any easement known to the law".[81]

In *Harmer v. Jumbil* Younger L.J. considered that the right acquired could be "infinitely varied in kind".[82] The approach of the courts suggests that even where an easement is not acquired the grantee acquires a proprietary right. In *Harmer*, the application of non-derogation from grant created a right, "plainly not capable of existing as an easement".[83] Notwithstanding it was readily accepted by the court that the right was enforceable against the grantor's successor. Commentators have expressed opposing views on the authorities. In Elliott's view,[84] the authorities establish that the application of non-derogation could create a proprietary right which does not have the characteristics of an easement, but which binds successors on the same basis as a legal easement. At the time he wrote, non-derogation was considered limited to imposing negative requirements.[85] In light of this, Elliott considered that the right acquired by the grantee has, "the easement's characteristics of transmissibility with the restrictive covenant's characteristics as to nature".[86] Although Elliott does not discuss the point, it is apparent that the right he describes is a proprietary right *sui generis*. It is not possible to create a right expressly which does not have the characteristics of an easement but is enforceable as an easement. Michael A. Peel argued that the authorities did not support Elliott's conclusion. On Peel's view, non-derogation is, "a convenient formula to explain the origin of rights which may be implied easements, covenants or merely contractual rights according to the circumstances".[87] He argued that the grantee does not necessarily acquire proprietary rights by the application of non-derogation. On appropriate facts, the right may be contractual.

---

[81] See above n.21 at 225–226.
[82] See above n.4 at 226.
[83] Michael A. Peel, "The Nature of Rights Arising Under the Doctrine of Non-Derogation from Grant" (1965) 81, L.Q.R. 28 at 28.
[84] See above n.28 at 264–267.
[85] See above n.61 and text.
[86] See above n.28 at 265.
[87] See above n.83 at 28.

Further, that if a proprietary right is acquired, then the transmissibility of the right should be determined by reference to the usual rules relating to such rights. For example, if the right acquired is a restrictive covenant, then the usual rules relating to restrictive covenants should apply.

It is submitted that, following *Johnston v. Holland*, Elliott's view should be supported to the extent he recognises that in all cases in which non-derogation is applied the grantee obtains a proprietary right. However, the right created may be an easement, a restrictive covenant or a right *sui generis*. Where an easement or restrictive covenant is acquired, then (as Peel argued) the transmissibility of the right should be determined by the usual rules applicable to such rights. Where an easement is acquired, the easement is legal if acquired on the grant of a legal right,[88] and is otherwise equitable. In *Johnston*, as has been seen, the duty not to derogate prevented the obstruction of the grantee's advertisements. In essence, this was a restrictive duty which limited the grantor's ability to build on neighbouring land. However, on the facts of the case, the parties could not have entered a restrictive covenant enforceable as a proprietary right under the rule in *Tulk v. Moxhay*. The important factor is that the duty not to derogate was applied in relation to land the grantor did not own at the time of the grant. For a restrictive covenant to be proprietary there must be a servient tenement. Nicholls L.J. explained that as the grantor did not own the land at the time of the grant, "there can be no question of any obligation undertaken by him operating in the nature of a restrictive covenant over that land so as to bind successive owners of that land as such".[89] Notwithstanding, the application of non-derogation created a proprietary right. The limitation on building was enforceable against the company as the grantor's successor in title to the lease out of which the advertising rights had been granted.

4. DURATION OF THE RIGHT ACQUIRED

The duration of the duty not to derogate, and therefore of the right acquired by imposing that duty, is dependent in part on the duration

---

[88] *cf.* Peter Sparkes, *A New Land Law* (1999), p. 622.

[89] See above n.1 at 268. Equally, this would preclude treating the right acquired as an easement. In relation to restrictive covenants and easements, the after acquired land could not form part of the servient tenement. Contrast Sparkes above n.88, p. 621. He seems to treat the right acquired as a negative easement.

of the interest granted. The duty not to derogate determines, at the latest, with the expiration of the interest. For example, the grantor of a lease is under a duty not to derogate for the duration of the lease. However, as has been seen, non-derogation from grant is dependent upon the grantor holding an interest in neighbouring land and controls his use of that land. Therefore the duration of the duty must also be measured by reference to the duration of the grantor's interest in the neighbouring land. Elliott notes that, "the rule seems firmly engrafted on to the doctrine of non-derogation that it is only in his capacity as estate owner in the adjoining land that the grantor's conscience is touched".[90] This rule is derived from the "unsatisfactory" decision in *Booth v. Alcock*.[91] The effect of the rule is that if the grantor's interest in neighbouring land is limited, then the duty not to derogate ends on the termination of that interest. The net effect of measuring the duty by reference to both the grantor's and grantee's interests is that the duty ends on the earlier of two events: the termination of the interest granted or the termination of the grantor's interest in neighbouring land. This is subject to one overriding limitation. The duty not to derogate applies only while the land granted is being used for the intended purpose.[92] The duration can be illustrated by the following example. Say, L grants a ten year lease of Blackacre to T and, at the time of the grant, L is the tenant of neighbouring Whiteacre under a lease with five years remaining. For the remaining five years of his lease, L is under a duty not to use Whiteacre in a manner which would derogate from his grant to T (assuming T continues to use Blackacre for the purpose intended by the grant). When L's lease expires the holder of the reversion is under no duty to T as he holds under a different estate to L's lease. Such a set of facts raises one contentious issue: if L terminates his lease of Whiteacre prematurely, then does this also end the duty not to derogate? There are two principal ways in which L may terminate his lease: by surrendering the lease to his landlord or by purchasing his landlord's reversion. The effect of each will now be considered.[93]

---

[90] See above n.28 at 253–254.
[91] (1873) 8 Ch. App. 663. Elliott above n.28 at 252 considers the case unsatisfactory as, "neither of the members of the [Court of Appeal] dealt with or even mentioned the doctrine of derogation, although it had been argued before them, and indeed had formed the basis of the judgment of the Vice-Chancellor which was being appealed against".
[92] Elliott above n.28 at 251.
[93] If forfeiture is obtained of L's lease, then any duty not to derogate will terminate: *Beddington v. Atlee* (1887) 35 Ch. D. 317 at 323. Forfeiture generally determines both the lease and any interest derived from the lease.

A surrender by L of his lease of Whiteacre operates as an assignment of the lease to the landlord. Once assigned, the lease is determined by being merged into the freehold. As the lease is determined, Elliott says that the "clear implication" of *Booth v. Alcock* is that the surrender terminates the duty not to derogate.[94] The current author has argued[95] that Elliott's comments on surrender do not take into account that the surrendered estate is not determined *in toto*. It continues to exist between the reversioner and those third parties who had an interest in the surrendered lease and whose interest now binds the reversioner.[96] This argument was used to establish that where, prior to a surrender, L had granted interests in his lease of Whiteacre to third parties, the reversioner is bound by the duty not to derogate from those interests for the remainder of the surrendered term. It is submitted that the surrendered estate should also be seen as continuing to subsist in favour of third parties such as T to whom, prior to the surrender, L had granted an interest in other land. As far as the application of non-derogation from grant is concerned it is irrelevant whether L granted interests in the surrendered estate (Whiteacre) or in other land (Blackacre). In both situations, the burden of the consequent duty not to derogate is attached to the surrendered estate. To the extent that the surrendered estate continues to subsist the reversioner, as successor in title to that estate, should be bound.

If L purchases the reversionary estate in Whiteacre, then the lease is determined as it is "drowned" in the freehold.[97] *Booth v. Alcock*[98] is authority for the proposition that when L purchases the reversion the duty not to derogate terminates.[99] L no longer holds the land in the capacity in which he granted the interest but holds it under a different estate. However as L, the grantor, remains interested in the land the argument for maintaining the duty seems strong. It is submitted that, by analogy with a surrender, the lease should be treated as continuing to subsist in relations between L and third parties, including T, to whom L has granted an interest.

Elliott is critical of the "hard legalistic"[1] rule that the duty not to derogate terminates with the grantor's interest in the neighbouring

---

[94] Elliott above n.28 at 253.
[95] In the paper referred to above n.45.
[96] See above n.45 at 287–288.
[97] *Pennell v. Payne* [1995] 2 W.L.R. 261 at 265, *per* Simon Brown L.J.
[98] See above n.91.
[99] The decision is criticised above n.91.
[1] See above n.28 at 253.

land. He considers it would be more consistent with, "the notions of common honesty upon which the doctrine of non-derogation is supposed to be founded" to measure the duration of the duty by reference to the intentions of the parties at the time of the grant.[2] Elliott's argument, broadly stated, seems to be that where a grantor has a limited interest in neighbouring land, the duty not to derogate should endure for the anticipated period of that interest (regardless, for example, of a surrender) as that would be the expectations of the parties. The argument made above enables this to be achieved within the confines of the established rule. However, a further argument may be made by reference to the intentions of the parties where the duration of the grantor's interest in neighbouring land is extended.[3] As has been seen, in *Johnston v. Holland* the court held that the duty not to derogate can apply to land acquired by the grantor after the date of the grant. It may be possible to treat the acquisition of a new estate in the same way as the acquisition of new land. Hence a grantor who acquires a new estate may be under a duty not to derogate for the duration of the new estate, not merely for the anticipated duration of the grantor's original estate. As with the acquisition of new land it would have to be shown that it was necessarily implicit at the time of the grant that the duty would apply to the new estate.[4] The courts may be more reluctant to extend the duration of the duty than they are to extend its geographical scope. Where the grantor is the tenant of neighbouring land, and subsequently acquires the freehold, holding the grantor bound may transform a temporary duty into a permanent burden on the land.

III. Specific rules derived from non-derogation from grant

The rule of non-derogation from grant is seen as the basis for three specific rules enabling the acquisition of an easement. As with the

---

[2] *ibid*.

[3] Where, *e.g.* the grantor is a tenant and subsequently buys the freehold.

[4] Elliott above n.28 at 253 suggests that where the grantor has only a limited interest in the neighbouring land, "that would be taken as showing an intent in both parties that the obligation should last only while the grantor or his assigns are interested in the land". However he wrote prior to *Johnston v. Holland* and consequently in the belief (stated at 252) that non-derogation did not apply to land acquired after the grant.

general rule, the easement acquired is legal where it is implied pursuant to the grant of a legal right and equitable when implied on the grant of an equitable interest. The general rule itself may give rise to the acquisition of easements. Therefore, the question arises to what extent there is an overlap between the general and specific rules. It seems that there are three characteristics that separate the specific rules. First, each specific rule has its own requirements which are distinct, in some respects, from the general rule. Secondly, in each case the right claimed must fulfil the general characteristics of an easement. The specific rules are not the source of proprietary rights *sui generis*. In these respects, the specific rules are more restrictive in their application than the general rule. However, thirdly, it seems that the specific rules alone can create positive easements.[5] The general rule may be limited to enabling the creation of negative easements. In addition to the three rules derived from non-derogation from grant, there is a fourth, related, rule enabling the acquisition of a legal easement[6] by words implied into a conveyance by statute. All four rules will be discussed in this section.

Only two of the rules to be discussed enable the implied reservation of an easement in favour of a grantor; necessity and common intention. Generally, courts are more reluctant to imply the reservation of an easement than to imply a grant. In *Wheeldon v. Burrows* Thesiger L.J. explained, "if the grantor intends to reserve any right over the tenement granted, it is his duty to reserve it expressly in the grant".[7] Thesiger L.J. based this on non-derogation from grant: to enable a grantor to claim rights over land granted is to enable him to derogate from the grant.[8] However, Thesiger L.J. acknowledged that an easement may be impliedly reserved in exceptional circumstances.[9]

1. WHERE AN EASEMENT IS NECESSARY TO PROVIDE ACCESS TO LAND

Where land is granted to which there is no means of access, but the grantor retains neighbouring land, an easement across the grantor's land is implied to provide access. This is an easement of necessity "strictly so-called".[10] It is an easement, "without which the [land

---

[5] Sparkes above n.88, p. 621.
[6] Or a profit.
[7] See above n.18 at 49.
[8] See also, *e.g. Peckham v. Ellison* (2000) P.&C.R. 276 at 291.
[9] See above n.18 at 49.
[10] *Nickerson v. Barraclough* [1980] Ch 325 at 332, *per* Megarry V.-C.

granted] cannot be used at all".[11] The implication of the easement of necessity, "clearly emanates from the principle against derogation from grant".[12] It would be a clear derogation to refuse access to land granted.[13] An easement of necessity may also be impliedly reserved where a grantor retains some land without reserving a means of access. To provide a right of access an easement will be implied across the land granted.

To claim an easement of necessity the principal requirement is that there is no other means of access to the land.[14] As with the general rule of non-derogation, the implication of an easement of necessity is dependent upon the grantor owning neighbouring land: the grantor is able to provide access only when he retains land physically contiguous to the land granted. It must be shown that, at the time of the grant, the grantor had a title to the neighbouring land which would enable him to grant the easement expressly. This requirement was confirmed by the Privy Council in *Manjang v. Drammeh*.[15] There, a grantor argued that an easement of necessity was impliedly reserved to provide him with access to land neighbouring the land he had granted. His claim failed because, at the time of the grant, he had no title to the neighbouring land.[16] Further, as with the general rule, it is necessary to establish the purpose of the grant. Save for exceptional

---

[11] *Union Lighterage Co v. London Graving Dock Co* [1902] 2 Ch. 557 at 573, *per* Stirling L.J. Whether easements of necessity may be implied other than to give access remain unclear. The possibility of other claims is discussed by Jackson, "Easements of Necessity" [1981] C.L.P. 133 at 148–152. Adopting a strict definition, other easements may be claimed as easements based on common intention discussed below, Part III 2.

[12] Gray, p. 1092.

[13] *Nickerson v. Barraclough* above n.10 at 335.

[14] The availability of an alternative means of access will defeat the claim, even though the alternative is less convenient. See, *e.g. Manjang v. Drammeh* (1991) 61 P. & C.R. 194 PC at 197: a means of access by river defeats a claim to an easement of necessity over land. However the existence of permissive access, not based on a legal right, will not defeat a claim: *Barry v. Hasseldine* [1952] Ch. 835 at 839.

[15] See above n.14 at 197. The Privy Council required the grantor, at the time of the grant, to hold a legal estate in both the land granted and the land retained.

[16] The claimant was in occupation at the time of the grant but only subsequently acquired title. *Manjang v. Drammeh* should be contrasted with *Johnston v. Holland* where, as seen above n.37 and text, the Court of Appeal applied the general rule in relation to land acquired by the grantor subsequent to the grant. *Johnston v. Holland* was not discussed in *Manjang v. Drammeh*. In *Johnston v. Holland* the after acquired land was the servient tenement. The court may not be prepared to apply the case where, as in *Manjang v. Drammeh*, the after acquired land is the dominant tenement.

circumstances, access will be required regardless of the purpose.[17] However, an easement of necessity may be used only for the purpose for which the land granted was in fact used at the time of the grant or for other purposes contemplated by the parties.[18]

There is some doubt whether easements of necessity are based on the presumed intentions of the parties to the grant or on a rule of public policy that, "no transaction should, without good reason, be treated as being effectual to deprive any land of a suitable means of access".[19] The practical importance of the debate is that if the easement is based on the parties' intentions, then it should be possible to preclude its creation by an express negation.[20] In *Nickerson v. Barraclough* Megarry V.-C., at first instance, considered easements of necessity to be based on public policy. He seemed to treat public policy as operating separately from non-derogation from grant.[21] The Court of Appeal, reversing Megarry V.-C., said that easements of necessity are based on the presumed intentions of the parties.[22] The discussion in that case of easements of necessity is *obiter* as limited access to the land was available.[23] However, it is submitted that only an analysis based on the intentions of the parties, which allows for the possibility of express negation, is consistent with non-derogation from grant. There could be no derogation by a grantor who refuses a right of access which is expressly precluded by the grant.

---

[17] *cf.* the examples given by Megarry V.-C. in *Nickerson v. Barraclough* above n.10 at 334. He comments that access could be denied, consistent with public policy, where land is granted for use as a bird sanctuary or where the land contains toxic substances. Although the test of public policy he advocated has been rejected, see below n.22 and text, an easement of necessity may be denied on the basis that access is not required to use the land for the purpose of the grant.

[18] Jackson above n.11 at 143–44.

[19] *Nickerson v. Barraclough* above n.10 at 334–335, *per* Megarry V.-C.

[20] But see Letitia Crabb, "Necessity: The Mother of Intention" [1981] Conv. 442 at 443–444. She argues that even if easements of necessity are based on the parties' intentions, then notwithstanding it may still be possible to imply an easement following an express exclusion.

[21] See, *e.g.* above n.10 at 335: "The vendor must not derogate from his grant . . . If, therefore, the words of negation can be read in some way so as not to produce any derogation from grant, they should be so read. The rule of public policy requires the same approach". Further at 336: "If, then, in construing this provision I give proper weight to the doctrine against derogation from grant and the rule of public policy. . .".

[22] [1981] 1 Ch. 426 at 440, *per* Brightman L.J. with whom, on this point, Eveleigh L.J. at 446–447, and Buckley L.J. at 447 agreed.

[23] *ibid.* at 437, *per* Brightman L.J. Access was available for agricultural and sporting purposes. The claimant sought to extend access to facilitate building on the land.

2. WHERE THE EASEMENT IS NECESSARY FOR THE LAND TO BE USED CONSISTENT WITH THE COMMON INTENTIONS OF THE PARTIES

An easement will be impliedly granted in two situations where the easement is necessary to enable land to be used as intended by the parties to the grant.[24] It would be a derogation from grant to refuse an easement necessary to enable the land to be used as intended. The first situation is where there is a grant of rights in land and an easement is necessary to enjoy those rights. For example, "the right of drawing water from a spring necessarily involves the right of going to the spring for the purpose".[25] The second, and more important situation, is where land is granted to be used for a particular purpose and the easement is necessary to enable the land to be used for that purpose. A strict test of necessity is applied, in light of which there is a close relationship between this category and easements of necessity. An easement based on common intention is sometimes seen as a wider specie of easements of necessity.[26] The relationship between them is illustrated by *Nickerson v. Barraclough*.[27] There, the plaintiff had limited access to her land, but wanted access to be extended to facilitate building. As access was available, she did not claim an easement of necessity in the strict sense. Instead, the plaintiff claimed that the implication of an easement was necessary to give effect to the purpose of the grant.[28]

The requirements of an easement of common intention are, to an extent, a stricter version of the elements of a claim under the general rule of non-derogation. As with the general rule, the purpose of the grant must be established. In *Pwllbach Colliery Co Ltd v. Woodman* Lord Parker explained that the parties must have intended the land granted (or retained) to be used in a, "definite and particular manner".[29] It is insufficient if the land is to be used in a manner, "which may or may not involve this definite and particular use".[30]

---

[24] Explained by Lord Parker in *Pwllbach Colliery Co Ltd v. Woodman* [1915] A.C. 634 at 646–647.

[25] *ibid.* 646 *per* Lord Parker.

[26] See, *e.g.* the discussion by Megarry V.-C. in *Nickerson v. Barraclough* above n.10 at 332.

[27] See above n.10 (at first instance), and n.22 (Court of Appeal).

[28] See above n.22 at 437. The claim in that case failed as the easement was expressly precluded in the grant.

[29] See above n.24 at 647.

[30] *ibid.*

Once the purpose is established an easement will be implied (as there would otherwise be a derogation from the grant) in two situations.[31] First, where the land could not practically be used for that purpose without the easement. Secondly where the purpose may be achieved without the easement, but the parties intended it to be achieved in a particular manner which does require an easement. A successful claim was made in *Wong v. Beaumont Property Trust Ltd*.[32] There, a lease of premises was granted to be used as a restaurant. The tenant covenanted to "control and eliminate all smells". The Court of Appeal considered that this was the, "definite and particular manner" in which the business was to be conducted.[33] As smells could be eliminated only by the installation of a ventilation duct up the wall of the grantor's neighbouring land, an easement to do so was implied.[34]

The circumstances in which the reservation of an easement will be implied were considered by the Court of Appeal in *Peckham v. Ellison*.[35] The court agreed that the correct test, as formulated by counsel, was "whether the circumstances raise a necessary inference of an intention common to both parties that [the grantor] should have the right of way reserved to it. . .".[36] This inference could be drawn only where the facts are not consistent with any other explanation. In upholding the claim to an easement, the court emphasised that the case was "exceptional".[37]

3. WHERE THE EASEMENT (OR QUASI-EASEMENT) WAS ENJOYED BY THE GRANTOR PRIOR TO THE GRANT

This rule can be explained by reference to an example. Say, X is the owner of neighbouring lands, Blackacre and Whiteacre. To further the enjoyment of Whiteacre, X exercises "rights" over Blackacre. These "rights" would have the characteristics of an easement but for

---

[31] *cf Pwllbach Colliery Co Ltd v. Woodman* above n.24 at 639.
[32] [1965] 1 Q.B. 173.
[33] See the discussion by Lord Denning M.R., *ibid*. at 181.
[34] The Court of Appeal treated the case as an easement of necessity. However, the Court applied *Pwllbach Colliery Co Ltd v. Woodman* above n.24, which itself was based on common intention. It is submitted that *Wong v. Beaumont* above n.32 is correctly interpreted as an easement based on common intention. *cf*. Megarry V.-C.'s comments in *Nickerson v. Barraclough* above n.10 at 332.
[35] See above n.8.
[36] See above n.8 at 291.
[37] See above n.8 at 298.

the fact the lands are in common ownership. Therefore, they are referred to as quasi-easements. X then transfers Whiteacre to Y. If certain conditions are met, then Y will acquire easements over Blackacre based on X's use during the period of common ownership. Hence, on the transfer of Whiteacre, the quasi-easements are transformed into easements. The informal acquisition of easements in this way is known as the rule in *Wheeldon v. Burrows*.[38] The application of the rule is subject to an express provision to the contrary.[39] This is consistent with non-derogation from grant: a grantor does not derogate by refusing an easement which is expressly precluded in the grant. However, *Wheeldon v. Burrows* enables only the implied grant of easements. If, in the above example, X transferred Blackacre and retained Whiteacre, then no easement would be impliedly reserved in X's favour by application of the rule in *Wheeldon v. Burrows*.

In explaining the rule, Thesiger L.J., in *Wheeldon v. Burrows*, considered it to be founded in non-derogation from grant.[40] The extent to which the rule continues to reflect the general rule of non-derogation from grant is uncertain. Jackson considers that the rule has taken, "a life of its own".[41] However, as will be seen, the rule may notwithstanding still be interpreted in a manner consistent with non-derogation from grant. The uncertainty arises as a result of doubt concerning the relationship between the first two of three requirements which must be met for *Wheeldon v. Burrows* to apply. This will be considered following an explanation of the requirements.

For the rule in *Wheeldon v. Burrows* to apply, the easement claimed must be continuous and apparent, necessary for the reasonable enjoyment of the land granted and must have been used by the grantor at the time of the grant for the benefit of the land granted. A continuous easement is one which benefits the dominant tenement without human activity; for example, a right to light. An easement is apparent where it is visible on an inspection of the land; for example, a right of way represented by a path.[42] It is probably sufficient for the

---

[38] See above n.18.
[39] See, *e.g. Millman v. Ellis* (1996) 71 P. & C.R. 158. There, the Court of Appeal held the mere fact an easement had been granted did not preclude the application of *Wheeldon v. Burrows* to claim an implied easement which, in effect, extended the scope of the servient tenement. See John West, *"Wheeldon v. Burrows* Revisited" [1995] Conv. 346 at 347–348.
[40] See above n.18 at 49.
[41] See above n.35, p. 76.
[42] See, *e.g. Borman v. Griffith* above n.20.

application of the rule for the easement to be apparent. In *Borman v. Griffith*[43] a right of way, which was visible on an inspection of the land, was acquired under the rule even though a right of way is not continuous. Whether an easement is "reasonably necessary" is a far less strict test than the test of necessity applied when an easement is claimed based on necessity or common intention.[44] M.P. Thompson suggests that the degree of necessity which must be established lies at an "ill-defined point" between a strict test of necessity and an easement which "merely accommodates" the land granted.[45] The need for the easement to have been used at the time of the grant ensures that rights claimed do in fact reflect use of the land by the common owner. The requirement may be satisfied despite several months of non-use immediately prior to the grant.[46]

It is the first requirement, the need for the easement to be continuous and apparent, which separates *Wheeldon v. Burrows* from non-derogation from grant.[47] The test is not derived from non-derogation but has been incorporated from French law. Charles Harpum explains that, applied in the context of *Wheeldon v. Burrows*, it is a rule of conveyancing convenience which facilitates the discovery of encumbrances.[48] Non-derogation from grant is reflected in the second requirement, that the easement is necessary for the reasonable enjoyment of the land.[49] The relationship between these two requirements is uncertain,[50] but the prevailing view is that both must be satisfied. This is suggested by *Wheeler v. J.J. Saunders Ltd*[51] in which, for the first time since 1950,[52] the application of the second

---

[43] See above n.20.
[44] *Wheeler v. J.J. Saunders Ltd* [1995] 2 All E.R. 697 at 702, *per* Staughton L.J., "even to a novice in the law of easements, it seems clear that the class of easements implied in favour of a grantee is wider than easements of necessity". There, a claim to an easement to provide access to land failed as the claimant enjoyed an alternative access which, "would do just as well".
[45] M.P. Thompson, "Paths and Pigs" [1995] Conv. 239 at 240.
[46] *Costagliola v. English* (1969) 210 E.G. 1425.
[47] Megarry and Wade, para. 18–104; Smith, p. 474.
[48] Charles Harpum, "Easements and Centre Point: Old Problems Resolved in a Novel Setting" [1977] Conv. 415 at 422.
[49] Smith, p. 474.
[50] Three possible interpretations are discussed by Graham J. Ferris, "Problems Postponed: The Rule in *Wheeldon v. Burrows* and *Wheeler v. Saunders*" (1996) 3 Web J.C.L.I.
[51] See above n.44. This approach is supported by Thompson above n.45 at 240, and Harpum above n.48 at 422.
[52] *Goldberg v. Edwards* [1950] 1 Ch. 247.

requirement independently from the first operated to defeat a claim.[53] If this view is correct, then it seems to confirm the separation of the rule in *Wheeldon v. Burrows* from non-derogation from grant. In *Wheeler v. Saunders*, the claim under *Wheeldon v. Burrows* failed because the easement claimed was not necessary for the reasonable enjoyment of the land. As it failed on this requirement, denying the easement did not in fact constitute a derogation from the grant. However if, as the case suggests, both requirements must be fulfilled, then merely to establish that denying the easement would be a derogation (because the easement is necessary for reasonable enjoyment of the land) will be insufficient to establish a claim. It must also be established that the easement is continuous and apparent. Ferris notes that in *Wheeler v. Saunders* the Court of Appeal neither considered the relevant authorities nor clearly determined the relationship between the two requirements.[54] Roger J. Smith suggests an interpretation of the requirements which is consistent with non-derogation from grant. He suggests that both should be seen merely as guidelines as to when the refusal of an easement will be a derogation.[55]

4. EASEMENTS ACQUIRED BY STATUTORY WORDS IMPLIED INTO A CONVEYANCE

When land is conveyed, section 62(1) of the Law of Property Act 1925 operates to ensure that the conveyance includes: "[all] liberties, privileges, easements, rights and advantages whatsoever, appertaining or reputed to appertain to the land". The section is considered sufficiently broad to transform into easements rights which did not exist as easements prior to the conveyance. It applies only on the conveyance[56] of a legal right. Although not apparent on the face of section 62, its application has been restricted to where the lands which become the dominant and servient tenement are not both

---

[53] Ferris above n.50.
[54] See above n.50.
[55] Smith, p. 474.
[56] "Conveyance" is defined in the Law of Property Act 1925, s.205(1)(ii) as, "a mortgage, charge, lease, assent, vesting declaration, vesting instrument, disclaimer, release and every assurance of property or of an interest therein, by any instrument, except a will". In registered land, s.62 applies on the disposition of a registered estate: Land Registration Act 1925, ss.19(3) (freehold) and 22(3) (leasehold).

owned and occupied by the vendor prior to the grant.[57] Unlike the other rules discussed in this chapter, section 62 is not derived from non-derogation from grant. Further, the section may not in fact enable the *informal* acquisition of easements. The section is a word saving clause, the contents of which are implied into every conveyance unless expressly excluded. An easement acquired by section 62 is therefore created by the interpretation of the words in a conveyance. Such easements may be considered to be expressly granted.[58] Notwithstanding, the section is discussed here as it is closely related to the rule in *Wheeldon v. Burrows*.

The application of section 62 can be illustrated by example. Say, *X* owns neighbouring lands, Blackacre and Whiteacre. Whiteacre is, however, occupied by *Y* as tenant. *X* allows *Y* to exercise "rights" across Blackacre which have the characteristics of an easement although no easement is created. *X* then conveys Whiteacre to *Y*. On the conveyance, by section 62, *Y* acquires legal easements reflecting his previous use of Blackacre.[59] In contrast to the rule in *Wheeldon v. Burrows*, it is not necessary to show that the easement is continuous and apparent or is necessary for reasonable enjoyment of the land.[60] However, if the easement claimed is continuous and apparent, then it is arguable an easement could be claimed under section 62 where, prior to the conveyance, *X* both owned and occupied the lands.[61] If this is correct, then the range of cases in which it is necessary to rely on the rule in *Wheeldon v. Burrows* will be reduced.[62] Section 62 will enable an easement to be acquired on a legal transfer, in cases such as *Wheeler v. Saunders*, where a claim under *Wheeldon v. Burrows* fails as the easement is not necessary for reasonable enjoyment of the land. As that requirement reflects non-derogation from grant, enabling a claim under section 62 to succeed when the requirement is not met

---

[57] *Long v. Gowlett* [1923] 2 Ch. 177, affirmed in *Sovmots Investments Ltd v. Secretary of State for the Environment* above n.17.

[58] J.T. Farrand, *Contract and Conveyance*, (1980), p. 301. The Law of Property Act 1925, s.62 is described as an express grant by Megarry and Wade, para. 18.092 and as an implied grant by Gray, p. 1100. Peter Sparkes, *A New Land Law*, p. 586 describes s.62 as a "use-based grant" in contra-distinction to an express grant.

[59] See, *e.g. International Tea Stores v. Hobbs* [1903] 2 Ch. 165.

[60] As this requirement reflects non-derogation from grant, its absence reflects the fact that s.62 is not derived from that rule.

[61] Harpum, "*Long* v. *Gowlett*: A Strong Fortress" [1979] Conv. 113; Thompson, "The Acquisition of Easements" [1997] Conv. 453.

[62] It would remain necessary to rely on *Wheeldon v. Burrows* where, *e.g.* the claim is made on the transfer of an equitable interest.

further demonstrates the separation of section 62 from derogation from grant.[63]

IV. Conclusion

When rights in land are created or acquired for a particular purpose, and the grantor owns neighbouring land, the grantor is placed under a duty not to derogate from those rights. The duty is given effect by the acquisition of proprietary rights by the grantee which ensures that the duty is enforceable against the grantor's successors in title. Although in the majority of cases the right acquired is likely to be an easement or restrictive covenant, non-derogation is also the source for the acquisition of proprietary rights *sui generis*. This means, paradoxically, that the right acquired to protect a grant may not itself be capable of being granted expressly.[64] The justification for the acquisition of rights is that it ensures a general standard of fairness by the grantor, who is prevented from taking away enjoyment of the right granted. This broad, common sense rationale has been more influential in the development of the rule than technical considerations such as the definition of "grant" or of a "servitude".

The specific rules derived from non-derogation may be seen as situations in which it would be a derogation from grant to deny an easement. The fact these rules are derived from the general rule may be an aid to their application and interpretation. For example, reference to the general rule may help clarify the basis of an easement of necessity and explain the relationship between the requirements for a claim under the rule in *Wheeldon v. Burrows*.

---

[63] No claim under s.62 was made in *Wheeler v. Saunders*. See Thompson above n.45 at 240–242.

[64] Megarry and Wade, para. 18–076.

Chapter 10.

To Recognise Use of a Right

I. Introduction

In limited circumstances a proprietary right may be acquired because the claimant (*C*) has exercised the right. There are two ways in which rights may be acquired in this way by use. First, where the use has the effect of creating a new right in favour of *C* and defeating pre-existing rights. This is recognised in the English law of adverse possession, which enables *C* to acquire a freehold estate by taking possession of land, and by continued use to defeat or extinguish existing titles. Secondly where use of a right for a given period of time is considered to be evidence that a right has in fact been granted. This is recognised in the English law of prescription, which enables the acquisition of an easement or profit. These are the only rights in land that it is possible to acquire through use.[1] This may in part reflect an overriding policy that a right cannot be derived from use unless its exercise is reasonably apparent to the person against whom it is asserted. This policy is manifested most clearly in the nature of the use required for a claim to succeed. A claim will fail where *C*'s possession of land (in the context of adverse possession) or exercise of an easement or profit (in a claim to prescription) is not reasonably discoverable by the person against whom the claim is made (hereafter the paper owner, or *PO* in relation to adverse possession; servient

---

[1] In both rules, long use is required. In prescription it is only after a long period of use that any right is acquired. In adverse possession, although rights are acquired by the taking of possession, it is only by long use that earlier titles are defeated and therefore that the right acquired ceases to be vulnerable. It is because of the significance of the initial possession in a claim to adverse possession that this chapter refers to "use" rather than "long use" as the common foundation of the rules.

owner, or *SO* in relation to prescription). This requirement ensures that *PO* or *SO* has the opportunity to assert their legal rights and prevent (or put an end to) *C*'s claim. The nature of an easement or profit is such that their exercise is usually visible. In contrast, it would not generally be possible to discover whether a restrictive covenant was being asserted. For example, if land is not used for business purposes, there will be no visible indication whether that is the choice of the legal owner or the result of a neighbouring landowner's restrictive covenant.[2] Further, the types of right recognised as easements are sufficiently defined that their acquisition is unlikely to sterilise *SO*'s use of his land.[3] In contrast, if non-use of land for a particular purpose was seen as the exercise of a restrictive covenant, then land may be sterilised as being restricted to its prevailing use. A proprietary right acquired by use is necessarily legal. An easement or profit acquired by prescription is legal because it is based on an implied grant. The title to land acquired through adverse possession is generally thought to be a legal freehold[4] by virtue of the concept of relativity of title, discussed below.[5]

The key distinction between adverse possession and prescription is the different way in which the two rules analyse the effect of use.[6] In *Lovett v. Fairclough* Mummery J. suggested that the similarity between the rules ends with their common basis in recognising long use.[7] However, as a result of their common basis in recognising use of a right, the rules do share a number of important features[8] and, to an extent, are based on common justifications. Both rules may initially appear difficult to justify. Both seem to legitimise the "theft" of rights in land. Together with the rules discussed in Chapters 2 and 3 (concerned respectively with giving effect to gifts and preventing the use of statute for fraud) and exceptional cases in Chapter 4, (where a

---

[2] Negative easements, in contrast to a restrictive covenant, may be visible, *e.g.* an easement to support may be apparent from the existence of the supporting wall. See Part III 2 (b).

[3] A claim which imposed an undue burden on the servient land would fail as not being within the general characteristics of an easement.

[4] This is debated. The debate is summarised by the Law Commission in Law Com. No. 254 *Land Registration for the Twenty First Century*, para. 10.23.

[5] Part II 1.

[6] *Buckingham C.C. v. Moran* [1990] 1 Ch. 623 at 644; *Lovett v. Fairclough* (1991) 61 P. & C.R. 385 at 398–399.

[7] See above n.6 at 398.

[8] Herbert Wallace, "Limitation, Prescription and Unsolicited Permission" [1994] Conv. 196 at 197.

purchaser expressly takes land "subject to" certain rights) use of a right enables rights to be acquired by a claimant who has neither provided consideration nor acted to his or her detriment. The rules discussed in Chapter 2 may be justified as they give effect to a gift intended by the legal owner. In the rules discussed in Chapters 3 and 4 rights are granted because of an overriding need to prevent a type of conduct considered to be fraudulent. Neither justification is applicable to claims based on use. However, rules based on use are common to many legal jurisdictions and their legitimacy has long been accepted by English courts.

In *Moody v. Steggles*[9] Fry J. explained: "Where there has been long enjoyment of property in a particular manner it is the habit, and, in my view, the duty, of the court, so far as it lawfully can, to clothe the fact with right".[10] This duty may be seen as the common foundation of adverse possession and prescription.[11] The initial difficulty in justifying the rules stems from a perspective of seeing them as "taking" from the legal owner. The difficulties become less apparent if the rules are viewed in terms of "confirming" to C that he has the rights he has been exercising. The rules ensure that formal ownership of land reflects actual occupation and use.[12] Reality is given preference above formal legal ownership. There are a number of further justifications which, although generally discussed in relation to adverse possession, may be equally applicable to prescription.[13] Both rules may be justified on the basis that they protect against stale claims which may cause evidentiary difficulties; encourage legal owners to assert their rights; avoid the hardship and resentment which may result from taking away a right long considered to exist; reward those who maximise use of land. Apart from these common

---

[9] (1879) 12 Ch.D. 261.
[10] See above n.9 at 265.
[11] Wallace above n.8 at 196.
[12] The "curative" effect of adverse possession is explained by Michael J. Goodman, "Adverse Possession of Land—Morality and Motive" (1970) 33 M.L.R. 281.
[13] Paul Jackson, *The Law of Easements and Profits* (1978), p. 110. See Martin Dockray, "Why Do We Need Adverse Possession?" [1985] Conv. 272 (justifications for adverse possession) and the Law Reform Committee's Fourteenth Report on *The Acquisition of Easements and Profits*, discussed by H.W. Wilkinson, "Law Reform Committee: Fourteenth Report on Aquisition of Easements and Profits by Prescription" (1967) 30 M.L.R 189 (justifications for prescription).

justifications, the Law Commission considers the strongest justification for adverse possession to be its role in facilitating the investigation of unregistered titles to land.[14] Prescription is perhaps more
readily accepted viewed in the broader context of other rules through
which the grant of an easement may be implied.[15]

In this chapter, adverse possession and prescription are discussed
in parallel. It will be apparent that while there is no uniform principle
enabling the acquisition of rights by use, the reliance each rule places
on use provides some common requirements and difficulties.

II. Sources of the rules

1. ADVERSE POSSESSION

Adverse possession is the combined effect of limitation of actions and
relativity of title. In English law, at least in the context of unregistered land, title is relative based on who has the superior (that is,
earlier) right to possess land. By entering into possession (in the
manner explained below)[16] C immediately acquires a legal fee simple
title, superior to that of any subsequent possessor, but subject to
earlier claims, including that of PO. The ability of holders of superior
titles to assert their claim against C is subject to rules governing
limitation of actions. Section 15(1) of the Limitation Act 1980
imposes a 12 year limitation period on actions to recover land.[17]
Hence, from the date C enters into possession, holders of superior
titles have 12 years to assert their claim. If they fail to do so, then
their claim becomes time barred and C's title is no longer vulnerable
to a challenge by them. Further, it is irrelevant whether the same

---

[14] See above n.4, para. 10.10, expressing agreement with Dockray above n.13 at 277–
278. As the period of use required to defeat a pre-existing title (12 years) is less than
the period of investigation required to establish good root of title (15 years plus one
conveyance), a good root of title virtually guarantees that there are no outstanding
claims.

[15] Discussed in Chapter 9 Part III.

[16] Part III 1 (b).

[17] In the context of a review of the law of limitation periods, the Law Commission has
made the preliminary recommendation that the period of limitation in an action to
recover land should be reduced to 10 years. The recommendation is made in the
context of providing a single limitation period for all types of action. See Law Com,
No. 151 *Limitation of Actions*, para. 13.117.

claimant remains in possession throughout the limitation period, or whether that period is marked by the successive (though uninterrupted) possession of two or more claimants. In any action, the question for the court is which party to the action has the relatively better title. It is irrelevant in an action between *C* and *PO* that a person who is not a party to the action has a title relatively superior to that held by both of the parties.

These principles may be illustrated by reference to the opinion of the Privy Council in *Sze To Chun Keung v. Kung Kwok Wai David*,[18] a case based on parallel provisions in Hong Kong law. There, the Crown was in possession of land adverse to *PO*. Throughout the Crown's possession, the land was physically occupied by *C*, as the Crown's licensee (and therefore on behalf of the Crown). For a short period of time prior to the action, the Crown relinquished its possession and *C* became an adverse possessor in his own right. In an action between *PO* and *C*, *C* was considered to be entitled to possession as *PO*'s title was time-barred. *C*'s title, which dated only from the time the Crown ceased possession, was not vulnerable to a claim by *PO* who had been excluded for the requisite limitation period. As the Crown was in possession prior to *C*, the Crown would have a superior title which it could assert against *C* until it had been excluded for the limitation period. However, the fact the Crown had a superior title was irrelevant to settling the dispute between *C* and *PO*.[19]

2. PRESCRIPTION

Unlike adverse possession, the mere exercise of an easement or profit does not immediately confer any rights. Instead, if use continues for the requisite period of time, then the right crystallises and the grant of an easement is implied. Hence, the claimant to an easement or profit by prescription either has a legal easement or has nothing. There is no "intermediate stage which has any legal existence".[20]

---

[18] [1997] 1 W.L.R. 1232.

[19] The case arose on a preliminary ruling to strike out *C*'s defence in an action for possession by *PO*. The Privy Council's opinion is therefore based on the facts as pleaded.

[20] *Greenhalgh v. Brindley* [1901] 2 Ch. 324 at 328, *per* Farwell J., cited in *Lovett* above n.6 at 399. The Law Commission has provisionally recommended above n.4, para. 5.17 that rights in the course of being acquired by prescription should be overriding interests, to put beyond doubt that a change in the ownership of the servient land does not affect a claim. There is a clear anomaly in protecting as an overriding interest a right with no legal existence.

There are three different methods by which an easement or profit may be acquired by prescription.[21]

First, at common law an easement was originally implied where use had continued since time immemorial, a date fixed by the Statute of Westminster as 1189. In recognition of the difficulty in satisfying that test, 20 years' use came to be considered to give rise to a presumption of use since 1189. However, the presumption was rebuttable and the claim would fail if shown that use could not have continued since that time. Hence, for example, easements could not be claimed in relation to a building constructed since 1189.[22] The second method of prescription, the doctrine of lost modern grant, was created by judges in response to the inadequacies of the original common law rule.[23] The doctrine, which was accepted by the House of Lords in *Dalton v. Henry Angus & Co,*[24] removed the need to refer to 1189. Instead, applying the doctrine, 20 years' use is generally seen as evidence that an easement has been granted after 1189, but the grant has been lost.[25] The doctrine operates by drawing a presumption of grant. As it is based on a presumption of grant, the doctrine does not apply where the right claimed is enjoyed as a natural incident of land.[26] Further, the presumption may be rebutted by, for example, evidence of incapacity to grant the easement.[27] However, the presumption is not rebutted by proof that in fact there was no

---

[21] The co-existence of these three methods is described ironically by the Law Commission, above n.4, para. 10.79 as an "extraordinary luxury". More pointedly, in *Tehidy Minerals Ltd v. Norman* [1971] 2 Q.B. 528 at 529 Buckley L.J. commented that it is, "anomalous and undesirable, for it results in much unnecessary complication and confusion". The Law Commission has provisionally recommended, above n.4, para. 10.91 that only one of the three methods, the Prescription Act 1832, should continue to apply to registered land.

[22] See, *e.g.* the discussion in *Simmons v. Dobson* [1991] 1 W.L.R. 720 at 723.

[23] See the explanation in *Simmons v. Dobson* above n.22 at 723.

[24] (1881) 6 App. Cas. 740. The effect of that case is summarised in *Tehidy* above n.21 at 552.

[25] The overarching principle is that there must be sufficient use to draw the presumption a grant was made. As a rule of thumb, 20 years' use is considered sufficient.

[26] *Palmer v. Bowman* [2000] 1 All E.R. 22. There, a claim to an easement of prescription for water to drain from *SO's* higher land to *C's* lower land was rejected. There was no need to assume a lost grant, as *C's* previous enjoyment of the claimed right was explicable as an incident of his ownership of the lower land.

[27] *Oakley v. Boston* [1975] 3 W.L.R. 478: during the relevant period, the land was vested in a Rector as a corporation sole who could not grant an easement without the consent of the Church Commissioners. *C*'s claim to a prescriptive easement based on lost modern grant therefore failed.

grant. This epitomises the artificial nature of lost modern grant.[28] In *Simmons v. Dobson* Fox L.J. explained, "nobody believed that there ever was a grant. But it was a convenient and workable fiction".[29] There is some debate as regards the relationship between these two methods of prescription. In *Mills v. Silver*[30] both parties accepted that, "in this, as in virtually every other case, the claim founded on prescription at common law ... adds nothing to the claim of presumed lost grant; they stand or fall together".[31] This assertion is not strictly true,[32] as a claim to lost modern grant alone will not fail merely because use began after 1189. However, it may be correct to state (and, in context, may have been the intention underlying the assertion in *Mills*) that as a claim to lost modern grant is easier to establish, the failure of such a claim would necessarily mean that there could be no claim based on common law prescription.

The third method is statutory prescription provided by the Prescription Act 1832. The Act has, "long been criticised as one of the worst drafted Acts on the Statute Books".[33] The Act provides different rules for easements and profits. In relation to easements, the general rule, in section 2 of the Act, is that an easement is acquired after 20 years' use and, after 40 years' use is "absolute and indefeasible". This general rule does not apply to rights of light, which are subject to a separate regime.[34] There also seems some doubt whether it applies to negative easements.[35] In relation to profits, under section 1 these are acquired by 30 years' use and are, "absolute and indefeasible" after 60 years. However, the Act applies only to profits appurtenant, and not to profits in gross. In all cases, the effect of use for the shorter period is that the easement or profit cannot be defeated merely by virtue of the fact use does not extend to time immemorial. In this way, it seems that the Act sought to cure the difficulty with common law prescription which had, in any event, been resolved by the doctrine of lost modern grant.[36] However, the

---

[28] *Dalton v. Angus* above n.24. See *Tehidy* above n.21 at 552; J. Gaunt and P. Morgan, *Gale on Easements* (16th ed., 1997), para. 4.12.

[29] See above n.22 at 723.

[30] [1991] 1 Ch. 271.

[31] See above n.30 at 278, *per* Dillon L.J.

[32] Noted by the Law Commission above n.4, para. 10.81.

[33] Law Reform Committee above n.13, para. 40.

[34] On which see Gale above n.28, paras. 4.21–4.24.

[35] Jackson above n.13, p. 124, seems confident that doubts as regards the application of the Act to negative easements have been removed. Gale above n.28, para. 4.20 is more cautious.

[36] Gale above n.28, para. 4.17.

claim remains vulnerable on any ground which may defeat a claim under the common law.[37] For example, on the ground that the use was consensual.

Apart from the period of use, there are three principal differences in the respective scope of the Prescription Act and the other two methods of prescription. First, the Prescription Act alone provides different rules in relation to easements and profits. Secondly, any interruption of use by SO is likely to defeat a claim under the common law or lost modern grant on the basis that subsequent use would be forceful.[38] However, under the Prescription Act, only an interruption of at least a year's duration is specifically considered to defeat a claim.[39] The third, and perhaps the most significant difference, relates to the time of the use. The Prescription Act applies only when the easement or profit has been used for the requisite period, "next before some suit or action".[40] The only relevant use is that which has taken place in the period immediately before the claim is considered in court. Under the common law and lost modern grant, use for 20 years at any time is sufficient, subject only to a challenge that the easement has been abandoned. In *Tehidy*, in an action commenced in 1966, the court relied upon use between 1920-1941 to enable a number of claimants to establish a prescriptive easement by lost modern grant. Subsequent events, which included the requisition of the land for a period of time by the MAFF, did not affect the claim. It is, perhaps, a failure to appreciate this difference which explains the decision in *Newnham v. Willison*.[41] There, an easement had been exercised for 20 years, but its use had then been interrupted by SO for more than a year prior to the action. A claim to the easement based on the Prescription Act failed because of the interruption. The fact that there had been 20 year's use was irrelevant in a claim under that Act because the use had not been "next before some suit or action". It is submitted, however, that as there had been 20 years' use the claim should have succeeded on the basis of lost modern grant.[42] On this analysis, the "interruption" of

---

[37] Prescription Act 1832, ss.1 and 2.

[38] See below, Part III 2 (a).

[39] Prescription Act 1832, s.4. The definition of interruption and the possible significance of a lesser period of interruption are discussed below n.10 and text.

[40] Prescription Act 1832, s.4.

[41] (1988) 56 P. & C.R. 8.

[42] Common law prescription was not considered by the Court, and it is not immediately apparent why the Prescription Act alone was discussed. In *Pugh v. Savage* [1970] 2 Q.B. 373 at 384 the Court of Appeal indicated that it is not necessary to plead all three grounds individually.

the easement could in fact have been interpreted as a trespass against the easement.

III. Elements of a claim

Although both adverse possession and prescription are based on use of the right, the elements of a claim and the nature of the use required, differ. In this part, the individual elements will first be considered, followed by a requirement common to both rules: the failure of *PO* or *SO* to assert their rights within the relevant period of use.

1. The Elements of a Claim to Adverse Possession

The elements of a claim to adverse possession are derived from the Limitation Act 1980. Section 15 of that Act provides that a person's right of action to recover land is time barred 12 years "from the date on which the right of action accrues to him". The date of accrual is defined in Schedule 1 paragraphs 1 and 8. Paragraph 1 explains that the right of action accrues on the date the person seeking to recover the land has been, "dispossessed or discontinued his possession". This is subject to paragraph 8, which provides: "No right of action to recover land shall be treated as accruing unless the land is in the possession of some person in whose favour the period of limitation can run (referred to . . . as adverse possession)". Hence, for a claim to succeed, *C* must establish adverse possession of land preceded by the dispossession or discontinuance in possession of the person against whom *C* asserts title. These elements will now be discussed in turn. However, in practice, it seems that if *C* establishes adverse possession, then this will necessarily demonstrate that PO has been dispossessed or has discontinued possession.[43]

(a) Dispossession or discontinuance in possession

The distinction between dispossession and discontinuance in possession was explained by Nourse L.J. in *Moran*,[44] adopting a distinction

---

[43] See above n.4, para. 10.81.
[44] See above n.6.

225

first drawn by Fry J. in *Rains v. Buxton*.[45] Nourse L.J. explained that dispossession arises, "where the squatter comes in and drives out the true owner from possession" and discontinuance, "where the true owner goes out of possession and is followed in by the squatter".[46] Dispossession is therefore based on the acts of *C* and his successors, while discontinuance looks to the acts of *PO* and his successors.[47] Discontinuance must be considered against the background of a presumption that, in the absence of evidence to the contrary, *PO* is deemed to be in possession.[48] The "slightest acts done" by or on behalf of *PO* will negative discontinuance.[49] The distinction between dispossession and discontinuance is illustrated by a comparison of *Moran* and *The Mayor and Burgess of the London Borough of Hounslow v. Minchinton*.[50] In both cases *C* successfully acquired title by adverse possession to a small parcel of land used as part of the claimants' gardens against *PO*, a Council. In *Moran*, *C* had enclosed the land and excluded access by the Council. The Court of Appeal held that although the Council had not discontinued its possession, it had been dispossessed by *C*'s acts. In *Minchinton*, the Council's predecessors in title had fenced the land in such a way as to deny themselves access. This was considered to be strong evidence that *PO* had discontinued possession. The Court rejected an argument that *PO* remained in possession through the presence of a tree and hedge.

(b) Adverse possession

To be "adverse", possession must not be based on permission (licence) or on a lawful title[51] and must be open. The requirement possession is open is necessary to ensure that *PO* has every opportunity to assert his title.[52] Possession is comprised of two elements:

---

[45] (1880) 14 Ch.D. 537 at 539–540.
[46] See above n.6 at 644.
[47] See, *e.g. The Mayor and Burgess of the London Borough of Hounslow v. Minchinton* (1997) 74 P. & C.R. 221 at 230. In view of this distinction, *C* could not rely on acts by *PO* to establish dispossession of *PO*.
[48] *Powell v. McFarlane* (1979) 38 P. & C.R. 452 at 470.
[49] *Powell* above n.48 at 472.
[50] See above n.47.
[51] *Moran* above n.6 at 636.
[52] Gray, p. 298. Where a claim is based on dispossession, establishing dispossession may necessarily involve showing that possession was open. See D.J. Cusine, "Adverse Possession of Land in Scots and English Law" (1996) 45 I.C.L.Q. 667 at 668.

factual possession and an intention to possess (or *animus possidendi*). In *Powell*, Slade J. defined factual possession as "an appropriate degree of exclusive physical control".[53] In determining whether factual possession is established, *C's* acts are assessed by reference to, "the nature of the land and the manner in which land of that nature is commonly used or enjoyed".[54] For example, in *Minchinton*[55] *C's* acts consisted of keeping a compost heap, weeding and trimming a hedge. These acts, despite appearing minimal, were considered sufficient in light of the nature of the land. The land in question was rough ground at the end of a garden, in relation to which *C's* acts constituted "the only sensible use".[56] *C* must also establish sole possession. In particular, *C's* claim will fail if he is in possession jointly with *PO*.[57] However, it is possible for sole possession to be exercised by or on behalf of several persons (other than *PO*) jointly.[58] *C* may rely on acts performed by a third party, where they are done at *C's* instigation or with his consent.[59]

The requisite intent was defined by Slade J. in *Powell* as: "the intention, in one's own name and on one's own behalf, to exclude the world at large, including the owner with the paper title . . . so far as is reasonably practicable and so far as the processes of the law will allow".[60] It is not necessary to establish an intention to own, or to acquire ownership, but merely an intention to "possess" the land.[61] The test of intent provided by Slade J. has been criticised insofar as it refers to an intent to exclude *PO*. Martin Dockray[62] notes that, due to relativity of title, *C* cannot logically be required to intend to exclude *PO*, who has a superior title. At most, *C* should be required to

---

[53] See above n.48 at 470.
[54] See above n.48 at 471. Slade L.J. adopted this earlier definition in *Moran* above n.6 at 641.
[55] See above n.47.
[56] See above n.47 at 233.
[57] *Powell* above n.48 at 470.
[58] *Powell* above n.48 at 470.
[59] *cf. Powell* above n.48 at 477. There, Slade J. indicated that he would have accepted an argument that *C* had acted on behalf of his grandfather if *C* had acted at his grandfather's instigation or with his consent. However, the argument failed on the facts.
[60] See above n.48 at 471–472.
[61] *Moran* above n.6 at 643. This formulation of the requisite intent is criticised by Louise Tee, "Adverse Possession and the Intention to Possess" [2000] Conv. 113. She argues the requisite intent is an intention to own the land, which would be presumed (subject to express written evidence to the contrary) by factual possession.
[62] Martin Dockray, "Adverse Possession and Intention—I" [1982] Conv. 256.

demonstrate an intent to exclude those with inferior titles.[63] Notwithstanding, the test was repeated by Slade L.J. in *Moran*.[64] Whether C can demonstrate such an intent is dependent upon the inference drawn from the acts used to establish factual possession. The courts will not place emphasis on "self-serving" declarations of an intent to possess.[65] In *J.A. Pye (Oxford) Ltd v. Graham*,[66] the test of intent was relied upon by the court in holding that adverse possession can be established despite the fact C has indicated to PO a willingness to enter into a lease or licence. Neuberger J. explained: "Given that the well informed squatter will know that he cannot lawfully exclude the owner . . . I see nothing inconsistent in the squatter having an intention to possess at the same time as making an offer to take a tenancy or a licence". Such an offer does not necessarily preclude an intention to exclude PO, "so far as is reasonably practical and so far as the processes of the law will allow".

Further, C's *intent* is not dependent upon his *motive*. In *Minchinton*, C's acts were held to infer an intention to exclude the world at large, notwithstanding C's motive for carrying out the acts was to keep their dogs within their garden and not to keep other people out.[67] In *Powell*, Slade J. indicated that the courts will require, "clear and affirmative evidence" of C's intent. If C's acts are open to interpretation, then the courts will lean against an interpretation which establishes intent.[68] In that case, C started to use the land in question, as a 14-year-old boy, to graze the family's cow. The court considered that his acts, in particular in light of his age when he began to use the land, did not demonstrate the requisite intent.[69] His acts were equivocal, as they could be interpreted simply as demonstrating an intent to use the land for such time as PO took no action.[70] Few acts are considered to point unequivocally, in the absence of evidence to the contrary, to the requisite intent.[71] One exception, however, is enclosure of the land, which is considered to be the clearest evidence of intent.[72]

---

[63] See above n.62 at 259.
[64] See above n.6 at 641.
[65] *Powell* above n.48 at 476. In contrast, however, an admission of an absence of intent will defeat a claim.
[66] Judgment, February 4, 2000.
[67] See above n.47 at 233.
[68] See above n.48 at 472.
[69] See above n.48 at 480.
[70] See above n.48 at 478.
[71] *Powell* above n.48 at 477–478.
[72] *Moran* above n.6 at 641–642.

The requirements of adverse possession, revealed though these authorities, are not easy to satisfy. The strictness of the tests may reflect a perceived judicial antipathy towards claimants. As Gerard McCormack observed, adverse possession, "smells of stealing, squatters and all things not nice".[73] Although the general test of possession remains strict, in *Central London Commercial Estates Ltd v. Kato Kagaku Co Ltd*[74] Sedley J. sought to assert judicial neutrality towards claims. He explained:

> "Parliament has prescribed the effects of a sufficient period of adverse possession without reference to circumstances, and enough examples have been canvassed in the course of the submissions to demonstrate that the deserving and the undeserving alike may be caught or spared by the operation of the Limitation Acts. The law, correspondingly, leans neither towards nor against the extinction of titles by prescription: for policy reasons it simply provides for it to happen in certain situations".[75]

Despite this modern reassurance, previous judicial antipathy towards adverse possession may explain the introduction of two doctrines which challenged the ability of claimants either to demonstrate that their possession was "adverse" or that their use constituted "possession". These are the doctrines of implied licence and specific future use.

(i) Implied licence

The doctrine of implied licence was introduced by the Court of Appeal in *Wallis' Cayton Bay Holiday Camp Ltd v. Shell-Mex and B.P. Ltd.*[76] There, the majority of the court (Stamp L.J. dissenting) indicated that in certain circumstances, where *C* establishes possession of land, the court will imply that *PO* granted *C* a licence. As a

---

[73] Gerard McCormack, "Adverse Possession—The Future Enjoyment Fallacy" [1989] Conv. 211 at 211. See also Paul Jackson, "The Animus of Squatting" (1980) 96 L.Q.R. 333 at 334. He suggests that parts of the judgment in *Powell*, "suggest a test for the existence of *animus* so strict that few squatters, if any, could satisfy it".

[74] [1998] 4 All E.R. 948.

[75] See above n.74 at 958. An apparent change in judicial attitude is also noted by H.W. Wilkinson, "'Possession as of Wrong'" (1997) N.L.J. 1662 at 1663.

[76] [1975] 1 Q.B. 94.

result of the implied licence, *C*'s possession would be permissive and therefore not adverse. The licence would be implied where *PO* left land unoccupied pending use for some purpose in the future, and *C*'s possession did not interfere with the intended future use. Subsequently, it was established that it was not necessary for *PO* to have in mind a specific use of the land.[77] In *Wallis' Cayton Bay* Lord Denning M.R. considered the implication of a licence to be justified on the basis that: "It does not lie in . . . [*C*'s] mouth to assert that he used the land of his own wrong as a trespasser. Rather his user is to be ascribed to the licence or permission of the true owner. By using the land, knowing that it does not belong to him, he impliedly assumes that the owner will permit it: and the owner, by not turning him off, impliedly gives permission".[78] In *Wallis' Cayton Bay*, *C*'s possession of land was held to be by licence because it did not interfere with *PO*'s intended use of the land in future in connection with a road.

There is no doubt that the existence of a licence, whether express or implied, defeats a claim to adverse possession. The controversy surrounding the implied licence is that it was to be implied, "even though no licence has been given and even though no licence could be implied on the facts for any purposes other than those of the [Limitation] Act".[79] The artificiality of the licence is highlighted by *Powell*.[80] There, Slade J. accepted that even if *C* had established possession, he would be bound by authority to imply that *C*'s possession was by implied licence, because his activities were not inconsistent with any use to which *PO* might have put the land in future. The licence would be implied despite the fact that, outside the *Wallis' Cayton Bay* principle, it was "manifestly impossible under any general principles of law to imply any licence or consent given to . . . [*C* by *PO*] who at that time was in Germany and had no knowledge of his existence".[81] The doctrine was finally repealed by paragraph 8(4) of Schedule 1 to the Limitation Act 1980. That provides: "For the purpose of determining whether a person occupying any land is in adverse possession of the land it shall not be assumed by implication of law that his occupation is by permission of

---

[77] The development of the implied licence is discussed in *Powell* above n.48 at 481–485.
[78] See above n.76 at 103.
[79] *Powell* above n.48 at 482–483, *per* Slade J.
[80] See above n.48.
[81] See above n.48 at 470, *per* Slade J.

the person entitled to the land merely by virtue of the fact that his occupation is not inconsistent with the latter's present or future enjoyment of the land". The provision expressly preserves the possibility of a licence being implied where such implication is justified on the facts.

(ii) Specific future use

The doctrine of specific future use was the source for the introduction of the implied licence in *Wallis' Cayton Bay*. It is a much narrower doctrine and was not affected by the statutory repeal of the implied licence.[82] It was thought to provide that if *PO* intends to use land for a particular purpose in the future, and *C* is aware of that intended use, then *C* will not be held to have dispossessed *PO*.[83] The doctrine stemmed from *Leigh v. Jack*.[84] There, *C* claimed title by adverse possession to land that *PO* intended to dedicate in the future for use as a public highway. *C*'s claim failed as the manner in which he had used the land was not inconsistent with *PO*'s future intended use. As such, Bramwell L.J. considered *C* had not "dispossessed" *PO*. Bramwell L.J. explained, that "in order to defeat a title by dispossessing the former owner, acts must be done which are inconsistent with his enjoyment of the soil for the purposes for which he intended to use it".[85] In *Powell*, Slade J. indicated that he considered *Leigh v. Jack* to be concerned with *C*'s ability to demonstrate the requisite intention to possess.[86] *C* was aware of *PO*'s intended use and, in light of that knowledge, his acts did not demonstrate an intention to disposes *PO*.[87] Subsequently, the significance of a specific future use was discussed by Slade L.J. in *Moran*.

---

[82] Although the doctrine of specific future use is not based on the implication of a licence, whether it was affected by the Limitation Act 1980 sched. 1 para. 8(4) remained uncertain until the decision in *Moran* above n.6. See Gerard McCormack, "Adverse Possession—The Future Enjoyment Fallacy" [1989] Conv. 211 at 213–214.

[83] For a discussion of specific future use, and its relationship with *Wallis's Cayton Bay* see Martin Dockray "Adverse Possession and Intention—II" [1982] Conv. 345.

[84] (1879) 5 Ex.D. 264.

[85] See above n.84 at 273. See, *e.g. J.A. Pye (Oxford) Ltd v. Graham* above n.66. There, *C*'s knowledge of *PO*'s specific future use of the land for development did not prevent their claim to adverse possession succeeding. *C* knew that their use of the land for agricultural purposes would in fact affect *PO*'s application for planning permission.

[86] See above n.48 at 473.

[87] See above n.48 at 473.

In *Moran*, *PO* argued that *C*'s acts did not constitute dispossession because (as in *Leigh v. Jack*) the land had been retained with the specific future purpose of being used as a road; a purpose with which *C*'s acts were not inconsistent. Slade L.J. rejected the existence of a special rule that a specific future use necessarily precluded claims to adverse possession.[88] However, he accepted that where (as was the case on the facts) *C* is aware of the specific future use, that knowledge is a factor to take into account when considering whether *C* has the requisite intent. In *Moran*, *C* had enclosed the land by placing a lock and chain on a gate. Slade L.J. considered this to be, "a final unequivocal demonstration of . . . [*C*'s] intention to possess the land".[89]

2. ELEMENTS OF A CLAIM TO PRESCRIPTION

For a claim to prescription to succeed, there must be use (in the manner to be discussed) of a right which has the characteristics of an easement[90] or profit.[91] Prescription does not enable the acquisition of proprietary rights *sui generis*.[92] This necessarily means that, unlike a claim to adverse possession, use will be concurrent with the owner of the servient land.[93] The requisite use is the same for all claims to prescription except a right to light under the Prescription Act 1832.[94]

The requisite use is use as of right (that is, based on an assumption the right exists) in which *SO* has acquiesced.[95] The use must usually be by and against a fee simple owner.[96] The need for use to be based on an assumption or right reflects the distinction between adverse

---

[88] See above n.6 at 639.
[89] See above n.6 at 642. See Tee above n.61 at 116–117. She notes the inconsistency in taking into account knowledge of a 'future' use in determining whether *C* has the requisite intent to possess the land for the time being.
[90] These are explained in *Re Ellenborough Park* [1956] Ch. 131.
[91] See Jackson above n.13, Chapter 2.
[92] However, prior to *Dalton v. Angus* above n.24, there was not a complete overlap between rights which could be prescribed and granted. See Stuart Anderson, "Easements and Prescription—Changing Perspectives in Classification" (1975) 38 M.L.R. 641.
[93] A claim to exclusivity is contrary to the general requirement that an easement must be capable of forming the subject of a grant. The requirement is discussed by Gray, pp. 1076–1079.
[94] Rights to light are governed by the Prescription Act 1832, s.3 and are claimed on the basis of use actually enjoyed.
[95] *Mills v. Silver* above n.30 at 281.
[96] See below, Part V 2.

possession and prescription. As has been seen,[97] prescription operates positively by implying that a grant was made. The courts are prepared to imply a grant only against a background of presumed legal entitlement.[98] *SO*'s acquiescence "lies at the heart of prescription, and of the fiction of a lost grant".[99] For there to be acquiescence, *SO* must know of *C*'s use, be able to prevent it and refrain from doing so. In *Sturges v. Bridgman*, *C* claimed an easement to make a noise caused by a pestle and mortar used in his confectionery business. *C*'s claim failed. Although the noise had continued for more than 20 years, it did not become an actionable nuisance until *SO* erected a doctor's surgery on his land. It was only from that time (a period much shorter than 20 years) that *SO* had the power to prevent the noise.

Save in exceptional cases, use based on a mistaken belief the right exists does not defeat a claim. In *Bridle v. Ruby*[1] *C*'s claim to a prescriptive easement succeeded, notwithstanding he had acted in the mistaken belief the easement had been expressly reserved. Ralph Gibson L.J. considered that for a mistake as to the source of a right to defeat a claim, "it must be such as to be capable of affecting the way in which the user of the right is conducted by the claimant or in which that user is seen by the owner of the land over which the right is asserted".[2] This may be the case where, for example, *C* mistakenly believed that he was the owner of the servient land.[3] A mistake may also defeat a claim where both *C* and *SO* believe that *C* is asserting a right for a limited term (such as the duration of a lease).[4]

The need for use to be as of right is generally explained by the requirement use must be without force, openly and without permission (*nec vi, nec clam, nec precario*). Only if these requirements are met will *SO* be considered to have acquiesced in *C*'s use. In *Sturges v. Bridgman* Thesiger L.J. explained: "a man cannot, as a general rule, be said to consent to or acquiesce in the acquisition by his neighbour of

---

[97] See above, Part I.

[98] Gray, p. 1108.

[99] *Sturges v. Bridgman* (1879) 11 Ch.D. 852 at 863 *per* Thesiger L.J.

[1] [1988] 3 W.L.R. 191.

[2] See above n.1 at 198.

[3] This is suggested by Gilbert Kodilinye, "Prescription Under Mistake" [1989] Conv. 261 at 265.

[4] This is the basis upon which *Chamber Colliery v. Hopwood* (1886) 32 Ch.D. 549 was distinguished in *Bridle v. Ruby*. The earlier case was previously thought to suggest that *C*'s mistaken belief as to the origin of a right would defeat a claim to prescription. See Gale above n.28, para. 4.80.

an easement through an enjoyment of which he has no knowledge, actual or constructive, or which he contests and endeavours to interrupt, or which he temporarily licences".[5] Each of these requirements will now be explained.

(a) Without force

In contrast to a claim to adverse possession which, as has been seen, may begin by the forceful dispossession of PO,[6] prescriptive use must be without force. If force is necessary to exercise the right, then it is clear that SO does not acquiesce. In *Newnham v. Willison* the Court of Appeal considered use would be forceful, "once there is knowledge on the part of the person seeking to establish prescription that his user is being objected to and that the use which he claims has become contentious".[7] If, for example, SO blocks the exercise of the easement, and C removes the obstruction: "then that is sufficient evidence to show that on the one hand . . . [SO] was objecting to the use, so that the user was no longer as of right, and on the other hand that . . . [C] was aware that he was not exercising it as of right but in the face of objections by . . . [SO]".[8] In *Newnham v. Willison*, C had an established right of way over a driveway and track on SO's land. C claimed by prescription an easement to turn from the driveway onto the track by means of a "swept curve" rather than a "sharp angle". A swept curve was essential to enable C to drive his horsebox along the right of way. It was held that C's use was not as of right as he had used "quite minor" force by removing obstructions place by SO.[9]

At common law and under the doctrine of lost modern grant, any interruption of C's use by PO makes subsequent use forceful. Section 4 of the Prescription Act 1832 indicates that an interruption will defeat a claim under that Act only when it has lasted for at least a year and has been "submitted to or acquiesced in" by C. The decision in *Newnham v. Willison* casts doubt on the effectiveness of the section. There, C had used the swept curve for more than 20

---

[5] See above n.99 at 863.
[6] See above, Part III 1 (a).
[7] See above n.41 at 19, *per* Kerr L.J.
[8] *Newnham* above n.41 at 19, *per* Kerr L.J.
[9] See above n.41 at 20. A.H. Hudson, "Mistake and Prescription" (1989) 40 N.I.L.Q. 64 at 70, suggests that the strict approach to use without force accords with the general approach of courts in discouraging self-help.

years before the dispute developed. As has been seen, C's exercise of the easement in the face of SO's objection was held to be forceful and therefore the claim failed. However, as Jill Martin notes, C's actions demonstrated that he did not submit to or acquiesce in SO's interruption.[10] Therefore, his acts should have been interpreted as establishing that there had not been an interruption within section 4 of the Act. In *Newnham v. Willison*, the interruption had continued for more than a year prior to the action. However, it seems equally possible, following that case, that an interruption for a lesser period would defeat a claim under the Prescription Act insofar as it could be interpreted as making C's use forceful.[11]

(b) Openly

SO will not be considered to acquiesce in use which is not reasonably discoverable. This requirement ensures, as does the analogous requirement in relation to adverse possession,[12] that SO has the opportunity to challenge C's claim. In *Union Lighterage Co v. London Graving Dock Co*,[13] Romer L.J. explained that to be open, use must be: "of such a character that an ordinary owner of the land, diligent in the protection of his interests, would have, or must be taken to have, a reasonable opportunity of becoming aware of that enjoyment".[14] The requirement may cause particular difficulty in a claim to a negative easement. In *Union Lighterage*, C claimed an easement for support for a dock which, for more than 20 years, had been attached to SO's wharf by a number of tie-rods. C's claim failed on the ground the use was not open. The tie-rods were not visible, save for two nuts used to fasten them. The nature of the support was extraordinary, and may have been apparent only to, "a skilled expert informed of the nature of the dock".[15] A more usual easement of support, such as that reasonably expected from neighbouring houses, may be acquired through prescription.

---

[10] [1989] Conv. 355 at 358.
[11] Gale above n.28, para. 4.70.
[12] See above, Part III 1 (b).
[13] [1902] 2 Ch. 557.
[14] See above n.13 at 571.
[15] See above n.13 at 559 from the judgment at first instance by Cozens-Hardy J.

235

(c) **Without permission**

As with adverse possession, permissive use defeats a claim to prescription. The reasoning underlying the requirement in prescription is that use based on permission necessarily is not based on an assumption of right. However, it can be difficult to draw a clear distinction between permission (which defeats a claim) and acquiescence (which is essential to a claim). Use based on an express agreement or in return for payment of money is clearly permissive. For a period of time, it seemed possible that SO could defeat a claim merely by establishing that he had "tolerated" C use.[16] This argument was finally rejected in *Mills v. Silver*.[17] There, C claimed a prescriptive easement for vehicular access across a track on SO's farm. The track had been used for vehicles by C's predecessors in title for 60 years. The court rejected SO's argument that no easement had arisen because the use had been tolerated. Parker L.J. explained that if use is established for the relevant period: "It is no answer for [C] to say 'I tolerated it'. If he does nothing he will be taken to have recognised the right and not intended to resist it. He will have consented to it or acquiesced in it".[18] Although "toleration" and "acquiescence" are not synonymous,[19] the concepts are closely related. Use is not made permissive merely because SO could have brought action against C to stop his use.[20]

3. Failure of PO or SO to Assert Their Rights

PO or SO may prevent C's claim from succeeding by asserting their title. In the context of adverse possession, PO's title remains superior to that held by C until the expiration of the limitation period. In *Mount Carmel Investments Ltd v. Peter Thurlow Ltd*[21] the Court of Appeal explained that within the limitation period PO must commence proceedings to recover possession. There, within the limitation period, PO had written to C demanding delivery of possession, but had not brought proceedings until the limitation period expired.

---

[16] Charles Harpum, "The Acquisition of Easements" [1992] C.L.J. 220 at 221.
[17] See above n.30.
[18] See above n.30 at 288.
[19] Harpum above n.16 at 222.
[20] *Mills v. Silver* above n.30 at 282.
[21] [1988] 1 W.L.R. 1078.

The court rejected an argument that by sending the letter *C* recovered "constructive possession". A letter would be effective only in two circumstances.[22] First, if *C* did in fact vacate the land; in which case adverse possession would cease. Secondly if *C* acknowledged *PO*'s title. To be effective the acknowledgement of title must be in writing. By sections 29-30 of the Limitation Act 1980, a written acknowledgement has the effect that a fresh right of action accrues in *PO*'s favour. In relation to the commencement of proceedings, where it is possible to do so the proceedings must be for the recovery of possession. In *J.A. Pye (Oxford) Ltd v. Graham*,[23] *C* had entered cautions against the register of *PO's* title in respect of his claim to adverse possession. Proceedings brought by *PO* for the cautions to be removed were ineffective to end the adverse possession, even though the proceedings demonstrated that *PO* disputed *C's* claim.[24]

In the context of prescription, *SO* may assert his title by, for example, bringing an action for trespass against *C*. In a claim based on common law or lost modern grant, *SO* must act before there has been 20 years' use. As has been seen,[25] a claim under those methods of prescription may relate to 20 years' use at any time. In a claim based on the Prescription Act 1832, the relevant period is the 20 years immediately prior to the action. Even without bringing an action for trespass, a denial or interruption of *C*'s right by *SO* may defeat the claim as *C*'s use would thereby become contentious and, therefore, forceful.[26]

Hence in relation to both adverse possession and prescription *C*'s claim will be defeated by placing his acts on a permissive footing.[27] Further, it has been held that a unilateral and unsolicited grant of permission by *C* may be sufficient to make use permissive. In relation to adverse possession, the issue arose in *B.P. Properties Ltd v. Buckler*.[28] There, *PO* wrote to *C* and said they were prepared to allow her to remain in the property to which she had claimed ownership by

---

[22] See above n.21 at 1086.
[23] See above n.66.
[24] Contrast *Walters v. Webb* (1870) LR 5 Ch. App. 531 and *Vandeleur v. Slone* [1919] I.R. 116 (Irish Court of Appeal). Those cases were distinguished in *J.A. Pye (Oxford) Ltd v. Graham* on the basis that proceedings to recover possession were not in fact possible.
[25] See above n.40 and text.
[26] See above, Part III 2 (a).
[27] However, oral permission will not defeat a claim based on a longer period of use (40 or 60 years) under the Prescription Act 1932.
[28] (1988) 55 P. & C.R. 337.

adverse possession, rent free, for life. *C* took no action[29] and, following her death, *PO* sought possession against her son. Dillon L.J. noted that giving effect to a unilateral licence could be contrary to the Limitation Act 1980. It, "would enable a person who is not prepared to incur the obloquy of bringing proceedings for possession, or of enforcing a possession order, to keep his title alive for very many years until it suits him to evict".[30] Notwithstanding, the court held that "whether [*C*] liked it or not, from the time of her receipt of the letters, [*C*] was in possession of the farmhouse and garden by the licence of [*PO*] and her possession was no longer adverse".[31] The court acknowledged that the decision might have been different if *C* had made clear to *PO* that she maintained her claim to ownership.[32] The limitation period may then have continued to operate in her favour.[33] The decision has been criticised by Wallace, who notes that its effect is that a unilateral grant of permission prevents *C*'s possession being adverse notwithstanding permission, "was neither sought, acknowledged nor accepted".[34] Further, that following the decision, even an oral grant of permission may defeat a claim.[35] Read in parallel with *Mount Carmel Investments*, a curious conclusion is reached whereby a letter from *PO,* within the limitation period, demanding that *C* gives up possession is entirely ineffective, while a letter granting *C* permission to continue to occupy will prevent *C*'s claim. This is notwithstanding the fact that the latter, like the former, could be used as a means of "extending" *PO*'s right of action beyond the statutory limitation period.

In *Rafique v. Trustees of the Walton Estate*[36] the possible effect of a unilateral grant of permission arose in the context of prescription. The point arose on an application to amend an interlocutory injunction which restrained *SO* from interfering with *C*'s use of a right of way pending the final hearing. *SO* sought to erect a locked barrier (for which *C* would be given a key) to prevent other

---

[29] See above n.28 at 346. *PO* neither sought nor awaited *C*'s acceptance. The court considered it would be artificial to suggest that *C* had accepted.

[30] See above n.28 at 346.

[31] See above n.28 at 346–347.

[32] See above n.28 at 346.

[33] Wallace above n.8 at 206. However, as Wallace notes, n.50 *PO* may then have sought possession immediately.

[34] See above n.8 at 200.

[35] See above n.8 at 203.

[36] (1993) 65 P. & C.R. 356.

claimants from acquiring rights. Warner J. rejected SO's application, on the basis other claims could be prevented by erecting a notice which stated that anybody using the road did so by permission.[37] The decision indicates that unsolicited permission will prevent C, who is in the process of acquiring rights by prescription, from completing the requisite period of use as of right.[38] The impact of a unilateral grant of permission is perhaps greater in the context of prescription. As has been seen,[39] in *Buckler* the court indicated that the decision would have been different if the claimant to adverse possession disputed the permission. In a claim for prescription, such a dispute may itself be sufficient to defeat a claim by establishing that use is contentious and therefore is not as of right.[40]

IV. Effect of use of the right

1. ADVERSE POSSESSION

On orthodox principles, once C completes 12 years' adverse possession, PO's title is extinguished. There is no "Parliamentary conveyance" of PO's title to C.[41] C's title, acquired by entering into adverse possession, is no longer vulnerable to a challenge from PO. This orthodoxy is challenged in two respects. First, in *Colchester B.C. v. Smith*[42] the court effectively enabled a title extinguished by adverse possession to be "resurrected".[43] There, following expiration of the limitation period, PO entered into an agreement to grant C a lease of the land. Under the terms of the agreement, C acknowledged PO's title and that no right had been acquired by adverse possession. In subsequent possession proceedings the court held that C was estopped[44] from claiming a title other than as provided by the

---

[37] See above n.36 at 357.

[38] Wallace above n.8 at 209.

[39] See above n.32 and text.

[40] See above n.7 and text.

[41] *Tichborne v. Weir* (1892) 67 L.T. 735 at 736; *St Marylebone Property Co Ltd v. Fairweather* [1963] A.C. 510 at 535.

[42] [1992] Ch. 421.

[43] *cf.* A.R.H. Brierley, "Adverse Possession: A Case of Death and Regrettable Resurrection" [1991] Conv. 397, commenting on the first instance decision affirmed by the Court of Appeal.

[44] The species of estoppel applied was estoppel by contract or by convention. For criticism of the application of estoppel in the case see Martin Dixon, "Title By Adverse Possession Lost by Estoppel" [1991] C.L.J. 234 at 235 commenting on the first instance decision affirmed by the Court of Appeal.

agreement. The decision is logically difficult to justify on the basis of adverse possession. There is no conceptual ground upon which *PO*'s title, once extinguished, can be resurrected.[45] It seems to have been influenced by a policy of giving effect to compromises entered into between parties to settle disputes.[46]

The second, and more far-reaching challenge, is the application of adverse possession to registered land. The rules of adverse possession provided for in the Limitation Act were developed in the context of a, "possession-based system of title".[47] In registered land, title is based on registration and not possession. Notwithstanding this fundamental distinction, the current approach has been to graft onto the system of registration of title the possession-based rules governing adverse possession. The resultant provisions, while generally successful, are not without difficulties. The Law Commission has recommended a new system of adverse possession to deal specifically with registered land.[48]

In registered land, the orthodox rule that adverse possession extinguishes title is in direct conflict with the guarantee of title provided by registration. As the register is deemed correct,[49] *PO*'s title can be extinguished only by being removed from the register. This basic conflict is resolved by section 75 of the Land Registration Act 1925. By section 75(1), upon the expiry of the limitation period, the registered proprietor holds the estate on trust for *C*. Subsections (2) and (3) then provide for *C* to apply to be registered as proprietors. Two main difficulties have emerged from this solution. First, there are doubts as to the nature of the trusteeship imposed. In particular, it may be thought unfair to impose upon *PO* the usual fiduciary duties associated with trusteeship.[50] The issues surrounding the trust remain largely unresolved.[51] Secondly, there is uncertainty surrounding the relationship between the interest held on trust and the

---

[45] Brierley above n.43 at 403.

[46] Dillon L.J. above n.42 at 434–435; Butler-Sloss L.J. at 435.

[47] Law Com, above n.4, para. 10.11.

[48] Law Com, above n.4, Part X.

[49] Land Registration Act 1925, s.69.

[50] In Chapter 2, Part II 1 it has been argued that following *Westdeutsche Landesbank Girozentrale v. Islington L.B.C.* [1996] 2 All E.R. 961 a trust can be imposed without fiduciary duties. While this makes the imposition of a trust more acceptable, the argument is not pursued here in light of the Law Commission's recommendations (considered below n.56 and text) to remove the s.75 trust.

[51] For a full discussion of these, see Elizabeth Cooke, "Adverse Possession—Problems of Title in Registered Land" (1994) 14 L.S. 1 at 2–4; Law Com, above n.4, 10.29–10.39.

interest acquired by *C* by adverse possession. Section 75 indicates that *PO* holds his registered title on trust.[52] However, by adverse possession, *C* acquires a title distinct from that of *PO*. When *C* applies to be registered, should he be registered with the estate held on trust or with his independent freehold?[53] In practice, where *C* establishes adverse possession against a freeholder, he is registered with a freehold title under a new title number and *PO*'s title is closed.[54] This conforms to the orthodoxy that there has been no Parliamentary conveyance to *C*. As will be seen below,[55] greater uncertainties arise when *C* establishes adverse possession against the registered proprietor of a lease. The Law Commission has recommended that a trust should no longer be used to give effect to adverse possession.[56] Pending registration, adequate protection is provided to *C* against possible dealings with *PO*'s title as a title acquired, or in the course of being acquired, by adverse possession is an overriding interest.[57]

The Law Commission has recommended a scheme for adverse possession in registered land in which registration alone, and not mere long use, will extinguish a registered title. This is a free-standing proposal and the Law Commission's recommendations on removing the section 75 trust are not dependent upon its acceptance. Under the proposed scheme, adverse possession for the limitation period will not automatically extinguish *PO*'s title. The superiority of *PO*'s title is maintained unless or until *C* becomes registered proprietor. Upon *C*'s application, *PO* can stop *C*'s claim by objecting to his registration. *PO* then has a further two years to evict *C* or to regularise his possession. *C* will be registered as proprietor, and *PO*'s title will be extinguished, only in three circumstances. First, where *PO* does not object to *C*'s application for registration. Secondly, where, following *PO*'s successful objection, *C* remains in adverse possession for a further two years. Thirdly, in exceptional cases in

---

[52] Cooke above n.51 at 5.

[53] Cooke above n.51 at 5–6.

[54] Cooke above n.51 at 6. The title awarded is usually an absolute freehold: Law Com, above n.4, para. 10.41

[55] Part V 1.

[56] See above n.4, paras. 10.70–10.77. The proposals would apply whether or not the Law Commission's proposed new scheme for adverse possession in registered land is adopted.

[57] Land Registration Act 1925, s.70(1)(f). The Law Commission recommends above n.4, para. 5.55 that *C* should be protected only if in actual occupation.

which the Law Commission considers that there are compelling reasons for *PO*'s registered title to give way to *C*.[58] In these cases, *C* may obtain registration despite *PO*'s objection. The significance of these proposals is that they provide a basis for adverse possession in registered land distinct from the current rules. The mere fact of long use will not enable *C* to defeat *PO*'s title. Title acquired by adverse possession will remain vulnerable against *PO*'s superior title unless *C* successfully obtains registration, regardless of the number of years' adverse possession.

2. PRESCRIPTION

As has been seen,[59] once there has been use for the requisite period or, in a claim based on the Prescription Act 1832, the right has been established in an action, the grant of an easement or profit is implied. Once established, the right is subject to the usual rules for the passing of the benefit or burden of such a right, however created. It remains unclear whether the easement is considered to date from the time the period of prescriptive use is completed, or is back-dated to the time of the presumed grant. The timing of the easement may be important in terms of determining *C*'s status where the dominant land is sold within the prescriptive period. If the easement does in fact date from the time of the presumed grant, then, *C* may correctly be seen as the successor in title to the easement. It seems preferable for the easement to date from the time the period of prescription is completed. This is because, in the majority of cases, it would be difficult to identify with any certainty the appropriate time for the grant to be presumed.[60]

V. Applying claims based on use of a right to leaseholds

Particular difficulties arise in applying rules based on long use in the context of leaseholds. The difficulties may be seen to stem from a

---

[58] The exceptional cases are outlined by the Law Commission above n.4, para. 10.50. They are: (i) where *PO* is estopped from objecting to *C*'s registration because it would be unconscionable for him to do so; (ii) where *C* has an independent right entitling him to registration; (iii) where *C* entered adverse possession under a reasonable mistake as to his rights.
[59] See above, Part II 2.
[60] An exceptional case, where the time of the presumed grant could fairly be identified, is *Tehidy* above n.21.

common conceptual problem. It is established as a general rule that, "a person cannot give what he does not have" (*nemo dat quod non habet*). Equally, it is illogical to suggest that *C* can acquire from long use more than *PO* or *SO* have. In relation to adverse possession, the basic proposition that by entering into possession *C* acquires a fee simple estate is difficult to apply where the land in question is subject to a lease. An easement or profit acquired through long use is of unlimited duration. The holder of a limited right in land is an incapable grantee or grantor of a right which endures beyond their entitlement.

1. Adverse Possession

When *C* enters into adverse possession against a tenant (*T*), *C* acquires a fee simple, notwithstanding *T*'s limited title. On the expiry of the limitation period, *T*'s title is extinguished. However, the landlord's (*L*'s) reversionary estate is unaffected by the adverse possession. By schedule 1 paragraph 4 of the Limitation Act 1980, a right of action to recover land accrues only when an estate falls into possession. *L*'s reversionary estate falls into possession on the termination of the lease. From that date, *L* has 12 years to assert his freehold against that held by *C*. *L*'s freehold is relatively superior because it pre-dates that acquired by *C*. Two difficulties have become apparent. First, the consequences of these facts where *T* is registered proprietor of a lease. Secondly the circumstances in which *L*'s reversionary estate may come into possession otherwise than by effluxion of time.

(a) Application to registered land

In registered land, once *C* completes the period of adverse possession against *T*, section 75 of the Land Registration Act 1925 operates and *T* holds his lease on trust for *C*. Hence, *C* has an independent freehold acquired by possession but is also a beneficiary under a trust of *T*'s registered lease. When *C* applies to be registered, should he be registered as proprietor of a freehold or leasehold estate? There is no uniform practice for dealing with such applications.[61] Browne-

---

[61] Law Com, above, n.4, para. 10.38.

Wilkinson J. suggested in *Spectrum Investment Co v. Holmes*[62] that the claimant in that case had been correctly registered with a lease.[63] If this is the case, then there appears in fact to have been a Parliamentary conveyance of *T*'s title.[64] In *Central London Estates v. Kato*,[65] Sedley J. suggested that the effect of the section 75 trust is that: "The squatter becomes entitled . . . to be placed in the same relationship with the freeholder as had previously been enjoyed by the leaseholder . . . This is to all appearances a statutory conveyance of the entire leasehold interest".[66] This apparent departure from orthodoxy may be more illusory than real. *C* is not *T*'s "successor" in title and is registered with a new leasehold title.[67] However, if *C* is registered with a lease, the question arises as to what has happened to the freehold *C* acquired by entering into adverse possession.[68] In *Central London Estates v. Kato* Sedley J. suggested that it is "nullified" by the trust.[69] These difficulties are removed if *C* is registered with a freehold title. Cooke suggested that the appropriate form of registration is a qualified freehold,[70] which is subject to the reversioner's interest. The principal objection to such registration is that, as a result, *L*'s freehold title will be closed, which may bar dealings with the reversion. *L*'s title is closed, despite being unaffected by the adverse possession, because it is not considered possible to have two freehold titles registered in relation to land. In *Spectrum Investment v. Holmes* Browne-Wilkinson J. suggested that the concurrent registration of two freeholds, "runs contrary to the whole scheme of the [Land Registration Act]".[71] In the context of proposals to replace the section 75 trust, the Law Commission has recommended, as Cooke suggested, that *C* should be registered with a qualified freehold title. However, contrary to Browne-Wilkinson J.'s view, the Law Commission considers that there may be more than one registered

---

[62] [1981] 1 W.L.R. 221.
[63] See above n.62 at 230. However, as Cooke notes above n.51 at 9 the case does not establish as *ratio* that *C* is entitled to such registration.
[64] Cooke above n.51 at 9.
[65] See above n.74.
[66] See above n.74 at 959. See Charles Harpum, "Estates in the Clouds—The Squatter, the Lease and the Car Park" (1999) 115 L.Q.R. 187 at 190.
[67] Law Com, above n.4, para. 10.39.
[68] Cooke above n.51 at 9.
[69] See above n.74 at 959–960.
[70] See above n.51 at 9–10.
[71] See above n.62 at 228. Contrast Graham Battersby, "Informally Created Interests in Land" in *Land Law Themes and Perspectives* (Susan Bright and John Dewar eds., 1998), p. 494.

freehold[72] and therefore that L's title should be unaffected by the registration.[73]

(b) Bringing L's reversionary estate into possession

It is possible that L's reversionary estate will come into possession otherwise than by effluxion of time. It is accepted that L may seek forfeiture against C for breach of covenants in the lease. In the absence of a Parliamentary conveyance of T's lease to C, there is no privity of contract or estate between C and L. However, a right of re-entry is a proprietary right independent of the lease, enforceable against C. More controversially, in some circumstances it is possible that T may be able to surrender his lease to L despite the fact the lease is "extinguished" by C's adverse possession, and that the surrender is effective to enable L immediately to assert his title against C. The possibility and effectiveness of a surrender is dependent upon whether the lease is registered or unregistered. In unregistered land, in *St Marylebone Property Co Ltd v. Fairweather*[74] the House of Lords, by a majority decision, held that a surrender did enable L to assert title. The House of Lords considered that although T's title had been extinguished in relation to C, it remained in existence as between T and L.[75] The decision was criticised by H.W.R. Wade as being in conflict with the basic *nemo dat* principle:[76] as T does not have a good title against C, he cannot give L a title good against C. In *Chung Ping Kwan v. Lam Island Development Co Ltd*[77] the Privy Council, referring to Wade's "powerful critique" left open the correctness of the decision.[78] As a decision of the House of Lords, *St Marylebone* does, notwithstanding, remain binding authority.

In registered land, the possibility of a surrender first arose in *Spectrum Investment v. Holmes*.[79] There C, who had completed a period of adverse possession against land subject to a registered lease, had

---

[72] See above n.4, para. 10.71.
[73] See above n.4, para. 10.73.
[74] See above n.41.
[75] See above n.41 at 539–540, *per* Lord Radcliffe; at 545, *per* Lord Denning.
[76] H.W.R. Wade, "Landlord, Tenant and Squatter" (1962) 78 L.Q.R. 541. See also N. Hopkins, "Surrender as an Assignment and the Protection of Third Parties" [1996] Conv. 284 at 291.
[77] [1997] A.C. 38.
[78] See above n.77 at 47.
[79] See above n.62.

applied and been registered as proprietor of a lease at the time of the purported surrender. *L*'s action for possession against *C* following a surrender failed. Browne-Wilkinson J. noted that at the time of the surrender, the lease was registered under a new title number in *C*'s name and *T*'s title had been closed. The effect of the registration, by section 69(1) of the Land Registration Act 1925 was, as against *T*, "to vest the term or deem it to be vested in [*C*]".[80] Therefore, *C* alone could surrender the lease, and only in the manner authorised by the Land Registration Act.[81] The decision is considered to be correct on the facts, in light of the *fait accompli* that *C* had been registered as proprietor of a lease.[82] However, it is generally considered that a surrender would be effective where *C* is registered with a qualified freehold title.[83] There is then no question of the lease being vested or deemed vested in *C*.[84] If the Law Commission's proposals to remove the section 75 trust are adopted,[85] *C* will invariably be registered with a qualified freehold title.

In *Spectrum Investment*, the purported surrender had been made after *C*'s application for registration. Browne-Wilkinson J. expressly left open the question of the effect of a surrender made during the period between completion of the limitation period and *C*'s application for registration; the period during which the section 75 trust subsists.[86] In *St Marylebone*, Lord Denning had expressed the view that the position would be the same as in unregistered land.[87] He explained that the trust, "is machinery so as to apply the Limitation Acts to registered land but it does not alter the substantive position very materially".[88] The issue arose for decision in *Central London Estates v. Kato*[89] and Sedley J. held that, during the subsistence of the trust, a surrender is ineffective. The failure of the surrender was considered to be a consequence of the nature of the interest held on trust. The decision in *St Marylebone* rests on the basis that following the period of limitation, *T*'s estate is divisible: the element of the

---

[80] See above n.62 at 228.
[81] *i.e.* by registered disposition: Land Registration Act 1925, ss.21 and 22.
[82] Cooke above n.51 at 9.
[83] Cooke above n.51 at 7; Law Com, above n.4, para. 10.74.
[84] Cooke above n.51 at 10.
[85] See above n.4, para. 10.71.
[86] See above n.62 at 231.
[87] See above n.41 at 548.
[88] *ibid*.
[89] See above n.74. See Harpum above n.66; Elizabeth Cooke, "Exploring the Section 75 Trust" [1999] Conv. 136.

estate connected with the relationship between *T* and *L* survives; that part connected with the relationship between *T* and *C* is extinguished.[90] The question for the court in *Central London Estates v. Kato* was the extent to which *T's* estate is held on trust. As Sedley J. stated the question: "Is the element of the estate which would otherwise be extinguished all that the statute saves, or is the estate indivisible for the purposes of [section 75] and so wholly subject to the trust?"[91] Only if the trust was restricted to the element of the estate that would otherwise be extinguished could the reasoning in *St Marylebone* apply, and a surrender be effective. Sedley J. held that, for the purposes of section 75, *T's* estate is indivisible. As the full estate was held on trust, the trusteeship passed to *L* upon the surrender[92] and *C's* interest under the trust bound *L* as an overriding interest.[93] Hence while, unlike in *Spectrum Investment*, it remained possible for *T* to surrender the lease, the surrender was not effective to enable *L* to assert his title against *C*. It should be noted that the decision in the case is a direct consequence of the imposition of a trust. The Law Commission has indicated that if, as it has proposed, a trust is removed, then a surrender prior to *C's* registration will be effective to enable *L* to assert his title.[94]

The adoption of the Law Commission's free-standing proposal for a new scheme of adverse possession in registered land[95] would alter the circumstances in which a surrender is effective. Under the proposed scheme, *T's* estate would not be extinguished unless and until *C* became registered proprietor. Therefore, the ability of *T* to surrender the lease would be unquestionable.[96] If *C* obtained registration, he would necessarily be registered with a freehold title.[97] *T's* title number would at that point be closed and treated as extinguished for all purposes. Hence, a surrender would not then be possible.[98]

2. PRESCRIPTION

It is an established principle that for prescription to operate use must be by and against a freehold estate. The principle was developed in

---

[90] *Central London Estates v. Kato* above n.74 at 959.
[91] See above n.74 at 958.
[92] See above n.74 at 960.
[93] *ibid.*
[94] See above n.4, para. 10.76.
[95] See above, Part IV 1.
[96] See above n.4, para. 10.76.
[97] See above n.4, para. 10.71.
[98] See above n.4, para. 10.74.

the context of common law prescription and reflected the fact that a claim under that method is based on use since time immemorial.[99] The same principle applies equally to a claim under the Prescription Act 1832, which is considered to be based on the same character of use as the common law.[1] More controversially, the rule was applied to the doctrine of lost modern grant in *Simmons v. Dobson*.[2] As the basis of a lost modern grant is a grant in recent time, it has been argued that it should be possible to imply the grant under that method of prescription of any easement capable of express creation.[3] A tenant is a capable grantor and grantee of an easement for the duration of his lease. However, in *Simmons v. Dobson* Fox L.J. noted that although there was no case directly deciding that lost modern grant could not apply by and against a tenant, there was, "strong and long standing" *dicta* to that effect, which represented the settled law.[4] He considered lost modern grant to be, "merely a form of common law prescription" which it would be anomalous to extend beyond the general principle of freehold use.[5]

Notwithstanding the general principle, in limited circumstances a claim by or against a tenant will succeed. These are not strictly exceptions to the general rule of freehold use. They are situations in which a grant is implied by or in favour of the freeholder, despite the fact the land is in the possession of a tenant. Where *T* exercises an easement against a freeholder, he is considered to act on behalf of his landlord.[6] Hence, *T* may acquire by prescription an easement against a freeholder on the basis that the easement is acquired for the freehold estate of his landlord, and not merely for the duration of his own lease.[7] However, because *T* acts on behalf of his landlord he cannot claim an easement by prescription over other land owned by his landlord:[8] this would be tantamount to enabling the landlord to

---

[99] V.T.H. Delany, "Leases and the Doctrine of Lost Grant" (1958) 74 L.Q.R. 82 at 87; Peter Sparkes, "Establishing Easements Against Leaseholds" [1992] Conv. 167; Harpum above n.16 at 223.

[1] Delany above n.99 at 87.

[2] See above n.22.

[3] Delany above n.99 at 88; Sparkes above n.99 at 172.

[4] See above n.22 at 725.

[5] See above n.22 at 725.

[6] *Pugh v. Savage* [1970] 2 Q.B. 373 at 380.

[7] *Pugh v. Savage* above n.6 at 380.

[8] *Gayford v. Moffatt* (1868) L.R. 4 Ch. App. 133. An extension of this principle was the basis upon which the claim failed in *Simmons v. Dobson* above n.22. There, one tenant claimed a prescriptive easement over neighbouring land in the possession of another tenant from the same landlord. See Harpum above n.16 at 222–223.

have the benefit of an easement over his own land. A claim to prescription by a freeholder against *T* will succeed only in one limited situation: where the use began against the freeholder who subsequently granted the tenancy. In *Pugh v. Savage*[9] the claimant had exercised the easement for eight years before the freeholder granted a lease of the alleged servient tenement to his son. The claim succeeded on the basis that, during the initial eight years, the freeholder had the opportunity to object to the claimant's use. The freeholder's opportunity to prevent the use is considered vital. Hence, in *Pugh v. Savage*, the claim would have failed if the freeholder had shown that he had been unaware of the use.[10] Where a claim succeeds, the freeholder and not *T* is considered to have made the lost grant.[11] Therefore, the easement acquired is not limited to the duration of *T*'s lease.

VI. Claims based on use of a right and estoppel

Debate has arisen as regards the relationship between claims based on use and claims to rights in land through estoppel, the rule discussed in Chapter 7. As has been seen,[12] a claim to prescription requires acquiescence by *SO* in *C*'s use of land. Acquiescence may also be interpreted as giving rise to an assurance of rights; one of the elements of a claim to estoppel. It may be difficult to determine whether *SO*'s acquiescence is correctly interpreted as an assurance *C* has (or will acquire) rights for the purposes of an estoppel claim, or as indicative that *C* is acting on an assumption that a right exists. Practical difficulties may be avoided because of the different nature of the two claims. For example, in a claim based on estoppel there must be a causative link between *C*'s act and *SO*'s representation (acquiescence). Further, *C*'s acts must be to his detriment.

In relation to adverse possession, an estoppel claimant may attempt to rely on use of land in that capacity to found a claim to adverse possession.[13] A claim may be made where the estoppel has not yet

---

[9] See above n.6.
[10] See above n.6 at 384.
[11] *Pugh v. Savage* above n.6 at 383–384.
[12] Part III 2 of this chapter.
[13] Mary Welstead, "Proprietary Estoppel and the Acquisition of Possessory Title" [1991] Conv. 280; Mark Powlowski, *The Doctrine of Proprietary Estoppel* (1996), Chapter 9.

been considered by a court, or where a court has not granted the claimant a positive remedy but has enabled the estoppel to be used to resist a claim to possession.[14] It is submitted that such a claim should be rejected. The remedial flexibility within estoppel suggests that it would be inappropriate for the doctrine to be used as a step in a claim to title by adverse possession. This is particularly the case where the court has considered the claim and, in the exercise of that discretion, has chosen not to award legal title.

VII. Conclusion

Although the different effect attributed to use by adverse possession and prescription precludes the existence of a uniform principle for the acquisition of rights based on use, there are links between adverse possession and prescription. Both enable the acquisition of rights in land through use which is discoverable and non-consensual. The common foundation in use of a right may lead to borderline cases where it is uncertain whether a claim is correctly based on adverse possession or prescription.[15] For example, use of a wall may be interpreted as a claim to title to the wall by adverse possession or as a claim to an easement of support.[16] Potential overlaps are limited by virtue of the different nature of the two claims; legal title (adverse possession) or limited use (easement). The nature of the use required will ensure that ultimately the two claims are mutually exclusive. Use cannot both be based on an assumption an easement exists and with an intention to exclude the world at large. As Goodman suggests, where borderline cases do arise, the court should assess C's acts objectively to determine the appropriate claim.

---

[14] Chapter 7, Part IV.
[15] Michael J. Goodman, "Adverse Possession or Prescription? Problems of Conflict" [1968] Conv. 270.
[16] See the discussion of *Phillipson v. Gibbon* (1871) L.R. 6 Ch. 428 by Goodman above n.15 at 274–275.

Chapter 11.

Conclusion

I. Introduction

The diversity of situations in which proprietary rights are acquired in the absence of a formal grant, and of the rules which provide the basis for the rights, precludes any suggestion of a single and coherent doctrine of informal acquisition. The purpose of this concluding chapter is to highlight, in light of this diversity, the relationship between the rules that have been discussed in this book and some recurring issues.

II. The nature of the informality and the relationship between the rules discussed

Rights informally acquired may be the result of original acquisition (for example, through adverse possession) or be imposed by the court, or be informally created by the acts of the parties. In relation to the creation of a right, it was noted in the Introduction to this book that the need to comply with formalities may arise in three distinct stages; contract, creation and registration. With only one exception, the rules discussed in this book are concerned with the absence of formalities in relation to the creation of a proprietary right. The exception is the rule in *Re Rose*,[1] which deals specifically with a gift of land which has not yet been completed by registration. None of the rules are concerned with circumventing formality

---

[1] Discussed in Chapter 2, Part II. See also Chapter 5 n.2.

requirements for a contract for sale of land. There are a number of reasons for this. In some situations there may in fact be a valid contract, and the absence of formality arises only in relation to the subsequent creation of the right. For example, in Chapter 5 it was seen that a valid, specifically enforceable contract may itself be the source of informal rights pending the formal creation of rights pursuant to the contract. The creation of a proprietary right is not necessarily preceded by a contract, and claims to informal rights may arise in situations in which there is no contract. For example, a gift of land would not be preceded by a contract; therefore no question of a valid contract arises in relation to the rules discussed in Chapter 2 through which rights are acquired to give effect to imperfect gifts. Further, it has been argued that where the basis upon which the informal acquisition of rights is claimed is not dependent upon a contract, no question of the existence of a valid contract should arise. This argument has been made in relation to claims based on estoppel and based on full payment of consideration pursuant to an informal sale.[2]

It is possible, where the elements of claims are similar, for the same set of facts to give rise to a claim under more than one of the rules discussed in this book. However, because of the diversity of the rules, it is important that they are distinguished in their application, so that the right acquired by a claimant is ultimately attributed to a particular rule. The outcome of a claim under each rule is likely to be different and it is therefore desirable, in the interests of certainty and consistency, to identify the limitations of each. A strict delimitation can also assist in determining the scope and purpose of individual rules. The relationship between proprietary estoppel and other means of informal acquisition has given rise to most discussion. Recognising the boundaries between estoppel and these other rules ensures that estoppel provides the basis of a claim only where there is a unilateral assurance of rights and detrimental reliance. Further that, given the scope of situations in which these elements are found, the courts' remedial flexibility is protected. Hence it has been argued that the distinction between constructive trusts (of the type discussed in Chapter 6) and estoppel should be strictly maintained. The similarity of the elements of a claim to each (the two are principally separated by the existence of a unilateral assurance of rights for an estoppel, as

---

[2] Chapter 5, Part III.

opposed to an agreement to share beneficial entitlement for a constructive trust) means that rights may commonly be claimed under both. However, once determined whether the claim should be interpreted as based on an agreement or an assurance, the application of the rules should be kept distinct. A successful claim to a constructive trust confers a beneficial interest dating from the time the elements to the trust were established. An estoppel claimant initially acquires only an inchoate equity, which is not itself proprietary. Whether proprietary rights are acquired, and the nature of those rights, is dependent upon the courts' exercise of its remedial discretion.

Similarly it has been seen that a direct contribution to the purchase of land may give rise either to a resulting trust or to an inferred agreement constructive trust, of the types discussed in Chapter 6. However, the distinction between these trust types should be maintained on the basis that each reflects a different purpose. The resulting trust is a means of reversing unjust enrichment while the constructive trust is imposed to give effect to an agreement to share beneficial entitlement. Finally, whether a claim based on use of a right is construed as being to an easement or a freehold title is dependent only on the nature of the use. Notwithstanding, a claim could not be interpreted both as being based on adverse possession and prescription because of the different interpretation each takes of use.

In *Lloyds Bank plc v. Carrick*,[3] the Court of Appeal went further and indicated that the existence of a specifically enforceable contract (enabling a claim based on *Walsh v. Lonsdale*) precluded a claim to estoppel or to a constructive trust of the type discussed in Chapter 6. The effect of the judgment is that even if the elements to a claim based on estoppel or constructive trust are fulfilled, a claim is precluded if, coincidentally, there is a specifically enforceable contract. Precluding such claims may be justified on the basis that, where parties have entered into a contract, they should be limited to claims derived from the contract. The aim of enabling the acquisition of rights in such a case is to regulate the parties' relationship pending formal execution of the contract.

---

[3] [1996] 4 All E.R. 630.

III. The nature and type of the right acquired

The majority of proprietary rights acquired informally are based on the intervention of equity and therefore are equitable proprietary rights. Intervention often takes the form of imposing a resulting or constructive trust. This is the case where legal and equitable entitlement to an estate is divided and where there is co-ownership of an estate (the situations discussed in Chapter 6). In relation to the division of legal and equitable entitlement, although the language of a trust has been used, it has been acknowledged, following *Westdeutsche Landesbank Girozentrale v. Islington L.B.C.*,[4] that such situations do not necessarily attract fiduciary obligations. In a limited number of situations it is possible for legal rights to be acquired informally. This may occur under the rule in *Strong v. Bird* (discussed in Chapter 2) where an intended donee is coincidentally appointed executor or administrator. A legal right is acquired as legal title vests in the donee. Exceptionally, legal title is acquired through a *donatio mortis causa*, where the donee is also appointed executor or administrator. Legal rights may also be acquired under the rules of corresponding benefit and burden and non-derogation from grant, considered in Chapters 8 and 9. Those rules create legal rights where they are applied following a transfer of legal title. Rights acquired through use of the right are invariably legal. An estoppel claimant may be awarded a legal right as a remedy by the court in the exercise of its remedial discretion.

As was noted in the introduction to this book, in exceptional cases proprietary rights acquired informally are *sui generis*, as they do not have the characteristics of a recognised proprietary right. Therefore such rights, if expressly created, would not have proprietary status. Only three situations have been discussed which may give rise to *sui generis* rights. First, in Chapter 4 where land is transferred "subject to" personal rights, such as a contractual licence. The authority for the application of the rule on such facts has been seen to be weak. If the rule does apply, then the rights are given effect through the mechanism of a constructive trust. The second and third situations concern the rules of corresponding benefit and burden and non-derogation from grant. These rules create proprietary rights *sui generis* where the burden of an agreement, or the scope of a duty not to

---

[4] [1996] 2 All E.R. 961. See Chapter 2, Part II.

derogate, does not meet the characteristics of recognised rights. The creation of *sui generis* rights by the application of these rules may be justified on the basis that those rules draw consequences from the fact rights are being enjoyed. For example, *sui generis* rights may be necessary to protect the grant of a recognised proprietary right.

IV. The common background to the informal acquisition of rights

The common background to the situations and rules discussed in this book is that they all concern the acquisition of proprietary rights as a result of the words or conduct of parties directly related to dealings with land. Chapters 2 and 5 deal respectively with the consequences of incomplete gifts and sales of land, and Chapter 10 with the use of land over a period of time. These chapters apart, the rules that have been considered may be seen broadly as enabling the informal acquisition of rights in response to forms of conduct which fall below a particular (if ill-defined) standard. In the rules discussed in Chapters 3 and 4 (the "instrument of fraud" doctrine and transfers of land "subject to" a person's rights) rights are acquired to prevent forms of conduct labelled as fraudulent. A concept of fraudulent or unconscionable conduct also pervades the acquisition of rights through the doctrines of trust and estoppel considered in Chapters 6 and 7. The rules discussed in Chapters 8 and 9, concerning benefits and burdens and non-derogation from grant, purport to impose a general standard of fairness or common honesty. The justification for granting proprietary rights in response to these forms of conduct has been considered in the context of each claim. It has been noted, for example, that only in Chapters 3 and exceptionally Chapter 4 does the prevention of fraud provide the sole justification for intervention. Further, in the discussion of estoppel in Chapter 7 it was suggested that in some situations restitution is the more appropriate response to unconscionable conduct. Again, however, in these chapters the fraud, unconscionability or unfairness concerns the conduct of the parties directly relating to their dealings with land. The fraud in Chapters 3 and 4 arises where a transferee of land reneges on an agreement pursuant to which the land was transferred. The unconscionable conduct in Chapters 6 and 7 arises from reneging on an agreement or assurance that the claimant has (or will have) rights in land. The standard of fairness in Chapters 8 and 9 is a standard relating to the exercise of rights in land.

V. Concluding comments

The introduction to this book noted the "policy of formality" that exists in relation to the creation of proprietary rights. It is submitted that the informal acquisition of proprietary rights does not preclude the assertion of such a policy. The formality requirements for the express grant of proprietary rights are "facilitative". They enable the grant of recognised proprietary rights to give effect to the intentions of parties in their dealings with land. Informal acquisition is, in contrast, reactive. Proprietary rights are acquired as a reaction to the words and conduct of parties in relation to land. The right acquired will not necessarily reflect the intentions of the parties.[5] Rarely would it be expected for parties consciously to choose to rely on informal acquisition.[6] The primary role of informal acquisition is to enable rights to be acquired where parties have not executed a formal grant. However, informal acquisition also arises in other circumstances. For example, non-derogation from grant uses informal acquisition to support or protect rights which have been granted.[7] The rule in *Re Rose* and *Walsh v. Lonsdale* pre-empt the formal grant of rights, pending completion of a (formally executed) gift or the performance of a contract the parties have entered. In these contexts, informal acquisition plays a role distinct from merely replacing a formal grant.

It is hoped that by presenting collectively the situations in which proprietary rights are informally acquired these situations, and their inter-relationship, will be better understood. To conclude, three factors can be highlighted that may have a future impact on the analysis of informal acquisition which has been provided. First, whether English courts embrace the concept of the remedial constructive trust. English law currently remains far from Lord Denning's vision of imposing constructive trusts (and therefore conferring proprietary rights) "whenever justice and good conscience requires it".[8] Secondly, it remains to be seen, in the context of the

---

[5] Only the rules discussed in Chapter 2 and the constructive trust in Chapter 6 are expressly concerned with giving effect to the parties' intentions.

[6] An exceptional case may be the rule discussed in Chapter 5, Part III, where parties may choose to rely on an informal sale. Claims made by parties in a familial or emotional relationship may arise where, as a result of the relationship, parties who are aware of formality requirements feel inhibited from insisting upon them.

[7] As has been seen, Chapter 9, Part II 1(a), the notion of grant is broadly construed.

[8] *Hussey v. Palmer* [1972] 1 W.L.R. 1286 at 1290.

situations discussed in this book, what consequences the courts draw from *Westdeutsche*[9] as regards the use of trusts. Thirdly informal acquisition will continue to be scrutinised by the Law Commission. In particular, the long awaited consultation paper on the property rights of homesharers will certainly have an impact on the application of the constructive and resulting trusts discussed in Chapter 6 and on proprietary estoppel.

[9] See above n.4.

Index

Introduction

The index covers Chapters 1 to 11. Index entries are to page numbers. Alphabetical arrangement is word-by-word, where a group of letters followed by a space is filed before the same group of letters followed by a letter, e.g. "Specific performance" will appear before "Specifically enforceable contracts". Initial articles, conjunctions and prepositions are ignored in determining filing order.

Acquiescence
  prescription, 232–236, 249
  proprietary estoppel, 140–141, 163–165
Administrators
  donees appointed as, 18–20, 24
Advancement, presumption of, 101–103
Adverse possession, 217–220, 251
  discontinuance in possession, 225–226
  dispossession, 225–226
  effect of use, 239–242
  elements of claims, 225–232
  estoppel and, 249–250
  failure to assert rights, 236–238
  implied licence, 229–231
  Law Commission recommendations, 241–242
  leaseholds, 242–243
    landlords' reversionary interests, bringing into possession, 245–247
    registered land, 243–245
    surrender, 245–247
  registered land, 240–242, 243–245
  sources of rules, 220–221
  specific future use, 231–232
  unilateral grant of permission, 238–9
Agreements
  constructive trusts, 162
  non-beneficial interests, 42–44
  non-proprietary rights, 44–45
Apparent easements, 211–213

Assignment
  agreements to create leases, 72–3
  future book debts, 76
  legal interests, 62
Assurance of rights
  constructive trusts, 134–135, 136
  proprietary estoppel *see* **Proprietary estoppel**

Bare licences, 45
Bare trustees, 74
Beneficial interests, 71
  acquisition on basis of agreements to share beneficial ownership *see* **Beneficial ownership**
  constructive trusts, 160
  trusts
    fraud prevention, 39, 41–42
    purchasers taking land "subject to" personal rights, 57
  unjust enrichment prevention by conferring *see* **Unjust enrichment**
Beneficial ownership
  agreements to share, 89–91, 253
    evidence of, 95
    excuses for sole name acquisitions, 107–109
    express, establishing beneficial interests detrimental reliance, 109–114
    establishing agreements, 104–109

Beneficial ownership—*cont.*
  agreements to share—*cont.*
    inferred, establishing beneficial
      interests, 115–118
    quantifying beneficial interests,
      118–124
    uncompleted sales, 83–85
    unjust enrichment prevention,
      103–104
  gender roles and discrimination,
    113–114
Benefit and burden, 88, 254–255
  choice, element of, 175–176, 177
  conditional, 167, 169–171, 172–174
  contracts, specifically enforceable,
    difference from, 180
  development of principle, 168–171
  effect of principle, 177–182
  equity, 181–2
  express conditions, 171, 172
  implied conditions, 171, 173
  mere equities, 180–181
  proprietary estoppel and, 153, 179
  pure principle, 167–168, 169–171
  relevance of burden to benefit, 173–4
  requirements of principle
    conditional benefit and burden,
      172–174
    enjoyment of benefit, 174–177
Book debts
  future, assignment of, 76
Breakdown of relationships
  family homes, 88–89
Burden *see* **Benefit and burden**

Chattels, *donatio mortis causa*, 21
Choses in action, gifts of. 25
Common expectation cases
  proprietary estoppel, 129–133
Common intention, easements of,
  209–210
Common law
  prescription, 222, 224, 234, 248
Compulsory purchase
  derogation from grant, rule against,
    189
Concurrent interests, 39
Conditional benefit and burden *see*
  Benefit and burden
Consideration, 17, 35–37, 54–55
  uncompleted sales, 74–83
Constructive trusts, 252–253, 254
  agreement, 162

Constructive trusts—*cont.*
  assurance of future rights, 134–135,
    136
  beneficial interests, 160
  fraud prevention 35–36, 39–40, 42–43
  imperfect gifts, giving effect to,
    22–23, 26
  inferred agreement trusts, 95–98, 253
  proprietary estoppel, 152, 154
    distinguishing, 160–163
    doctrine approaching, 120–121
  purchasers taking land "subject to"
    personal rights, 56, 57
  remedial, 256
  sub-trusts, 65–67
  uncompleted sales, 64–65, 82
  voluntary transfers of land, 99–101
Continuous easements, 211–213
Contracts, 3, 64, 252
  see also **Equitable interests; Legal
    estates; Legal rights**
  oral, 44, 68, 79
  part performance, 40
  privity, 53
  specifically enforceable, 252, 253
    see also **Uncompleted sales**
    acquisition of rights, 187–188, 189
    difference from benefit and
      burden, 180
  stages in acquisition of rights, 75
  validity requirements, 68–69
  in writing, 79
Contractual licences, 56–58, 159, 254
  proprietary estoppel and,
    distinguishing, 160–163
Contribution
  direct 95–98, 116–118
  indirect, 109–110, 117–18
  to initial deposit, 121–122
  to purchase price, 116
  restitution against unjust enrichment,
    89–91, 92
Conveyances, 64, 75
  easements acquired by statutory
    words implied into, 213–215

Death
  gifts of land *see* **Gifts of land**
Debtors
  appointed as executors, 18–19
Deed
  estoppel by, 165
  legal estates and interests, creation
    by, 3–4

Delivery to donees, 24–26
Derogation from grant, rule against, 185–186, 254–255
compulsory purchase, 189
easements
acquisition rules, 206–215
apparent, 211–213
of common intention, 209–210
conformation with characteristics of, 200–201
continuous, 211–213
enjoyed by grantors prior to grant, 210–213
of necessity, 206–208
reservations, 188
statutory words implied into conveyances, acquired by, 213–215
economic interference, 198–199
failure to act, 197
general rule
requirements
duration of rights acquired, 202–205
giving effect: acquisition of proprietary rights, 199–202
grantor owning neighbouring land, 191–194, 203
purpose of grant, 189–191
scope of duty, 194–199
interpretation of term "grant", 186–189
leases, 193–194
reservations, 188
restrictive covenants, 202
servitudes, 191, 199–200
sui generis rights, 201–202
Detriment
financial, 145
gender roles and discrimination, 113–114, 147
net loss, 144–145
personal services constituting, 146
proprietary estoppel, 128, 144–147, 164
reliance on agreements to share beneficial interests, 89–91, 104, 109–114, 120, 122
Discontinuance in possession, 225–226
Discrimination
detrimental reliance, effects on, 113–114, 147
Dispossession, 225–226

Divorce, 89
Dominant tenements, 199–200, 211
Donatio mortis causa, 21–27, 45, 254

Easements, 42–43
apparent, 211–213
of common intention, 209–210
continuous, 211–213
derogation from grant, rule against *see* **Derogation from grant, rule against**
equitable, 63
prescription, 223–224
quasi-easements, 210–213
of necessity, 206–208
reservations, 188
statutory words implied into conveyances, acquired by, 213–215
Economic interference
derogation from grant, rule against, 198–199
Encumbrancers' claims, 89, 90–91, 122–123
Equitable easements, 63
Equitable estoppel *see* **Proprietary estoppel**
Equitable interests, 2, 61–62
contracts for sale, 65–68
in personal property, 77
Equitable leases, 63, 73
Equitable mortgages, 63, 80
Equitable rights in land, 26–27
Equity, 62, 74, 254
see also **Inchoate equity; Mere equities**
benefit and burden, 181–2
floating, 158
gifts of land, 9–10, 11–27
"naked and alone", 181
proprietary estoppel, 127–128
Estate contracts, 50, 57, 70, 83–84
Estates, 2, 3
Estoppel, 36, 252, 254, 255
adverse possession and, 249–250
by deed, 165
equitable *see* **Proprietary estoppel**
prescription and, 249
promissary, 165
proprietary *see* **Proprietary estoppel**
by representation, 165–166
Estoppel licences, 159, 160–161

Executors
debtors appointed as, 18–19
donees appointed as, 18–20, 24
Express conditions, benefit and
burden, 171, 172
Express trusts, 39–41

Factual possession, 227
Family assets, doctrine of, 123–124
Family homes
beneficial ownership, agreements to
share, 104–124
breakdown of relationships, 88–89
encumbrancers' claims, 89, 90–91,
122–123
proprietary rights, 88–91
Fiduciary obligations, 254
constructive trusts, 64–65
trusts of land, 14–15, 23
uncompleted sales, 74–75, 79
Financial detriment, 145
Floating equity, 158
Formality requirements, 1
enforcing, justification for, 88
estoppel by deed, 165
facilitative nature, 256
gifts of land, 10
nature and purpose, 3–5
non-compliance, 32
proprietary estoppel circumventing,
128, 157
trusts of land, 22
Fraud, 255
definition, 30–33, 51–52
inchoate equity, denial of, 154
prevention, 29–46
purchasers taking land "subject to"
personal rights, 48, 51–52, 58
statutes, use as instruments of, 30–33
transfers of land on trust, 33–34
Fulfilment of expectations
proprietary estoppel remedy,
156–158

Gender roles
detriment, assessing by reference to,
113–114, 147
Gifts of land, 251, 252
absence of intention to make 96, 97
advancement, presumption of, and,
101–103

Gifts of land—*cont.*
imperfect
death of donors, 18
gifts made in contemplation of,
and conditional upon, 20–27
delivery to donees, 24–26
donatio mortis causa, 21–27
donees appointed executors or
administrators, 18–20, 24
donors doing all in power to
complete transfers, 10–18
equitable rights in land, 26–27
equity, 9–10, 11–27
formal requirements, 10
Land Certificates, delivery of,
25–26
registered land, 10, 15–16
Rose, Re, rule in, 12–18, 20, 27
Strong v. Bird, rule in, 19–20, 24
third party action required, 16
title deeds, delivery of, 25
transfers on trust, 27
unregistered land, 10, 16
informal, proprietary estoppel, 129
mistaken, 93–95
trusts *see* **Trusts**
Gifts of shares in private companies,
11–13
Grants
derogation from *see* **Derogation from
grant, rule against**
interpretation of term, 186–189
proprietary rights following
proprietary estoppel, 128
of rights, estoppel by deed, 165

Implied conditions, benefit and
burden, 171, 173
Implied licences
adverse possession, 229–231
Inchoate equity, 127–128, 150–155, 159
Independent proprietary rights
uncompleted sales, 70–73
Inferred agreement constructive trusts,
95–98, 253
Informal acquisition
common background, 255
justifying, 5–6
nature and type of rights acquired,
254–55
nature of informality and
relationship between rules,
251–253

Intention to possess, 227–228
Interests in land, 2, 3
  creation in writing, 43–44
  see also Equitable interests; Legal
    interests

Joint tenants, 87, 92

Land Certificates, delivery of, 25–26
Land charges, 70–71, 72, 83
Law Commission
  abolition of part-performance, and,
    69, 81–82
  adverse possession
    recommendations, 241–242
Leases
  adverse possession see Adverse
    possession
  assignment of agreements to create
    72–73
  derogation from grant, rule against,
    193–194
  division of legal and equitable
    entitlement, 71
  equitable, 63, 73
  prescription, 242–243, 247–249
Legal estates, 61–62
  contracts for sale, 62, 64
  deed, creation by, 3–4
  definition, 3
  separation from equitable ownership,
    23, 64–65, 71, 254
Legal interests, 61–62
  contracts to assign, 62
  deed, creation by, 3–4
Legal rights, 61–62
  contracts to create, 62–63
  uncompleted sales, 62–65
Licences, 72
  contractual see Contractual licences
  estoppel, 159, 160–161
  implied, adverse possession, 229–231
Limitation of actions, 220–221, 225
Lost modern grant see Prescription

Maritime law, 54, 58
Matrimonial homes, 123–124
Mere equities
  inchoate equity, 153–155
  benefit and burden, 180–181
Mining rights, 169
Misprediction
  proprietary estoppel, 140, 164–5

Mistaken belief
  prescription, 233
Mortgagees' claims, 122–123
Mortgages
  direct contribution to, 116–118
  donatio mortis causa, 26
  equitable, 63, 80
  indirect contribution to, 109–110,
    117–118

Necessity, easements of, 206–208
Net loss
  detriment, 144–145
Non-beneficial interests, 42–44
Non-derogation from grant see
  Derogation from grant, rule
  against
Non-proprietary rights, 44–45

Part performance, 36
  constructive trusts and, 40–41
  oral evidence of contracts, 44
  uncompleted sales, 68–69, 80–81
Permission
  adverse possession and prescription,
    238–239
Personal property
  equitable interests, 77
Personal rights
  proprietary estoppel, 158–159
  purchasers taking land "subject to",
    47–48, 59–60, 254
    elements of claims, 48–49
    enforceability of acquired rights,
      57–58
    fraud, 51–52
    implied requirements, 52–55
    nature of rights acquired 57–58
    new rights, intention to create,
      49–51
    scope of rule, 55–57
    time of acquisition of rights, 58–59
Personal services constituting
  detriment, 144–145
Positive covenants, 173
Possession
  adverse see Adverse possession
  factual, 227
  intention to possess, 227–228
Pre-contractual negotiations, 137–138
Prescription, 217–220
  acquiescence, 232–236, 249
  common law, 222, 224, 234, 248

Prescription—*cont.*
effect of use, 242
elements of claims, 232–234
open use, 235
use without force, 234–235
use without permission, 236
estoppel and, 249
failure to assert rights, 237
leaseholds, 242–243, 247–249
lost modern grant, 222–223, 224–225, 234, 248
mistaken belief, 233
sources of rules, 221–225
statutory, 223–224, 248
unilateral grant of permission, 238–9
Private companies, gifts of shares in, 11–13
Privity of contract, 53
Profits, prescription, 217, 223–224
Promissary estoppel, 165
Proprietary estoppel, 127–128, 252–253
assurance of rights
acquiescence, 140–141, 163–165
active, 139
establishing, 139–141
future, 134–137
misprediction, 140, 164–5
nature of, 133–139
pre-contractual negotiations, 137–138
unilateral, 161, 164
benefit and burden and, 153, 179
common expectation cases, 129–133
constructive trusts, 152, 154
distinguishing, 160–163
doctrine approaching, 120–121
contractual licences and, distinguishing, 160–163
detriment, 128, 144–147, 164
elements of claims, 128–150
formality requirements circumvention by, 157
gifts of land, informal, 129
historical application, 129
inchoate equity, 127–128, 150–155, 159
reliance, 141–144, 156–157, 164
remedies, 155–156, 254
fulfilment of expectations, 156–158
personal rights, 158–159
proprietary rights, 158–159
purpose, 156–158
restitution, 156–157

Proprietary estoppel—*cont.*
restitution, 156–157
distinguishing, 163–165
uncompleted sales, 81–82
unconscionability, 127–128, 147–150
unilateral mistake cases, 129–133, 140
Proprietary rights
characteristics necessary for, 1
creation, 2
family homes, 88–91
meaning, 2
non-derogation from grant, duty, 199–202
proprietary estoppel, 158–159
recognised, 1–2
sui generis see **Sui generis rights**
uncompleted sales, 69–74
Purchasers for value
inchoate equity, enforceability, 152–153
Pure principle of benefit and burden, 167–168, 169–171

Quasi-easements, 210–213

Redistributive justice, 91, 124
Registered land
adverse possession, 240–242, 243–245
gifts of land, 10, 15–16
Relativity of title, 220
Reliance
detrimental *see* **Detriment**
proprietary estoppel, 141–144, 156–157, 164
Remedial constructive trusts, 256
Representation, estoppel by, 165–166
Reservations, 188
Restitution, 255
proprietary estoppel, 156–157
distinguishing, 163–165
unconscionability, 163–165
unjust enrichment, 89–91, 92
Restitutionary resulting trusts, 92–95
Restrictive covenants, 2
derogation from grant, rule against, 202
Resulting trusts, 253, 254
inferred agreement constructive trusts and, 95–98
and mistaken gifts, 93–95
no presumption of, 98–103
restitutionary, 92–95

Rights of light, 223
Rights *sui generis* *see* ***Sui generis* rights**
***Rochefoucauld v. Boustead,* rule in,** 31–33, 34–36, 40–41, 43–44, 51
***Rose, Re,* rule in,** 12–18, 20, 27, 45, 251, 256

Sale transfers of land, 17
Secret trusts, 32
Servient tenements, 199–200
Servitudes, 191, 199–200
Settled land, 39
Shares in private companies, gifts of, 11–13
Specific future use
adverse possession, 231–232
Specific performance, 44
uncompleted sales, 62, 68–69, 73–75, 77–78, 79
Specifically enforceable contracts *see* **Contracts; Uncompleted sales**
Statutory prescription, 223–224, 248
***Strong v. Bird,* rule in,** 19–20, 24, 45, 254
Sub-trusts, 65–67
Successive interests, 39
***Sui generis* rights**, 2, 254–255
non-derogation from grant, 201–202
personal rights, purchasers taking land "subject to", 55, 58
prescription, 232
proprietary estoppel, 159
uncompleted sales, 69

Tenancy in common, 92
Third parties
enforcement of agreements, 52–55, 59–60
enforcement of rights against, 70, 72
gifts of land, 16
Title deeds, delivery of, 25
Trusts
see also **Constructive trusts; Resulting trusts**
adverse possession, registered land, 240–241
beneficial interests under, 39, 41–42
declaration of, 4, 21
donors holding for donees, 13, 14–15, 16, 23
express, 39–41
fiduciary obligations, 14–15, 23

Trusts—*cont.*
formality requirements, 22
fraudulent claims, 30
"in full sense and without more", 76
oral, 30–33
restitutionary resulting, 92–95
secret, 32
sub modo, 76
sub-trusts, 65–67
transfers of land, 33–34
use of, 257
in writing, 21, 27

Uncompleted sales, 61–62
consideration paid in full by purchasers, 74–83
relationship with other means of acquiring proprietary rights, 83–85
specifically enforceable contracts
independent proprietary rights, 70–73
proprietary rights, nature of, 69–74
sale of equitable interests in land, 65–68
sale of legal rights in land, 62–65
specific performance, 68–69, 73–74
Unconscionability, 36, 255
proprietary estoppel, 127–128, 147–150
restitution, 163–165
Unilateral assurance of rights, estoppel following *see* **Proprietary estoppel**
Unilateral grant of permission
adverse possession and prescription, 238–9
Unilateral mistake cases
proprietary estoppel, 129–133, 140
Unjust enrichment, 253
and mistaken gifts, 93–95
prevention by conferring beneficial interest
inferred agreement constructive trusts, 95–98
restitutionary resulting trusts, 92–95
resulting trusts, 95–98
no presumption of, 98–103
restitution, 89–91
Unregistered land, 10, 16
Use of rights *see* **Adverse possession; Prescription**

Voluntary transfers of land, 99–101
   see also **Gifts of land**

Walsh v. Lonsdale, **rule in**, 63, 73, 253, 256
Wheeldon v. Burrows, **rule in**, 211–214